THE RIGHT TO LIFE AND CONFLICTING INTERESTS

The Right to Life and Conflicting Interests

ELIZABETH WICKS

OXFORD
UNIVERSITY PRESS

OXFORD
UNIVERSITY PRESS

Great Clarendon Street, Oxford, OX2 6DP,
United Kingdom

Oxford University Press is a department of the University of Oxford.
It furthers the University's objective of excellence in research, scholarship,
and education by publishing worldwide. Oxford is a registered trade mark of
Oxford University Press in the UK and in certain other countries

Published in the United States of America by Oxford University Press
198 Madison Avenue, New York, NY 10016, United States of America

British Library Cataloguing in Publication Data
Data available

ISBN 978-0-19-954739-5

Preface

The right to life has received remarkably little attention in the legal academic press. It has typically been treated either as one of many rights protected in the international human rights treaties or as a small element of a broader ethical investigation into the value of life. This is surprising given the apparent importance of the right to life. It is often regarded as the most fundamental of all rights, not just because without its protection any other human rights protection is ineffective, but also because it seeks to protect a principle regarded as sacred by many: the inherent value in human life. The religious and philosophical underpinnings of the right to life are an important aspect of its nature and development. They give the right a context and purpose but they are not the whole story, and this book will primarily be investigating the right to life as a legal right: a merging of national and international human rights law with the ethical principle of the value of human life.

Despite the importance of the right to life, it is far from absolute. In the abstract it may be difficult to identify any interest that might outweigh the need to protect human life but when we consider some specific circumstances we soon become aware of the existence of potential conflicts. If we consider, for example, the shooting of a suspected suicide bomber in order to prevent the detonation of a bomb, or the withdrawal of life-sustaining medical treatment from a permanently comatose patient, or the shooting down of a hijacked plane targeting thousands of people on the ground, we begin to appreciate that there may be some circumstances in which the legal protection for human life should not be absolute. Of course the above examples are not uncontroversial. There is room for a great deal of argument about whether suspicion of a threat to others is sufficient, and whether there is still value in a comatose life, but such argument acknowledges that there are potentially conflicting interests at play here: one life against the life of many, or the sanctity of life versus the quality of life, for example. This book seeks to identify the interests that may conflict with the right to life, and to consider when and why the right may be limited by some other value. Potentially conflicting interests identified in the following pages include the prevention of crime, the rights of others, autonomy, quality of life, limited public resources and the special circumstances inherent in armed conflict. Not all of these will be regarded as capable of outweighing the right to life in all circumstances but the need for a balancing exercise to take place is clear. A single human life cannot be protected by the state in complete disregard of the rights of others in society, the wishes of that individual and the cost (financial and otherwise) of doing so. That may be a sobering thought but it is also a realistic one that is based on a recognition that the right to life will be a stronger and more meaningful force if its limitations are explicitly acknowledged.

The interests that potentially conflict with the right to life are diverse and so the following pages will touch upon a variety of legal and ethical subjects. We will encounter international humanitarian law, criminal law and medical law, as well as human rights law. The situations in which the right to life conflicts with other interests are some of the most topical and controversial facing the disciplines of law, ethics and politics today, including the killing of civilians in another state, the death penalty, the use of lethal force against suspected terrorists, abortion, and assisted suicide. Explicit recognition of the conflict between the right to life and other interests in these situations may help to cast light upon both the nature of the right and its limits of application. It may also move us a small step closer to the resolution of such conflicts.

In writing this book I have benefited from discussions with many people but I am particularly grateful to Jon Yorke from Birmingham City University and Adrian Hunt and Stephen Smith from the University of Birmingham for their valuable comments on various aspects of this book. My partner, Frank, has also offered valuable advice and guidance, often by forcing me to reconsider my instinctive reactions, which has undoubtedly resulted in a better book. I am also grateful, as always, to my Mum and Dad for their support and encouragement. I have sought to take into account developments up to September 2009.

Liz Wicks

Contents

Table of Cases

ENGLAND AND WALES

OTHER JURISDICTIONS

INTERNATIONAL AND REGIONAL JURISDICTIONS

Table of Legislation

1

An Introduction to the Meaning
of Life

This first chapter will serve as an introduction to the concept of life. The following chapter will then trace the historical and philosophical protection for the concept of life before later chapters address the enforcement of a right to life and other interests which may conflict with it. Before any of these issues can be considered, however, it is necessary to identify the boundaries of life: when does it begin and end? In addition, some attention needs to be paid to the issue of why human life should be singled out for special treatment. As part of this search, the first chapter will also consider the complex issue of human consciousness and the challenges that it presents to a complete understanding of how the human brain works. In order to address these issues, the expertise of different disciplines will be drawn upon, beginning with anthropology.

A. Human life: an evolutionary perspective

Life on earth is varied and abundant. From simple bacteria and viruses through to the more complex mammals, it has survived numerous global catastrophes from ice ages to mass extinctions. Life has endured. In the context of this book, and the right to life, however, we are not concerned with the diversity of life on earth (or elsewhere) but the special legal and ethical protection accorded to human life.[1] As Jared Diamond explains, 'Somewhere along the scale from bacteria to humans, we have to decide where killing becomes murder, and where

---

[1] Albert Schweitzer's 'reverence for life' ethic extends moral concern to all living things equally. (*Civilisation and Ethics: The Philosophy of Civilization Part II* (London: A & C Black, 1929)). This controversial ethic's core element, and fundamental flaw, is that it opposes any attempt to establish a principled compromise between the ethical requirement to respect all life and the practical requirement, which Schweitzer recognizes, sometimes to take life. ('In order to preserve my own existence, I must defend against the existence which injures it. I become the hunter of the mouse which inhabits my house, a murderer of the insect which wants to have its nest there, a mass-murderer of the bacteria which may endanger my life. I get my food by destroying plants and animals.' (pp. 254–5.)) See M.A. Warren, *Moral Status: Obligations to Persons and Other Living Things* (Oxford: Clarendon Press, 1997), pp. 30–41 for an interesting discussion of this view.

eating becomes cannibalism.'[2] A preliminary question that must be addressed, therefore, is: what makes human life special within a world where life abounds? The difficulty of selecting humanity for special treatment is well expressed by Diamond:

> If our ethical code makes a purely arbitrary distinction between humans and all other species, then we have a code based on naked selfishness devoid of any higher principle. If our code instead makes distinctions based on our superior intelligence, social relationships, and capacity for feeling pain, then it becomes difficult to defend an all-or-nothing code that draws a line between all humans and all animals.[3]

The closest 'animal' relatives to humans are chimpanzees (of which there are two types: common and pygmy). Humans split from chimpanzees about seven million years ago, which in evolutionary terms is remarkably recent. We still share 98.4 per cent of our DNA, meaning that there is only a 1.6 per cent difference in the genetic make-up of humans and chimps. Our common ancestor split from gorillas about ten million years ago (with whom modern humans still share 97.7 per cent of our DNA). This earlier split in the evolutionary development of primates devastates the traditional distinction between humans and 'apes' because, if we look at the issue from the chimpanzees' perspective, their closest relative is not the gorilla or any other so-called 'ape' (such as the orang-utans or gibbons) but humans. Jared Diamond notes that there is a small dichotomy between the slightly lower apes (gorillas, orang-utans and gibbons) and the slightly higher apes (the three chimpanzees: common, pygmy and...human). In the title of his book, humans are the 'third chimpanzee'.[4] For many people, this is a startling new perspective.

The difference between the other chimpanzees and humans has been supplemented by an evolutionary distance between our common ancestor and modern humans. The evolution has, on the whole, been slow, with the occasional burst of change. By about four million years ago—three million years after we split from the other chimpanzees—our ancestors were walking upright, thus enabling the use of the forelimbs for other activities such as tool making. By three million years ago, our lineage had split again into at least two and possibly three separate species. By two and a half million years ago, our ancestors were making regular use of stone tools. By around one million years ago, the surviving ancestor, *homo erectus*, first moved beyond Africa. By 500,000 years ago, the *homo sapiens* had evolved, looking more recognizably like modern humans and with larger brains. But, despite these significant changes, culturally, progress was exceedingly slow. The leap forward happened a mere 40,000 years ago with the emergence of the Cro-Magnons in Western Europe utilizing

---

[2] J. Diamond, *The Third Chimpanzee: The Evolution and Future of the Human Animal* (New York: HarperCollins, 1992), p. 30.   [3] ibid.

[4] The above discussion, and that in the following few paragraphs, is drawn from Diamond's book.

more advanced tools and art. As Diamond explains: 'They constitute the most important innovation that came with our rise to humanity: namely, the capacity for innovation itself.'[5] Their emergence also coincided with the extinction of the Neanderthals: evidence of humanity's first genocide, perhaps.[6] Since that time, cultural change has proceeded at a rapid pace, independent of genetic change.

What made the difference? The evidence remains unclear on this point, although the development of language seems to be the forerunner in potential theories. Is it possible that mutations in the vocal tract, thus enabling greater control over a wider variety of sounds, is the key to humanity? It may be relevant to point out here that evidence exists that some other animal species have developed language. For example, studies of vervant monkeys have enabled at least ten different 'words' to be identified.[7] Furthermore, a select few apes have been successfully taught sign language. Perhaps language, and even complex language, is not a solely human trait? What is unique about human life then? There is no critical component in the human brain which is missing from the chimpanzee's brain. The difference between a modern human's brain and a chimpanzee's brain is not in relation to structure, but merely in relation to size. Put bluntly, we have much bigger brains. The larger brains did not evolve immediately, however. Until about two and a half million years ago, our ancestors survived with ape-sized brains. Then, over a relatively short period of time, the brains increased in size until by 150,000 years ago, the human brain was four times the size of the ape brain. Note that this is long before the great leap forward 40,000 years ago—before the development of language, agriculture, art and civilization. Those later advances did not spurt from genetic changes such as the enlargement of the brain, but rather must have occurred due to a harnessing of the plasticity of the brain (which had, on a genetic basis, completed its evolution to its modern state by 150,000 years ago).[8]

It has been argued that 'human uniqueness lies in our radically improved conscious capacity'.[9] Our heightened sense of consciousness may be what

---

[5] Diamond, n. 2 above, p. 50.

[6] See Diamond, ibid, p. 364 for discussion of this possibility: 'Although we usually think of the Cro-Magnons as the first bearers of our noblest traits, they also bore the two traits that lie at the root of our current problems: our propensities to murder each other en masse and to destroy our environment. Even before Cro-Magnon times, fossil human skulls punctured by sharp objects and cracked to extract the brains bear witness to murder and cannibalism. The suddenness with which Neanderthals disappeared after Cro-Magnons arrived hints that genocide had now become efficient. Our efficiency at destroying our own resource base is suggested by extinctions of almost all large Australian animals following our colonization of Australia fifty thousand years ago...'

[7] See Diamond, ibid, Chapter 8.

[8] See D.C. Dennett, *Consciousness Explained* (London: Penguin, 1991), pp. 189–90 for discussion of this point.

[9] M. Donald, *A Mind So Rare: The Evolution of Human Consciousness* (New York: W.W. Norton & Co, 2001), p. 202.

distinguishes us from the other primates but we are certainly not alone in being conscious entities:

Human conscious capacity is the end product of a very long evolution. The idea is incompatible with the idea that humans are the only conscious beings in the terrestrial biosphere. Humans have more of everything. We might be called superconscious. But other species may share component features of our conscious capacity.[10]

The first step towards the evolution of consciousness has been identified as self-preservation: 'if you are setting out to preserve yourself, you don't want to squander effort trying to preserve the whole world: you draw the line. You become, in a word, selfish. This primordial form of selfishness...is one of the marks of life'.[11] This idea of self; of 'me against the world'[12] is the first step towards consciousness. Subsequent steps include the development of a basic nervous system to control activities in time and space; touch for info-proximal anticipation; short range anticipation (for example, through the ducking mechanism); vision (especially a sensitivity to patterns with a vertical axis of symmetry); the so-called 'fight or flight' mode of heightened vigilance. The latter led to more general vigilance, which in turn led to information gathering, which led to a division of labour in the brain (between the 'dorsal' which takes responsibility for keeping the organism out of harm's way, and the 'ventral' which is thus freed to concentrate on the identification of various objects in the world).[13] Once these genetic variations have occurred, the next step in the evolution of consciousness is 'phenotypic plasticity': learning which takes place within the brain during an organism's lifetime.

Three levels of basic awareness enjoyed variously by many different species have been identified by Merlin Donald:[14] first, selective binding or the power of perception which may be possessed by many species of animals; second, short-term control which requires a short-term working memory to extend the brain's perceptual framework over several seconds and is restricted to more advanced species, including mammals; and third, intermediate and long-term governance which extends awareness into the domain of voluntary movement or self-initiated action, and also adds a supervisory, or evaluative, dimension and is complete only in primates, and fully developed only in humans. This third level of awareness is particularly significant in its addition of a supervisory dimension which enables scrutiny of the level two awareness and an increased perception of time and space, including into the domain of imagination. Even within this third level of awareness, consciousness continues to be refined. The more precise and self-conscious control of action

---

[10] ibid, p. 130.   [11] Dennett, n. 8 above, p. 174.

[12] ibid. Dennett further explains that 'this distinction between everything on the inside of a closed boundary and everything in the external world is at the heart of all biological processes, not just ingestion and excretion, respiration and transpiration. Consider, for instance, the immune system, with its millions of different antibodies arrayed in defense of the body against millions of different alien intruders. This army must solve the fundamental problem of recognition: telling one's self (and one's friends) from everything else'. (p. 174.)

[13] The list is taken from Dennett, ibid, pp. 177–81.   [14] Donald, n. 9 above, Chapter 5.

evident in early humans evolved through the development of language and the accumulation of cultural knowledge until, by the great leap forward of 40,000 years ago, our ancestors had developed much more powerful and abstract reflective cultures driven by symbolic technology.[15] For many writers, the development of symbolism is a key capacity of humans but whether it is the result, or the cause, of our heightened consciousness remains unclear.[16] Donald argues that the main difference between apes and humans is 'symbolic culture' and he further asserts that this is 'largely outside, not inside, the brain box'.[17] This alludes to an important and challenging issue which will now be investigated: can human consciousness be explained entirely in terms of brain capacity? Or, to put the query in even more challenging terms: is there a distinction between the self and the brain?

B. Human consciousness: the key to human life?

The scientific debate on the nature of consciousness is played out against the backdrop of the dualism theory. This is the view that 'there are two metaphysically different kinds of phenomena in the universe, the mental and the physical'.[18] In terms of understanding how the brain works, dualism asserts that there is a mind/brain distinction, under which the 'mind' is not explainable in purely physical terms. The theory originates from the seventeenth-century distinction between physical reality as described by science and the mental reality of the soul.[19] Today, John Searle has identified four possible theoretical positions on the dualism issue. First, there are two types of dualists: 'substance dualists' who regard the mind and body as two different kinds of substance (the only scientists who adopt this position are those with a strong religious commitment to the idea of a human soul);[20] and 'property dualists' who view 'mental' and 'physical' as two different kinds of properties or features in a manner that enables a single substance to have both (this is a more popular position with scientists, including Searle himself, as it requires everything in the brain to be explainable in physical terms but also leaves open the possibility that there is something else more intangible beyond that physical explanation, such as, for example, consciousness).[21] Then, Searle identifies two types of monists: 'idealists' who regard everything as mental (which is not a view adopted by scientists); and 'materialists' who regard everything as physical. Many scientists adopt this latter view, including Daniel Dennett who points out that if the mind and body are distinct, they must

---

[15] ibid, Chapter 7.   [16] ibid, p. 117.   [17] ibid, p. 153.

[18] J.R. Searle, *The Mystery of Consciousness* (London: Granta Books, 1997), p. xii.

[19] Both Descartes and Galileo were proponents of this distinction.

[20] Searle gives the example of the Nobel laureate neurobiologist, Sir John Eccles, who believes that God attaches the soul to the fetus at about three weeks (Searle, n. 18 above, pp. 6–7).

[21] Searle argues that consciousness is 'both a qualitative, subjective "mental" phenomenon, and at the same time a natural part of the "physical" world' (ibid, p. xiv).

nevertheless interact, and yet anything that has an effect on physical matter must itself be physical.[22] Dennett's rejection of dualism entails a rejection of the idea of a 'self' distinct from the brain. While he acknowledges that the distinction seems natural, he regards it as a fallacy: 'It is very natural to think of our own bodies as mere hand puppets of sorts that "we" control "from inside". I make the hand puppet wave to the audience by wiggling my finger; I wiggle my finger by...what, wiggling my soul?'[23]

The concept of dualism is inherent in many of our social and legal norms. For example, a sleepwalker's actions may be regarded as non-culpable and yet they are still controlled by the brain. The buck seems to stop not at the brain but at the self that owns the brain.[24] A cursory reference to our own assumptions indicates that many of us instinctively believe in a type of 'mini-me' located somewhere inside our brains that controls our every conscious action. But if the 'mini-me' is not identifiable in a physical examination of the brain—and it is not, even in the sense of a localized area making executive decisions—then we are instinctively adopting a dualist perspective. The existence of a 'mini-me' is a divisive issue in the consciousness debate. Dennett explains his rejection of it as follows: 'The brain is Headquarters, the place where the ultimate observer is, but there is no reason to believe that the brain itself has any deeper headquarters, any inner sanctum, arrival at which is the necessary or sufficient condition for conscious experience. In short, there is no observer inside the brain.'[25] Searle rejects this argument, comparing Dennett's theory of the brain to 'a performance of Hamlet without the Prince of Denmark'.[26] Donald also argues in favour of a homunculus—a 'complex egocenter'—to tie all the brain's functions together.[27] Why is this issue relevant to our foolishly ambitious search for the meaning of 'life'? It was suggested above that the distinguishing feature of human life may be a heightened sense of consciousness. We remain largely in the dark in relation to this elusive mental state, however, and very different conclusions might be reached on the issue depending on whether it arises from a physical action of the whole human brain or from an entirely metaphysical construction of self existing somewhere both within and outside the human brain. If the entity that we wish to protect in some manner through the law is conscious life, then we need some basic idea of what consciousness is so that we can begin to draw some boundaries between what is to be protected and what is not to be protected.

Dennett's controversial view of consciousness is based on his rejection of a central headquarters within the brain where 'it all comes together for the perusal of a Central Meaner'.[28] Therefore, he argues that there is no single, definitive stream of consciousness but rather 'multiple channels in which specialist circuits try, in

---

[22] Dennett, n. 8 above, pp. 34–5.   [23] Dennett, ibid, p. 32.   [24] ibid.
[25] ibid, p. 106. Dennett argues that the idea of a 'special center in the brain is the most tenacious bad idea bedevilling our attempts to think about consciousness' (p. 108).
[26] Searle, n. 18 above, p. 100.   [27] Donald, n. 9 above, p. 135.
[28] Dennett, n. 8 above, p. 253.

parallel pandemoniums, to do their various things, creating Multiple Drafts as they go'.[29] It seems to us that there should be storage within our brains for both a working memory and long-term memory (somewhere the executive 'mini-me' can send her minions to retrieve previously stored files of information) but, as Dennett points out, there are not two distinct places in the brain to house these storage facilities. The only plausible location for memory storage is, surprisingly, the whole cortex (or higher brain).[30] Multiple functionality such as this is extremely difficult to explain for it is by nature counter-intuitive. As Dennett explains, 'It is proving to be fiendishly difficult—but not impossible—to figure out how the brain works, in part because it was designed by a process that can thrive on multiple, superimposed functionality, something systematically difficult to discern from the perspective of reverse engineering.'[31] Dennett clarifies the matter somewhat when he makes a comparison (albeit controversial) with computers. He argues that consciousness is analogous to a computer software program, with the brain itself as the hardware. He explains that with the computer, as with the brain, it is easy to miss the forest for the trees: micro details of instructions (streams of data on a computer; electrical brain activity, as we shall shortly see, in the brain) hide the virtual things (blocks of text or files in a computer; specific memories in the brain) and virtual places (directories or menus in a computer; memory storage facilities in the brain), connected by virtual paths (such as ESC to DOS or entering the print menu from the main menu on a computer; retrieving a specific memory in the brain) and permitting various virtual operations to be performed (such as searching a file for a word on a computer; searching a retrieved memory for a person's name, for example, in the brain).[32]

This analogy goes some way towards explaining how consciousness might co-exist within the hardware of the brain. It is a useful thought process at least. However, it is hard to escape from the question of how exactly consciousness can arise from seemingly unconnected brain activity. (This, of course, is Dennett's point.) The brain is not an obvious machine for creating consciousness. As Searle states, 'If you were designing an organic machine to pump blood you might come up with something like a heart, but if you were designing a machine to produce consciousness, who would think of a hundred billion neurons?'[33] The question is even more apposite when it is realized that all these hundred billion neurons ever do is to increase or decrease their rates of firing electrical signals. That is all the brain is. Where is the consciousness coming from? How am I composing this sentence? How do I know that I am doing so? Where am *I*? Scientists have studied the activity of the brain in great detail and a link has been clearly established

---

[29] ibid, pp. 253–4.   [30] ibid, pp. 270–1.
[31] Dennett, n. 8 above, p. 273. Dennett's book (*Consciousness Explained*), one of a growing number trying to explain consciousness, is an enlightening and fascinating read, even if the theory Dennett proposes remains extremely controversial.
[32] The computer software analogy is discussed in Dennett, ibid, pp. 209–26.
[33] Searle, n. 18 above, p. 22.

between consciousness and electrical brain activity. As Donald explains, 'conscious effort is the single most reliable predictor of the patterns of brain activity.'[34] So, science can tell us what causes consciousness but it still cannot tell us why: 'Brains that pulse with certain patterns of electrical activity are conscious. Why? They just are.'[35]

The search for *me* in this context—the core of the life that might be protected by law—remains unfulfilled. Is the electrical brain activity—the rapidity of the firing of billions of neurons—really all that exists of me? Because that is not what I, or anyone else, values. I don't want to ensure the continuation of electrical activity in one of the organs of my body; I want to live. One view of the person behind—or perhaps in front of—the electrical activity is that the self is merely a 'valuable abstraction'.[36] This is Dennett's view and sits alongside his view of human consciousness as the operations of a virtual machine (an evolving computer program that shapes the activities of the brain) and his rejection of any central meaner or executive body or 'mini-me' sitting inside the brain. The apparent existence of multiple 'selfs' within a person suffering from multiple personality disorder (although the selfs may not be as fully developed) certainly suggests that the self may be a construction. One of the consequences of such a view is that the self-as-a-construction need not always reside within the body as it is not an inherent part of it, nor the source of its actions, but rather a product of it. As such, it could survive beyond the existence of the body:

> If you think of yourself as a center of narrative gravity, . . . your existence depends on the persistence of that narrative . . . which could theoretically survive indefinitely many switches of medium, be teleported as readily (in principle) as the evening news, and stored indefinitely as sheer information. If what you are is that organization of information that has structured your body's control system (or, to put it in its more usual provocative form, if what you are is the program that runs on your brain's computer), then you could in principle survive the death of your body as intact as a program can survive the destruction of the computer on which it was created and first run.[37]

This view opens the door to a number of opportunities and problems. If death of the body need not inevitably mean death of the self then we will need to be clearer, both ethically and legally, on when life ends. If the self is truly distinct from the body, then the death of the self may also not inevitably signify death of the body. Again, in that scenario, when does life end?

This brief discussion of the role of human consciousness in human life has, unsurprisingly perhaps, raised more questions than it has answered. It has, however, revealed the nature of the ongoing academic debate on consciousness. The importance of consciousness lies in what it may reveal about the nature and meaning of human life. As we do not yet have a clear explanation for how

---

[34] Donald, n. 9 above, p. 178. For details of the established link between consciousness and electrical brain activity, see Donald's discussion at pp. 168–78.   [35] ibid.
[36] Dennett, n. 8 above, p. 431.   [37] ibid, p. 430.

consciousness arises or why, any search for a definitive explanation of life itself is destined to fail. Some lessons can be learned from this discussion, however, and regarded as tentative conclusions to take forward into the subsequent discussion of the boundaries of life. First, consciousness is inextricably linked to electrical brain activity—the firing of neurons may not be 'me' but there is little doubt that it (at least) enables the functioning of the living organism in which I reside and is indicative of conscious awareness. Second, whether regarded as the traditional mini-me sitting in the throne room of the brain (if we could only locate it), or as a self-as-a-construction analogous to a computer software program running on the hardware of the brain, there is an intangible 'something' that comprises the individual that is in some (again intangible) way distinct from the living organism of the (rest of) the body. While the future might bring with it the possibility of dividing these two entities, a human life today comprises both working in tandem. Against this backdrop, it is now necessary to turn our attention to the issue of the boundaries of human life; the age-old questions of when does life begin, and when does it end?

C. The end of life: defining death

Perhaps counter-intuitively, discussion of the boundaries of life will begin with the question of when life ends. (The reason for this structure will become clear as the section concludes.) At first glance it may appear to be obvious when life ends, because there is often perceived to be a clear distinction between life and death. Traditionally, death occurs when an individual ceases breathing or when his or her heart stops beating. This is known as cardio-respiratory failure. It is far from a complete answer to when life ends, however. Advances in medical technology have enabled the restarting of a heart that has stopped beating, as well as artificial respiration to counter a cessation in breathing independently. The consequence of these advances is that a person who would previously have been regarded as dead—one who is not breathing and/or whose heart is not beating—can now be revived. The incursion of death into life has been halted and pushed back. This leaves the question, however, of what death means if it no longer means cardio-respiratory failure. The question was first addressed by an ad hoc committee of the Harvard Medical School in 1968.[38] The committee, chaired by anaesthesiologist Henry Beecher, reached two significant recommendations. First, it offered a set of criteria by which doctors could establish that a patient had suffered permanent loss of all brain functions. Second, it proposed those criteria as a diagnosis of death.

The criteria offered by the Harvard committee specified the termination of all functions of the whole brain, including both conscious activities and unconscious,

---

[38] The committee's findings were published in 'A Definition of Irreversible Coma' (1968) 205 *Journal of American Medical Association* 337.

or reflexive, activities. Some opponents of these criteria would, as we shall see, have preferred a focus solely upon the activities of the so-called higher brain and the irreversible loss of consciousness. As Martin Pernick explains, the 'ensuing controversy between advocates of whole-brain and higher-brain criteria for diagnosing brain death often reflected a much older conceptual contest over whether mental activity or bodily integration constituted the essence of human life'.[39] At the time of the committee's investigation, it was not surprising that the criteria for brain death focused upon the cessation of all functions of the whole brain, because there was at that time no test for whether higher-brain activity had ceased. The Harvard committee did not conclusively advocate a whole-brain definition of death, however, as there is an important distinction between criteria for death and a definition of death. It is not an easy distinction to apply, as Pernick goes on to explain:

A capacity like the ability to breathe, to integrate bodily functions, or to experience consciousness can be seen simply as a marker that indicates whether a more basic something else called *life* is still present. But the ability to perform these very same functions can also be considered not the indicator but the essence of life.[40]

The Harvard committee seemed to adopt the former approach but when, in 1981, another US committee, the President's Commission for the Study of Ethical Problems in Medicine and Biomedical and Behavioral Research, explicitly rejected the higher-brain definition of death, the distinction between criteria and definition—and thus between an indicator and the essence of life—was blurred. The President's Commission reached its conclusions against the backdrop of an important sea change in the reason for needing a clear definition of death. Originally, as cardio-respiratory failure became outdated, brain death was seen as a means of protecting doctors from legal liability for removing organs for transplant; by the 1980s there was a new and equally important need for an unambiguous definition: to protect the public from futile medical treatment.[41] The President's Commission proposed a uniform model death law.[42] The Uniform Determination of Death Act is now law in thirty-six US jurisdictions. It contains a bifurcated legal standard: both cardio-respiratory failure and whole-brain death are regarded as legal death. This does not mean that there are two different ways to die in the United States; rather, that there are two different ways for doctors to determine that somebody has died. This is an important distinction which will be returned to below.

The whole-brain death criteria has been somewhat modified within the UK where the clinical and legal emphasis is on brain stem death. The brain stem's

---

[39] M.S. Pernick, 'Brain Death in a Cultural Context: The Reconstruction of Death 1967–1981' in S.J. Younger, R.M. Arnold & R. Schapiro (eds), *The Definition of Death: Contemporary Controversies* (Baltimore: Johns Hopkins University Press, 1999), p. 12.   [40] ibid, p. 22.
[41] ibid, p. 17.
[42] *Defining Death: Medical, Legal and Ethical Issues in the Determination of Death* (Washington DC: Government Printing Office, 1981).

functions include crucial centres responsible for generating the capacity for consciousness and the respiratory centre. It is also the part of the brain least affected by a lack of oxygen. Therefore, it can be assumed that if the brain stem is irreversibly destroyed by a lack of oxygen, so too are the other parts of the brain. David Lamb is a strong proponent of brain stem death criteria. He describes the 'death of the critical system as measured by tests for the irreversible cessation of brainstem functions' as the appropriate criterion for death, which he defines more broadly as the 'irreversible loss of function of the organism as a whole'.[43] Brain stem death (BSD) has been accepted by the courts in the UK as the legal definition of death. In *Re A*,[44] a young boy was taken to hospital with head injuries which suggested a non-accidental injury. He was placed on a ventilator but was subsequently declared brain stem dead. His parents wanted him to be maintained on the ventilator to enable their own experts to examine him in the light of potential legal proceedings. The court refused, however, holding that the boy was legally dead and the doctors would not be acting unlawfully by disconnecting the ventilator. This judicial acceptance of BSD as legal death was subsequently confirmed by the House of Lords in *Airedale NHS Trust v Bland*. Lord Keith, for example, said that 'In the eyes of the medical world and of the law a person is not clinically dead so long as the brain stem retains its function.'[45]

Brain stem death is not without its critics, however. Martyn Evans, for example, opposes BSD as he regards it as counter-intuitive to classify an individual with a heartbeat as dead.[46] He notes that BSD is not always the approach taken to death and that it is only in the intensive care unit scenario, where an individual's cardio-respiratory functions are artificially maintained, that the BSD approach is necessary in order to 'penetrate the mask of maintained functions and to diagnose the true underlying state of the unfortunate patient'.[47] Ultimately, Evans takes the view that a BSD diagnosis regards a dying patient as already dead.[48] If true, this would be a serious encroachment into any ethical or legal protection of life, such as through a right to life, and would amount to unsustainable ambiguity on such a fundamental issue as death. Underlying this issue is the question of whether death is most appropriately described as a process or an event.

The view that death is a process is based upon the fact that individual cells in the body cease to function at different times depending on their sensitivity to a lack of oxygen. This leads some commentators to argue that we should not seek a single point of death, nor a comprehensive definition of it, but instead should answer various relevant questions, such as when life support can be withdrawn, when organs can be harvested and when a body can be buried or cremated, on

[43] D. Lamb, *Death, Brain Death and Ethics* (London: Croom Helm, 1985), p. 14.
[44] (1992) 3 Med.L.R. 303.   [45] [1993] 1 All ER 831, p. 859.
[46] M. Evans, 'Against the Definition of Brain Stem Death' in R. Lee & D. Morgan (eds), *Death Rites: Law and Ethics at the End of Life* (London: Routledge, 1994).   [47] ibid, p. 1.
[48] ibid, p. 9.

their own merits.[49] In Baruch Brody's view, the respective answers to these three questions should be (a) that life support can be withdrawn when an organism is no longer a person, (b) that organs can be harvested when cortical function has been lost and the organism can no longer breathe on its own, and (c) that an organism can be buried or cremated only after asystole when the organism is fully dead.[50] These answers, and indeed the posing of the separate questions, immediately reveal the often hidden complexity of the seemingly simple question of when life ends. For some commentators, the recognition of such complexity is unwelcome and a single point of death should be sought. James Bernat, for example, rejects Brody's idea of death as a process and argues that a singular event of death needs to be identified.[51] Lamb also argues that a clear-cut distinction between life and death is needed, for when it is abandoned 'there is nothing to prevent a step on a slippery slope where ethical imperatives to preserve life may cease to apply with the onset of any serious illness or permanent handicap'.[52] A clear distinction between life and death is indeed desirable, especially from this book's perspective of a right to life, but Lamb's argument on this point is not always convincing. He tries to explain, for example, that a view of death as a process implies either that the process starts when the person is still living or that it starts when the person is already dead. In Lamb's view, the former would confuse the process of death with the process of dying, while the latter would confuse it with the process of disintegration.[53] This is a circular argument, however, for it depends upon a distinction between dying and disintegration: it assumes that dying is something that happens while a person is still alive and that disintegration of the body happens after death. But the view that Lamb is criticizing denies that there exists a clear distinction between dying, death and disintegration. Under the death-as-a-process view, the process does not start either when the patient is alive or when he is dead because such a clear dividing line cannot be drawn. Regarding death as a process inevitably causes difficulties for the law and ethics but it cannot be criticized for failing to respect the life/death boundary because that is its entire point: there is no single such boundary.

The societal need for a clear line between life and death is obvious to many: organ transplants, inheritance rules, criminal liability and disposal of the body all require clarity on this issue, as does the need for a deceased's loved ones to

---

[49] B.A. Brody, 'How much of the Brain must be Dead?' in Younger, Arnold & Schapiro, n. 39 above, at pp. 79–81.   [50] ibid.
[51] J.L. Bernat, 'Refinements in the Definition and Criterion of Death' in Younger, Arnold & Schapiro, n. 39 above, at pp. 84–5. Bernat makes the point that death does not usually seem like a process. It is only in some chronic conditions that it does so and the general definition of death should not focus only on this rare scenario.
[52] Lamb, n. 43 above, p. 75. Lamb actually makes a distinction between 'clinical death' (the cessation of integrative action between all organ systems of the body) which he regards as an event and 'biological death' (the irreversible loss of function of all of the body's organs) which he accepts as a process.   [53] See Lamb, ibid, pp. 81–2.

grieve. Alexander Capron explains that viewing death as a process in medical terms does not preclude a clear legal and social definition of death:

although dying is a process (since not all parts of the body cease functioning equally and synchronously), a line can and must be drawn between those beings who are alive and those who are dead. The ability of modern biomedicine to extend the functioning of various organ systems may have made knowing which side of the line a patient is on more problematic, but it has not erased the line.[54]

In this context, the line may be somewhat arbitrary. It is needed in order to regulate certain legal, social and ethical issues but could conceivably be drawn at various different points. If this is the case, could there be an element of individual choice in determining when life ends?

One of the leading proponents of a subjective definition of death is Robert Veatch who has argued in favour of a conscience clause to enable individuals to accept or reject a brain death criterion for death. Veatch justifies the argument as follows:

A great deal is at stake in determining exactly when someone dies. Wills will be read, assets distributed, and the timing of the occurrence of the death, which may be critical for determining inheritance, prosecution of crimes, and other things, will be established. These are not neurological issues; they are social, normative issues about which all citizens may reasonably voice a position relying on their personal religious, philosophical, and ethical view of the world.[55]

The fact that views upon death vary greatly can be seen when the approach in certain different cultures is compared. While many people in western states accept the development of a brain death definition, others stridently reject it. The main examples of cultures rejecting the brain death concept are Orthodox Jews, Native Americans and the Japanese. Orthodox Jews and Native Americans both place great value upon respiration and traditionally find it unacceptable to regard someone as dead if he or she is still breathing, whether artificially assisted or not. David Novak explains that, for Judaism, this view originates in Genesis 2:7 ('The Lord God... breathed into his nostrils the breath of life...') which is interpreted as meaning that 'human life is still human as long as its human subject is still breathing'.[56] The Japanese opposition to brain death is also based upon a lack

---

[54] A.M. Capron, 'The Bifurcated Legal Standard for Determining Death: Does it Work?' in Younger, Arnold & Schapiro, n. 39 above, p. 128.

[55] R.M. Veatch, 'The Conscience Clause: How much Individual Choice in Defining Death can our Society Tolerate?' in Younger, Arnold & Schapiro, n. 39 above, pp. 140–1.

[56] D. Novak, *The Sanctity of Human Life* (Washington DC: Georgetown University Press, 2007), p. 40. The ethical consequences of this view are well explained by Clive Lawton: 'Maimonides, who besides being a great rabbi was a great physician, commented that the only way of being absolutely sure that somebody was dead was if their head was missing. Certainly, the view seems to be that principles such as brain death are not clear and objective enough. A doctor needs irrefutable evidence that the individual is not likely to be so again—particularly when the doctor is driven by the urgent possibility of saving another life through organ transplant.'

of faith in neurological criteria for death that do not pay attention to the most obvious indicators of life: breathing, heartbeat, a warm body. As Noel Williams describes, an academic debate on the respective merits of the traditional approach to death and the new theory of Nōshi (brain death) remains unresolved.[57] Japan has not incorporated brain death into its law, but most other states have done so. One US jurisdiction has an interesting approach, however. The New Jersey Declaration of Death Act 1991 sets out a whole brain criterion for death but also expressly permits religious objection to the use of this criterion in favour of a cardiac criterion. New Jersey is the only jurisdiction to legislate so that death is not uniform. Imagine two patients in identical medical conditions: one may be regarded as deceased because of the irreversible cessation of all critical brain functions; while the other, due to a rejection of brain death, may be treated as still living. Whatever the merits of such an approach in terms of religious and cultural freedom and self-autonomy, any law which encourages such ambiguity on the vital issue of life and death is ultimately unsatisfactory. If a line is to be drawn between life and death (even if it is to be an arbitrary line), it must be drawn in the same place for everyone; any other approach fails to respect the life of all in equal terms.

The acceptance of brain death has led some commentators to go further and propose a concept of higher-brain death. John Lizza raises the issue of why so many of us accept brain death: 'we have been willing to accept brain death as death not because we have been certain that it constitutes the irreversible loss of organic integration but because we have been certain that it entails the irreversible loss of consciousness and every other mental function...'[58] Under this argument, it is the irreversible loss of consciousness which signifies the end of life. An example of such a loss is a patient in persistent vegetative state (PVS). This condition entails irreversible damage to the higher brain when the brain stem is still functioning. The normal functioning of the brain stem means that the patient may be breathing independently but the destruction of other parts of the brain means that the patient will have no awareness or consciousness of the world around him or her. This PVS condition poses considerable ethical and legal dilemmas across the world. The patient does not meet the criteria for either whole brain death or brain stem death but everything that made that patient a person has gone: memories, the ability to communicate, conscious awareness. Is

P. Morgan & C.A. Lawton (eds), *Ethical Issues in Six Religious Traditions* (Edinburgh: Edinburgh University Press, 2007, 2nd edn.), p. 188.

[57] See N. Williams, *The Right to Life in Japan* (London: Routledge, 1997), p. 25. Williams also notes that the Japanese have traditionally seen death as connected with beauty and so how a person dies is considered to be of fundamental importance: 'whereas the sacrifice of one's life in a beautiful way is honourable, the mere clinging onto life for its own sake is considered ugly and vulgar' (pp. 93–4).

[58] J.P. Lizza, *Persons, Humanity and the Definition of Death* (Baltimore: Johns Hopkins University Press, 2006), p. 163.

this patient really still alive or is death of the person that he or she used to be a sufficient criterion for the end of life?

Jeff McMahan takes this view and regards patients in PVS as already dead, due to the loss of their higher brain functions, even though their organism, or body, lives on.[59] He argues that this organism should be treated as a dead body because 'a mere organism does not have interests and cannot itself be benefited or harmed. To end its life is no more objectionable than it is to kill a plant, provided that what is done does not contravene the posthumous interests of, or manifest disrespect for, the person who once animated the organism'.[60] Lizza also regards the continuation of the organism that once constituted the person as a non-critical issue. He distinguishes between the life of the person and the life of the human organism and argues that organic integration is insufficient for the continued life of a person.[61] What of the problematic issue of the 'dead' person still breathing without assistance? For Lizza this is a minor inconvenience:

Whereas a person is normally transformed into a corpse at his or her death, technology has intervened in this natural process...Instead of a person's death resulting in remains in the form of an inanimate corpse, a person's remains can now take the form of a living being devoid of the capacity for consciousness and any other mental function.[62]

This does not fully appreciate the practical difficulties of dealing with a dead body that is still breathing or the emotional challenge for relatives to accept their loved one as dead when the body is still so alive. Nevertheless, the distinction between a human organism and a person is well supported in philosophical thought. The concept of personhood carrying with it moral value is a common theme. John Harris, for example, argues that 'what we need to know is not when life begins, but rather when life begins to matter morally. And the correlated question is not "when does life end?" but rather "when does life cease to matter morally?"' and he asserts that the entity that is valuable in this way is classed a 'person'.[63] Peter Singer takes a similar view and expressly states that the right to life 'is not a right of members of the species Homo sapiens; it is...a right that properly belongs to persons'.[64] Mary Anne Warren explains that personhood is 'a psychological concept, not a biological one. It is a being's mental and behavioural capacities that make it a person, not the shape of its body, the microstructure of its chromosomes, or any other strictly physiological characteristic.'[65] There is, therefore, some strong academic support for a distinction between the human living organism and the entity that has moral value, namely the person. Unfortunately, there is

[59] J. McMahan, 'Brain Death, Cortical Death and Persistent Vegetative State' in H. Kuhse & P. Singer, *Companion to Bioethics* (Oxford: Blackwell, 1998).   [60] ibid, p. 258.

[61] Lizza, n. 58 above, p. 13 and generally.   [62] ibid, p. 15.

[63] J. Harris, *The Value of Life: An Introduction to Medical Ethics* (London: Routledge, 1985), p. 8.

[64] P. Singer, *Rethinking Life and Death: The Collapse of Our Traditional Ethics* (Oxford: Oxford University Press, 1995), p. 206. In Singer's view, personhood need not be confined to the species homo sapiens and he is a strong proponent of animal rights.

[65] Warren, n. 1 above, pp. 93–4.

very little agreement on what qualities are needed for personhood. Consciousness is widely regarded as a minimum characteristic, at least in the sense of basic self-awareness. Other proposed criteria include capacity for reason (Singer), capacity to value one's own existence (Harris) and moral agency (Kant). The problem with these theories is that they either include many other species within the concept of personhood (not necessarily objectionable in itself but requiring significant changes to our treatment of other species) or they exclude many human beings. Both Singer and Harris are comfortable with excluding infants and PVS patients from personhood, and thus from moral status, although Warren proposes a multi-criterial approach to moral status which would explain 'why it is appropriate to accord full moral status to infants and other sentient human beings who are not moral agents, while denying it to most non-human animals—including many whose mental capacities are more impressive than those of a human infant'.[66] This seems to be the key issue: when the nature of human life, including its individual capacity for consciousness and self-awareness, as well as reasoning ability, varies so widely between different individuals, how can a single test for morally valuable life be appropriate? A better solution seems to be to divide the issue into two distinct questions: why does human life matter morally? And, why does an individual's life matter morally? From the answers to these two questions, we can develop a working model of when life ends (as well as when life begins).

The question of why human life matters seems to be tied inextricably to the concept of consciousness. As we have seen above, ambiguity still surrounds this concept. For example, the simplistic distinction between whole-brain death and higher-brain death is undermined by recent findings in neuroscience that consciousness is not anatomically grounded exclusively in the neocortex, not to mention that we still do not (and may never) understand why the rapidity of electrical firings of neurons results in self-awareness. Nevertheless, consciousness stakes a good claim to being the key to human life. The higher level of consciousness enjoyed by humans as compared to many other species is the underlying reason why human life should be regarded as more valuable and given greater protection, morally and legally, than the life of a virus, a plant, an insect and even a pig. (A chimpanzee is another matter entirely, as discussed above.) Human life matters because of human consciousness. But—and here is the key—if human life matters, then it *always matters*, regardless of personhood, rationality, moral agency or consciousness. The life of an individual human being matters morally not because that organism is sentient or rational (or free of pain, or values its own existence) but because it is a human life. This point is supported by the ethical and legal principle of equality which is well established in the field of human rights, with perhaps Ronald Dworkin providing the strongest support for it.[67] It comes into play here as a convincing ethical justification for the proposition

---

[66] Warren, ibid, p. 181.
[67] See, for example, R. Dworkin, *Taking Rights Seriously* (London: Duckworth, 1977).

that if human life matters, then the life of each human matters equally, regardless of differences in rationality or the level of consciousness. From an end of life perspective, this means that life ends only when the human organism dies. This cannot sensibly require the death of all of the body's cells but rather the death of the organism as a whole. In other words, life comes to an end when the integrative action between the organs of the body is irreversibly lost. It is the life of the organism which matters, not its living component parts, and thus it is the permanent destruction of that integrative organism which signifies the end of the organism's life. That end is inevitable, complex, but discernible. The death of the brain, or the brain stem (provided we can retain a reasonable level of scientific certainty that the death of the brain stem inevitably means the earlier death of the rest of the brain), is one means of discerning that end. And it is not negotiable on an individual basis.

D. The beginning of life: life before birth?

Having established a workable theory for when life ends, it is now necessary to consider the other boundary of life: its beginning. As a preliminary note, it should be mentioned that this is not the place for an in-depth analysis of the conflicting rights of a fetus and its mother. Chapter 6 will discuss the right to life when it comes into conflict with the rights of others and this will include consideration of a conflict between the right to life of a fetus and the conflicting rights of its mother. In this section, we are only seeking to determine when life begins, for the purposes of the right to life. If it is decided that life begins at conception then the potential conflict with the mother's rights to be discussed in chapter 6 becomes a huge issue; if, on the other hand, life is regarded as beginning at birth then there will be no need for any discussion of the conflicting rights of the mother for there will be no fetal right to life at issue. If life begins at some point between conception and birth then the discussion in chapter 6 will be adjusted accordingly.

The question of when life begins is one that has challenged many commentators over the years. The three main theories for the beginning of life are conception, viability and birth. All of these have some individual merit but there is a sense in which choosing any one of them is a purely arbitrary decision. The beginning of human life is a process, not an event, and the progress is relatively continuous throughout the nine months of pregnancy and, crucially, beyond. As Jonathan Glover notes, 'Conventional lines for social or legal purposes could always be drawn, but we would be mistaken if we took the shadows cast by these lines for boundaries in biological reality.'[68] To some extent, the human organism that will later be born can have its life traced back to conception. Many people believe, often for religious reasons, that human life begins, and should be protected, at

[68] J. Glover, *Causing Death and Saving Lives* (London: Penguin, 1977) at p. 127.

this point. This view presents both practical and theoretical difficulties, however. On a practical level, if such a view were legally accepted, it would mean that not only abortion, but also some contraceptive methods, would conflict with fetal life. The contraceptive pill, for example, not only works to prevent fertilization but also changes the womb lining to make it reject fertilized eggs and thus prevent implantation. It thus has the potential to destroy the human life created at conception. Furthermore, each menstrual period has a similar potential to cause mourning for the loss of human life.[69] It is the futility of any attempt to protect all human life from conception that makes this such a problematic starting point for life. There is also a theoretical difficulty, however, because, while it is true that a fertilized egg is potentially a human being, so too are the unfertilized egg and the sperm:

> To say that a fertilised egg is potentially a human being is just to say that if certain things happen to it (like implantation), and certain other things do not (like spontaneous abortion), it will eventually become a human being. But the same is also true of the unfertilised egg and the sperm. If certain things happen to the egg (like meeting a sperm) and certain things happen to the sperm (like meeting an egg) and thereafter certain other things do not (like meeting a contraceptive), then they will eventually become a new human being.[70]

Drawing a theoretical line between potential human beings and reproductive products of existing human beings is, therefore, an extremely difficult, and possibly misconceived, task.

At the other extreme, we could regard life as beginning at birth. This has the advantage of clarity and certainty. (It also, although that should not concern us here, avoids any issue of conflict with the interests of another human being within whose body the fetus resides.) An unavoidable difficulty, however, is that the newborn baby is nearly identical to the full-term fetus. Only the geography has changed. Why should we value the life of one and not the other? Furthermore, if life begins at birth, does it matter when birth occurs? Does a baby born at twenty-two weeks have a life worthy of protection, while a fetus at thirty-six weeks does not? This is obviously ridiculous. The location of the organism should be irrelevant to a determination of whether it is a human life. (It is, of course, very relevant to the issue of a conflict of rights with the mother.)

An intermediary step between conception and birth which draws considerable support as the starting point of life is viability. This describes the state at which a fetus is capable of being born alive and has the potential to survive independently of its mother's body. When the fetus has reached this stage of development, there is a strong argument that it has acquired a human life and that that life deserves some protection. Viability is not without difficulties, however, because it is a shifting boundary, dependent upon the state of modern technology and its

---

[69] J.K. Mason, *Medico-Legal Aspects of Reproduction and Parenthood* (Aldershot: Dartmouth Publishing, 1998, 2nd edn.), pp. 109–10.   [70] Harris, n. 63 above, pp. 11–12.

availability to a particular fetus. As Glover argues, there 'seems to be something absurd about a moving boundary, so that we might say "last year this fetus would not have been a person at this stage, but since they re-equipped the intensive care unit, it is one".[71] Furthermore, viability of any one individual baby will depend greatly upon its country of birth and the medical facilities available there. Nevertheless, viability has some merit as the boundary for the beginning of life. This can be demonstrated by drawing upon the conclusions from the previous section on the end of life.

It was proposed in the previous section that human life matters because of the species' capacity for consciousness. An obvious line of thought here, therefore, is to consider when a fetus (or baby) acquires consciousness. This is a far from simple question, however. Brain waves first appear at about eight weeks' gestation but this in itself is not a significant development. As Bonnie Steinbock explains, brain function is only significant because it is a necessary condition for mental states such as sentience and conscious awareness and these mental states cannot occur until much later when the neural pathways to the cortex are further developed.[72] This is estimated to occur at around twenty-two to twenty-four weeks' gestation.[73] Warren also explains that, while we cannot be certain when human sentience begins, it is fairly certain that it is not before the late second or third trimester because, before that stage, neither the sense organs nor the parts of the central nervous system necessary for the processing of sensory information are sufficiently developed.[74] McMahan adopts a similar view: 'Most neurologists accept that the earliest point at which consciousness is possible is around the twentieth week of pregnancy, which is when synaptic connections begin to form among the cortical neurons. It is, however, unlikely that consciousness becomes possible until after at least another month.'[75] In support of this, McMahan quotes the neurologist Julius Korein who explains that the fundamental core of brain function develops gradually between the twentieth and twenty-eighth week of pregnancy, culminating in the unequivocal presence of consciousness.[76] In addition to the difficulty in determining exactly when consciousness develops, there is a further more fundamental problem with this approach to the beginning of

---

[71] Glover, n. 68 above, p. 125.

[72] B. Steinbock, *Life Before Birth: The Moral and Legal Status of Embryos and Fetuses* (Oxford: Oxford University Press, 1992), p. 50.   [73] ibid.

[74] Warren, n. 1 above, p. 205.

[75] J. McMahan, *The Ethics of Killing: Problems at the Margins of Life* (Oxford: Oxford University Press, 2002), p. 267.

[76] 'Neurons in the cortical plate first begin to form cortical synapses at about 20 weeks. These neurons then form synaptic connections between other intracerebral structures such as the thalamus and the brain stem, resulting in sensory reception and more patterned spontaneous and induced motor activity. Cortical EEG activity can be first recorded at about 21–22 weeks after fertilization; the blink-startle response, with eyes opening, to auditory stimuli can be demonstrated at 24 weeks; and cortical sensory evoked potentials appear at about 25–27 weeks' (J. Korein, 'Ontogenesis of the Brain in the Human Organism: Definitions of Life and Death of the Human Being and Person' (1997) 2 Advances in Bioethics 1, at pp. 25–6).

life. It was argued in the previous section that, while human life in general matters because of consciousness, an individual's life matters because it is a human
life. A fetus is a human being in development and therefore it would be inconsistent with the conclusions posited above about when life ends to deny that a fetus is
a human life merely because it is not yet conscious.

A better approach would be to focus on the other conclusion in the previous section, namely that life ends when the human organism no longer retains
integrative function. By corollary, we might assert that life begins once a fetus
develops organic integration. When is this? Viability asserts a strong claim to
represent this stage of development. At present, in developed countries where
neonatal intensive care is available, viability stands at about twenty-two weeks.
A baby born earlier than that will be unable to survive due to its poorly developed
lungs which will prevent breathing even with the aid of an artificial ventilator.[77]
Even after twenty-two weeks the chances of long-term survival are slim but, with
medical assistance, the baby's body has the potential to function effectively. Until
the lungs are sufficiently developed to enable the supply of oxygen to the other
organs (with assistance if necessary), the body cannot be regarded as capable of
functioning as an integrated organism. To mirror the conclusions about the end
of life, we could thus assert that until viability there is no human life. We have
thus arrived at two proposed boundaries to life: from viability to the death of
the brain. The key to an individual organism's life is integrative function (governed by the brain and requiring sufficiently developed lungs to supply oxygen
to the major organs) while the key to human life—the justification for it being
rewarded with greater protection than most other forms of life on the planet—is
the high level of consciousness which we as a species (together, perhaps, with our
closest ape relatives) enjoy.

E. Conclusion

The purpose of this introductory chapter has been to consider the concept of
life itself. This will serve as a useful backdrop to later consideration of the legal
and ethical protection of a right to life. The discussion of life has drawn upon
a wide variety of disciplines (anthropology, neuroscience, psychology, philosophy) and has only been able to skim the surface of many of the complex questions surrounding the concept of life. Issues addressed include the questions of
what distinguishes human life from other animal life; how that human life has
evolved into its current state; the significance of consciousness for human life
and how that has evolved; whether the mind is distinct from the body; and when

---

[77] In the case of *C v S* in 1987 ([1987] 1 All ER 1230), it was held by the court that a fetus of
18–21 weeks' gestation was not capable of being born alive because it was incapable of breathing by
the use of its own lungs, even with the assistance of a ventilator.

life begins and ends. Many of these questions are not susceptible to a definitive answer at this stage in human development. However, a few important conclusions have been reached which will cast a shadow over the remainder of this book. First, it has been proposed that the fundamental value of life for homo sapiens as a species is the high level of consciousness which the species enjoys. This invisible power of our mind has been the key to our rapid evolution and distinguishes us from most, but perhaps not all, other species on earth. The possibility that other apes have evolved a comparable capacity for consciousness issues a note of caution for our treatment of our closest animal relatives. While consciousness lies at the core of the human life that, as we shall see, the law seeks to protect, not all members of the species have an equal capacity for consciousness. The second conclusion of this chapter is that limited, or even irreversibly damaged, consciousness should not prevent an individual benefiting from the protection given to human life in general. (The argument that protection of life may not always be beneficial to an individual in such a state will be considered in later chapters.) Instead, the core requirement for an individual human being to be regarded as possessing a life is basic integrative function of the organism. In other words, from viability to brain death, while a human organism has the potential to function in an integrative manner, an individual has a life equal to that of all other human organisms. Later chapters of this book consider at length the types of conflicting interests that will justify the deprivation of a human life (and it is possible that the permanent destruction of consciousness or the conflicting rights of a viable fetus's mother may suffice for such a justification), but the main argument to be drawn from this introductory chapter is that the boundaries of life are not dependent on consciousness or birth. From viability to brain death a human organism has a life. Now we can begin to consider whether, and if so why, that life should be legally protected.

2
The Right to Life: Religious, Philosophical, and Legal Origins

In the previous chapter, the concept of human life was discussed and it was concluded that the fundamental value of this is the high level of consciousness which homo sapiens as a species enjoy. It was also concluded that from viability to brain death, an individual member of that species has a life equal to that of all other human organisms. In this chapter, it is now necessary to investigate the human origins of the idea that human life has an inherent value. This concept has religious and philosophical roots and serves as the underlying principle for the modern-day right to life. We will see its development from a religious belief in the sanctity of human life, through philosophical musings about why human life is valuable and whether individuals enjoy certain rights by virtue of their human-ity, to the gradual development of a right to life in international law. This chap-ter is in large part an analysis of the rhetoric of the right to life: why do people believe that human life is a valuable asset and why do they seek to protect that life through human rights law? This is only half of the overall picture, however, and the remainder will be revealed in chapter 3 when the practical enforcement of the right to life is discussed. Without such implementation, the rhetoric of a right to life as revealed in this chapter is ultimately hollow and illusory. This danger should be borne in mind through the following pages as the human belief in the value of human life, as expressed by words rather than actions, is exposed.

A. Religious origins of a right to life

The contribution paid by religion to the development of a concept of a moral and legal right to life cannot be ignored. It has been argued that 'all of the great religious traditions share a universal dissatisfaction with the world as it is and a determination to make it better by addressing the meaning of human life, the worth and dignity of all persons, and, consequently, the duty toward those who suffer.'[1] It is from this perspective that we must investigate the role of the world's

---

[1] P.G. Lauren, *The Evolution of International Human Rights: Visions Seen* (Philadelphia: University of Pennsylvania Press, 2003, 2nd edn.), p. 5.

major religions in prioritizing a sacred value for human life. Perhaps most significantly, the sanctity of human life lies at the core of the Judaeo-Christian tradition which has so dominated the development of contemporary western standards. Therefore, it is with this tradition that we will start.

(1) The Judaeo-Christian tradition

A good starting point for consideration of this issue is the first book of both the Christian Old Testament and the Jewish Torah: the Book of Genesis. This shared notion of the origin of humanity leaves no doubt that human life is of peculiar value and should be treated as such. For example, the first command from God to Adam and Eve concerning the tree of knowledge—'On the day you eat from it you shall surely die'[2]—is described by the Jewish writer, David Novak, as 'a beneficent warning to humans about how to avoid death'.[3] Furthermore, it is in the Book of Genesis that God punishes Cain for murdering his brother Abel. This has raised the question of how, at this apparently early stage in human history, Cain could have been expected to know that taking a human life was prohibited by God. Novak argues that 'the answer seems to be that Cain and Abel were both expected to be aware of the fact that they had been created in the image of God...As such, an assault on the image is tantamount to an assault on the One whose image has been assaulted.'[4] This point is more explicit in Genesis 9:6 where it is stated that 'whosoever sheds human blood by humans shall his blood be shed because in the image of God He made humankind'. This has been described as 'a re-presentation of a norm that has no single historical origin but is coterminous with human being in the world, at all times and everywhere'.[5] It is also an early expression of the now infamous equation of 'a life for a life'.[6] This severe punishment for killing another human being serves both to highlight the value placed upon human life in both the Old Testament and the Torah, as well as to imply that some killings are justified: the issue at the core of this book. In the context of the Book of Genesis, it is clear that the pronouncement that 'whosoever sheds human blood by humans shall his blood be shed' is not merely an issue of the punishment fitting the crime, but that the killing of human life is an assault on God in whose image mankind is made.[7] This is a fundamental principle both in Genesis and in the Judaeo-Christian tradition. Clive Lawton reveals a Talmudic discussion between Rabbi Akiva and Ben Zoma on the issue of the most important line in the Torah. They finally agreed upon a relatively obscure line from Genesis: 'These are the generations of Adam.' The reason for this choice was

---

[2] Genesis 2:17.
[3] D. Novak, *The Sanctity of Human Life* (Washington DC: Georgetown University Press, 2007), p. 37.   [4] ibid, p. 36.
[5] ibid, p. 39.   [6] Exodus 21:23; Leviticus 24:18.   [7] See Novak, n. 3 above, p. 36.

twofold. First, it 'reminds us that all people are descended from Adam (thereby making them all of equal ancestry)'.[8] Second, it reminds us that 'Adam was created in the image of God (thereby making it clear that all human beings deserve respect as descended from someone created in the image of God)…'[9] If this can be regarded by Talmudic authorities as the most important line in the entire Torah, it is clear that the principle of the value of human life as made in the image of God will have had a profound impact on the development of western laws and morals. Modern Christianity also continues to assert a similar principle as of fundamental value. In his 1995 encyclical, Pope John Paul II declared that 'Man's life comes from God; it is his gift, his image and imprint, a sharing in his breath of life. God therefore is the sole Lord of this life: Man cannot do with it as he wills…the sacredness of life has its foundation in God and in his creative activity: "For God made man in his own image".'[10]

As Pope John Paul II implies, in conjunction with the concept that God created human beings in His own image, lays the concept of God as the giver of life. From this belief stems a moral obligation to protect human life, including one's own. For example, in Genesis 2:7, it is stated that God 'breathed into his nostrils the breath of life…'. Novak regards this as 'solid scriptural support for the position that God alone has the right to take back the breath of any of his human creatures because God alone directly gave it or placed it in the human body'.[11] This means that humans should neither take their own lives nor the lives of others because to do so would cause offence to God: 'Only the Giver of the gift can take back what He has given; the recipient of the gift, whose charge is to care for it, is not allowed to hand back the gift or cause the gift to be handed back to the Giver.'[12] The religious prohibition on taking one's own life—or handing back God's gift of life—is more explicitly stated in the Book of Deuteronomy where it is commanded that humans 'be very careful with your own lives'[13] and 'surely be very diligent to care for your own life'.[14] It should be briefly noted, however, that taking one's own life is not an unambiguous issue, in ancient times or today. Glanville Williams points out that the Old Testament contains four cases of suicide (Samson, Saul, Abimelech and Ahitophel) and 'gives no indication that they were frowned upon'.[15]

The most well-known assertion of the sanctity of human life in both the Christian Bible and the Jewish Torah is to be found in the Ten Commandments, the sixth of which commands 'Thou shalt not kill'.[16] Even the origin of this commandment is regarded as being found in the Book of Genesis. Genesis 2:16—'And

[8] C. Lawton, 'Judaism' in P. Morgan & C. Lawton (eds), *Ethical Issues in Six Religious Traditions* (Edinburgh: Edinburgh University Press, 2007, 2nd edn.), p. 192.   [9] ibid.
[10] *Evangelium Vitae (The Gospel of Life)*, para. 39. (The document is available at <http://www.vatican.va/holy_father/john_paul_ii/encyclicals/documents/hf_jp-ii_enc_25031995_evangelium-vitae_en.html>.)   [11] Novak, n. 3 above, p. 124.
[12] ibid, pp. 124–5.   [13] Deuteronomy 4:15.   [14] Deuteronomy 4:9.
[15] G. Williams, *The Sanctity of Life and the Criminal Law* (London: Faber & Faber, 1958), p. 225.   [16] Exodus 20:2–17; Deuteronomy 5:6–21.

the Lord God commanded the humans'—has been interpreted by rabbis to mean that God commanded concerning the humans or, in other words, that God commanded what may or may not be done to humans. Therefore, as Novak explains, an assumption has arisen that this verse is the original version of the sixth commandment.[17] The Ten Commandments, or 'Ethical Decalogue', were revealed by Moses on Mount Sinai. In Jewish thought, before this revelation there existed the seven Noahide commandments, regarded by some as a form of natural law. One of these commandments included a prohibition on the shedding of the blood of innocents.[18] It is the Ten Commandments, however, whose legacy has endured. The commandment that 'thou shalt not kill' has a somewhat contentious interpretation. For Jews, as well as in later Protestant versions, it is interpreted as 'thou shalt not murder', whereas Roman Catholic and earlier Protestant translations use the verb 'kill' rather than 'murder'. The more limited nature of a prohibition on murder is obvious but nevertheless for our purposes it cannot be doubted that the sixth commandment, in either form, serves as an early protection for the sanctity of human life. In the Christian tradition, the Sermon on the Mount also re-iterates the commandment that thou shall not kill, adding the crucial but challenging instructions of turning the other cheek and loving thine enemy.[19]

Beyond the negative obligation not to kill, or murder, there is some evidence in both the Old Testament and the Torah for a more positive obligation to protect human life. Leviticus 19:16 declares that 'thou shalt not stand idly by the blood of your neighbour'. This seems to imply a moral duty to preserve life where possible. Furthermore, Lawton notes that although the Torah includes a total of 613 rules or commandments about how to live, all but three of these may be broken if the purpose in doing so is to save life. Only the prohibitions on murder, idolatry and incest must be upheld even at the cost of human life.[20] The extensive regulations which form the heart of the Torah and Jewish law more broadly raise an important distinction which should be noted here to preclude rash conclusions: respect for the sanctity of life does not necessarily imply a right to life. Lawton explains that 'Jewish law exists to keep society stable and protect the individual from exploitation . . . It is more interested in people's responsibilities than in people's rights and the personal fulfilment of the individual.'[21] The undoubted value given to human life in Jewish thought is far removed from the modern-day right to life, even if it ultimately served as a first step in that direction. Similarly in Christian thought, the sanctity of life is not primarily about an individual right to life but about the value of a life given by God: 'Many Christians argue that people do not own their own lives. Life is God's gift and no one has the right to terminate it.'[22] It would be erroneous, therefore, to regard a right to life as stemming from the Judaeo-Christian emphasis on the sanctity of human life. Nevertheless, that tradition is

---

[17] Novak, n. 3 above, p. 37.   [18] ibid, pp. 31–2.   [19] Matthew 5.
[20] Lawton, n. 8 above, pp. 190–1.   [21] ibid, p. 191.
[22] A. Brown, 'Christianity' in Morgan & Lawton, n. 8 above, p. 251.

influential in the context of the right to life, both in terms of serving as a popular justification for the modern-day right and more indirectly by helping to develop western laws and morals which protected human life, leading the violation of such protection to be viewed with repulsion. From this emotional response, via the Nazi death camps, an internationally enforced right to life would eventually emerge in the modern rights era.

(2) Other religious traditions

The value placed upon human life in the Judaeo-Christian tradition is not unique. All of the major religions of the world share a belief in the value of life. In Islam, for example, it has been acknowledged that there are 'many verses of the Qur'an and Traditions of the Prophet Muhammad that acknowledge the sanctity of human life, enjoin its protection and prohibit its arbitrary deprivation'.[23] The sanctity of life in Islamic thought is regarded as having a divinely ordained purpose and destiny.[24] The Qur'an states that 'From God we are and to God is our return.'[25] It also regards the taking of one life as a harm caused to all of humanity: 'If anyone slew a person—unless it be for murder or for spreading mischief in the land—it would be as if he slew humanity as a whole; and if anyone saved a life, it would be as if he saved humanity as a whole.'[26] The taking of life is expressly prohibited elsewhere in the Qur'an: 'Take not life which God has made sacred, except by way of justice and law';[27] 'Nor take life—which God has made sacred—except for just cause.'[28] It will be noted, however, that each of these statements of prohibition on the taking of life incorporates a wide exception where the taking of a life is justified. This limited protection for life is reflected in the 1990 Cairo Declaration on Human Rights. The Cairo Declaration is the response of Islamic states to the Universal Declaration of Human Rights and reveals a reconciliation between Muslim values and individual rights. Although the international protection of the right to life is an issue which will be considered later, it is useful at this stage to mention the protection of the right to life in the Cairo Declaration due to its unique nature as an explicitly Islamic manifestation of the right to life. Article 2 states that 'Life is a God-given gift and the right to life is guaranteed to every human being. It is the duty of individuals, societies and states to safeguard this right against any violation, and it is prohibited to take away life except for a shari'ah prescribed reason.' Baderin explains that in practice the 'shari'ah prescribed reason' exception refers to the death penalty which has only been abolished in two Muslim states (Azerbaijan and Turkey).[29] It is clear that the Islamic tradition does not envisage an absolute sanctity of life but it is not

---

[23] M.A. Baderin, *International Human Rights and Islamic Law* (Oxford: Oxford University Press, 2003), p. 67.   [24] A. Nanji, 'Islam' in Morgan & Lawton, n. 8 above, p. 314.
[25] Qur'an 2:156.   [26] ibid, 5:32.   [27] ibid, 6:151.   [28] ibid, 17:33.
[29] Baderin, n. 23 above, p. 70.

alone amongst the major religions in that approach. Even the Judaeo-Christian tradition which has been so explicit in the value it accords to human life adheres to the 'life for a life' concept and the Old Testament and the Torah sanction the taking of life in numerous situations notwithstanding the commandment not to kill. The protection for human life in Islam is limited but shares with other religions the view that human life is in some way special due to its creation as a gift by God.

In Hinduism, preserving and promoting human life, in particular by pro-creating, is regarded as a central aspect of dharma and thus is the duty of each individual Hindu.[30] The religion advocates respect for all life, although the caste system facilitates discrimination and may undermine the idea that all human life is equal. Sikhism also places a high value on human life, while Buddhism places the value of life at the core of its philosophy, although it emphasizes respect for all living things rather than just human life. The first precept for a Buddhist is 'I undertake the rule of training to refrain from harming any living things' although issues such as intention, the definition of living beings and whether some lives are more important than others are acknowledged in Buddhist think-ing.[31] The reverence for life in Buddhism is related to the concept of *karma*. As Morgan explains, 'Taking life is thought to be morally harmful to those who make the decision and brings negative *karma*.'[32] However, she also emphasizes that each individual case is taken on its merits and that the intention of the per-son taking a life will be relevant: 'If suicide or abortion is an expression of despair, hatred or selfishness then it will be seen to produce nothing but bad *karma*. If, however, the actions are rooted in selfless compassion for others, they cannot be seen as entirely wrong. There is always some *karmic* responsibility for the taking of life, but it is balanced by good intentions.'[33] This rather pragmatic view means that moral absolutes are rare in Buddhist thinking.[34] It is also worth noting that for a Buddhist, a person's *karma* continues into another life and so euthanasia, for example, would not be an effective means of escape from suffering.[35]

---

[30] W. Menski, 'Hinduism' in Morgan & Lawton, n. 8 above, p. 36. Some concern has been expressed, however, that the strong preference for sons rather than daughters in Indian culture has led not only to widespread abortion of female fetuses but even neonaticide: 'since medical tech-nology now makes it possible to determine the sex of an unborn child early in pregnancy through amniocentesis or ultrasound techniques, female foetuses are being aborted in large numbers...It is also not unknown that newborn girls are killed at once...Poor parents often justify this practice by arguing that a little suffering at this early stage is better than a life of misery later' (ibid, pp. 36–7). This worrying practice is not unique to Hinduism and similar concern has been expressed about it within Sikh culture: 'Abortions frequently occur because, despite Sikh teaching, sons are more prized than daughters as they carry on the family name, look after their parents and do not require dowries. It was for these reasons that in previous generations many female babies were suffocated at birth' ('Sikhism' in Morgan & Lawton, n. 8 above, p. 143). The author of this quotation makes clear that such practices are contrary to Sikh teaching but does acknowledge that the ratio of female to male births in Sikh culture remains less than 8 to 10.

[31] P. Morgan, 'Buddhism' in Morgan & Lawton, n. 8 above, p. 63.   [32] ibid, p. 88.

[33] ibid, pp. 88–9.   [34] ibid.   [35] ibid, p. 90.

(3) Beyond religion

This brief investigation of the value placed upon human life in the major religious traditions demonstrates that religion has contributed greatly to the protection afforded to human life in national, and indeed pre-national, laws across the world. There is also evidence that primitive societies without formal religions frequently adopt a similar high value for human life. It is claimed, for example, that a principle of sanctity of life and of the human body was well established in Dinka society.[36] The Dinka are the largest ethnic group in Sudan and are regarded as among the African people least touched by Western or Islamic civilization.[37] Similarly, the Akan, an ethnic group living predominantly in Ghana and parts of the Ivory Coast, apparently have a strong concept of an intrinsic value in human life. This stems from belief in the life principle of *okra*, which is part of a three-fold union believed to contribute to the Akan conception of a person: 'the *okra* is held to come directly from God. It is supposed to be an actual speck of God that he gives out of himself as a gift of life along with a specific destiny... By virtue of possessing an *okra*, a divine element, every person has an intrinsic value, the same in each, which he does not owe to any earthly circumstance.'[38] The parallels with the Jewish and Christian views of life as a gift from God are obvious. The Akans do believe in the concept of a noble suicide, however, and reject the idea of artificially prolonging a painful life.[39] They also in earlier times practised human sacrifice, seemingly inconsistent with the concept of *okra*. The juxtaposition of sacrificing human life while asserting its inherent value is not unique to African cultures, however. Even Christianity is based upon the idea of God sacrificing the life of his son for humankind.

This evidence that a broad cross section of human cultures operates from a starting point of according special value to human life, despite not always living up to their ideals, suggests that it is, and always has been, a global value. The Jewish writer Novak, when discussing the proposition in Genesis 9:6 that killing another human being is prohibited, refers to it as '*a priori* in the sense that there is no time when a morally astute person could assume that this norm does not obtain—although, of course, it often is violated in practice and even mandated by positive laws...'[40] This may, perhaps, be overstating the point slightly but the argument that the sanctity of human life is not specific to any one human tradition or culture is hard to deny. We have seen traces of it in a variety of religious and ethnic traditions. This point is convincingly expressed by Lauren in his book on the evolution of human rights when he argues that it is 'essential to recognise

---

[36] F.M. Deng, 'A Cultural Approach to Human Rights among the Dinka' in A.A. An-Na'Im & F.M. Deng (eds), *Human Rights in Africa: Cross-Cultural Perspectives* (Washington DC: Brookings Institution, 1990), p. 272.   [37] ibid, p. 264.
[38] K. Wiredu, 'An Akan Perspective on Human Rights' in An-Na'Im & Deng, n. 36 above, p. 244.   [39] ibid, p. 253.
[40] Novak, n. 3 above, p. 39.

that the moral worth of each person is a belief that no single civilization, or people, or nation, or geographical area, or even century can claim as uniquely its own'.[41] As an idea which has endured in various cultures throughout many centuries, the value to be accorded to human life is an issue which has been debated by many diverse thinkers. It will now be useful to consider the philosophical foundations for a right to life stemming from the writings of a selection of famous philosophers from different places and times.

B. Philosophical origins of a right to life

(1) Suicide in ancient times

The death of the Ancient Greek philosopher Socrates, by his own hand while imprisoned, is described in detail by Plato in his *Phaedo*.[42] Indeed, all we know of Socrates is what has been written about him by his pupil Plato. According to Plato, Socrates mused at length upon life and death and the immortality of the soul before famously drinking hemlock. Some commentators question whether Socrates really spent his last day on Earth trying to prove the immortality of the soul, particularly as Socrates appeared to be agnostic in Plato's earlier 'Apology'. It is possible, therefore, that much of the Socratic musings on this issue are an invention by Plato.[43] According to Plato, Socrates begins by contemplating the issue dominant in religious thinking about the value of life, namely that our lives are a gift from the gods: 'the gods are our guardians and...men are one of their possessions...Perhaps then, put in this way, it is not unreasonable that one should not kill oneself before a god had indicated some necessity to do so, like the necessity now put upon us.'[44] Socrates continues, however, by arguing that philosophers should be ready and willing to die because death will separate the soul from the body which is the ultimate aim of all true philosophers: 'if we are ever to have pure knowledge, we must escape from the body and observe matters in themselves with the soul by itself. It seems likely that we shall, only then, when we are dead, attain that which we desire and of which we claim to be lovers, namely, wisdom...'[45] Socrates, at least according to Plato, made clear that he did not regard death as the end: 'I have good hope that some future awaits men after death, as we have been told for years, a much better future for the good than for the wicked.'[46] This pseudo-religious belief in an afterlife takes the sting out of the end of life, and continues to provide comfort to many today. Socrates seems to go

---

[41] Lauren, n. 1 above, p. 12. This point is preceded, however, by a warning that 'it is necessary to guard against the shallow and unhistorical view that all societies somehow have always subscribed to the same basic beliefs and values'.

[42] Plato, *Five Dialogues: Euthyphro, Apology, Crito, Meno Phaedo* (translated by G.M.A. Grube) (Indianapolis: Hackett Publishing, 2002).

[43] See D. Bostock, *Plato's Phaedo* (Oxford: Clarendon Press, 1986), pp. 9–10 for discussion.

[44] Plato, n. 42 above, p. 62b–c.   [45] ibid, p. 66e.   [46] ibid, p. 63c.

further, however, and regards life as a mere preparation, or dress rehearsal, for the afterlife, at least for philosophers who will value the separation of their soul from their human form.

The acceptance of suicide was common in Ancient Greece, and Roman philosophy also adopted the view that suicide was often justified by the surrounding circumstances. Seneca, in particular, writes frequently and eloquently of death as a favourable escape from a miserable life. He writes, for example, that 'Slavery loses its bitterness when by a step I can pass to liberty. Against all the injuries of life, I have the refuge of death.'[47] The contrast between Seneca's view of the value of life and that of the Judaeo-Christian tradition is stark. For Seneca, human life is a choice which it is entirely within our own hands to reject. Glanville Williams, in his influential 1958 book on the sanctity of life and the criminal law, notes that other Roman writers of this period shared Seneca's view (including Cato, Epictetus and Marcus Aurelius) and that consequently suicide was a common occurrence under the first Roman Emperors.[48] Indeed, even early Christians viewed suicide favourably because it hastened one's journey to the afterlife for which life on earth was a mere rehearsal (and, furthermore, a short life on earth would reduce the chances of committing sins that might jeopardize one's existence thereafter).[49] It was only in the fifth century, initially with Augustine's *City of God*, that suicide came to be condemned in Christian thought on the basis that the sixth commandment prohibited killing oneself as well as killing another.[50] The philosophical protection of human life even from the hands of its inhabitant is a theme more recently developed by Immanuel Kant in the eighteenth century.

(2) Kant and human life as an end in itself

In *Groundwork of the Metaphysics of Morals*, Kant argues that man is an end in himself and should never be treated merely as a means to an end.[51] More specifically, he applies this rule to rational beings, or 'persons', 'because their nature already marks them out as ends in themselves'. He further explains that this imposes a limit on all arbitrary treatment of persons: 'Persons, therefore, are not merely subjective ends whose existence as an object of our actions has a value for us: they are objective ends—that is, things whose existence is in itself an end, and indeed an end such that in its place we can put no other end to which they should serve

---

[47] Seneca, *The Laws*, Book 9, Section 843.
[48] G. Williams, *The Sanctity of Life and the Criminal Law* (London: Faber & Faber, 1958), p. 228.   [49] ibid, p. 229.
[50] Augustine, *City of God* (translated by H. Bettenson) (London: Penguin Classics, rev. edn., 2003).
[51] *Immanuel Kant: Groundwork of the Metaphysics of Morals: In Focus* (ed. L. Pasternack) (London: Routledge, 2002).

simply as means...'[52] This idea of human existence as an end in itself (regardless of potential limitations on the concept in respect of human beings lacking rationality) has important consequences not only for the way we treat others, but also for the way we treat ourselves. In stark contrast with Seneca's view of the continuation of life as a choice, Kant describes it as a moral duty. He recognizes that to preserve one's life is also usually in line with our immediate inclination, and so its nature as a moral duty is often obscured from view. However, when life brings no other reward, the moral duty to preserve an unwanted life comes into play: 'When...disappointments and hopeless misery have quite taken away the taste for life; when a wretched man, strong in soul and more angered at his fate than faint-hearted or cast down, longs for death and still preserves his life without loving it—not from inclination or fear but from duty; then indeed his maxim has a moral content.'[53] Suicide, in Kant's view, violates his concept of human existence as an end in itself; it treats life as a means to an end. If a man takes his own life, he is 'making use of a person merely as a means to maintain a tolerable state of affairs till the end of his life'.[54] The concept of a human life as an end in itself is an important one in the history of ideas. It supplements the Judaeo-Christian tradition of the sanctity of human life but, significantly, it values life in itself rather than as a reflection of God. Life as an intrinsic, rather than instrumental, value is at the heart of later legal protection for a right to life. Shortly, we will begin to trace the development of this right in international law when we see the conjunction of the religious and philosophical value of the sanctity of life with the philosophical concept of legally protected human rights. First, however, it is worth looking at a more recent attempt to analyse the value of human life: that of Ronald Dworkin.

(3) Dworkin and investment in life

In his book, *Life's Dominion*, Dworkin investigates the concept of the sanctity of life against the backdrop of the heated debates on abortion and euthanasia in the United States, and many other countries, during the twentieth century.[55] Fundamentally, Dworkin recognizes a concept of investment in human life. This investment comes in two forms: a natural investment in life and a human investment in life. Dworkin regards the question of the appropriate balance between these two investments as being at the core of the abortion and euthanasia debate. The natural investment in life is the idea with which we have become familiar in the preceding discussion: the idea of life as having an inherent value, due either to our relation to God or to nature itself. Dworkin expresses it in the following terms:

The dominant Western religious traditions insist that God made humankind 'in His own image', and that each individual human being is a representation and not merely a

---

[52] ibid, p. 428.   [53] ibid, p. 398.   [54] ibid, p. 429.
[55] R. Dworkin, *Life's Dominion: An Argument about Abortion and Euthanasia* (London: HarperCollins, 1993).

product of a divine creator, and people who accept that Article of faith will understandably think that each human being, not just the species as a whole, is a creative masterpiece. A secular form of the same idea, which assigns the masterpiece to nature rather
than God, is also a staple of our culture—the image of a human being as the highest
product of natural creation is one of Shakespeare's most powerful, for example. 'What a
piece of work is a man!' says Hamlet...[56]

Dworkin adds an important new dimension to the issue, however, when he also
identifies the extensive human investments in life. These human investments
take a number of forms. Dworkin writes about the life of a human organism
commanding respect and protection not only because of the complex creative
investment it represents (whether by God or evolution) but also,

because of our wonder at the divine or evolutionary processes that produce new lives
from old ones, at the processes of nation and community and language through which a
human being will come to absorb and continue hundreds of generations of cultures and
forms of life and value, and, finally, when mental life has begun and flourishes, at the process of internal personal creation and judgments by which a person will make and remake
himself.[57]

Human life, therefore, is not just of value because it is a life created by God
or nature (although that does make it valuable) but because there is a human
investment—a non-divine effort that can be discerned in every life, but especially those that entail mental reasoning. Dworkin's theory suggests that my
life is something worthy of value for a variety of reasons, including that it is
the culmination of millennia of evolution; that I am part of, and contribute
to, generations of human cultural development; and that I have made my life
unique, by my choices, priorities and values. My life today is not just created by
the science of evolution (or God, if one prefers) but by my past choices—by the
investment that I, and others, have put into my life. And the value to be placed
on the continuation of that life depends upon a delicate balancing of those different investments, and the investments that have contributed to other people's
lives as well.

Dworkin also discusses the issue of whether human life has an incremental
value. On the one hand, he recognizes the unarticulated basic premise of our
society that the human race must endure. This, he argues, is also due to the dual
investments of nature and humanity. We are the highest achievements of either
God's creation or evolution and there is a feeling that for this reason humanity
should strive to survive, but we are also aware that the destruction of humanity
would mean the loss of all knowledge, art and culture that previous generations
have created.[58] So, each life is valuable and so is humanity in general. But does
this need for humanity to survive mean that we should aim for more human lives.
If a human life is a prima facie good, are not more lives even better? And yet even

[56] ibid, p. 82.   [57] ibid, p. 84.   [58] ibid, p. 82.

though so many of us view human life as intrinsically valuable, we do not tend to think there should be more of it in the world. Dworkin explains that the sanctity of human life does not entail it being valued incrementally: 'The hallmark of the sacred as distinct from the incrementally valuable is that the sacred is intrinsically valuable because—and therefore only once—it exists. It is inviolable because of what it represents or embodies. It is not important that there be more people. But once a human life has begun, it is very important that it flourish and not be wasted.'[59] The fact that Dworkin's argument about investment in life is proposed within the context of the divisive abortion and euthanasia debates illustrates that the issue is a complex and often subjective one, but there is much to learn from the core idea that the intrinsic value of life stems from both the natural and human investment in that life.

(4) Locke and the natural law of the preservation of life

If we now travel back in time to the seventeenth century, we can investigate the link between philosophic thought and the origins of legal protection for the right to life. John Locke, in his *Two Treatises of Government*, sets out an influential theory of government, often used as a post facto justification for the 1688 'glorious' revolution which deposed King James II from the throne of England. Much of the content was written earlier, however, as a criticism of the government of James' brother, King Charles II. We shall see in the following section that Locke's theory of government and concept of natural rights was extremely influential across the Atlantic, inspiring the founding fathers of the United States of America. Locke's influence on the development of human rights is well known, but it is particularly interesting in the context of our discussion, to recognize the primary role Locke assigned to the preservation of human life. One of the leading commentators on Locke's theory, Peter Laslett, even comments that 'preservation, of oneself and all mankind, is a natural law for Locke, perhaps the natural law'.[60] Why was this so important in Locke's thinking?

In his *First Treatise*, Locke acknowledges the Judaeo-Christian tradition of the value of human life:

God having made Man, and planted in him, as in all other animals, a strong desire of self-preservation, and furnished the World with things fit for Food and Rayment and other Necessities of Life, subservient to his design, that Man should live and abide for some time upon the Face of the Earth, and not so curious and wonderful a piece of Workmanship by its own Negligence, or want of Necessities, should perish again, presently after a few moments continuance...[61]

---

[59] ibid, pp. 73–4.
[60] Locke's *Two Treatises of Government* (ed. P. Laslett) (Cambridge: Cambridge University Press, 1988), footnote on p. 205.   [61] ibid, *1st Treatise*, section 86.

In other words, Locke believed that humanity, as God's greatest achievement, should endure on Earth. He states more clearly his belief in the need to preserve life when he claims that the 'first and strongest desire God planted in Men, and wrought into the very Principles of their Nature being that of self-preservation'.[62] In a similar vein to Kant's later writings, Locke takes the view that every human being 'is bound to preserve himself, and not to quit his station wilfully'.[63] The preservation of life goes further than this, of course, and Locke also acknowledges that we are all obligated to preserve the rest of mankind. This means that (subject, Locke says, to the need to 'do Justice on an offender') nobody should 'take away, or impair the life, or what tends to the Preservation of the Life, Liberty, Health, Limb or Goods of another'.[64] We can begin to see an ancestor of a right to life here, as also when Locke states clearly that 'men, being once born, have a right to their preservation'.[65] Locke's theory of natural law is perhaps the most famous aspect of his work. He proposes a state of nature, which exists outside of positive laws, and which is governed by the law of nature. He argues that men naturally are in a 'state of perfect freedom' and 'a state also of Equality'[66] and that reason, which is the law of nature, 'teaches all mankind, who will but consult it, that all being equal and independent, no one ought to harm another in his Life, Health, Liberty or Possessions'.[67] Locke believes all men in this state of nature to hold a natural right to execute the natural law[68] and that each contractually transfers this right to public authorities.[69] This is a conditional transfer, limited by the ends for which it is made, namely to protect rights and freedoms. A government, under Locke's theory, is only legitimate if it protects individual rights. This very idea would ultimately lead to the first constitutional protection for human life, due to its influence in eighteenth-century America in general, and to Thomas Jefferson in particular.

Before we proceed to map the development of a constitutional protection for life in America, and beyond to an international legal protection for the right to life, it will be useful to reflect upon the philosophical origins of this protection. We have seen that in ancient times, death was often viewed as a welcome refuge from life, whether to escape misery or pain, or to facilitate a search for true wisdom by the disembodied soul, or to avoid the temptation of sin and hasten entrance to the afterlife. Since that time, however, respected thinkers have recognized the special value that is inherent in human life, in a development which mirrors religious beliefs but is distinct from them, founded upon secular ideas of natural law, man as an end in himself, and human investment in life. Writers such as Locke, Kant and, more recently, Dworkin, have expressed our unthinking instincts in fluent prose. Reason has joined faith to champion the value of

---

[62] ibid, section 88. Locke adds that the second strongest desire God planted in men is 'a strong desire also of propagating their kind, and continuing themselves in their posterity'.
[63] ibid, *2nd Treatise*, section 6.   [64] ibid.   [65] ibid, section 25.
[66] ibid, section 4.   [67] ibid, section 6.   [68] ibid, sections 7–11.
[69] ibid, sections 87–9.

human life. In eighteenth-century revolutionary America, it first began to take hold as a legal right.

C. Legal origins of a right to life

(1) The American Declaration of Independence and Bill of Rights

As mentioned above, the theory of John Locke was very influential amongst eighteenth-century Americans who welcomed his argument that all governments derive their power from the consent of those they govern. In colonies whose inhabitants felt increasingly removed from, and taken for granted by, their rulers across the sea, this idea took root. When the American colonies declared independence from Great Britain, Locke's theory could be seen within the words of Jefferson's famous Declaration; a document the purpose of which was not so much to declare independence as to 'proclaim to the world the reasons for declaring independence. It was intended as a formal justification of an act already accomplished.'[70] Becker explains that the Lockean background was almost inevitable: 'Whenever men become sufficiently dissatisfied with what is, with the existing regime of positive law and custom, they will be found reaching out beyond it for the rational basis of what they conceive ought to be. This is what the Americans did in their controversy with Great Britain; and this rational basis they found in that underlying preconception which shaped the thought of their age—the idea of natural law and natural rights.'[71] The fact that the separation from Britain was justified on the basis of the natural rights of man, rather than the narrower basis of the treatment of the colonists by the British government, means that the rights expressed in the Declaration of Independence are intended to have wider application. As Becker further explains, in the Declaration 'the foundation of the United States is indissolubly associated with a theory of politics, a philosophy of human rights which is valid, if at all, not for Americans only, but for all men'.[72] Perhaps now is the best time to issue the vital note of caution, however, that the phrase 'all men' in this context is not only as limited as it sounds (excluding all women) but also even more limited for it also excludes all black slaves and Native Americans. Not even all men, it appears, were created equal in the minds of the political leaders of the time.[73]

---

[70] C. Becker, *The Declaration of Independence: A Study in the History of Political Ideas* (New York: Peter Smith, 1933), p. 5.

[71] ibid, p. 134. Thomas Jefferson, the primary author of the Declaration, subsequently explained the intention of his wording: 'Neither aiming at originality of principles or sentiments, nor yet copied from any particular and previous writing, it was intended to be an expression of the American mind' (*The Writings of Thomas Jefferson* (edn. 1869), VII, p. 407, quoted in Becker, ibid, at p. 26).

[72] Becker, ibid, p. 225.

[73] See H. Zinn, *A People's History of the United States: 1492–Present* (New York: HarperPerennial, 1999) for a realistic view of the place of the wider people in the advances in human rights of this, and later, eras.

The key extract from the Declaration for our purposes—the first part of the second paragraph—sets out a general political philosophy which is both a legacy of its time and an enduring message to future generations: the right of a people to establish, and ultimately overturn, their own government.[74] This paragraph of the Declaration of Independence begins as follows:

We hold these truths to be self-evident, that all men are created equal, that they are endowed by their Creator with certain unalienable Rights, that among these are Life, Liberty and the pursuit of Happiness.—That to secure these rights, Governments are instituted among Men, deriving their just powers from the consent of the governed,—That whenever any Form of Government becomes destructive of these ends, it is the Right of the People to alter or to abolish it, and to institute new Government, laying its foundation on such principles and organizing its powers in such form, as to them shall seem most likely to effect their Safety and Happiness.[75]

The Declaration introduces into the new arena of American constitutional law the fundamental idea that all men are endowed by God with certain unalienable rights, including (as the first mentioned) a right to life. It is interesting to see the development of this extract through various drafts. Jefferson's so-called 'rough draft' which was sent to Benjamin Franklin did not originally include the word 'self-evident', which is now a famous part of the passage, and instead contained the phrase, 'We hold these truths to be sacred and undeniable'. In this rough draft, these words had been crossed out (whether by Franklin or Jefferson himself is not clear) and replaced with the word 'self-evident'.[76] The rough draft then continues as follows 'that all men are created equal and independent; that from that equal creation they derive rights inherent and inalienable, among which are the preservation of life, and liberty, and the pursuit of happiness'. The three major differences here—that men are created independent; that inherent rights derive from men's equal creation; and that the right to life is a right to the 'preservation of life'—are all subsequently crossed out in the so-called 'fair copy' of the Declaration presented to Congress on the 28 June 1776. Becker takes the view that these changes were for linguistic, rather than substantive, reasons.[77] For example, the word 'indepen*dent*' is removed once 'self-evid*ent*' is added in close proximity and 'preservation' is omitted because it is superfluous: 'If a man has a right to life, the right to preserve life is manifestly included.'[78] The fair copy also contains, for the first time, the important phrase 'they are endowed by their creator' suggesting a fundamental role for religious faith in the natural rights theory of the Declaration.[79] The Declaration was adopted by Congress with some amendment

---

[74] See Becker, n. 70 above, p. 8.

[75] Becker makes an interesting comment on the unusual capitalization and punctuation reproduced in this quotation: 'the capitalization and punctuation, following neither previous copies, nor reason, nor the custom of any age known to man, is one of the irremediable evils of life to be accepted with becoming resignation' (ibid, p. 185).

[76] See discussion in Becker, ibid, pp. 140–2.   [77] ibid, pp. 198–9.   [78] ibid, p. 199.

[79] ibid, p. 161.

on 4 July. The Declaration adopted can be seen in the rough Journal of Congress for that day and the only relevant change to the first part of the second paragraph is the replacement of 'inherent and inalienable' with 'certain unalienable'.[80] Congress also omitted a later phrase which expressly referred to the right to life in the context of the list of grievances against the King. The part omitted included the accusation that 'he has waged cruel war against human nature itself, violating its most sacred rights of life and liberty in the persons of a distant people'. This reference was in the context of slavery and was for that reason removed but it highlights the fundamental nature of the 'most sacred' right of life and its connection with the concept of human nature itself.

Despite the central role of rights, including a right to life, in the Declaration of Independence, the US Constitution drafted in 1787 failed to offer explicit rights protection. During the drafting of the Constitution at the Philadelphia Constitutional Convention, a deliberate decision was taken to omit a bill of rights. Some argued in favour of such a bill, including Thomas Jefferson, and George Mason, who had drafted the Virginia Bill of Rights, one of the first to emerge from the states, which explicitly stated that all men were created free and equal and were entitled to the enjoyment of life and liberty. The majority view at the Philadelphia Convention was opposed to a bill of rights, however. There were a variety of reasons for this but perhaps the most pressing was the view that 'they had planned a government of limited, enumerated powers, making unnecessary, they reasoned, a list of restraints on powers that did not exist'.[81] As Levy recognizes, this argument was 'plausible, but neither convincing nor politic' and the 'usually masterful politicians who dominated the Convention had seriously erred'.[82] It very quickly became obvious that a bill of rights needed to be added to the US Constitution and when this was done, by means of the addition of ten constitutional amendments introduced during the first United States Congress in 1789 by James Madison, protection for the right to life was included. The Fifth Amendment, famous for offering constitutional protection against self-incrimination (as in the phrase 'pleading the fifth') also includes the following prohibition: 'No person shall be . . . deprived of life, liberty, or property, without due process of law.' As Levy notes, this was a curious inclusion as no state had a constitutional guarantee along these lines.[83] The Fifth Amendment applies against the federal government only but the Fourteenth Amendment ratified in 1868 after the American civil war, extended the protection against states. We should not overlook the fact, however, that this constitutional protection for life remains limited, and not only because of the many people excluded from its ambit at the time of its drafting. Both the Fifth and Fourteenth Amendments are due process clauses, prohibiting the deprivation of life without due process.

---

[80] ibid, p. 175.
[81] L.W. Levy, *Origins of the Fifth Amendment: The Right Against Self-incrimination* (New York: Macmillan, 1986), p. 415.   [82] ibid.
[83] ibid, pp. 422–3.

While substantive elements of due process claims have been recognized, these clauses remain distinct in nature from the right to life that was to emerge in international law following the Second World War.

(2) The Universal Declaration of Human Rights

The natural law philosophy which underlied the great eighteenth-century documents such as the US Declaration of Independence and the French Declaration of the Rights of Man also has a role to play in the first international expression of human rights, the Universal Declaration of Rights. This important document stemmed from the new United Nations organization established following the Second World War. The Charter of the United Nations which was agreed and signed at San Francisco on 26 June 1945 included respect for human rights as one of the basic purposes of the new organization. Its Preamble includes the following: 'to reaffirm faith in fundamental human rights, in the dignity and worth of the human person, in the equal rights of men and women and of nations large and small...' This emphasis on the 'dignity and worth of the human person' is a significant development, as we shall soon see, stemming largely from revulsion at the horrors of the Nazi concentration camps. The UN Charter also established a Human Rights Commission which, under the chairmanship of Eleanor Roosevelt, decided to draft an international bill of rights. Unable to agree upon the means of implementation of a legally enforceable covenant, the Commission agreed to a compromise under which a non-binding declaration would be drafted first, followed by a legally enforceable covenant. The first stage became the Universal Declaration of Human Rights (UDHR) which was adopted by the General Assembly of the United Nations on 10 December 1948.[84]

A number of forces shaped the UDHR, including the beginnings of the cold war, the women's lobby and the tradition of Latin American socialism, but by far the most important factor was the Holocaust.[85] The Preamble includes the 'recognition of the inherent dignity and of the equal and inalienable rights of all members of the human family', while Article 1 states that 'All human beings are born free and equal in dignity and rights. They are endowed with reason and conscience and should act towards one another in a spirit of brotherhood.' These phrases owe a legacy to the natural law theory so evident in the US Declaration of Independence but, as Morsink recognizes, they are not mere natural law or Enlightenment reflexes, 'they are deep truths rediscovered in the midst of the Holocaust and put on paper again shortly thereafter'.[86] This can be seen particularly in relation to the protection for the right to life. Article 3 of the UDHR

---

[84] Forty-eight states agreed to this list of human rights, while eight abstained: USSR, Byelorussia, Czechoslovakia, Poland, Saudi Arabia, Ukraine, South Africa and Yugoslavia.
[85] See J. Morsink, *The Universal Declaration of Human Rights: Origins, Drafting, and Intent* (Philadelphia: University of Pennsylvania Press, 2000), p. 37.   [86] ibid, p. 38.

states that 'Everyone has the right to life, liberty and security of person.' This is one of the first clear statements of an international right to life.[87] When drafting the Declaration, the Human Rights Commission relied upon the War Crimes Commission report of November 1947.[88] This report explicitly identified some of the Nazi policies which had so undervalued human life, including 'the policy which was in existence in Germany by the summer of 1940, under which all aged, insane, and incurable people, "useless eaters", were transferred to special institutions where they were killed.'[89] It also identified the policy of shooting between fifty and one hundred hostages for any one German life taken, and the dramatic rise in the death penalty, which had risen from thirty-two in 1937 to 5,191 in 1944, and was imposed for offences such as undermining morale, spreading malicious propaganda, or saying that the war is lost.[90] As Morsink succinctly notes after reciting this information, 'Life was cheap to the Nazis.'[91] Morsink continues, however, by noting that life was also cheap to others; for example, the USSR delegate referred to British colonial policies and the US lynching of African Americans, while the UK delegate responded by referring to Stalinist concentration camps.[92] Many states had lived in glasshouses for years and should not have been throwing stones but, the point remains, that the Holocaust was distinctive in its scope and blatant disregard for the value of human life. It is not surprising, therefore, that it served as the catalyst both for international protection of human rights in general, and a right to life in particular. As discussed above, the religious tradition of the sanctity of life led to a strong revulsion at the disregard of human life by the Nazis and thus centuries of religious and philosophical thought culminated in a declaratory international document unambiguously stating for the first time a human right to life.

The unsettling information about the mistreatment imposed by the Nazis led the Chilean delegation to propose a specific amendment to Article 3 stating that 'unborn children, incurable, mentally defectives and lunatics shall have the right to life'.[93] This proposal was not accepted, presumably because it was felt that many of these individuals would be included automatically in the word 'everyone' (although, as we shall see in due course, the argument as to whether everyone includes the unborn still rages today). The protection offered by Article 3 was supplemented, however, by positive rights to food, clothing, housing and medical care in Article 25.[94] It later become rare for such economic and social rights

[87] The American Declaration of Rights and Duties of Man, adopted in April 1948, was actually the first human rights treaty albeit a regional rather than universal document.
[88] 'Information Concerning Human Rights Arising from Trials of War Criminals' (E/CN.4/W.20). [89] See Morsink, n. 85 above, p. 40.
[90] ibid. [91] ibid. [92] ibid, pp. 40–1.
[93] 21/Annex F. See Morsink, ibid, p. 40.
[94] Article 25(1): 'Everyone has the right to a standard of living adequate for the health and well-being of himself and of his family, including food, clothing, housing and medical care and necessary social services, and the right to security in the event of unemployment, sickness, disability, widowhood, old age or other lack of livelihood in circumstances beyond his control.'

(the so-called second generation of rights) to be included in the same document as civil and political rights (the so-called first generation of rights) but, as we shall discover, the right to life may need to be more than a mere prohibition on arbitrary killing by state officials if it is to genuinely reflect the ethical value afforded to human life.

The Universal Declaration of Human Rights is, as its name suggest, a mere declaration. It is not a binding legal covenant—that was to follow, eventually, twenty years later—but its influence on the development of international human rights was unprecedented.[95] It is a legacy of its time, as so many of these documents are, but it continues to send a strong message that the rights it lists, including the right to life, are inherent in every human being. It is this natural law background to the UDHR which has been so influential because it asserts that the rights declared in the UDHR apply to everyone, regardless of their state, race, religion or any other defining characteristic; regardless of whether any positive law of their state accords them these rights. As Morsink explains, 'It is precisely because these rights are inherent in people and not the gifts of history or circumstance that they can be used as standards against which history and circumstance are to be judged.'[96] And the UDHR, drafted as it was against the backdrop of the Holocaust, leaves no room for doubt that the right to life is a right at the very heart of this new order. As the preamble of the UN Charter declares, 'the dignity and worth of the human person' is now a matter of international concern. It was soon to be a matter of international legal concern as well.

(3) The International Covenant on Civil and Political Rights

The Human Rights Commission was established under the UN Charter with the task of drafting an international bill of rights. It soon decided, however, to split this task into two stages: a declaration of rights that would set out general principles and a binding convention that would define specific rights and their limitations. The first stage was quickly completed by means of the UDHR but the second stage took far longer. The main source of disagreement during the intervening period concerned the question of appropriate implementation and whether the rights should be split into two covenants (upon the basis of the two generations of rights). The lengthy drafting process was also complicated by the changing balance of power within the United Nations during the two turbulent decades of the 1950s and 1960s. McGoldrick notes that the drafting

---

[95] Views on the significance of the UDHR continue to differ drastically. Simpson says it 'represented little more than an exhalation of pious hot air' (A.W.B. Simpson, *Human Rights and the End of Empire: Britain and the Genesis of the European Convention* (Oxford: Oxford University Press, 2001), p. 11) while Lauren claims that it 'enormously accelerated the evolution of international human rights' (Lauren, n.1 above, p. 239). These two points of view are not, of course, mutually exclusive. It is entirely possible that the UDHR is 'pious hot air' that nevertheless accelerated the development of international human rights.   [96] Morsink, n. 85 above, pp. 295–6.

of the covenants 'largely coincided with the depths of cold war confrontation, the explosive development of notions of self-determination and independence, the accompanying political tensions of large scale decolonization, and the consequential effects of a rapidly altering balance of diplomatic power within the United Nations'.[97] Within this context, the eventual successful completion of two covenants is in itself an impressive task. The International Covenant on Civil and Political Rights (ICCPR) and the International Covenant on Economic, Social and Cultural Rights (ICESCR) were both finally adopted by the General Assembly of the UN in Resolution 2200 (XI) on 16 December 1966. The ICCPR includes a right to life.

Article 6(1) ICCPR states that 'Every human being has the inherent right to life. This right shall be protected by law. No one shall be arbitrarily deprived of his life.' The remainder of Article 6 goes into greater detail on the right, especially in the context of the death penalty. The *travaux préparatoires* make clear that the basic affirmation of the inherent right of everyone to life (originally proposed in amendments submitted by Columbia and Uruguay) garnered wide support amongst the state representatives on the Third Committee (Social, Humanitarian and Cultural Questions) of the General Assembly. This was largely because the message of the UDHR, and the earlier natural rights theory, that human rights existed outside of positive law, had been taken on board: 'It was held that the right to life was not a right conferred on the individual by society. Society, in fact, owed a duty to the individual—that of protecting his right to life.'[98] The first sentence of Article 6(1) was adopted by sixty-five votes to three with four abstentions. The *travaux préparatoires* also make clear that even those states opposing the clause 'did not disagree with the principle it enunciated; they objected to its inclusion, since it was a declaratory statement and, therefore, out of place in a legal instrument'.[99] Therefore, Article 6 sends out a clear message, similar to that enunciated in the UDHR, that the right to life is inherent and inalienable; it comes from our nature as human beings and not from the laws of any particular state.[100]

A greater source of disagreement during the lengthy drafting process of the Covenant was whether it should include an absolute or limited protection for life. One view was that it was important that the right to life should enunciate the principle that no one should be deprived of life under any circumstances. This view was based upon a belief that 'in drafting an Article on the right to life, which was the most fundamental of all rights, no mention should be made of

---

[97] D. McGoldrick, *The Human Rights Committee: Its Role in the Development of the International Covenant on Civil and Political Rights* (Oxford: Clarendon Press, 1994), p. 14.

[98] M.J. Bossuyt, *Guide to the 'Travaux Préparatoires' of the International Covenant on Civil and Political Rights* (Dordrecht: Martinus Nijhoff, 1987), p. 119 (Third Committee, 12th Session (1957), A/3764, section 112). [99] ibid.

[100] A proposed amendment to add the phrase 'human life is sacred' was, however, defeated (Commission on Human Rights, 6th session (1950), E/CN.4/365; Bossuyt, ibid, p. 115). Perhaps the use of the word 'sacred' in a Covenant which eschewed religious terminology was considered inappropriate.

circumstances under which the taking of life might seem to be condoned'.[101] This is a somewhat naïve view, however, because, as this book seeks to demonstrate throughout, there are numerous situations in which a right to life is outweighed by other considerations. This led to an opposing view among the drafters that the Covenant must not only be idealistic, but also realistic, and that it should, therefore, explicitly recognize the circumstances under which the taking of life was justified.[102] A compromise between these two views is apparent in the third sentence of Article 6(1): 'No one shall be arbitrarily deprived of his life.' The use of the word 'arbitrarily' was intended to indicate that the right to life is not absolute without the need to set out the potential exceptions in detail. The use of the word was criticized by some representatives, however, 'on the ground that it did not express a generally recognised idea and that it was ambiguous and open to several interpretations'.[103] The latter point is true, although whether that is necessarily a problem remains to be investigated. The wording of Article 6(1) does successfully indicate that (a) the right to life is a moral, or natural law, right which pre-dates positive protection in the laws of the contracting states; (b) that it is inherent in all human beings; and (c) that it is not an absolute right and is only infringed if the state arbitrarily takes an individual's life. Perhaps most importantly, the inclusion of the right to life in the ICCPR removed any doubt that the right is a legally enforceable right at international law. The way in which the previously stated three principles shaped the legal enforcement of the right to life will be investigated in the next chapter. First, however, it is important to consider the regional protection for the right to life which began in 1948 in the Americas and moved later to Europe and then Africa. If the international development of the right to life has placed it on the map as an inherent right for all, it is the regional protection systems which often offer the most practical protection for the value of human life.

(4) The regional human rights systems

The European Convention on Human Rights was always intended to transform the admirable theory of the UDHR (or at least some parts of it) into practical, enforceable reality. The Preamble of the Convention made clear that it sought to 'take the first steps for the collective enforcement of certain of the Rights stated in the Universal Declaration.' The ECHR emerged in the early 1950s from a new European organization called the Council of Europe.[104] The Statute of

---

[101] ibid, p. 115 (Commission on Human Rights, 5th Session (1949), 6th Session (1950) and 8th session (1952)—A/2929, Chapter VI, section 1).   [102] ibid.

[103] ibid, pp. 121–3 (Commission on Human Rights, 5th Session (1949), 6th Session (1950) and 8th session (1952)—A/2929, Chapter VI, section 3); (Third Committee, 5th Session (1950), 9th session (1954), 12th Session (1957), A/3764, section 114).

[104] For detailed discussion of the drafting of the ECHR, see A. Lester, 'Fundamental Rights: The United Kingdom Isolated?' [1984] P.L. 46; G. Marston, 'The United Kingdom's Part in

the Council of Europe was signed in London in May 1949 by the UK, France, Netherlands, Belgium, Luxembourg, Italy, Ireland, Sweden, Denmark and Norway. The Statute included an emphasis upon human rights and the first session of the consultative assembly of the Council, held in Strasbourg on 10 August 1949, included a debate on human rights. It was immediately clear that the document to be drafted under the auspices of the Council of Europe would not be innovative in terms of the rights protected but rather due to its aim of ensuring the protection of the rights through common commitments undertaken by contracting states. To this end, the European scheme would include the establishment of a European Court.[105]

The first draft of the Convention, prepared by Teitgen, was submitted to the Council of Europe in July 1949. It included 'security of life and limb' but contained no further detail or definitions in relation to the protection of life.[106] The Committee on Legal and Administrative Questions, with Maxwell-Fyfe as Chairman, met between 22 August and 5 September 1949 and the draft to emerge from this body did not include any mention of the right to life at all. The report went to the Consultative Assembly which accepted the proposals. A legally binding Convention without the right to life in its terms was nearly a reality. However, the UK government retained some misgivings about the whole project and, at its suggestion, a Committee of Experts was set up to produce a new draft. In fact, two distinct drafts were to emerge from this body by March 1950. Alternative A was based upon the earlier draft but included the phrase 'Everyone has the right to life, liberty and security of person.'[107] Alternative B, based upon a slightly amended UK draft convention, included a much narrower right to life with tightly defined exceptions.[108] This was the version of the right that was to ultimately gain a place in the final Convention, with only one difference: an additional exception to the prohibition on intentional killing for deaths resulting from necessary force used to prohibit entry to a clearly defined place to which access is forbidden on grounds of national security. This exception did not survive into the final version of the right, but all of the other exceptions listed in alternative B remain in the final text. The Committee of Ministers agreed to compose a Conference of Senior Officials to choose between alternatives A and B. The conference met in June 1950 and was able to produce a single draft convention

the Preparation of the European Convention on Human Rights, 1950' (1993) 42 I.C.L.Q. 796; E. Wicks, 'The UK Government's Perceptions of the European Convention on Human Rights at the Time of Entry' [2000] P.L. 438; A.W.B. Simpson, *Human Rights and the End of Empire: Britain and the Genesis of the European Convention*, n. 95 above.

[105] The implementation measures of the new Convention were the most controversial during the drafting process. The UK, among other states, strongly opposed the establishment of a European Court and the concept of individual petition, leading to these measures being framed in optional terms in the final text of the Convention. For further discussion, see Wicks, n. 104 above, pp. 448–52.   [106] Simpson, n. 95 above, pp. 659–60.

[107] Art 2(1)(b): G. Robertson, *Collected Edition of the Travaux Préparatoires* (The Hague: Martinus Nijhoff, 1977), Vol. IV, p. 52.   [108] Art 3, ibid, p. 58.

with majority support. The compromise draft was much closer to alternative B: it defined the rights, rather than merely enumerating them. This compromise draft was agreed to by the Committee of Ministers, and was finally signed on 4 November 1950. The right to life provision is in Article 2. It states:

(1) Everyone's right to life shall be protected by law. No one shall be deprived of his life intentionally save in the execution of a sentence of a court following his conviction of a crime for which this penalty is provided by law.

(2) Deprivation of life shall not be regarded as inflicted in contravention of this Article when it results from the use of force which is no more than absolutely necessary:

(a) in defence of any person from unlawful violence;
(b) in order to effect a lawful arrest or to prevent the escape of a person lawfully detained;
(c) in action lawfully taken for the purpose of quelling a riot or insurrection.

The exceptions are broad, and include the death penalty and lethal force in some circumstances of law enforcement, but the right itself is also broad. In contrast to the later ICCPR, all intentional deprivation of life by the state is prohibited (whereas the ICCPR only prohibits arbitrary killings). Article 2 also retains the natural rights philosophy seen in earlier documents by failing to declare a right to life but rather recognizing a pre-existing right to life and requiring that it be protected by law. The enforcement of this right will be considered in depth in the next chapter.

Before the ECHR had even been imagined, however, another regional document had already been created. The American Declaration of Rights and Duties of Man was adopted in Bogotá in April 1948 by the Organisation of American States. It therefore pre-dates even the UDHR and can be regarded as the first human rights treaty in international law. The first provision of this first human rights treaty is the right to life. Article 1 states: 'Every human being has the right to life, liberty and the security of his person.' The terms of the American Declaration are very similar to that of the UDHR except that ten so-called duties are also listed, including duties to acquire an elementary education and to vote. The American Declaration was subsequently superseded by the American Convention of Human Rights, signed in San José in 1969. Article 4(1) of the ACHR protects the right to life: 'Every person has the right to have his life respected. This right shall be protected by law and, in general, from the moment of conception. No one shall be arbitrarily deprived of his life.' Two interesting points emerge from this provision. First, the ACHR follows the ICCPR rather than the ECHR in prohibiting only arbitrary deprivation of life and, secondly, the ACHR is the only human rights treaty which purports to resolve the controversial issue of when the right to life begins (although the manner in which it does so, with the use of the phrase 'in general' still leaves room for debate). The ACHR came into force in 1978 and is enforced by the Inter-American Commission of

Human Rights (established in 1959) and the American Court of Human Rights (established by the Convention). For most American states, the ACHR has superseded the American Declaration but the latter remains of relevance to the few states that have not ratified the Convention. These include the US and Canada, as well as Cuba which has been suspended from the Organisation of American States. The enforcement of the ACHR will be considered in the next chapter, but it is worth noting here that the American system faces very different challenges to that of the European system as it has to deal with more large-scale violations, states of emergency and the ambivalence of some governments. It may be a tougher challenge but, as David Harris has pointed out, the right to life is of greater need in Latin America: 'Human rights issues in the Americas have often concerned gross, as opposed to ordinary, violations of human rights. They have been much more to do with the forced disappearance, killing, torture and arbitrary detention of political opponents and terrorists than with particular issues concerning, for example, the right to a fair trial or freedom of expression that are the stock in trade of the European Commission and Court.'[109] As if to prove this point, the first contentious case initiated by an individual under the ACHR concerned a violation of the right to life in respect of the practice of disappearances in Honduras.[110]

The final region to obtain its own human rights treaty was Africa. Africa has a distinct tradition of rights and duties which was not particularly reflected in the UDHR because many of the present African states were still colonies at the time it was drafted (as too were many Asian states). It is often argued that the African emphasis in respect of rights is more community or group based rather than individualistic.[111] This is reflected to some extent in the African Charter on Human and Peoples' Rights which was approved by the Organisation of African Unity in 1981 and came into force in 1986. Article 4 of this document protects the right to life: 'Human beings are inviolable. Every human being shall be entitled to respect for his life and the integrity of his person. No one may be arbitrarily deprived of this right.' The emphasis on the inviolability of human life is supplemented by explicit protection for human dignity in Article 5: 'Every individual shall have the right to the respect of the dignity inherent in a human being.' This Article then proceeds to prohibit 'all forms of exploitation and degradation of man'. Taken together it is clear that these two Articles send a strong message that human life has a special value and dignity which requires legal protection.

---

[109] D. Harris, 'Regional Protection of Human Rights: The Inter-American Achievement' in D. Harris & S. Livingstone (eds), *The Inter-American System of Human Rights* (Oxford: Clarendon Press, 1998), p. 2.

[110] *Velásquez Rodríguez Case* (Judgment of 29 July 1988, Inter-Am Ct. H.R. (Ser. C) No. 4 (1989)).

[111] For analysis of this view, see R.E. Howard, 'Group versus Individual Identity in the African Debate on Human Rights' in An-Na'Im & Deng, n. 36 above.

(5) International protection beyond treaties

As we have seen, the three regions of Europe, the Americas, and Africa all have explicit protection for the right to life within their regional human rights treaties. The enforcement of these provisions will be considered in the following chapter. For now, it is sufficient to note that the long legacy of sanctity of life, drawn from both religious and secular viewpoints finally found international law enforcement during the second half of the twentieth century. Even beyond the confines of the international treaties (which are, after all, optional commitments for states), it appears that at least some aspects of the right to life have found legal protection on the international plane. The Vienna Convention on the Law of Treaties describes a peremptory norm of general international law as 'a norm accepted and recognised by the international community of states as a whole as a norm from which no derogation is permitted and which can be modified only by a subsequent norm of general international law having the same character'.[112] The right to life is not regarded as a peremptory norm in its entirety but widespread violations may fall foul of such a norm. As Hannikainen explains, 'the international community of states has not left any doubt that it considers mass extermination, arbitrary killings and summary executions grave offences against elementary considerations of humanity and gross violations of international law'.[113] Whether the international community, or the United Nations, is able to effectively enforce such a norm in practice is more subject to doubt but the fact remains that some aspects of the right to life exist in international law beyond the confines of treaty law, and hence the legal protection offered to human life throughout the planet is increased. The (albeit limited) protection for life by means of peremptory norms also reaffirms the existence of a right to life beyond positive law. The mass extermination of life (at least) violates some fundamental human value that cannot be extinguished by state laws or international treaties.

D. Conclusion

The development of an international, legally enforced, right to life has been a slow process which only came to fruition in the latter half of the twentieth century but it was built upon millennia of religious and philosophical thought. There is little doubt that the concept of the sanctity of human life is at the heart of the Judaeo-Christian tradition, built upon the dual beliefs that man is made in the image of God and that God is the giver of life (as well as being equally reflected in

---

[112] Article 53, Vienna Convention on the Law of Treaties.

[113] L. Hannikainen, *Peremptory Norms (Jus Cogens) in International Law: Historical Development, Criteria, Present Status* (Helsinki: Finnish Lawyers' Publishing Company, 1988), at p. 519.

other religious traditions). A secular version of the sanctity of life, affording some inherent value to human life has also developed over the centuries. This is still a large step removed from a legal right to life, however. The adoption of a natural rights philosophy first encouraged the constitutional and later international recognition of fundamental human rights, of which life was one. The legal protection of the right to life is based upon the idea that all human life is of equal value. The nature of that value builds upon ideas drawn from religion, philosophy and science. The emphasis on the importance of human consciousness in the previous chapter can now be combined with the emphasis on the sanctity of human life in religious and philosophical thought to provide a justification for the special value of human life. Once the concept of human rights, including the right to life, became established, the focus moved, in more recent decades, to the question of enforcement. Two millennia of human history have led to widespread agreement that human life has a special value; but can such a moral belief be transformed into a legal obligation, not only upon individuals but also, most significantly and problematically, upon governments? It is to this issue of enforcement we will now turn, in order to investigate whether the developments discussed in this chapter are anything more than mere rhetoric.

3

The Enforcement of the Right to Life

This chapter will focus upon the legal implementation of the right to life, within both domestic and international legal systems. It will identify the diverse range of circumstances which may give rise to a right to life claim and will present some of the difficulties faced by states and international organs in seeking to implement the right. The previous two chapters have established that each human life has some value and that that inherent value has long been recognized in religious and philosophical thought. We discovered at the end of the previous chapter that the right to life emerged as an internationally respected human right in the latter half of the twentieth century but we cannot ignore the fact that the twentieth century is notorious for widespread deprivations of life, including through both new technologies and old political and philosophical conflicts. This chapter addresses the crucial practical question of whether, and if so how, the right to life can be enforced in a world where the loss of life is so commonplace.

A. Means of implementation

(1) Domestic implementation

The most effective means of ensuring protection for the right to life is through the mechanisms of domestic law. International law provides essential oversight but it is at the domestic legal level, within the state, that an individual's life can be best be protected, as well as most easily destroyed. The most fundamental protection afforded to the right to life by domestic law will be a general prohibition on the taking of human life. Indeed, the widespread implementation of such a prohibition is one of the best indicators that the right to life, and the concept of the sanctity of human life, is universal. The need for domestic legal systems to impose criminal sanctions upon the deprivation of human life is now recognized at an international level as an international obligation upon states party to human rights treaties. The Human Rights Committee, for example, in its General Comment No. 6 explained that the right to life provision within the International Covenant on Civil and Political Rights requires that state parties take measures 'to prevent and punish deprivation of life by criminal acts'.[1] This will require an effective policing system to seek to prevent the criminal deprivation of life, a legal prohibition on criminal activities resulting in the deprivation of life, and sufficient punishment of those individuals convicted of such offences.

In England and Wales, the criminal prohibition on the taking of life focuses upon the two offences of murder and manslaughter.[2] Murder is any act that causes the death of another where the intention is to kill or cause grievous bodily harm. It carries a mandatory sentence of life imprisonment. Manslaughter covers a disparate range of killings, including where death results from an unlawful and dangerous act of the defendant, or where the defendant was subjectively reckless as to death or grievous bodily harm, or grossly negligent as to death. Traditionally murder and manslaughter have dominated the law on homicide in England and Wales, although there are in addition specific offences such as infanticide and causing death by dangerous driving that are designed to apply to the taking of life in specific circumstances. In recent years, however, dissatisfaction with the traditional system has increased, due in part to the false equality implied by a mandatory life sentence for all intentional killings (which can operate particularly harshly against, for example, so-called mercy killers) and in part to the extremely broad range of activities encompassed by the offence of manslaughter. The Law Commission has recently proposed a radical change to the law on homicide in England and Wales involving a move from the current two-tier system to a new three-tier system.[3] This proposed change would introduce a new distinction between first degree and second degree murder with the more serious category reserved for intentional killings and killings with an intention to do serious injury in the awareness that there is a serious risk of causing death. The differentiation of two degrees of murder is a common feature in other countries. In the United States, for example, many states regard premeditated murder as murder in the first degree, although it is far from clear whether premeditation is always an aggravating factor. Again the example of 'mercy-killings' is illuminating here for they will, by definition, be premeditated but are not generally regarded as the most serious of murders. In the state of New York, first degree murder, which makes the defendant eligible for the death penalty, is defined by means of special victims or circumstances such as where the victim is a police officer, the defendant is confined in a state correctional facility, the killing is performed for money or in the course of a felony, or is a second offence.[4] Why are these killings worse than others? Why, for example, is killing for money worse than killing for pleasure? Why does the death of a police officer deserve greater punishment than the death of a postman? Why is a killing within the violent and threatening environment of

---

[1] General Comment No. 6: The Right to Life (1982), para. 3.

[2] In Scotland, the two offences are murder and culpable homicide.

[3] Law Commission for England and Wales, 'Murder, Manslaughter and Infanticide' (Law Com. No. 304 London, 2006).

[4] These are just a few of the many circumstances listed in the New York Penal Code, s. 125.27.

a prison treated as more serious than a killing within a family home? There are no easy answers to these questions but, as we have seen, premeditation is not necessarily any more logically consistent. As Clare Finkelstein recognizes, 'Aligning the category of first degree murder with the killings that reflect greatest moral turpitude is a significant challenge for any jurisdiction that identifies degrees of murder.'[5]

Within England and Wales, in addition to the applicability of general defences such as insanity, there are specific 'partial defences' to murder which reduce the prohibited behaviour to manslaughter (or second degree murder in the Law Commission's proposals). These partial defences are provocation, diminished responsibility and a half-completed suicide pact. Deaths caused in circumstances where one of these partial defences apply are still prohibited but the convicted perpetrator is convicted of a lesser offence and will serve a lesser sentence (possibly even a non-custodial one). Does this reduce the legal protection for life and fail to provide adequate respect for the right to life? In Scotland, where the provocation defence is much stricter than in England and Wales—applying only to provocation by physical violence rather than by any words or deeds—there is an explicit exception for the discovery of infidelity by the defendant's partner.[6] That this partial defence is intended to apply in modern society is evident by the fact that 'partner' has been interpreted as including a partner in a same-sex couple,[7] but does infidelity really help to justify killing, or even make it slightly less objectionable? The crucial equality of human life, identified in the previous chapters, would suggest not. The point could be made, however, that defences such as provocation, and also insanity and diminished responsibility, only apply to situations where the killing was not the result of a rational choice. As Joseph has noted, 'deterrence is a rational choice, so defences such as insanity, diminished responsibility and provocation will often protect persons who were not, at the time of the homicide, capable of being deterred'.[8] The availability of such defences does not, therefore, prevent a state from performing its obligation under international law to take measures to prevent deprivations of life and, furthermore, it is only fitting that the punishment of such deprivations reflects, at least to some extent, the moral wrong involved. A defence that goes more directly to the heart of whether the taking of life is ever justified is duress. Traditionally, duress is not available as a defence to murder,[9] and neither is necessity, but the Court of Appeal judgment

---

[5] C. Finkelstein, 'Two Models of Murder: Patterns of Criminalisation in the United States' in J. Horder (ed.), *Homicide Law in Comparative Perspective* (Oxford: Hart Publishing, 2007), p. 104.

[6] *HMA v Hill* 1941 JC 59.

[7] Victor Tadros regards this as 'an ironically modern and politically correct evolution in an arguably anachronistic and perhaps even sexist context' ('The Scots Law of Murder' in Holder, n. 5 above, p. 204).

[8] S. Joseph, 'The Right to Life' in D. Harris & S. Joseph (eds), *The International Covenant on Civil and Political Rights and United Kingdom Law* (Oxford: Clarendon Press, 1995), at pp. 161–2.

[9] *R v Howe* [1987] AC 417.

in *Re A (conjoined twins)*[10] suggests that a defence of necessity is available to a charge of murder if only in the specific circumstances of that case. (These issues will be discussed in much more detail in chapter 6.)

The international obligation to punish criminal deprivations of life is most commonly satisfied by the imposition of lengthy sentences of imprisonment. In the UK, the mandatory life sentence for murder replaced the death penalty in the Homicide Act 1957. The abolition of the death penalty is increasingly seen as an important goal in international law, although it is retained in a number of states. The mandatory life sentence avoids the complication, from the right to life perspective, of punishing one deprivation of life by performing another,[11] but, as noted above, the mandatory nature of the sentence causes problems of its own. The Law Commission's proposal of a three-tier homicide law system is one solution to the problem; the abolition of the mandatory sentence is another. In the meantime, Parliament has created de facto differences between types of murder for sentencing purposes. For example, intentionally killing more than one victim, or a police officer while on duty, or with a sadistic motive will garner a longer minimum term in custody.[12] Some differentiation between types of killings is evident within sentencing for murder, therefore (although increasingly by Parliament rather than the individual judge), and even more so for manslaughter where a sentence may range from probation to life imprisonment. It is interesting to note that in France, a Western European state with comparable social problems and priorities, there is no mandatory life sentence for murder (*meurtre*) even though the offence is defined more restrictively than in the UK (by requiring an intention to kill).[13] Indeed, only aggravated forms of murder (such as those that are premeditated, involve victims under the age of fifteen or with racist intent) carry a maximum penalty of life imprisonment.[14] The French code also regards the causation of death as an aggravating factor for other offences against the person. For example, a death after rape will be classified as an aggravated form of rape rather than a murder in its own right.[15] It could be queried whether this awards sufficient weight to the sanctity of human life or risks blurring the line between homicides and other offences. A clearer value is placed upon human life by dealing with all killings as primarily homicide offences, with an aggravating factor of, for example, rape, rather than allowing them to be treated as primarily other offences, such as rape, with an aggravating factor of causing death. A rape followed by the murder of the victim is not a particularly heinous case of rape, but rather a murder by a rapist.

[10] *Re A (children)(conjoined twins: surgical separation)* [2000] 4 All ER 961.
[11] The complex relationship between the right to life and the death penalty will be discussed fully in chapter 5.
[12] See J. Horder & D. Hughes, 'Comparative Issues in the Law of Homicide' in Horder, n. 5 above, at pp. 5–6.
[13] See J.R. Spencer, 'Intentional Killings in French Law', in Horder, n. 5 above.
[14] Article 221 *Code Pénal*.   [15] Articles 221–3 *Code Pénal*.

It is, it could be argued, an important if subtle difference of great relevance to the enforcement of the right to life.[16]

In the context of a state's obligations to protect the right to life, one of the most important elements of the need to prevent, prohibit and punish deprivations of life occurs when the perpetrator acts on behalf of the state. The fact that in the UK, unlike in many states, most ordinary police officers are not armed goes some way towards discouraging the use of lethal force, although the possession and use of firearms by police has increased significantly in recent decades.[17] In general, the use of force by the police is governed by a requirement of reasonableness. The Criminal Law Act 1967 states in section 3(1) that 'A person may use such force as is reasonable in the circumstances in the prevention of crime or assisting in the lawful arrest of offenders or suspected offenders or of persons unlawfully at large' and section 117 of the Police and Criminal Evidence Act 1984 permits the use of reasonable force in the exercise of the powers conferred by that Act.[18] This reasonableness test has been criticized for being 'unsatisfactorily imprecise'. Joseph continues by arguing that 'lack of clarity may breach the Article 6 [ICCPR] duty to protect the right to life "by law"'.[19] David Feldman adds that the traditional reasonableness test for force sits uneasily with the 'absolutely necessary' test under Article 2 ECHR. He queries whether there should be a distinction between what is acceptable for a private citizen acting in self-defence and law enforcement officers performing their professional duties. Reasonable force may be an appropriate test for the private citizen: 'The state should not be obliged to criminalise behaviour based on an honest and reasonable reaction to a pressing danger, even if someone dies as a result.'[20] By contrast, a more demanding standard, perhaps that of necessity or absolute necessity, may be appropriate for trained agents of the state when using lethal force. Joseph notes that in practice police and government policy restricts the use of force to that which is perceived as being necessary, but that the reasonable test continues to be used to defend police officers against allegations of excessive force, and as such remains a potentially significant shortcoming in English law's enforcement of the right to life.[21] The difficulty in obtaining convictions against the police for the use of lethal force is a further problem in this context. Even if a mistake is made and the force used is not objectively reasonable, it will be extremely difficult to prove that the individual police officer did not honestly believe the use of such force to be reasonable at the time.[22] The difficulty

---

[16] Another distinguishing factor of French criminal law is the offence of failing to help a person in danger, which applies regardless of whether any harm is caused (Arts 223–6 *Code Pénal*).

[17] Joseph, n. 8 above, p. 165.

[18] In Scotland the rules are similar but regulated by the common law rather than statute.

[19] Joseph, n. 8 above, pp. 165–6.

[20] D.J. Feldman, *Civil Liberties and Human Rights in England and Wales* (Oxford: Oxford University Press, 2002, 2nd edn.), p. 191.

[21] Joseph, n. 8 above, p. 166. These issues will be considered in more detail in chapter 5.

[22] Exactly this situation is at the heart of the important case of *McCann v United Kingdom* (1995) Series A, No. 324; 21 EHRR 97.

in obtaining convictions against the use of lethal force by the security forces was particularly evident during the conflict in Northern Ireland. As Rodley explains, between 1969 and 1991, there were twenty-one prosecutions of members of the security forces for killings using firearms while on duty in Northern Ireland and all but two were found not guilty. Of those two, one was found guilty of manslaughter and given a suspended sentence and the other was convicted of murder but had his life sentence commuted and was reinstated in the army after serving only two years in prison.[23] Rodley comments as follows: 'In a state governed by the rule of law, the security forces, however cruelly and ruthlessly challenged by the paramilitaries, must not be and must be seen not to be above the law. Our institutions have not always succeeded in achieving this goal.'[24] The situation in Northern Ireland has now, thankfully, moved on to a more peaceful and democratic plane, but the lessons to be drawn from the failings there remain. Criminal prohibitions on intentional deprivations of human life are of little value unless they apply equally (albeit possibly with some necessary exceptions) to agents of the state, both on paper and, crucially, in practice.

The mainly criminal sanctions on the taking of life discussed above are only a small part of the overall role of the state in protecting the lives, and right to life, of its citizens. The criminal sanctions must be backed up by an effective police force and criminal justice system. The civil law will play a part in regulating the taking of life, for example in the context of negligent deaths or the award of compensation to the deceased's relatives. The armed forces will seek to protect the lives of all citizens of the state from external threats and government diplomacy will seek to prevent threats to life at home and abroad. The protection of human life also requires broader social assistance from the government. As Feldman notes, 'Life depends on a range of support mechanisms in society to advance health, combat disease, and protect against violence. Decent nutrition and clean water are at least as important to most people's prospects of life as therapeutic intervention or policing.'[25] Such disparate issues contribute to the protection of human life that the success or failure of any particular state in protecting the right to life of its citizens is often difficult to measure. International oversight, of both the big picture and individual allegations of failures, is therefore essential.

(2) International implementation

As noted in the previous chapter, the right to life is protected in a number of international human rights treaties, including the International Covenant on Civil and Political Rights (ICCPR), the European Convention on Human Rights (ECHR), the American Convention on Human Rights (ACHR) and the African

---

[23] N.S. Rodley, 'Rights and Responses to Terrorism in Northern Ireland', in Harris & Joseph, n. 8 above, at pp. 140–1.   [24] ibid, pp. 139–40.
[25] Feldman, n. 20 above, p. 179.

Charter on Human and Peoples' Rights (AfCh). The previous chapter discussed the evolution of the right to life in international law but stopped short of any consideration of the means of implementation of this right. Without implementation, the right to life at international law is a mere declaration. The main implementation methods utilized by these human rights treaties are a reporting system, inter-state complaints and individual petitions. Each of these mechanisms will now be considered in turn, with particular focus on how they work in respect of the right to life.

(a) State reports

The requirement of periodic state reports, which is the only compulsory implementation measure under the ICCPR and is also required under the ACHR and the AfCh, has the primary role of identifying the shortcomings in the state parties' domestic implementation of the treaty provisions. The obligation to submit reports under Article 40 ICCPR requires an initial report to be submitted within one year of ratification and then subsequent reports 'whenever the Committee so requests'.[26] The reports are examined by the Human Rights Committee in public dialogue with the reporting state's representatives and then (since 1992 only) so-called concluding observations are issued by the HRC. The reporting system does not guarantee domestic protection for the right to life or any other right but it does send an important message to states that the international community is monitoring the domestic human rights situation. As David Harris explains, at the least, it 'serves as a symbol of the international community's commitment to human rights and a medium for educating or reminding governments of the standards to which they are subject'.[27] It may also focus the minds of members of a government upon human rights issues which, although of limited use in a state with little respect for human rights, may be valuable in states already committed to effective protection of rights but distracted on a daily basis by other societal concerns. The need to report to an international body on progress made in implementing human rights will concentrate the minds of those governments with generally good intentions (or a desire to give a good impression).

The major failing of the reporting system in practice, however, is non-compliance by the states. Under the ICCPR, very few state reports are submitted on time and the delay may be anything from a few months to over a decade. Reports overdue in 2009 included one from Somalia eighteen years overdue and one from Equatorial Guinea twenty-one years overdue. Perhaps even more objectionable are the overdue reports from European countries, including a report

---

[26] Article 40(1)(b). A rule had previously been established requiring periodic reports every five years ('Decisions on Periodicity', Report of the HRC, A136/40 (81) Annex V) but the HRC reverted to the original requirement in 2000 (Report of the HRC, UN Doc A/55/40, Vol. 1, Annex III, 113, para B.1).

[27] D. Harris, 'The ICCPR and the UK: An Introduction' in Harris & Joseph, n. 8 above, p. 29.

four years overdue from Switzerland and one thirteen years overdue from Malta.[28] Various reasons are given for such delays, including 'unforeseen preparatory diffi- culties, pending constitutional or governmental reforms, co-ordination between the various domestic ministries, consultations required under federal systems, status as a developing country, and concurrent obligations to other international forums'.[29] Such excuses should not detract from the fact that states are bound under international law to meet their treaty obligations. The failure to submit reports on time seems to reflect a reluctance to prioritize human rights obliga- tions and, as such, is cause for concern. If many states are not willing or able to meet the reporting obligations of human rights treaties, which is, at least on the surface, more of a presentational requirement than a substantive one, they may be equally unwilling or unable to guarantee the rights themselves. The signifi- cant delays and failure to submit reports under the ICCPR has led the Human Rights Committee to make the momentous decision that it will consider the human rights situation within states in the absence of reports. General Comment No. 30 makes clear that the HRC is now willing both to examine reports in the absence of state delegations and even to examine a state's implementation record and produce its concluding observations without the submission of a report. The HRC followed this new procedure in 2002 in respect of Gambia.[30] This pro- active approach enables greater monitoring of recalcitrant states but it lacks the voluntary commitment element that gives the reporting system its main value.

(b) Inter-state complaints

The possibility of a state party bringing a complaint against another state party exists under the ICCPR, ECHR, ACHR and AfCh. It is the most rarely used enforcement measure, however. Under Article 41 ICCPR, the inter-state com- plaints system is reciprocally optional: a complaint can only be heard by the HRC if both the complaining and responding states have issued optional dec- larations. The procedure remains un-utilized, despite the fact that the HRC's conclusions under other procedures indicate that serious and widespread viola- tions of the Covenant's provisions have occurred in some states. The obstacles to effective use of inter-state complaints are numerous,[31] but the two most import- ant considerations are, first, the lack of interest by one state in the human rights

---

[28] Information on overdue reports drawn from <http://www.unhchr.ch/tbs/doc.nsf/>.

[29] D. McGoldrick, *The Human Rights Committee: Its Role in the Development of the International Covenant on Civil and Political Rights* (Oxford: Clarendon Press, 1991), pp. 71–2.

[30] S. Joseph, J. Schultz & M. Castan, *The International Covenant on Civil and Political Rights: Cases, Materials and Commentary* (Oxford: Oxford University Press, 2004, 2nd edn.), p. 20.

[31] Other reasons include the failure of states with the worst human rights records to accept the Article 41 procedure; the considerable time delay in pursuing a complaint to its conclusion, thereby prolonging the political difficulties suffered by the complaining state; and the existence of other less extreme options such as diplomacy, financial sanctions, trade embargoes and the suspension of diplomatic relations (S. Leckie, 'The Inter-State Complaint Procedure in International Human Rights Law: Hopeful Prospects or Wishful Thinking?' (1988) 10 H.R.Q. 249).

situation in another and, secondly, the political, and possibly economic, difficulties stemming from the alienation of another state. In short, both the lack of self-interest in initiating a complaint and the existence of self-interest in not doing so have ensured that the Article 41 procedure, as well as the comparable inter-state complaints systems in the ACHR and AfCh, remain in disuse. The missed opportunity presented by this is recognized by the HRC which has expressly reminded state parties of the existence and potential value of the inter-state complaints procedure.[32]

Under the ECHR, the inter-state complaints procedure in Article 33 is not subject to optional declarations and so any state party may submit a complaint against any other state party. In practice, however, use of this procedure remains rare. On the rare occasions when states do resort to the use of this procedure, there is often a political agenda in addition to what may be legitimate human rights concerns, as for example in respect of Ireland against the UK in the context of Northern Ireland or Cyprus against Turkey. It is apparent, however, that although many of the inter-state complaints have been politically motivated, they have virtually all been based on genuine and serious human rights violations. For example, *Cyprus v Turkey* resulted in the finding of a number of serious violations of the rights of Greek Cypriots, including a violation of the right to life under Article 2 due to Turkey's failure to mount an effective investigation of the whereabouts of Greek Cypriot missing persons.[33] It is cases such as these, in which widespread violations are in issue, that the inter-state complaints procedure can play a vital role in publicizing and condemning violations of rights such as the right to life. Far greater will on the parts of governments under the ECHR and other treaties is needed, however, in order for inter-state complaints procedures to live up to their potential.

(c) Individual petitions

Traditionally, international law governed only the relations between states. Human rights treaties are a good example of how this traditional approach has changed. The relationship between states and individuals is at the core of such treaties and it is perhaps not surprising, therefore, that individuals are involved in the implementation of their provisions. Human rights treaties are for the benefit of individuals. By ratifying such a treaty, state parties are guaranteeing to protect the human rights, including the right to life, of the individuals within their borders. It is only appropriate that these beneficiaries should be able to take action against their state if they become victims of violations of the treaty provisions. While reporting systems or inter-state complaints may be more effective at drawing attention to large scale human rights abuses, individual complaints

---

[32] General Comment No. 31: 'The Nature of the General Legal Obligation Imposed on States Parties to the Covenant' (2004), para. 2.   [33] *Cyprus v Turkey* ECHR 2001-IV 172.

have value as relating to individual instances of alleged violations of rights and, given the importance of each human life and the potential threat to all life from a single arbitrary deprivation of life by the state, are equally important. Indeed, an individual petition system may be the most reliable means of policing a state's observance of its treaty obligations because, unlike the reporting system, it does not rely on the state authorities' own views of the human rights situation and, unlike the inter-state complaints system, it does not rely on another state over-coming its apathy and endangering its own international relations. Individual petition relies upon the people who matter most under human rights treaties: the potential victims. It is this point that was recognized as particularly significant during the drafting of the ECHR when individual petition was proposed for the first time in an international treaty.[34]

The ECHR is the human rights treaty under which individual petition has most prospered. Although (largely at the UK's request) the acceptance of individual petition is optional under the Convention, all state parties have accepted it. Individual petition has been described as 'the essence of the Strasbourg experience' and as representing 'the mainstay of activity'.[35] Cases involving Article 2's protection for the right to life have been relatively common and in some important judgments the European Court of Human Rights has found the UK in violation for the planning and control of an operation which resulted in the fatal shootings of three suspected terrorists,[36] Russia in violation for the killings of civilians by use of combat weapons in Chechnya,[37] and Turkey in violation for the use of excessive force in quelling a riot.[38] These are just a few examples, illustrating both the diverse issues raised in individual complaints and the important role of the Strasbourg institutions in seeking to enforce the internationally recognized right to life.

The individual petition systems under other treaties have been less extensively used. The HRC, a non-judicial body, hears communications from individuals but only those from state parties which have ratified the First Optional Protocol. The Committee issues its 'views' on the merits of the complaint and, even though these are not legally binding, as 'the pre-eminent interpreter' of the ICCPR, their decisions are 'strong indicators of legal obligations, so rejection of those decisions

---

[34] One of the representatives expressed this most effectively: 'That the international machinery should be at the disposal of the victims is...the only means we have of persuading the men and women of Europe that something new has been done and that an advance has been achieved. We must say to them that even if the states take no further interest in them, and even if no one takes any action on their behalf, they may, by virtue of their dignity as men, avail themselves on their own behalf of an international organ of protection' (Teitgen, quoted in G. Robertson, *Collected Edition of the Travaux Préparatoires* (The Hague: Martinus Nijhoff, 1977), Vol. 2, p. 178).

[35] L. Heffernan, 'A Comparative View of Individual Petition Procedures under the European Convention on Human Rights and the International Covenant on Civil and Political Rights' (1997) 19 H.R.Q. 78, at p. 87.

[36] *McCann v United Kingdom* (1995) Series A No. 324; 21 E.H.R.R. 97.

[37] *Isayeva, Yusopova & Bazayeva v Russia* (2005) 41 E.H.R.R. 347.

[38] *Guleç v Turkey* (1998) 28 E.H.R.R. 121; Reps 1998-IV.

is good evidence of a state's bad faith attitude towards its ICCPR obligations'.[39] The HRC has considered communications in respect of the death penalty, police shootings and deaths in custody, amongst many other issues. The role of individual petitions under the ACHR has increased in recent decades, probably due both to the creation of a court with authority to make legally binding decisions, and the restoration of democracy in many south and central American states. The court is required to submit an annual report to the General Assembly of the Organisation of American states indicating which state parties have not complied with its judgments and making 'pertinent recommendations'.[40] The number of complaints under the American system remains very low compared to the European system but even the limited growth in recent years has presented practical difficulties for the Inter-American organs which remain severely under-resourced. Nevertheless, important decisions have been made by the Inter-American Court, including the case of *Velásquez Rodríguez* which concerned the practice of disappearances in Honduras and resulted in the finding of a violation of the right to life.[41] The case has been described by Steiner and Alston as 'one of the most influential and cited decisions of an international human rights tribunal'.[42] Under the African Charter, individual complaints are heard by the African Commission on Human and Peoples' Rights. Although a new African Court has recently been created, it is not yet hearing cases under the Charter. The African Commission, although hampered by a lack of resources and the limited political will of the state parties, has heard a number of complaints relating to serious right to life violations including massacres, extrajudicial executions, disappearances and police killings. If nothing else, the use of the individual complaints systems under all four of these human rights treaties poignantly illustrates the widespread failings at the domestic level in protecting the right to life.

One particular issue with great relevance to the effective enforcement of the right to life is the availability of interim measures. The HRC considers the need for interim action where the performance of certain actions by a state would cause irreparable damage to the author of a communication.[43] In other words, if a communication is alleging that an imminent death will be contrary to the ICCPR, as for example with an allegation that a death penalty has been improperly imposed, the state can be asked to refrain from causing the death until the HRC has had the opportunity to consider the matter. Such requests for interim relief are usually complied with but there are exceptions. For example, in *Paindiong v Philippines*,[44] the state executed the three authors of a complaint after receiving the HRC's request. The HRC responded by issuing a strong

---

[39] Joseph, Schultz & Castan, n. 30 above, p. 24.   [40] Article 85 ACHR.

[41] Judgment of July 29, 1988, Inter-Am Ct. H.R. (Ser. C) No. 4 (1989).

[42] H.J. Steiner, P. Alston & R. Goodman, *International Human Rights Law in Context: Law, Politics, Morals* (Oxford: Oxford University Press, 2008, 3rd edn.), p. 1042.

[43] Rule 86 of the HRC's Rules of Procedure (UN Doc. CCPR/C/3/Rev.6, 24 April 2001).

[44] Communication 869/1999.

condemnation of the state's actions, describing them as 'grave breaches of its obligations under the Optional Protocol'[45] and emphasizing that the availability of interim measures is 'essential to the Committee's role' and the flouting of such measures 'undermines the protection of Covenant rights through the Optional Protocol'.[46] Similar condemnation followed the execution by Trinidad and Tobago of the author of a pending communication in *Ashley v Trinidad & Tobago*.[47] The HRC expressed its 'indignation' at the execution which followed a request from the HRC Special Rapporteur for New Communications that the death penalty should not be carried out while the communication remained pending.[48] The HRC's frustration in respect of such matters is understandable. It is essential that state parties who are obligated to respect both the right to life and the right of individual petition to the Committee are willing to delay executions that are subject to communications alleging an infringement of the Covenant. If the complaint is unfounded, the execution can proceed at a later date, but a life taken cannot be returned. The deliberate disregard of a request for interim relief in right to life cases not only shows a lack of respect to the HRC but also undermines the very core of the right to life which incorporates an assumption of the inherent value in human life.[49]

(d) International relations

So far discussion has concentrated upon the treaty-based regimes which protect a right to life in international law but broader considerations of international relations, including the political organs of the United Nations, can also play a role in protecting this right. Under the United Nations system, the most important body in this regard is the Human Rights Council (which replaced the Commission on Human Rights in 2006).[50] Unlike the HRC, the HRCouncil is a United Nations Charter-based body: 'the Charter-based bodies are political organs which have a much broader mandate to promote awareness, to foster respect, and to respond to violations of human rights standards. They derive their legitimacy and their mandate, in the broadest sense, from the human rights provisions of the Charter.'[51] A number of procedures are available to the HRCouncil and many of these have particular relevance to the right to life. For example, the 1503 procedure enables the examination of communications relating to 'situations which appear to reveal

---

[45] ibid, para. 5.2. [46] ibid, para. 5.4. [47] Communication 580/1994.
[48] ibid, para. 411.
[49] It is not only requests by the HRC that have been ignored. The US breached a provisional measures order of the ICJ which requested that the US refrain from executing a German citizen denied consular access upon arrest contrary to international law (*Germany v USA (LaGrand)* (Order of 3 Mar 1999) [1999] ICJ Rep 9).
[50] The Human Rights Council was established by GA Resolution 60/251 (2006) to replace the largely discredited Commission on Human Rights. The Council is a body with 47 member governments elected by the General Assembly, on the basis of regional groupings (Asia, Africa, Eastern Europe, Latin America, Western European and others).
[51] Steiner & Alston, n. 42 above, p. 740.

a consistent pattern of gross and reliably attested violations of human rights'.[52] This procedure is shrouded in secrecy, however, due to the confidential nature of the examinations. The so-called 'special procedures' avoid this pitfall and have increased in importance in recent years. They involve an annual report, fact-finding missions to states and the sending of communications. By 2007, there were twenty-eight of these thematic procedures including, of direct relevance to the right to life, special procedures on disappearances, extrajudicial executions, the right to food and the right to health. The Report of the Special Rapporteur on Extrajudicial, Summary and Arbitrary Executions on his mission to Nigeria in 2005 is extracted in Steiner and Alston's book and makes interesting reading.[53] The report raises concerns about deaths by stoning for the offence of sodomy: 'the imposition of the death sentence for a private sexual practice is clearly incompatible with Nigeria's international obligations'.[54] The response by the Nigerian ambassador is to dispute the relevance of such death sentences to the subject of the report, claiming that these deaths 'should not be equated with extrajudicial killings' and that 'the notion that executions for offences such as homosexuality and lesbianism are excessive is judgemental rather than objective'.[55] The serious concern raised by the rapporteur is too easily dismissed by the representative of Nigeria, whose response highlights the difficulties posed to effective protection of human life by varying cultural beliefs, but at least reports such as these encourage dialogue on matters of concern to the international community on the issue of the right to life.

Perhaps surprisingly, the Security Council of the United Nations also has a central role in respect of the right to life both in terms of seeking peaceful settlements to conflicts and in authorizing the use of force (particularly as the UN Charter only permits force in self-defence without Security Council approval). Indeed, it is in the context of conflicts, international or increasingly domestic, that the right to life is most threatened. The 1994 genocide in Rwanda resulted in 800,000 people being killed in approximately 100 days. The UN's failure to intervene at any stage during that period is perhaps the most blatant failure of the international community to protect human life. An independent inquiry has concluded that this failure to intervene was a failing of the UN system as a whole and has blamed this upon a lack of both resources and political commitment.[56] A similar lack of commitment could be discerned in relation to Bosnia, while the intervention in Kosovo (by means of military action, which inevitably brings its own right to life

---

[52] The 1503 procedure is named after Economic and Social Council Resolution 1503 (XLVIII) (1970). The procedure was reviewed in 2007 and the HRCouncil has decided to retain at least the essence of it. See Steiner & Alston, ibid, pp. 754–9 for discussion.

[53] Report of the Special Rapporteur on Extrajudicial, Summary and Arbitrary Executions, Philip Alston, on his mission to Nigeria (27 Jun–8 Jul 2005) (UN Doc. E/CN.4/2006/53/Add.4), extracted in Steiner & Alston, ibid, pp. 779–82.   [54] ibid, para. 37.

[55] Steiner & Alston, ibid, p. 781.

[56] 'Report of the Independent Inquiry into the Actions of the United Nations during the 1994 Genocide in Rwanda' (UN Doc. S/1999/1257).

issues) was NATO based and proceeded without a Security Council resolution in order to bypass the inevitable veto from Russia. The UN has much to do to prove that it can, and will, intervene in a timely and effective manner to save lives from those acting with a manifest disregard for the right to life.

The European response to the conflicts in Chechnya and Turkey also raise questions as to the best approach to extensive loss of life during political conflicts within a state's borders. Greer argues that, despite the ECHR and an active individual petition system emerging from the Council of Europe, it is 'hard to deny that the European Union has had a much greater impact than the Council of Europe on the position of human rights in Turkey'.[57] While many cases on the right to life have been brought against Turkey by individuals, and even some states, due to its law enforcement agencies' tendency to adopt 'an excessively forceful approach to public protest and political unrest',[58] recent improvements have stemmed from EU accession negotiations rather than the ECHR obligations to which Turkey has been committed since its origin. The fact that Turkey has been found in violation of the ECHR, including Article 2's protection for the right to life, numerous times does not seem to have had as much positive impact on protecting human life as the country's desire to join the EU. The European Court of Human Rights has also more recently found Russia to be in violation of Article 2 in relation to the use of force in Chechnya,[59] but on this matter Greer raises the question as to whether the right to life, as well as democracy and human rights in general, would be 'better served in the long term by expelling Russia for such gross and flagrant violations, or by retaining it in spite of them?'[60] In a conflict which has cost an estimated 100,000 human lives, how does a human rights treaty system respond? When human life is treated so cheaply, what role is left for the right to life other than to declare loudly and repeatedly that life is something of value and should be protected, not eradicated, by the state? Ultimately, then, the right to life in international law remains a message rather than a deed. So, given the apparent widespread deviation from the preservation of life, what exactly is the message that the right to life seeks to send? What is the scope of this right?

B. The scope of the right to life

(1) Killings by state agents

At the core of the right to life is the prohibition of arbitrary killings by agents of the state. The HRC emphasized this aspect of Article 6 ICCPR in General

---

[57] S. Greer, *The European Convention on Human Rights: Achievements, Problems and Prospects* (Cambridge: Cambridge University Press, 2006), p. 102.   [58] ibid, p. 99.
[59] *Isayeva, Yusopova & Bazayeva v Russia* (2005) 41 E.H.R.R. 347.
[60] Greer, n. 57 above, p. 130.

Comment No. 6 by describing the protection against arbitrary deprivation of life as being of 'paramount importance'.[61] The Committee states that:

State parties should take measures not only to prevent and punish deprivation of life by criminal acts, but also to prevent arbitrary killing by their own security forces. The deprivation of life by the authorities of the State is a matter of the utmost gravity. Therefore, the law must strictly control and limit the circumstances in which a person may be deprived of his life by such authorities.[62]

The HRC had the opportunity to put this principle into practice when considering the communication of *Suarez de Guerrero v Colombia*[63] involving the killing of seven suspects by Colombian police officers. The police believed that a kidnapped former ambassador was being held at a particular house in Bogotá and so a raid of the property was authorized. Nobody was found at the house and the police patrol waited in hiding for the arrival of the suspected kidnappers. As each of seven victims entered the house, they were killed at point-blank range. The author of the communication was shot several times after she had already died from a heart attack. The actions of the police were lawful under domestic law but the HRC found a violation of the right to life under Article 6 ICCPR. The Committee regarded the killings as intentional and not proportionate to the requirements of law enforcement. In particular, the HRC had regard to the fact that there was no warning or opportunity to surrender given to the victims and that there was no evidence that the actions of the police were necessary in the defence of themselves or others or to effect the arrest or prevent the escape of the suspects. The HRC added that by arbitrarily killing these suspects, the police had denied them all of the protections of due process of law.[64] The HRC's views in respect of these communications are significant because they establish that in order to be regarded as 'arbitrary', a killing by a state agent does not necessarily need to be unlawful under the domestic law of the state. Furthermore, the introduction of the concepts of intentional killing, proportionality and necessity for law enforcement bring Article 6 much more in line with the provisions of Article 2 ECHR.

The leading case on this issue under the ECHR is *McCann v United Kingdom*.[65] This infamous case concerned the fatal shooting of three IRA terrorists in Gibraltar who were suspected of planning to activate a car-bomb. Article 2 expressly prohibits the intentional deprivation of life but the second paragraph of the Article permits the deprivation of life when it results from the use of force which is no more than absolutely necessary in defence of any person from unlawful violence. This case was one of the first opportunities for the European Court of Human Rights to consider the right to life and it confirmed that Article 2 is 'one of the most fundamental provisions in the Convention' which, together with

---

[61] General Comment No. 6: The Right to Life (1982), para. 3.   [62] ibid.
[63] Communication 45/1979.   [64] ibid, para. 13.2.
[65] (1995) Series A No. 324; 21 E.H.R.R. 97.

Article 3, 'enshrines one of the basic values of the democratic societies making up the Council of Europe' and thus 'its provisions must be strictly construed'.[66] The Court took the view that the term 'absolutely necessary' in Article 2(2) indicates that 'a stricter and more compelling test of necessity' must be applied in contrast to the test of necessity in other Convention Articles and that, therefore, the force used by state agents must be strictly proportionate to the aim pursued.[67] Perhaps the most significant finding of the Court, however, was that it must take into consideration not only the actions of the agents of the state who actually administer the force but also 'all the surrounding circumstances including such matters as the planning and control of the actions under examination'.[68] This extension of the Court's task proved crucial on the facts of the case because, while the Court concluded that the force used by the soldiers was justified under Article 2(2) as being based on an honest, but mistaken, belief of its necessity to prevent unlawful violence,[69] a majority found the planning and control of the operation to be unsatisfactory. In particular, the majority was critical of (a) the decision not to prevent the suspects from travelling into Gibraltar; (b) the failure of the authorities to make sufficient allowances for the possibility that their intelligence assessments might be erroneous; and (c) the automatic recourse to lethal force when the soldiers opened fire.[70] The latter point concerns the so-called shoot to kill policy of members of the SAS which, according to the Court, required greater care to be taken in ensuring that the information conveyed to the soldiers on the scene was accurate: 'the authorities were bound by their obligation to respect the right to life of the suspects to exercise the greatest care in evaluating the information at their disposal before transmitting it to soldiers whose use of firearms automatically involved shooting to kill'.[71] The Court found a violation of Article 2 by only ten votes to nine and the decision remains controversial, particularly in the UK, but many of the important points of interpretation were the subject of agreement by all members of the Court, such as the strict test of absolute necessity and the relevance of the planning and control of operations rather than just the actions directly responsible for the death. Ni Aolain makes the point that the Court 'signalled an equality approach' to the right to life in this case by making clear that the status of the victims, in this case as terrorists, does not lessen the protection afforded to their lives under Article 2.[72] The Court also set down an important rule of interpretation when it concluded that an honest mistake in relation to the necessity of lethal force by the actual shooter does not violate Article 2. This is a significant restriction upon the applicability of the right to life and it could be argued that trained professionals should be required to make, at least, reasonable assessment of the necessity of lethal force before engaging in shoot-to-kill actions. The understandable reluctance to place the blame with individual soldiers or

[66] ibid, para. 147. [67] ibid, para. 149. [68] ibid, para. 150.
[69] ibid, para. 200. [70] ibid, para. 213. [71] ibid, para. 211.
[72] F. Ni Aolain, 'Truth Telling, Accountability and the Right to Life in Northern Ireland' (2002) 5 E.H.R.L.R. 572, at p. 576.

police officers who are acting in the heat of the moment is no excuse when we are considering the liability of the state itself for an intentional killing by an agent of the state that was not objectively necessary.

The subsequent case of *Andronicou and Constantinou v Cyprus*[73] applied the principles from *McCann* to a rescue operation during which both a hostage-taker and his victim were fatally shot by the police. As in *McCann*, the shooting officers were entitled to rely on an honest but mistaken belief that lives were in danger and that the use of lethal force was necessary but, unlike in the earlier case, the planning and organization of this police operation was held to have minimized to the greatest extent possible the risk to life. This conclusion was based upon the fact that the officers were explicitly told to use proportionate force and to fire only if lives were in danger. The rescue operation as a whole, therefore, provided adequate protection for the right to life even though mistakes on the part of the officers involved led to two avoidable deaths. In *Isayeva, Yusopova and Bazayeva v Russia*,[74] the Court held that Article 2(2) may even justify the use of lethal force against illegal armed groups by means of heavy combat weapons but this requires both convincing evidence and efforts to minimize the risk to life. In this case, involving the deaths of innocent civilians during indiscriminate bombing by Russian military planes of a civilian convoy near Grozny in Chechnya, there was neither convincing evidence nor efforts to minimize the risk to life and a violation of Article 2 was found on the basis that the operation was not planned and executed with requisite care for the lives of the civilian population.

Article 2(2) not only justifies the use of lethal force in defence of unlawful violence but also to quell a riot or insurrection, in the context of which the force used must not be excessive,[75] and to effect a lawful arrest or prevent an escape. In *Nachova v Bulgaria*,[76] a sensible restriction was placed upon the latter exception when the Court concluded that it can never be absolutely necessary to use lethal force to arrest a non-violent suspect if he is posing no threat to life or limb, even if the failure to use lethal force will result in the suspect's escape. This represents a logical balancing of the need to protect life against the social benefit of other aspects of law enforcement. An intentional killing by a state agent in circumstances where there is no threat of unlawful violence now or in the future cannot be compatible with state protection for the right to life.

(2) Effective investigations for killings and disappearances

The influential case of *McCann*, discussed above, also established a further requirement of the right to life under the ECHR, namely the duty upon states to undertake effective investigations into killings.[77] The Court noted that 'a general legal

---

[73] (1997) 25 E.H.R.R. 491; 1997-VI.   [74] (2005) 41 E.H.R.R. 347.
[75] *Guleç v Turkey* (1998) 28 E.H.R.R. 121; Reps 1998-IV.   [76] ECHR 2005-VII.
[77] This obligation also exists under the ICCPR: *Baboeram et al v Suriname* (Communications 146, 148–154/1983); *Herrera Rubio v Colombia* (Communication 161/1983); *Sanjuán Arévalo v Colombia* (Communication 181/1984).

prohibition of arbitrary killing by the agents of the State would be ineffective, in practice, if there existed no procedure for reviewing the lawfulness of the use of lethal force by State authorities'.[78] For this reason, the Court held that Article 2 requires by implication that there be some form of effective official investigation when individuals have been killed by agents of the state or otherwise. On the facts of *McCann*, there was no breach of this particular requirement of Article 2 but in *Kaya v Turkey*[79] the Court considered this aspect further. It concluded that the accountability of state agents for the use of lethal force requires that their actions be subjected to independent and public scrutiny, capable of leading to a determination as to whether such force was justified in the circumstances.[80] The Court emphasized the need under Article 2 for effective and independent investigation into deaths arising out of clashes with security forces and stated that this need increased when the precise circumstances of the death remain unclear. Therefore, 'neither the prevalence of violent armed clashes nor the high incidence of fatalities' can displace the requirement of an effective investigation.[81] This point was particularly relevant in the case which concerned the killing of a man by the security forces who claimed that he was killed in a gun battle between members of the security forces and a group of terrorists, a claim denied by the deceased's family. Given the dispute over the circumstances of the death, an effective and independent investigation became all the more important. And this is not merely a procedural nicety; the failure of the Turkish authorities to provide such an investigation in this case was the basis for a finding of a violation of the right to life.

The difficulty of proof in cases allegedly involving killings by agents of the state was also an issue in the case of *Yasa v Turkey*.[82] In this case, it was not clear whether the death in question had been caused by agents of the state or not, but the Court clarified that the requirement of an effective investigation is not confined to cases where it has been established that the death was caused by agents of the state. The Court also held that the requirement of an effective investigation is not dependent on a formal complaint being lodged by the family of the deceased. The obligation to conduct an investigation arises from the mere fact of being informed of a murder.[83] The investigation carried out in this case was held to be insufficient for the purposes of Article 2 because it did not allow for the possibility that the security forces may have been implicated in the death and because there had been no credible progress made more than five years after the death.[84] A violation of the right to life is found even though it has not been proven that the death was caused by an agent of the state. The need for such an approach to the right is explained even more clearly in the later case of *Timurtas v Turkey*.[85]

Timurtas involved the disappearance of the applicant's son. It was alleged, although the state authorities denied it, that he had been apprehended by security forces and subsequently held in detention. The Court recognized that where

---

[78] *McCann*, n. 65 above, para. 161.   [79] (1998) 28 E.H.R.R. 1; Reps 1998-I.
[80] ibid, para. 87.   [81] ibid, para. 91.   [82] (1998) 28 E.H.R.R. 408; Reps 1998-VI.
[83] ibid, para. 100.   [84] ibid, para. 102.   [85] ECHR 2000-VI.

an applicant accuses agents of the state of violating his rights, the state alone may have access to relevant information proving or disproving the alleged facts, and a failure to submit such evidence without satisfactory explanation may lead to the drawing of inferences as to the well-foundedness of the allegations. The state's failure to provide a plausible explanation as to a detainee's fate, in the absence of a body, may raise issues under the right to life. The European Court of Human Rights has adopted this expansive approach in order to adequately deal with cases of disappearances, where the applicant is unable to prove that the state has caused a death, without assistance by the state itself. The Court explained that it will be looking for 'sufficient circumstantial evidence, based on concrete elements, from which it may be concluded to the requisite standard of proof that the detainee must be presumed to have died in custody'.[86] The period of time of detention will be a relevant factor; in this case, a period of six and a half years helped to engage Article 2.[87] The fact that the applicant's son was suspected of alleged terrorist activities was also relevant because the Court could not exclude the possibility that an unacknowledged detention of such a person would be life-threatening. The Court found Turkey to have violated the right to life on the basis that the applicant's son must be presumed dead following an unacknowledged detention by security forces. As the state did not admit this, there could be no justification under Article 2(2). In addition to this substantive violation of the right to life (on the basis of presumed facts), the Court also found a procedural violation due to the inadequacy of the state's investigation into the disappearance of the applicant's son and noted the importance in this context of the prompt judicial intervention required by Article 5 of the ECHR which may lead to the detection and prevention of life-threatening measures in violation of Article 2.[88]

The Inter-American Court of Human Rights has adopted a similar approach to the problematic issue of disappearances, an issue traditionally of far greater significance in Latin America where the problem is commonplace. In the *Velásquez Rodríguez* case of 1988, the Inter-American Court, while recognizing that disappearances are not new in the history of human rights violations, found 'their systematic and repeated nature and their use not only for causing certain individuals to disappear, either briefly or permanently, but also as a means of creating a general state of anguish, insecurity and fear, is a recent phenomenon' and one that 'has occurred with exceptional intensity in Latin America'.[89] The Inter-American Court recognized that the forced disappearance of individuals represents a multiple and continuous violation of many human rights, including the right to liberty and the prohibition on cruel and inhuman treatment, and also that the

---

[86] ibid, para. 82.

[87] An earlier case, *Kurt v Turkey* (ECHR 1998-III 1187; (1998) 27 E.H.R.R 91) involved a similar disappearance but for a shorter period of four and a half years. In that case the Court held that there was insufficient persuasive indications that the disappeared person had died in custody. The significance of the time difference appears overstated.   [88] *Timurtas*, n. 85 above, para. 89.

[89] Judgment of 29 July 1988, Inter-Am Ct. H.R. (Ser. C) No. 4 (1989), para. 149.

practice of disappearances 'often involves secret execution without trial, followed by concealment of the body to eliminate any material evidence of the crime' and this is a flagrant violation of the right to life.[90] The Court found a systematic practice of disappearances to have occurred in Honduras between 1981 and 1984 and that this was carried out or tolerated by state officials. As with the European Court many years later, the Inter-American Court accepted the need to rely upon circumstantial evidence in the context of disappearances 'because this type of repression is characterised by an attempt to suppress all information about the kidnapping or the whereabouts and fate of the victim'.[91] The Inter-American Court justified this use of circumstantial evidence on the basis that the objective of international human rights law is to protect victims and provide reparation for damages, not to punish individuals who are guilty of such violations. The burden of proof can, therefore, justifiably be lowered.

It is well established that the international implementation of the right to life includes a recognition of the relevance of disappeared persons to this right. It is notoriously difficult to prove that state agents have caused a death, unless the state authorities admit to this fact. The requirement of an effective investigation into deaths is an important procedural guarantee, which helps to cast light on the often murky circumstances of unacknowledged state killings, but the regional human rights courts have gone beyond this procedural requirement and lessened the burden of proof for individuals seeking to establish that a disappeared person has been killed by the state.[92] This is an essential protection for the values underlying the right to life and sends a strong message to state authorities that killings by state agents will not be tolerated even in circumstances where the state denies responsibility. We can begin to discern here the extent of the obligations imposed upon states under the right to life, extending beyond the negative obligation not to kill, to a series of positive obligations to investigate deaths and provide plausible explanations for the whereabouts of detained persons or face the consequences for not being able to do so. The extent of the positive obligations under the right to life will now be considered.

(3) Positive obligations to preserve life

In its first General Comment on the right to life under the ICCPR, the HRC noted that 'the right to life has been too often narrowly interpreted'.[93] The

---

[90] ibid, para. 157.   [91] ibid, para. 131.

[92] The particular problems posed by the practice of disappearances has also been recognized by the HRC, which has called upon state parties to the ICCPR to 'take specific and effective measures to prevent the disappearance of individuals, something which unfortunately has become all too frequent and leads too often to arbitrary deprivation of life. Furthermore, States should establish effective facilities and procedures to investigate thoroughly cases of missing and disappeared persons in circumstances which may involve a violation of the right to life.' (General Comment No. 6, para. 4.)

[93] General Comment No. 6, para. 5.

Committee explained that the expression 'inherent right to life' in Article 6 'cannot properly be understood in a restrictive manner' and 'requires that States adopt positive measures'.[94] In *Dermit Barbato v Uruguay*, the HRC found a violation of the right to life in respect of a death in custody on the basis that the state authorities were responsible, either by act or omission, for not taking adequate measures to protect life.[95] In the *Velásquez Rodríguez* case, discussed above, the Inter-American Court identified positive obligations as arising from Article 1(1) of the ACHR which requires state parties to 'undertake to respect the rights and freedoms recognised herein and to ensure to all persons subject to their jurisdiction the free and full exercise of those rights and freedoms'. This requires not only that states refrain from killing individuals (either through act or omission), but also that they ensure the free and full exercise of the right to life, by preventing, investigating and punishing any violation.[96] The jurisprudence of positive obligations under the right to life is most developed under the ECHR. The existence of positive obligations was first hinted at in *L.C.B. v United Kingdom* in 1998.[97] In this case concerning the testing of nuclear weapons, the Court held that the first sentence of Article 2 ('Everyone's right to life shall be protected by law') requires state parties to take appropriate steps to safeguard the lives of those in its jurisdiction. The key question for the Court will be whether the state did all that could have been required of it, in the circumstances of the case, to prevent the applicant's life being avoidably put at risk.[98] The answer, on the facts of this case, was held unanimously to be yes, but this approach has been developed in subsequent cases. In *Öneryildiz v Turkey*,[99] the Court recognized a duty on the state to put in place a legislative and administrative framework designed to provide effective deterrence against threats to the right to life. This applies even in the context of dangerous activities, such as, in this case, residing in slums near a household-refuse tip which was destroyed, along with much of the slum housing, in a methane explosion.[100] This case demonstrates the extent of the positive obligations upon the state which must, for example, safeguard the public from the possibility of a lethal explosion at a hazardous waste state not only by means of providing appropriate legal regulation of such sites, but also by ensuring the observance of these regulations and by informing the public about risks and taking reasonable preventive measures to protect any lives that are at risk.

One of the most common contexts of the imposition of positive obligations upon a state is in relation to policing and the criminal law. In the landmark case

---

[94] ibid. The Committee particularly mentions that it would be 'desirable' (although not, presumably, obligatory) for state parties 'to take all possible measures to reduce infant mortality and to increase life expectancy, especially in adopting measures to eliminate malnutrition and epidemics'. Information regarding such issues has been consistently sought under the reporting process (McGoldrick, n. 29 above, p. 329).   [95] Communication 84/1981.

[96] *Velásquez Rodríguez* case, n. 89 above, para. 166.

[97] (1998) 27 E.H.R.R. 212; Reps 1998-III.   [98] ibid, para. 36.

[99] [2004] ECHR 657; (2005) 41 E.H.R.R. 20.   [100] ibid, para. 90.

of *Osman v United Kingdom*,[101] the Court outlined the positive obligation upon a state party to the ECHR to preserve the lives of those in its jurisdiction. The case concerned a failure on the part of the police to prevent a death. The Court held that Article 2(1) 'enjoins the state not only to refrain from the intentional and unlawful taking of life, but also to take appropriate steps to safeguard the lives of those within its jurisdiction'.[102] While the primary duty is to provide effective criminal law provisions, backed up by law-enforcement machinery, the obligation may extend to the need for preventive operational measures to protect an individual whose life is at risk from the criminal acts of another individual.[103] However, any such obligation must be interpreted in a way which does not impose an impossible or disproportionate burden on the authorities.[104] This limitation was imposed by the Court due to a number of factors, such as the 'difficulties involved in policing modern societies, the unpredictability of human conduct and the operational choices which must be made in terms of priorities and resources'.[105] The Court also held that the positive obligation on the police to safeguard lives is subject to the requirements of due process, including those implied by the right to liberty (Article 5) and the right to respect for private life (Article 8). This recognition of the need to balance not only public resources but also the potentially conflicting Convention rights illustrates the limits of the positive aspect of the right to life. Nevertheless, the Court established an important principle that state authorities must do all that could reasonably be expected of them to avoid a real and immediate risk to life of which they have or ought to have knowledge.[106]

There was held to be no violation of Article 2 in *Osman*, but in *Mahmut Kaya v Turkey*, a violation of the right to life was found in the extreme circumstances of the absence of an effective criminal law regime in the south-east region of the state[107] and in *Gongadze v Ukraine* there was a violation in the context of major criminal behaviour amongst senior officials and politicians.[108] There are also positive obligations placed upon prison authorities to safeguard the lives of detainees,[109] including by providing timely and adequate medical care.[110] This point has also been confirmed by the HRC in *Lantsov v Russian Federation*, a case concerning the death of a detainee in pre-trial detention.[111] The HRC held that the state had failed to take appropriate measures to protect the detainee's life and that it was irrelevant that the detainee had not specifically requested medical assistance: 'the essential fact remains that the state party by arresting and detaining individuals takes the responsibility to care for their life. It is up to the state

---

[101] (1998) 29 E.H.R.R. 245; Reps 1998-VIII.   [102] ibid, para. 115.   [103] ibid.
[104] ibid, para. 116.   [105] ibid.   [106] ibid.   [107] [2000] ECHR 129.
[108] Judgment of 8 Nov 2005. In *Mastromatteo v Italy* ([2002] ECHR 694), the Court even considered, but ultimately rejected, the argument that the state was in violation of the right to life for permitting the early release of a prisoner who went on to kill.
[109] *Paul and Audrey Edwards v United Kingdom* ([2002] ECHR 303; (2002) 35 E.H.R.R. 19).
[110] *Augvelova v Bulgaria* (Judgment of 13 Jun 2002).   [111] Communication 763/1997.

party by organising its detention facilities to know about the state of health of the detainees as far as may be reasonably expected.'[112] Unlike the European Court of Human Rights, the HRC explicitly denied the relevance of financial resources, adding that 'lack of financial means cannot reduce this responsibility'.[113]

The positive obligation to safeguard lives is extensive and demanding but it is, in general, rooted in the real world, with the European Court (the body that has developed the most extensive jurisprudence upon the matter) taking into account the conflicting demands of public services and due process when imposing positive obligations upon state authorities.

(4) The death penalty

The complex relationship between the death penalty and the right to life will be considered in greater detail in chapter 5 but a brief overview is necessary here in order to establish the general scope of the right. It is first important to note that the right to life under both the ICCPR and the ECHR expressly permits the death penalty but optional protocols to both treaties have prohibited it and abolition is encouraged by the HRC.[114] Under Article 6(2) ICCPR, the death penalty can only be imposed for the 'most serious crimes'. This constraint must, according to the HRC, be 'read restrictively to mean that the death penalty should be a quite exceptional measure'.[115] Thus, in *Lubuto v Zambia*, a violation of the right to life was found in the context of a death sentence imposed for an aggravated robbery in which firearms were used but did not result in any injuries.[116] The HRC's views in this case suggest that the death penalty should not be imposed for crimes where no one is injured, although one member of the Committee expressly dissented on this point. In its concluding observations to a number of state reports, the Committee has also excluded the following from the category of most serious offences: drug-related offences, property offences and abetting suicide,[117] apostasy, committing a third homosexual act, embezzlement by officials and theft by force,[118] crimes of an economic nature, adultery and corruption.[119] It appears that only intentional killings or attempted killings, and perhaps intentional infliction of serious bodily harm, may attract the death penalty under Article 6(2).[120]

The mandatory imposition of a death penalty is also an issue on which the HRC has expressed strong views. In *Brown v Jamaica*, a mandatory death sentence for 'murder in aggravated circumstances' was held not to be contrary to

---

[112] ibid, para. 9.2.   [113] ibid.
[114] Second Optional Protocol of the ICCPR; Protocol No. 6 of the ECHR. In General Comment No. 6, para. 6, the HRC declares that 'all measures of abolition should be considered as progress in the enjoyment of the right to life'.   [115] General Comment No. 6, para. 7.
[116] Communication 390/1990.
[117] Concluding observations on Sri Lanka (1996) UN Doc. CCPR/C/79/Add. 56, para. 14.
[118] Concluding observations on Sudan (1997) UN Doc. CCPR/C/79/Add. 85, para. 8.
[119] Concluding observations on Islamic Republic of Iran (1995) UN Doc. CCPR/C/79/Add. 25, para. 8.   [120] Joseph, Schultz & Castan, n. 30 above, p. 167.

Article 6's protection for the right to life,[121] but in *Thompson v St. Vincent and the Grenadines*, a mandatory death sentence for all murders (defined broadly as an intentional act of violence resulting in death) was regarded as a violation.[122] The Committee's conclusion was based upon its view that 'such a system of mandatory capital punishment would deprive the author of the most fundamental of rights, the right to life, without considering whether this exceptional form of punishment is appropriate in the circumstances of his or her case'.[123] Five members of the Committee dissented on the basis that this view amounted to the addition of new conditions—such as requirements of proportionality in sentencing and judicial discretion in the imposition of the death penalty—which are not derived from Article 6(2)–(6). Two of these dissenting members did concur, however, with the HRC's later finding in *Kennedy v Trinidad and Tobago* that a mandatory death penalty for non-intentional killings is a violation of Article 6 on the basis that not all such killings will amount to the most serious crimes and a mandatory sentence deprives the courts of the opportunity to asses whether the individual's actions in a particular case can be categorized as a most serious crime or not.[124]

Article 6's protection for the right to life also expressly prohibits the execution of pregnant women and persons who were under eighteen years of age at the time of the crime. The latter restriction was enforced by the HRC in *Johnson v Jamaica* in which the applicant was only seventeen when he committed the crime and so his death sentence amounted to a violation of Article 6(5).[125] The HRC has also added its own restriction to Article 6 regarding mentally incompetent persons. This was evident in its concluding observations to a report from the US when it regretted the state's failure to protect such persons from the death penalty[126] and in *R.S. v Trinidad and Tobago* when it found that the imposition of the death penalty on an individual who is mentally incompetent would breach Article 6(1).[127]

The circumstances surrounding the imposition of the death penalty can also raise arguable issues. In *Mbenge v Zaire*, for example, a sentence of death which was imposed in circumstances breaching the fair trial requirements of Article 14 ICCPR was held to also be a violation of the right to life.[128] The African Commission on Human and Peoples' Rights has also found a violation of the right to life in respect of a death penalty imposed in circumstances breaching the fair trial provisions of the Charter.[129] However, under the ICCPR it is clear that not all violations of the fair trial provisions in capital trials will result in violations of the right to life. An unreasonable delay may be a breach of Article 14 but does

---

[121] Communication 775/1997.   [122] Communication 806/1998.
[123] ibid, para. 8.2.   [124] Communication 845/1998.
[125] Communication 592/ 1994.   [126] UN Doc. CCPR/C/79/Add. 50, para. 16.
[127] Communication 684/1996.
[128] Communication 16/1977. Many cases involving Caribbean states under the ICCPR have reached similar conclusions.
[129] *International Pen, Constitutional Rights Project, Interights on behalf of Ken Saro-Wiwa Jr and Civil Liberties Organisation v Nigeria* (137/94, 139/94, 154/96, 161/97).

not in itself mean that the trial was conducted in an unjust manner and so a sentence of death imposed in such circumstances may remain consistent with the right to life under Article 6.[130]

A final issue considered by the HRC, and perhaps the most controversial, is that of extradition from an abolitionist state to a state that retains the death penalty. In a series of cases in the early 1990s, Canada, which has abolished the death penalty, was found not to be in violation of the right to life for extraditing suspects to the United States where they may face the death penalty.[131] In *Judge v Canada*, however, the HRC changed its collective mind (and adopted a view expressed by a number of dissenters in the previous cases) and found that extradition to the US would be a violation of Article 6.[132] The Committee's reasoning is based upon a recognition of a 'broadening international consensus in favour of abolition'.[133] The HRC ingeniously argued that the right to life under the ICCPR comprises an obligation upon all state parties to protect the right to life under Article 6(1) and specific exceptions to that obligation under paragraphs 2 to 6 which are available only to those states that have not yet abolished the death penalty. Thus, while a state such as the US can continue to execute people provided that it complies with the requirements of those paragraphs, a state, such as Canada, that has already abolished the penalty has an obligation not to expose an individual to a real risk of execution.[134] The consequence of the HRC's views in this case is that abolitionist and retentionist states are treated differently under the ICCPR. The HRC even acknowledges this but regards it as 'an inevitable consequence of the wording of the provision itself, which ... sought to appease very divergent views on the issue of the death penalty'.[135] It is interesting that an approach regarded by the HRC as 'inevitable' should have been avoided in the previous cases involving Canada but the Committee is entirely correct in noting the nature of the right to life provision as a compromise between divergent views on the death penalty. The problem is that this has led the Committee into developing a logically inconsistent approach to the demands of the right to life. The right's coherence is seriously damaged by an interpretation that permits executions in many states but prohibits extradition to those states for individuals fortunate enough to be arrested in an abolitionist state.

A comparable inconsistency can be discerned in the European Court of Human Rights' approach to the death penalty under the right to life. The European Court is forced to implement a Convention that expressly permits the death penalty, without any of the restraints imposed by the ICCPR (although there is now widespread acceptance of Protocol No. 6 that prohibits the imposition of the penalty).[136] So, in *Soering v United Kingdom*,[137] concerning the UK's intention

---

[130] *Brown and Parish v Jamaica* (Communication 665/1995).
[131] *Kindler v Canada* (Communication 470/1991); *Ng v Canada* (Communication 469/1991); *Cox v Canada* (Communication 539/1993).   [132] Communication 829/1998.
[133] ibid, para. 10.3.   [134] ibid, para. 10.4.   [135] ibid, para. 10.5.
[136] Only Russia has not ratified Protocol 6.   [137] (1989) 11 E.H.R.R. 439.

to extradite a suspected murderer to the US where he may face the death penalty, the European Court was unable to regard such extradition as contrary to the right to life. The Court clearly wished to send a strong message of disapproval with the death penalty (one that would mirror the view of many of the Convention's state parties), however, and so it developed the problematic concept of the death row phenomenon. This phrase describes the conditions facing an individual on death row, including the often very long wait for execution. The Court held that this amounted to a violation of Article 3's prohibition on inhuman and degrading punishment and sent the very strange message that a long wait to be executed is a violation of the ECHR but an actual execution is not. As with the HRC, the European Court has faced interpretive difficulties in seeking to implement an outdated document that fails to adequately reflect either the Court's or the state parties' current aversion to the death penalty.

(5) Other issues of scope

A few further issues of the scope of the right to life remain: does the right extend before birth?; does it have any application to the use of non-lethal force?; is there a right to die inherent within the right to life? On the first issue, the right's prenatal application, most versions of the right to life in international law leave the question open. The ICCPR states that 'every human being has the inherent right to life', while the ECHR states that 'everyone's right to life shall be protected by law'. Neither document is clear on whether 'every human being' or 'everyone' includes a fetus and seems to leave the question open for the treaty bodies to determine. The European Court (and Commission) of Human Rights has had the opportunity to consider this issue but has brought us no nearer to an answer. In *Paton v United Kingdom* in 1980,[138] the European Commission of Human Rights considered the issue when a British father sought to prevent the abortion of his unborn child. The Commission noted that most uses of the term 'everyone' in the Convention can only apply postnatally[139] and that the remainder of Article 2, with its limitations of everyone's right to life in respect of the death penalty and law enforcement, suggests that Article 2 protects persons already born.[140] The Commission excluded the possibility that Article 2 recognizes an absolute right to life for the fetus on the basis that such an interpretation of Article 2 would be contrary to the object and purpose of the Convention because it would require the prohibition of abortion even when the mother's life is at risk. The mother, as an already existing person, is entitled to the full protection of the right to life subject only to the express limitations in Article 2. An absolute right to life for the fetus would add an additional implied limitation to the mother's right to

---

[138] (1980) 3 E.H.R.R. 408.
[139] ibid, para. 7. Other uses of 'everyone' include Articles 1, 5, 6, 8–11 and 13.
[140] ibid, para. 8.

life which would be contrary to the object and purpose of the Convention. The Commission was not willing, however, to rule out the possibility that the fetus may be entitled to some limited protection under Article 2[141] and thus the *Paton* decision left open the question of whether Article 2 extends any protection of the right to life to an unborn entity.

An opportunity for the European Court of Human Rights to reconsider this difficult issue finally presented itself in 2004 in the case of *Vo v France*[142] concerning a case of mistaken identity in a French hospital. Thi-Nho Vo, the applicant, attended Lyons General Hospital for a medical examination during her sixth month of pregnancy. At the same time, another Vietnamese woman, Thi Thanh Van Vo, was scheduled to have a coil removed at the same hospital. The applicant, who did not speak French, answered the doctor's call of 'Mrs Vo' and the doctor then sought to remove a coil without carrying out the medical examination which would have revealed her pregnancy. In the course of the procedure, the amniotic sac was pierced, causing the loss of a substantial amount of amniotic fluid. As a result, a few days later the applicant's pregnancy was terminated on health grounds. She lodged a criminal complaint against the doctor for the death of her child but the French courts held that a fetus could not be the victim of homicide. The European Court of Human Rights found no violation of Article 2 but steadfastly refused to decide whether the fetus has any protection under Article 2. The Court was able to evade the core issue, first, by concluding that it would be neither desirable nor possible to answer in the abstract whether an unborn child is given protection under Article 2 and, secondly, by concluding that it was also unnecessary to decide the issue on the facts of the case before it because, even if this fetus does have a right to life, it was not violated by the French laws.[143] The basis for this second argument is that a criminal sanction for unintentional homicides is not essential under Article 2. Other legal options such as negligence were held to be sufficient to satisfy the requirements of this Article. The difficulty with the Court's approach in *Vo* is that it seeks to discuss the requirements of a right to life for the fetus before deciding whether such a right even exists under Article 2. As such, it amounts to a regrettable abdication of judicial responsibility.[144] The question of whether the ECHR's protection of the right to life offers some limited

---

[141] It held that this issue did not have to be decided on the facts of the case before it because the abortion in question had occurred at an early stage in the pregnancy (10 weeks) and was performed on the basis of protecting the life or health of the mother which would amount to an implied limitation on any limited right to life a fetus might enjoy under Article 2.

[142] *Vo v France* (2005) 10 E.H.R.R. 12.   [143] ibid, para. 85.

[144] The Court's approach was not unanimous. Although there was officially a 14 to 3 majority for the decision that Article 2 had not been violated, a total of 9 judges expressed an opinion on the key question of whether Article 2's protection encompasses the fetus. The three officially dissenting judges (Judges Ress, Mularoni and Straznicka) all regarded Article 2 as extending protection to the fetus and concluded that Article 2 had been violated. Judge Costa agreed that a fetus has a right to life but held that it had not been violated on the facts of the case. Five other judges (Judges Rozakis, Caflisch, Fischbach, Lorenzen and Thomassen) wrote a separate opinion in which they concluded that the fetus does not have any protection under the right to life and so Article 2 was inapplicable

protection to a fetus remains unanswered nearly sixty years after its origin. The reluctance of the Court to decide this issue is understandable, given the variety of political, religious and ethical opinions on it across Europe. However, as one of the judges sitting in *Vo*, Judge Costa, has argued: 'Does the present inability of ethics to reach a consensus on what is a person and who is entitled to the right to life prevent the law from defining these terms? I think not. It is the task of lawyers, and in particular judges, especially human rights judges, to identify the notions…that correspond to the words or expressions in the relevant legal instruments.'[145] In other words, the Court should seek to define the term 'everyone' in Article 2 as it seeks to define other terms in the Convention.

The ACHR is distinct from the other human rights treaties on this issue because its drafters made an explicit effort to determine when the right to life begins. It is stated that the right to life shall be protected 'in general, from the moment of conception'. The phrase 'in general' leaves open the possibility that a right to life may not be enforced for fetuses in all circumstances and was added in order to produce a compromise. In the so-called *Baby-Boy* case in 1981,[146] the American Commission of Human Rights considered a case challenging the United States' abortion laws. The Commission looked predominantly at Article 1 of the American Declaration of Rights and Duties of Man as the US was bound by this declaration but not a party to the ACHR. The Commission noted that an earlier draft of the declaration included explicit protection of the right to life 'from moment of conception' and 'to the right to life of incurables, imbeciles and the insane'. This sentence was deleted as part of the drafting process and therefore the Commission concluded that a decision had been taken by the drafters not to extend protection to the fetus. This reasoning does, however, leave the question of the status of the other specific categories of persons identified in this sentence somewhat uncertain. The Commission was also swayed by the existence of abortion rights in some drafting states at the time of the declaration and thus concluded that Article 1 had not been intended to render abortion illegal. Although the US was not a party to the ACHR, the Commission also took this rare opportunity to consider the position of the fetus under this later document. It concluded that the wording of Article 4 represented a compromise and was thus not intended to deviate from the position agreed in the declaration. The question of whether the fetus enjoys protection for its life under the American regional documents remains open, although it is clear that they do not provide such protection as to render abortion illegal in all circumstances. Further consideration of this issue will take place in chapter 6.

to this case. This leaves only 8 out of the 17 judges on the Court who did not express an opinion on whether Article 2 encompasses protection for the life of the fetus.

[145] Para. 7 of Judge Costa's Separate Opinion.
[146] Case 2141, Res. No. 23/81 of 6 March 1981.

It might be assumed that the right to life will only come into play if there is a death. However, both the European Court of Human Rights and the HRC have recognized its application to the use of non-lethal force. In *Makaratzis v Greece*,[147] the applicant was not killed during a pursuit by the police and there was no intention to kill him but the degree and type of force used were held by the European Court to engage Article 2. It was held that the applicant was a victim of conduct which put his life at risk; the Court regarded the fact that he was not killed as 'fortuitous'.[148] Although the use of potentially lethal force was held to be justified on the facts, the Greek authorities had not provided sufficient safeguards against arbitrariness, abuse of force and avoidable accident[149] in order to avoid a real and immediate risk to life. A substantive violation of the right to life was, therefore, found by the Court despite the fact that nobody had died as a result of the police action. This is an important extension of the scope of the right to life as it requires state parties to the ECHR to provide sufficient safeguards to protect against risks to life, regardless of whether the risk materializes. In effect, this removes the element of moral luck from the equation under Article 2. A state party will be found in violation whenever its use of potentially lethal force is exercised in a manner which is insufficiently regulated so as to minimize risks to life. It sends a clear message that the justification of the use of potentially lethal force under Article 2(2) is not the end of the issue: even if the authorities are justified in using such force, they must still act to minimize the risk to life.

The HRC has also held that non-lethal force may amount to a violation of the right to life under the ICCPR. In *Chongwe v Zambia*, an unsuccessful assassination attempt by agents of the state was found to be a violation as the state authorities had authorized the use of lethal force without lawful reasons.[150] Under the African Charter, a case against Nigeria also enabled the African Commission on Human and Peoples' Rights to determine that the denial of medication to a prisoner to the extent that his life was seriously endangered could amount to a violation of the right to life even though it did not cause the death of the prisoner.[151]

Finally, the European Court of Human Rights has dismissed an argument that the right to life implies a right to die. In *Pretty v United Kingdom*,[152] the applicant, a motor neurone sufferer, sought to argue that Article 2 protects not merely life itself, but rather the choice of whether to live or not: a right to self-determination in relation to issues of life and death. The Court, however, could not escape the fact that Article 2 'cannot, without a distortion of language, be interpreted as conferring the diametrically opposite right, namely a right to

---

[147] [2004] ECHR 694; (2005) 41 E.H.R.R. 49.   [148] ibid, para. 54.
[149] ibid, para. 58.
[150] Communication 821/1998, para. 5.2. See also *Jiménez Vaca v Colombia* (Communication 859/1999).
[151] Case against Nigeria, n. 129 above. The African Commission also found in *Kazeem Aminu v Nigeria* (205/97) that arrests and detentions could violate the right to life in the absence of a loss of life.   [152] (2002) 35 E.H.R.R. 1.

die'.[153] Comparisons with Article 11's right to join a trade union, which was interpreted by the European Court of Human Rights in the case of *Young, James and Webster v United Kingdom* to incorporate the right *not* to join a trade union,[154] were ultimately held to be unhelpful. The Court refused to extrapolate from this that the right to life could also include its apparent opposite: a right to die. It held that Article 2 is distinguishable from Article 11 in respect of its interpretation to include a negative aspect because the right to life is not expressed as a freedom whereas the right to join a trade union is an aspect of Article 11's right to freedom of association.[155] The word 'freedom' implies a choice: to take advantage of the protected activity or not; whereas the right to life has no such choice at its heart. The Court was swayed, therefore, by the common-sense meaning of a right to life and its apparent incompatibility with a right to die, which is regarded as the antithesis of the right to life.[156]

C. Conclusion

The enforcement of the right to life in international law has so far developed to include the use of non-lethal force, to preclude the implication of a right to die, and to leave open the question of its application pre-birth. The death penalty has an uneasy relationship with the right to life that is likely to continue to develop, perhaps at the continued cost of endangering consistency and logic of decisions by the treaty bodies. At the core of the right, however, and as discussed above, lie three obligations upon the state: not to arbitrarily/intentionally kill individuals; to set up effective investigations into deaths and disappearances; and to take all reasonable measures to prevent real and immediate risks to life. The latter obligation has vast potential but has been interpreted in a relatively narrow manner thus far, with great weight being accorded to conflicting societal interests, including the limited nature of public funds. What is perhaps most remarkable in the enforcement of the right to life is the breadth of circumstances in which a death can occur for which the state holds some responsibility, whether or not it is held to be in violation of the right to life. The need to protect this most fundamental right by means of a voluntary system of human rights treaties, with under-resourced, and frequently non-judicial, enforcing bodies presents a considerable challenge to the courts, committees and commissions discussed above. The enforcement of the right to life in international law indicates clearly that it is far from an absolute right: an individual may be killed by the lawful imposition

---

[153] ibid, para. 39.
[154] (1981) Series A, No. 44; 4 E.H.R.R. 38.   [155] *Pretty v UK*, n. 152 above, para. 39.
[156] Unfortunately for Ms Pretty the European Court also dismissed her other arguments that a right to die could be implied in Articles 3, 8, 9 and 14. It is now clearly established that there is no right to die under the ECHR, although Article 8's right to respect for private life was held to include a right to make decisions about how we die.

of the death penalty; or in circumstances where the use of lethal force is honestly, even if mistakenly, regarded as necessary to achieve one of a number of goals of law enforcement; or where incompetence or misjudgements or a lack of resources prevent the state from protecting life. If the individual is not yet born, or disappears without trace, it may be even more difficult to rely on the right to life. For a fundamental right, its enforcement is plagued not only by lack of resources and political will, but also by a myriad of conflicting interests that require equal protection within democratic states. The difficulties presented, both ethically and legally, by the need to reconcile such conflicting interests are the subject of the remainder of the book.

4

The Right to Life in Times of War or Armed Conflict

None of the classic enactments of the right to life, such as that in the international human rights treaties discussed in the previous chapters, seem designed for application in times of war or armed conflict. Instead, they seem to envisage a peacetime context when the greatest state-sanctioned threat to human life comes in the form of criminal justice penalties and enforcement. But in reality, the threat to human life in peacetime usually fades into insignificance compared to the threat posed by armed conflict. One issue underlying the discussion in this chapter is whether human rights law, and thus the right to life, applies during armed conflict. If it does, then the question arises as to the nature and justification of the permissible limitations upon the prohibition of taking human life, for there is little doubt that armed conflict presents unique circumstances in which human life will be more vulnerable than at other times. This chapter will not focus on the justifications for the use of force by a state but, rather, on the taking of human life once an armed conflict has begun. Three main issues will be considered: the application of the right to life during armed conflict; the right to life under international humanitarian law; and the ethics of killing in war. The ultimate answer being sought in this chapter is the identification of the conflicting interest(s) that are seen to outweigh, in some circumstances, the right to life during times of war or armed conflict. The search is complicated both by the harsh realities of warfare and by the ambiguous relationship between human rights law and international humanitarian law.

A. The application of the right to life in times of war

War is synonymous with death and destruction and often heralds the loss of human life on a massive scale. The application of a right to life in this context is often viewed as academic and illusory. However, the right to life does not apply only when times are good: it is not a fair-weather friend to humanity. Thus, we need to consider whether, and if so, how and why, the right to life permits deaths during times of war or conflict. The first issue to be considered here is whether human rights law even applies within the context of war or armed conflict, given that a specific body of law known as international humanitarian law (IHL) has been developed to apply in this context. The relationship between IHL and human rights law has become a subject of academic debate in recent years. Some commentators argue forcefully that human rights law has no role to play during armed conflict,[1] but both human rights treaties, and the bodies enforcing them, seem to take a different view. Treaties such as the ECHR and the ACHR, for example, specifically permit the derogation of certain rights during times of war or other public emergency, suggesting that the non-derogable provisions are intended to apply in wartime.[2] It should be noted that state practice does not seem to support the need for a formal derogation, as European states did not derogate from the derogable rights of the ECHR in respect of conflicts in the Former Yugoslavia, Kosovo, Afghanistan or Iraq. However, the European Court of Human Rights has not shied away from enforcing the full extent of the Convention rights in times of conflict in the absence of a derogation. In *Isayeva v Russia*, the Court was prepared to find a violation of the right to life by Russia due to the use of heavy combat weapons on civilians in the context of an armed conflict.[3] As Russia had not derogated, the provisions of the ECHR continued to apply to their full extent. The Inter-American Court of Human Rights has also been prepared to apply human rights law during times of armed conflict and has even gone so far as to apply IHL alongside the provisions of the ACHR, by means of interpreting the Convention in light of the Geneva Conventions.[4] The bottom line, however, is that it is the very nature of human rights that requires their application in wartime. As Cordula Droege notes, 'if they are inherent to the human being, they cannot be dependent on a situation'.[5]

This is not the end of the matter, however, for there are two remaining issues to be considered in the context of the application of the right to life to deaths in wartime. The first is the issue of substantive jurisdiction: does the right to life, or positive manifestations of it, encompass an exception for deaths during war or international conflict? Or, in other words, is the right to life engaged when soldiers fire upon soldiers (or civilians) of an enemy state? The second issue is distinct from the first and focuses on what we might call the procedural aspect of the jurisdiction of the right to life: do the bodies enforcing the right to life under various human rights treaties have jurisdiction to consider alleged infringements of the right to life during a war, particularly (as we shall see) one fought outside

---

[1] M.J. Dennis, 'Non-Application of Civil and Political Rights Treaties Extraterritorially during Times of International Armed Conflict' (2007) 40 Isr.L.Rev. 453 makes this point in respect of acts by a state's armed forces beyond its own territory. See below for further discussion of the extra-territorial jurisdiction issue.   [2] See Article 15 ECHR and Article 27 ACHR.

[3] *Isayeva v Russia* (Application no. 57950/00; 24 February 2005).

[4] *Bámaca Velaquez v Guatemala* Case No. 11/129, paras 207–9.

[5] C. Droege, 'The Interplay between International Humanitarian Law and International Human Rights Law in Situations of Armed Conflict' (2007) 40 Isr.L.Rev. 310, at p. 324.

a state party's borders? In other words, this second issue focuses on whether a state committed to protecting the right to life at home needs to extend that protection to enemy combatants or civilians during an international conflict. The two issues are, therefore, whether the substance of the right to life is engaged by deaths in wartime and, if so, whether it can be relied upon before an international or regional treaty body. The latter issue has become a controversial one, particularly under the ECHR, in recent years, while the former remains inadequately investigated.

(1) The substantive issue: is the right to life engaged by deaths in wartime?

There is nothing in any of the international manifestations of the right to life which excludes the right's application during times of war or international conflict. However, the aim of this entire book is to emphasize the conflicting obligations that require or permit limitations upon the right to life; the fact that the right applies in times of war is a large step away from a recognition that it is violated by each and every wartime death. As was seen in the previous chapter, all of the international right to life provisions are non-absolute. They list express exceptions to the right (such as, for example, the death penalty) and prohibit only certain types of deaths, such as those that are arbitrary or intentional. These provisos open the door to the concept of permissible deaths (in war and peace). For example, under the ICCPR, only arbitrary deprivations of life are prohibited by Article 6. A death in wartime may or may not be arbitrary. How are we to assess arbitrariness in this context? The answer to this question was provided by the International Court of Justice (ICJ) in its advisory opinion in the *Nuclear Weapons* case:

whether a particular loss of life, through the use of a certain weapon in warfare, is to be considered an arbitrary deprivation of life contrary to Article 6 of the International Covenant on Civil and Political Rights, can only be decided by reference to the law applicable in armed conflict and not deduced from the terms of the Covenant itself.[6]

The (legal) answer to whether a death during war is arbitrary (and thus prima facie amounts to a violation of the right to life under the ICCPR) is, therefore, to be determined by its legality under the laws of international armed conflict. If a death is lawful under this special branch of law, then it will not be regarded as arbitrary under the right to life. The law of international armed conflict in relation to the loss of life will need to be looked at in detail later in this chapter. First, however, it is necessary to compare the scenario under the ECHR where the position is, arguably, rather different.

---

[6] (1996) ICJ Reps 226, at para. 25.

Unlike Article 6 ICCPR, the ECHR does not require that a deprivation of life be arbitrary in order to fall within the terms of Article 2's protection for the right to life. All intentional deprivations of life by a state party are violations of the right to life unless they fall within one of the four exceptions listed in Article 2 (and relating to law enforcement). On the surface, this seems to indicate that deaths on a wartime battlefield will amount to violations of the right to life under the ECHR (for the deaths caused will surely be intentional). The matter is complicated, however, by Article 15 ECHR which permits derogation from certain rights in times of war or public emergency. The right to life is one of only four Convention rights described, at least in part, as non-derogable, meaning that even in times of war, the right to life must be protected. There is an exception to the general non-derogability of the right to life, however, in respect of 'deaths resulting from lawful acts of war'.[7] This means that a deprivation of life which is a consequence of a lawful act of war (again engaging the body of law relating to international armed conflict) may be the subject of a derogation. Some commentators oversimplify this issue by describing deaths resulting from lawful acts of war as an exception to the right to life under the ECHR. This is not accurate, however. The phrase 'deaths resulting from lawful acts of war' is not to be found anywhere in Article 2's protection of the right to life; it is only contained within Article 15(2) as an exception to the general non-derogability of Article 2. Thus, it is only engaged when a state party derogates. Without a formal notice of derogation, all intentional deaths caused by the state (and not otherwise excepted from the terms of Article 2) will remain violations of the right to life. No state party to the ECHR has issued a notice of derogation in respect of Article 2 and so 'deaths resulting from lawful acts of war' is an irrelevant consideration at present in Europe. Furthermore, even if such a derogation was issued, it would need to satisfy the other requirements of Article 15, including the requirement that the measures taken in response to the specified war or public emergency be 'strictly required by the exigencies of the situation'. In other words, the deaths would not only need to result from 'lawful acts of war' but would also need to be 'strictly required' which, as we shall see later, may be a stricter test than that under the laws of international armed conflict.[8]

(2) The procedural issue: are deaths in wartime within the 'jurisdiction' of the state responsible?

The European Court of Human Rights has had a few opportunities in recent years to consider whether deaths in one state caused by military force exercised

---

[7] Article 15(2) ECHR.

[8] Under the ACHR, the right to life is non-derogable during times of war or other emergency (Article 27(2)). The AfCh has no derogation clause in its terms. Thus under neither the American nor African regional treaties is the right to life derogable during war.

by another state fall within the ambit of Article 2's protection for the right to life. In *Bankovic v Belgium*[9] the deprivations of life in question resulted from the NATO bombing of a television studio in Belgrade during the Kosovo crisis. The NATO forces included a number of European states who were obligated under Article 1 ECHR to 'secure to everyone within their jurisdiction the rights and freedoms' contained within the ECHR. On 23 April 1999, at approximately 2:00am, a missile launched by NATO forces hit an RTS (Radio Televizije Srbije) building. Sixteen people (all civilians) were killed. The bombing was part of a planned attack aimed at disrupting Serbia's military command, control and communications network.[10] This was not a case of a civilian building hit in error but rather a deliberate targeting of the offices of Serbian television. The European governments disputed the admissibility of a case brought by relatives of the deceased and others injured in the attack, claiming that the applicants did not fall within the jurisdiction of the respondent states as required by Article 1. A Grand Chamber of the European Court of Human Rights confirmed that 'the jurisdictional competence of a State is primarily territorial'.[11] This means that a state party to the ECHR will be required to protect the rights of everyone within its territory (whether nationals or not) but the extension of jurisdiction beyond a state's own borders will be rare. This is because, under international law, a state is generally prohibited from exercising jurisdiction on the territory of another state without the latter's consent, invitation or acquiescence.[12] The Grand Chamber confirmed that any non-territorial basis of jurisdiction would be exceptional. It would not, however, be impossible. In the earlier case of *Loizidou v Turkey*,[13] the Court had found that Turkey's obligation to secure the Convention rights and freedoms extended beyond its own territorial borders to encompass Northern Cyprus which was regarded as under Turkey's effective control.[14] In theory, this principle of effective control permits significant extra-territorial application of the Article 1 obligation. However, in *Bankovic* the Court was able to distinguish the position of Northern Cyprus, not only from that of Serbia during the NATO bombing, but also in terms that would today distinguish it from that of Iraq, Afghanistan and other non-European states. It is fairly obvious, and uncontroversial, that the European states of NATO were not exercising effective control over Belgrade merely because they were participating in the bombing of the city. The Court regarded the applicants' submissions in *Bankovic* on this issue to be 'tantamount to arguing that anyone adversely affected by an act imputable to a Contracting State, wherever in the world that act may have been committed or its consequences felt, is thereby brought within the jurisdiction of that State for the purpose of Article 1 of the Convention.'[15] Quite correctly, the Court

---

[9] ECHR 2001-XII.

[10] M. Happold, '*Bankovic v Belgium* and the Territorial Scope of the European Convention on Human Rights' (2003) 3 H.R.L.R. 77, at p. 77.   [11] *Bankovic*, n. 9 above, para. 59.

[12] ibid, para. 60.   [13] Reports 1996-VI.   [14] *Bankovic*, n. 9 above, para. 70.

[15] ibid, para. 75.

regarded such an interpretation of Article 1 to be unsupported and unsustainable. However, the Court did not stop at this point and instead added that there was a further relevant distinguishing feature between the citizens of Northern Cyprus and those of the Federal Republic of Yugoslavia, namely that the former had previously enjoyed the benefits of the Convention before the Turkish occupation and it was necessary to avoid 'a regrettable vacuum in the system of human rights protection' within Cyprus.[16] As the Federal Republic of Yugoslavia had never resided within the 'legal space' of the contracting states, no such concerns applied in the circumstances of *Bankovic*.[17]

The Court has thus opened the door to a regrettable distinction between the violation of rights within Europe (but beyond the current territory of the contracting states) and the violation of rights by the contracting states outside of Europe. The Court made clear that the Convention 'was not designed to be applied throughout the world, even in respect of the conduct of Contracting States'.[18] This seems to suggest that, while the bombing of Belgrade did not bring its victims within the jurisdiction of the attacking states, a similar violation of rights in a former contracting state could potentially do so. There are, therefore, two seemingly distinct paths towards the application of an extra-territorial jurisdiction under Article 1: effective control of a foreign territory; or a human rights vacuum in a formerly contracting state now occupied by another contracting state. While the general proposition from the *Bankovic* judgment—that individuals are not generally regarded as within the jurisdiction of a state merely because they have been affected by the impugned act—is reasonable, the additional propositions have been less well received. Happold, for example, argues that 'the effect of holding that the Convention only applies within the "legal space" of the Contracting Parties would be to erect a rather distasteful distinction between what Contracting parties can do "at home" and what they can do "abroad"'.[19] Happold argues more generally that *Bankovic* is the 'right decision for the wrong reasons'.[20] He would prefer a more encompassing concept of jurisdiction to require contracting parties to protect the rights of individuals whenever the state has jurisdiction over them, whether territorial or not.[21] So, for Happold, the Court's interpretation of the restraints of Article 1 in this case are too restrictive, but he agrees—indeed, it is difficult to disagree—that aerial bombing of a foreign city does not bring its inhabitants into the jurisdiction of the attacking state.

In the subsequent case of *Issa v Turkey*,[22] a Chamber of the Court went further than the Grand Chamber in *Bankovic* in its interpretation of extra-territorial jurisdiction. The case involved the killing of a number of individuals in Northern Iraq by Turkish forces. The Court acknowledged that, in exceptional circumstances, non-territorial bases for jurisdiction can be recognized.

---

[16] ibid, para. 80, quoting a passage from the *Cyprus v Turkey* judgment (ECHR 2001-IV 172, para. 78).   [17] ibid, para. 80.
[18] ibid.   [19] Happold, n. 10 above, p. 88.   [20] ibid, p. 90.   [21] ibid.
[22] Application no. 31821/96, judgment of 16 November 2004.

Referring to *Lozidou*, the Court said that 'a State's responsibility may be engaged where, as a consequence of military action—whether lawful or unlawful—that state in practice exercises effective control of an area outside its national territory', whether through its armed forces or a subordinate local administration.[23] The Court then went further and recognized that a state may also be held accountable for a violation of the Convention rights of individuals in the territory of another state but who are under the former state's authority and control through its agents operating in the latter state. Controversially, the Court then concluded that accountability in this situation stems from the fact that Article 1 'cannot be interpreted so as to allow a State party to perpetrate violations of the Convention on the territory of another State, which it could not perpetrate on its own territory'.[24] This seems to be in stark contrast to the Grand Chamber's comments in *Bankovic* that, notwithstanding other jurisdictional issues, the Convention rights can only have application within the 'legal space' of the Convention. Northern Iraq is not within that legal space. Furthermore, a literal interpretation of the Court's comments in *Issa* would extend the reach of Article 1 beyond any logical boundaries, for it seems to focus on the actions of the state rather than whether the alleged victims are within the state's jurisdiction. These issues are of crucial importance when considering the application of human rights in times of war because many of the deaths and injuries resulting from combat are likely to occur outside the state's own territory (and most commonly outside the 'legal space' of the Convention). On the facts of *Issa*, it was held that it had not been proven that Turkish troops held effective control of the precise territory on which the deaths occurred, although it was accepted in principle that Turkey may have exercised, temporarily, effective control of areas within Northern Iraq, as a result of military action there.[25] Notwithstanding the difficulties of establishing the exact whereabouts of invading forces (which will not be a problem unique to this situation), the judgment in *Issa* suggests that the mere fact of military action on the territory of another state may suffice to establish jurisdiction, and require appropriate protection for the rights to life of the citizens of the invaded state. There is, of course, a major distinction between ground forces and aerial bombing and the former is likely to be required, even under the broad approach evident in *Issa*, before non-territorial jurisdiction is established. Even so, the consequences, for example for the actions of British troops in Iraq and Afghanistan at present, are potentially vast.

The domestic case of *Al-Skeini v Secretary of State for Defence* considered this very point.[26] The case arose from the deaths of six Iraqi civilians by British armed forces in Basra. One of these deaths raised distinctive issues because it occurred while the deceased was in the custody of the British armed forces and following severe mistreatment. As such, there was little doubt that this deceased was within

---

[23] ibid, para. 69.   [24] ibid, para. 71.   [25] ibid, para. 74.
[26] [2007] UKHL 26.

the jurisdiction of the UK and his case was remitted to the Divisional Court by the House of Lords. The other deaths raised more problematic jurisdictional issues, however. The House of Lords identified two aspects of the question of jurisdiction relating, respectively, to the scope of the Convention and of the Human Rights Act 1998 (which brings the Convention rights into domestic law). Lord Rodger of Earlsferry described these two aspects of the question as follows:

> For the purposes of the extra-territorial effects of section 6 of the 1998 Act, the key question was whether a public authority—in this case the Army in Iraq—was within Parliament's legislative grasp when acting outside the United Kingdom. By contrast, for the purposes of deciding whether the Convention applies outside the territory of the United Kingdom, the key question is whether the deceased were linked to the United Kingdom when they were killed.[27]

On the HRA issue, the Law Lords held (with Lord Bingham of Cornhill dissenting) that the Act has extra-territorial effect. It applies to the actions of public authorities whether acting at home or abroad, provided that when acting abroad they are acting within the jurisdiction of the UK as defined under Article 1 ECHR.[28] The more problematic issue was to determine the correct interpretation of Article 1's use of 'jurisdiction' and this task was made considerably more difficult by the inconsistent authorities of *Bankovic* and *Issa*. The Law Lords were 'unable to reconcile'[29] the broad *Issa* approach with the narrower reasoning in *Bankovic* and they unanimously preferred the latter. Perhaps partly, and understandably, the preference for *Bankovic* stemmed from the weight of a Grand Chamber decision, but the House of Lords also seemed to prefer the narrower approach on its merits. Lord Rodger explained that the European Court of Human Rights 'had "so far" recognised jurisdiction based on effective control only in the case of territory which would normally be covered by the Convention. If it went further, the court would run the risk not only of colliding with the jurisdiction of other human rights bodies but of being accused of human rights imperialism'.[30] This final point refers to the origins of the ECHR as a peculiarly (Western) European document. It is, in the words of Lord Rodger, 'a body of law which may reflect the values of the contracting states, but which certainly does not reflect those in many other parts of the world'.[31] He gives the example of the Court's jurisprudence on issues such as the death penalty, sex discrimination, homosexuality and transsexuals.[32] The House of Lords thus seek to revive the

---

[27] ibid, para. 64.

[28] 'where a public authority has power to operate outside of the United Kingdom and does so legitimately—for example, with the consent of the other state—in the absence of any indication to the contrary, when construing any relevant legislation, it would only be sensible to treat the public authority, so far as possible, in the same way as when it operates at home.' (Lord Rodger, ibid, para. 53.)

[29] ibid, para. 75.   [30] ibid, para. 78.   [31] ibid.

[32] ibid. Perhaps a related point is being made when Lord Brown of Eaton-under-Heywood mentions an occupying force's obligations under Article 43 of the Hague Regulations to 'respect the laws in force' which he argues may not be consistent with the introduction of new laws to satisfy

most objectionable aspect of the *Bankovic* decision, namely that one rule applies to a European state's actions within Europe and another (less strict) rule applies to its actions elsewhere in the world. Within the context of deaths in wartime (and given the UK's military engagements in Iraq and Afghanistan), this is a particularly disquieting approach.

Lord Carswell makes a less objectionable point when he emphasizes that the degree of control necessary in order for the effective control test to enable extra-territorial jurisdiction is very demanding.[33] Beyond embassies, consulates and military prisons (as in Basra), a 'high degree of control by the agents of the state of an area of another state [would be required] before it could be said that that area was within the jurisdiction of the former'.[34] In Lord Carswell's view, shared by all of the other Law Lords in this case, 'the British presence in Iraq falls well short of that degree of control'.[35] While this conclusion may be arguable (especially given the length of time of the British and American presence there), it at least poses a more appropriate question than whether the victims are located within Europe because, without effective control, a state will be unable to ensure protection for the Convention rights. The legacy of *Al-Skeini* is that the UK will not be held responsible under the ECHR for a failure to respect the right to life, or any other Convention right, of Iraqi citizens. The right to life will, as will be discussed later, be protected indirectly (and to a limited extent only) by means of IHL but the full protection of human life provided by Article 2 will not apply. The *Al-Skeini* decision, while consistent with *Bankovic*, fails to follow the route recommended by the Council of Europe in this regard. The Parliamentary Assembly of the Council of Europe passed a resolution in 2004 calling upon those member states engaged in Iraq 'to accept the full applicability of the European Convention on Human Rights to the activities of their forces in Iraq, in so far as those forces exercised effective control over the areas in which they operated'.[36] The House of Lords regarded this resolution as 'irrelevant' to the correct interpretation of Article 1.[37]

The dire threat to human life inherent in the recent troubling situation in Iraq was raised again before the British courts in the case of *R (on application of Gentle) v The Prime Minister*.[38] This case under Article 2 was brought by the mothers of two British soldiers killed while serving in Iraq. The basis of the case is clearly explained (but not supported) by Lord Bingham:

Article 2 of the Convention imposes a duty on member states to protect life. This duty extends to the lives of soldiers. Armed conflict exposes soldiers to the risk of death. Therefore a state should take timely steps to obtain reliable legal advice before committing

the requirements of the ECHR (ibid, para. 129). This concern will not apply, however, to the issue of the right to life which, as we have seen in previous chapters is, at least in its core, universally recognized.

[33] ibid, para. 97.   [34] ibid.   [35] ibid.

[36] Resolution 1386, para. 18, adopted by Parliamentary Assembly of the Council of Europe on 24 June 2004.   [37] *Al-Skeini*, n. 26 above, para. 65 (Lord Rodger).

[38] [2008] UKHL 20.

its troops to armed conflict. Had the UK done this before invading Iraq in March 2003, it would arguably not have invaded. Had it not invaded, Fusilier Gentle and Trooper Clarke would not have been killed.[39]

The House of Lords was entirely unimpressed with such an argument. Crucially, the Lords held that the legality of a war is not relevant to the obligation on a state to protect the rights of its soldiers. It is certainly true that the legality of military action is, in practical terms, irrelevant to the protection of human life. The Japanese attack on Pearl Harbor, for example, was unlawful and yet minimized the threat to Japanese soldiers[40] while a more open, lawful attack may have entailed greater casualties. Lord Rodger explained this point:

> The risk to soldiers' lives is not affected...by whether a military operation is lawful or unlawful under international law. Indeed,... an unlawful attack enjoying the element of surprise may actually be safer for the invading forces. Therefore, while there may be all kinds of moral and political reasons why states should take care to ensure that their military operations are lawful under international law, reducing the risk to the lives of the troops whom they order into battle is not one of them.[41]

This point reflects a strongly established principle of international humanitarian law, namely that considerations of *jus ad bellum* (the rules on when to go to war) does not affect *jus in bello* (the rules on conduct during war). It proved to be fatal for the appellants' arguments in *Gentle*. If the argument that the legality of the invasion of Iraq was irrelevant to the UK's obligations to protect its soldiers' lives, then further evidence would be needed that the UK had failed to do so and this evidence was not forthcoming. The House of Lords was clear that the right to life is not violated 'simply by deploying servicemen and women on active service overseas as part of an organised military force which is properly equipped and capable of defending itself, even though the risk of being killed is inherent in what they are being asked to do'.[42] Presumably if one of these conditions was proven not to apply—for example, if the troops were not properly equipped—then a right to life issue might potentially arise. Even in that situation, however, there may be further obstacles. This is apparent from the stark difference of opinion evident within the House of Lords in *Gentle* on whether members of the British armed forces operating overseas are within the jurisdiction of the UK under Article 1 ECHR. Baroness Hale states what may appear to be the obvious answer to this issue when she says that she does not have much difficulty with the proposition that the deceased soldiers were within the jurisdiction of the UK: 'If Mr Baha Mousa, detained in a military detention facility in Basra, was within the jurisdiction, then a soldier serving under the command and control of his superiors must also be within the jurisdiction.'[43] Surprisingly, Lord Bingham disagreed and argued that although the deceased soldiers were subject to the authority of

---

[39] ibid, para. 3.   [40] ibid, para. 8.   [41] ibid, para. 43.
[42] ibid, para. 19 (per Lord Hope of Craighead).   [43] ibid, para. 60.

the UK government, as they were in Iraq, 'they were clearly not within the jurisdiction of the UK as that expression in the Convention has been interpreted'.[44] This issue was not crucial to the outcome of the case but raises concern about the responsibility of the UK government for the rights, including the right to life, of its troops when deployed abroad. It is hard to imagine an individual more within the jurisdiction of a state than a member of the state's own armed forces. While the issue of an invading state's responsibility for the citizens of the occupied state is an important and challenging one (as the deaths of Iraqi citizens highlight), a preliminary step in ensuring some minimal protection for the right to life, even in times of war, must be to recognize a state's responsibility for its own soldiers, especially when deployed in foreign war zones and required to risk their lives on a daily basis for a cause all too often obscure.

Under the ICCPR, Article 2(1) requires that state parties respect and ensure the Covenant rights 'to all individuals within its territory and subject to its jurisdiction'. Despite the apparent requirement of territorial jurisdiction in this provision, the HRC has clarified that it 'does not imply that the State party concerned cannot be held accountable for violations of rights under the Covenant which its agents commit upon the territory of another state, whether with the acquiescence of the government of that state or in opposition to it'.[45] More recently, in General Comment No. 31, the HRC has recognized effective control as the key for jurisdiction under the ICCPR (as it is under the ECHR).[46] The Inter-American Commission of Human Rights has set a much lower standard, however. In *Alejandro v Cuba*, the Commission held that Cuba had violated the right to life by shooting down two unarmed civilian light aircraft. The Commission explained that, although acting outside the territory of Cuba, the state agents had placed the civilian pilots 'under their authority' by targeting them.[47] This approach suggests that any infringement of human rights by a state agent beyond the territory of the state will satisfy jurisdiction requirements. This is in direct contradiction to the European Court's approach in *Bankovic* where such an approach was categorically rejected.

It has been seen that the issue of 'jurisdiction' under the ECHR has caused considerable difficulties in holding European states to account for their military activities around the world. The need to give some meaning to Article 1's restrictions is understood but, in the context of war, a focus on territorial jurisdiction is unhelpful. The recognition of extra-territorial jurisdiction in exceptional circumstances is welcome but these exceptional circumstances must be

---

[44] ibid, para. 8.   [45] *Burgos Lopez v Uruguay* No. 52/1979 (29 July 1981) at para. 12.3.

[46] 'A State Party must respect and ensure the rights laid down in the Covenant to anyone within the power or effective control of that State Party, even if not situated within the territory of the State Party.' (General Comment No. 31, (2004), para. 10.)

[47] Case 11.589, Inter-Am CHR, Report No. 86/99. See J. Cerone, 'Jurisdiction and Power: The Intersection of Human Rights Law and the Law of Non-International Armed Conflict in an Extraterritorial Context' (2007) 40 Isr.L.Rev. 396, pp. 425–6 for discussion of this case.

interpreted in a manner that acknowledges the extent of an occupying or invading state's control over the lives and liberties of those within the enemy state. Any distinction between responsibility for military acts within Europe and beyond is a mere distraction from the real issue of the power exercised over individuals outside the state's own territory, for good or ill, during times of armed conflict. Notwithstanding the difficulties of establishing jurisdiction for these acts, it was noted above that the right to life endures throughout an armed conflict but, at least under the ICCPR, there will be no violation of the right unless a death is unlawful under the special law relating to international armed conflict. A deprivation of life that is lawful under the rules of war will not be regarded as arbitrary under the Covenant (and, if a state has derogated under Article 15 ECHR, it will similarly be permissible as a lawful act of war under the Convention). And there are many deprivations of life that fall into this category during times of war.

B. Deprivation of life in times of war: the law of international armed conflict

When investigating this subject from a human rights perspective, and specifically from a right to life perspective, it takes some time to become accustomed to the very different viewpoint of the laws of international armed conflict (or international humanitarian law, hereafter IHL).[48] Instead of beginning with an assumption that human life has an inherent value and will be preserved, these laws acknowledge the grim reality that war inevitably means the loss of human life on a massive scale and any system of law that seeks to regulate the conduct of a war cannot hope to prevent this.[49] What the rules of war seek to regulate instead is which lives can be legitimately lost, and in what circumstances, and by what means. From a right to life perspective these are subsidiary questions, carefully framed to avoid the crux of the issue: why is human life expendable during war? What is the competing interest that outweighs the value of human life in this context? This book will attempt to address these key questions soon, but first it will be helpful to adopt the focus of IHL for a short time and ask which lives must be protected and which may be destroyed.

---

[48] On the differences between the two systems of law, see K. Watkin, 'Controlling the Use of Force: A Role for Human Rights Norms in Contemporary Armed Conflict' (2004) 98 Am.J.Int.L. 1.

[49] Dinstein explains this effectively: 'Some people, no doubt animated by the noblest humanitarian impulses, would like to see zero-casualty warfare. However, this is an impossible dream. War is not a chess game. Almost by definition, it entails human losses, suffering and pain. As long as it is waged, humanitarian considerations cannot be the sole legal arbiters of the conduct of hostilities. The law of international armed conflict can and does forbid some modes of behaviour, with a view to minimising the losses, the suffering and the pain. But it can do so only when there are realistic alternatives to achieving the military goal of victory in war.' (Y. Dinstein, *The Conduct of Hostilities under the Law of International Armed Conflict* (Cambridge: Cambridge University Press, 2004), p. 1.)

IHL is contained in a myriad of international documents, including the Hague Conventions 1899 and 1907, the four Geneva Conventions of 1949,[50] and Protocol I and II added in 1977.[51] Furthermore, much of it is now customary international law binding all states. The key to understanding the protection of human life under these laws is to accept the classification of individuals into different categories with varying protection for their lives. Whether an individual is a prisoner of war, a civilian, a lawful combatant or an unlawful combatant will affect the level of protection accorded to his or her life. While this seems inconsistent with the general principle of equality of rights, it enables a right to life to be retained by some, if not all, individuals affected by war.

The degree of protection for the lives of prisoners of war (POWs) is quite high. According to Geneva III, prisoners of war in custody must not be killed.[52] There is no doubt that this principle is also part of customary international law and therefore binding on all states of the world. Furthermore, POWs should, as soon as possible, be evacuated to camps far from the combat zone, a measure which will ensure greater protection for their lives.[53] Protocol I even adds that if POWs are captured by a small unit which cannot spare guards for a prompt evacuation, the prisoners should be released rather than killed.[54] Being a prisoner of war inevitably means a deprivation of liberty for the duration of the hostilities but, as Dinstein notes, 'While his liberty is temporarily denied, the decisive point is that the life, health and dignity of a prisoner of war are guaranteed.'[55]

A lawful combatant gains the benefits of prisoner of war status if captured but, while still actively participating in hostilities, a lawful combatant has very limited protection for his right to life. Attacks must be targeted at legitimate military objectives but IHL is clear that this can include human beings, so all enemy combatants can be targeted. If the death of human beings is to be an aim of a military attack, there are restraining principles of necessity and proportionality that need to be taken into account,[56] and it will be essential for the deaths to offer a definite military advantage.[57] Retreating troops are not secure from attack and specific individuals may also be targeted, provided that this is not done treacherously (for example, in civilian clothes).[58]

There are two ways to qualify for lawful combatancy: as a member of the armed forces of one of the parties to the conflict; or as a member of the irregular forces, such as guerrillas, partisans, resistance movements and so on. The latter is problematic. The Hague and Geneva Conventions set out six conditions for lawful

---

[50] Geneva I covers the wounded and sick in the armed forces in the field; Geneva II covers the wounded and sick in the armed forces at sea; Geneva III covers prisoners of war; Geneva IV covers the protection of civilians.

[51] Protocol I deals with the protection of victims of international armed conflicts, while Protocol II deals with non-international armed conflicts.   [52] Article 13 Geneva III.

[53] Article 19 Geneva III.   [54] Article 41(3) Protocol I.

[55] Dinstein, n. 49 above, p. 29.

[56] These principles will be discussed in more detail below.

[57] Dinstein, n. 49 above, p. 85.   [58] ibid, pp. 94–5.

combatancy: subordination to responsible command; fixed distinctive emblem; carrying of arms openly; conduct in accordance with IHL; organization; and belonging to a party to the conflict.[59] It is very difficult for members of irregular forces to meet these requirements as such forces depend upon secrecy in order to operate. If a participant in hostilities is not granted the status of lawful combatant, his or her life is at greater risk because, if captured, prisoner of war status will be withheld. The requirement to wear a military uniform (derived from the second condition above) was used by the United States government to justify the withholding of prisoner of war status from members of al-Qaeda and the Taliban captured by US forces. However, Article 44 of Protocol I undermines the distinction between lawful and unlawful combatants by extending protections equivalent to those offered to prisoners of war to members of irregular forces. The only requirement under this Article is that arms are carried openly during military engagement or deployment when visible to an adversary. The United States has refused to ratify this Protocol on the basis of this provision but it may well be customary law. The significance of the distinction between lawful and unlawful combatants is greatly reduced by Protocol 1 but the treatment of detainees at Guantánamo Bay demonstrates the continued practical importance of being categorized as a lawful combatant and thus a prisoner of war when captured.

The category of persons granted the greatest protection for their lives are civilians. In order to be classified as a civilian, an individual must not be a member of the armed forces and must not participate directly in the hostilities. The distinction between combatants and civilians is at the very core of IHL. While combatants may be attacked as legitimate military targets, attacks against civilians are prohibited.[60] This is a strong protection for the right to life of civilians during war. As Dinstein notes, the prohibition on killing civilians applies even if such an attack would bring the war to an end sooner, thus saving a greater number of lives: 'the prohibition of direct attacks against civilians applies irrespective of utilitarian considerations'.[61] In addition, not only direct attacks against civilians are prohibited but also indiscriminate attacks which are incapable of distinguishing between civilians and combatants. This includes firing imprecise missiles against military targets located near civilians. The concept of collateral damage—an unacceptable euphemism for the unintended (but often foreseeable) killing of innocent civilians—is only an acceptable part of modern warfare if the number of civilian deaths are proportionate to the military aim sought.[62]

---

[59] Article 4(A) Geneva III.

[60] Article 51(2) and 52(1) Protocol I. The prohibition of the killing of civilians was confirmed by the ICJ in the *Nuclear Weapons* case (n. 6 above, p. 257). In addition, intentional direct attacks against civilians is now a war crime under Article 8(2)(a)(i) Rome Statute of the International Criminal Court 1998.

[61] Dinstein, n. 49 above, p. 116.

[62] 'Excessive' damage to civilians (whatever that may mean) is expressly prohibited in Article 51(5)(b) Protocol I and is a war crime under Article 8(2)(b)(iv) Rome Statute of International Criminal Court 1998.

The most vulnerable civilians during an armed conflict will be those either work-ing within military targets (such as munitions factories) or living nearby. Even civilians working in munitions factories remain categorized as civilian and are thus prima facie exempt from attack but their deaths are unlikely to be regarded by IHL as excessive given the high military importance of the target.[63] This does not mean that precautions should not be taken to prevent (or reduce) such deaths, however, and attacking at night, for example, would be a valuable precaution. Protocol I also requires that advance warning be provided for civilian attacks unless the circumstances do not permit this.[64] The wide exception will frequently come into play given that surprise is often a key element of an attack. The limited protection provided to the life of a civilian against enemy forces under IHL is sup-plemented by means of restrictions on the actions of a civilian's own state which is required under Article 58 of Protocol I to endeavour to remove civilians from the vicinity of military objectives and avoid locating military objectives within or near densely populated areas. The use of civilians as a human shield is also clearly prohibited,[65] as is the use of starvation of civilians as a military tactic.[66] While civilian deaths in wartime seem to be inevitable, international humanitarian law treats the lives of civilians as worthy of protection. While enemy combatants can be killed with impunity; the killing of enemy civilians will only be permitted if an unintended consequence of an attack on a legitimate military target. It is not much comfort to civilians, especially those working or living near a target, but it is more comfort than is accorded to soldiers.

C. The ethics of killing in wartime

Much of the academic writing on IHL focuses on the reasons for granting immunity to the lives of civilians: why, it is often asked, are this category of per-sons offered protection from the full horrors of war when their compatriots on the frontline have no such protection? This is an important question but what is rarely asked is why non-civilians lose the usual protection for their life. What is it that distinguishes a civilian from a soldier, and if the former are regarded as inno-cent, where lies the guilt of the latter?[67] As Larry May acknowledges, 'One way to see the difficulty is by trying to distinguish between a reluctant conscripted soldier and a war-mongering munitions manufacturer. Is the latter someone who

---

[63] Dinstein, n. 49 above, p. 124.   [64] Article 57(2)(c) Protocol I.
[65] Article 51(7) Protocol I.   [66] Article 54 Protocol I.
[67] Noam Zohar describes this dilemma effectively: 'As long as the objective is to oppose shoot-ing at civilians, proclaiming that they are "innocent" seems straightforward; truly they do not deserve to die. The corollary of this is, however, that the "noninnocent" soldiers somehow *deserve* their deaths, but what can warrant such a sweeping imputation?' (N.J. Zohar, 'Collective War and Individualistic Ethics: Against the Conscription of "Self-Defense"' (1993) 21 Political Theory 606, at p. 607.)

should never be killed and the former someone who can always be killed?'[68] This raises the inescapable fact that it is often impossible to draw a clear moral line of culpability between the soldier and the civilian. Increasingly, in modern warfare, the lines are blurred. Anthony Coates tries to resolve this dilemma by explaining that 'innocence' in the context of distinguishing civilians from soldiers means not 'blameless' but rather 'harmless'.[69] In a subjective moral sense, many soldiers are blameless while some civilians may be blameworthy. But civilians do not generally pose a threat and in Coates' view, 'It is the threat that an unjust aggressor poses that results in the loss or suspension of that right of immunity from attack that all human beings are thought to possess.'[70] On this view, the non-threatening status of civilians preserves their natural immunity. Coates recognizes, however, that even this distinction is not easy to sustain in modern warfare. Many civilians may play an important role in the war effort, providing the means and instruments of combat.[71] Coates would use this fact not to remove the distinguishing line between soldier and civilian but rather to move it so that civilians contributing to the war effort—and thus posing a threat to the enemy—are re-categorized on the non-immunity side of the line. However, this seems an even more arbitrary line than the traditional one: factory workers, for example, do not choose the product they produce so drawing a distinction between a worker producing weapons and a worker producing food seems to do no more than provide a flimsy veil of justification for the killing of the former.

We are still circling the core of the issue here and if we can confront the issue of why some people lose the usual immunity from being killed—their right to life, in other words—then this may also reveal how to distinguish those who have lost their immunity from those who have not done so. Jeff McMahan proposes a radical answer to this core question. In doing so, he seeks to re-introduce issues of *jus ad bellum* to the conduct of war. He argues that individual soldiers bear moral culpability for acting in an unjust cause and this culpability justifies their loss of immunity. For McMahan, 'unjust combatants cannot participate in war without doing wrong'.[72] This approach overcomes the difficulty highlighted above in apportioning blame to soldiers which would justify their being distinguished from 'innocent' civilians. However, McMahan places too much responsibility on individual soldiers by failing to recognize two important issues. First, he fails to recognize the other conflicting ethical considerations, such as acting in the national interest, which may influence an individual's behaviour. Lackey presents an alternative view here when he identifies ethical justifications for killing enemy combatants regardless of whether the cause is just: 'If the war is fought for a just cause, the killing of enemy soldiers is justified as necessary to

---

[68] L. May, *War Crimes and Just War* (Cambridge: Cambridge University Press, 2007), p. 18.
[69] A.J. Coates, *The Ethics of War* (Manchester: Manchester University Press, 1997), p. 235.
[70] ibid.   [71] ibid, p. 237.
[72] J. McMahan, 'The Ethics of Killing in War' (2004) 114 Ethics 693, at p. 714.

the triumph of right. If the war is fought for an unjust cause, the killing of enemy soldiers is acceptable because it is considered an honourable thing to fight for one's country, right or wrong, provided that one fights well and clearly.'[73] Second, McMahan's argument also fails to recognize the practical restraints on a soldier's free will. The soldier may be conscripted and, even if he is a volunteer, he is likely to lack the information necessary to make an informed choice about the matter. The British and American soldiers fighting in Iraq, for example, could not have been expected to make a fully informed choice about the merits of the invasion at the time it occurred, given that crucial information was misrepresented by the governments. Debate still rages in political, legal and media circles as to the justi-fication for the invasion; can we really expect a sixteen-year-old soldier to be able to make a clear assessment of the case for war? Furthermore, the effect on military discipline of each individual soldier making individual assessments of the just-ice of the cause for each military engagement seems in itself to shift McMahan's theory from reality to the realms of fantasy. Rejection of McMahan's argument should not be seen as a rejection of the need for soldiers to act according to their consciences. It is a good thing for soldiers—and everyone else in society—to con-sider the merits of the cause for which they are being asked to fight. But it is a step too far to apportion moral blame to a soldier who fights according to the laws of war—killing only enemy combatants, and only when to do so is militarily neces-sary and proportionate—and who does so under constant threat to his own life, merely because his government has acted with arrogance, incompetence, or bad motives. There is good reason for keeping *jus ad bellum* considerations distinct from those of *jus in bello*.[74]

Perhaps the most obvious justification for killing in wartime is self-defence. Even in times of peace we accept that taking a life may be morally permissible if it is done in defence of one's self, although merely a life for a life equation will not be reconcilable with the right to life. As Zohar explains, 'Killing can never be morally justified by the result alone—that a life is saved; for just as surely a life is lost. Something more is required to tip the scales: a minimal measure of moral guilt (on the part of the aggressor), which distinguishes self-defense from mere substitution.'[75] Killing someone who poses a direct and immediate threat to your life is permissible (and, in right to life terms, can be excused from punishment by the state authorities without the state attracting condemnation). More broadly, as we shall see in chapter 6, the rights of others present a conflicting interest that needs to be taken into account when enforcing an individual's right to life. So,

---

[73] D.P. Lackey, *The Ethics of War and Peace* (New Jersey: Prentice-Hall, 1989), p. 18.
[74] Walzer explains this point effectively: 'the moral status of individual soldiers on both sides is very much the same: they are led to fight by their loyalty to their own states and by their lawful obedience. They are most likely to believe their wars are just, and while the basis of that belief is not necessarily rational inquiry but, more often, a kind of unquestioning acceptance of official propa-ganda, nevertheless they are not criminals; they face one another as moral equals.' (M. Walzer, *Just and Unjust Wars: A Moral Argument with Historical Illustrations* (New York: Basic Books, 2006, 4th edn.), p. 127.)   [75] Zohar, n. 67 above, p. 609.

it is not advisable to look at a wartime death in isolation; its moral justification, if there be any, will depend upon the wider circumstances of the death, including the threat posed by the deceased to his killer. Self-defence is not a complete answer, however, because while it may explain some deaths on the battlefield (where an individual soldier must kill or be killed), many deaths in wartime are perpetuated by someone safely removed from any immediate threat to his life. Modern destructive weapons operate at long range and enable the aggressor to be far removed from the immediate battlefield (or, indeed, to create a new one at the press of a button). Furthermore, the minimal element of moral guilt required to tip the balance of the 'life-for-a-life' scales will often be absent because, as argued above, the individual soldier does no wrong if he follows the rules of war regardless of the rights or wrongs of his government's entering into the war. There are significant problems, therefore, in applying the individualistic concept of self-defence to deaths in wartime. War is, after all, not an individualistic battle but rather a fight between two (or more) state parties (or possibly intra or supra state parties). As Zohar recognizes, the 'reality of international confrontation is not adequately described by reduction to individualistic terms. We are not only individuals facing other individuals but also a nation confronting another nation.'[76] This broader, and more realistic, perspective on war opens the door to the concept of collective self-defence: 'it is a collective that defends itself against attack from another collective rather than simply many individuals protecting their lives in a set of individual confrontations'.[77] The main problem with this view is that collectives cannot be killed; nations cannot be killed. The only entities to die during war are individuals. Why should some individuals—presumably soldiers—be identified as representatives of the collective, and killed? As Walzer eloquently reminds us, the war is not that of the soldier: 'War is not in fact his enterprise, but rather surviving this battle, avoiding the next. Mostly, he hides, is frightened, doesn't fire, prays for a minor wound, a voyage home, a long rest.'[78] In Zohar's view, the key factor is participation: 'combatants are those marked as participating in the collective war effort, whereas the rest of the enemy society retain their exclusive status as individuals'.[79] Larry May presents an opposing view:

why should those who are so enlisted be the ones who pay the price for what the state has planned and is trying to execute? We do not punish a state effectively by killing the soldiers of that state, because soldiers are so easily replaceable. And similarly, we do not reward a state by sparing its soldiers or civilians from death. These individuals should be spared or killed for reasons that have to do with them as individuals, for they are not automatically to be seen as extensions of the state.[80]

Walzer uses the principle of humanity to seek to explain the loss of immunity of the enemy soldier: 'An enemy has to be described differently, and though the

---

[76] ibid, p. 616.   [77] ibid, p. 615.   [78] Walzer, n. 74 above, pp. 142–3.
[79] Zohar, n. 67 above, p. 618.   [80] May, n. 68 above, p. 188.

stereotypes through which he is seen are often grotesque, they have a certain truth. He alienates himself from me when he tries to kill me, and from our common humanity. But the alienation is temporary, the humanity imminent.'[81] Walzer then gives a number of examples of instances when a soldier refused to kill an enemy soldier when provided with a clear opportunity. Each of these examples differs but, in each of them, the humanity of the soldier is restored, for example, by smoking a cigarette, holding up his pants, or taking a bath. Walzer describes these insignificant actions as restoring humanity but they could also be regarded as restoring the individuality of the enemy soldier, so that he is no longer seen merely as part of the enemy collective but rather as an individual, with a life as worthy of protection as anyone else.

From a human rights perspective, the idea of participants in a war losing their status as individuals and instead being viewed primarily as members of a collective is problematic. However, we have no difficulty in viewing the perpetrators as part of a collective rather than individuals acting alone. It is clearly a mistake to view killing in a war as a killing by one individual soldier; what distinguishes war is that the killings are authorized, and ultimately perpetrated, by the state. On this basis, if the victim is viewed merely as an individual, it will be almost impossible to find any justification for the state authorized killing. Only if the individual victim is regarded as a representative of the enemy state does the concept of war make any sense. It may be, of course, that war does not make any sense, but any attempt to identify and explain the laws regulating the conduct of war must recognize that war creates unique circumstances. And one of those, perhaps the most important one, is that those who participate in the war do not act individually but rather on behalf of a collective. The individual soldier kills in the name of the collective and the victim dies as a representative (perhaps an unwilling or unknowing one) of the enemy collective. Zohar's summary of his theory introduces another important concept for the justification of killing in wartime:

From the individual perspective, even the enemy soldiers ought not to be killed. The very license for killing them derives from a compromise, which subsumes them—the primary participants in the enemy war effort—under the collective identity of 'aggressors'. Collectively, we must and may act against the enemy war effort, despite the fact that this involves destroying innocent lives.[82]

The argument that we must act against the enemy introduces the concept of acting in the national interest.

Because of the conceptual difficulties in regarding individual self-defence as the ethical justification for killings in wartime, the idea of collective self-defence seems more fitting. It seems to open the door, however, to considerations of *jus ad bellum*, because not all national collectives will be fighting in self-defence; some will be illegal aggressors. The concept of acting in the national interest returns

[81] Walzer, n. 74 above, p. 142.   [82] Zohar, n. 67 above, p. 619.

the focus back to issues of *jus in bello* alone because even if a collective initially enters a war unjustly, once immersed in a fight, and under attack by the enemy, the national interest may require victory. The killing of enemy soldiers may then be justified in order to defend the collective's own civilians, justly acting soldiers, legitimate government and territory. This idea was expressed clearly by Lackey in the quotation above: 'the killing of enemy soldiers is acceptable because it is considered an honourable thing to fight for one's country, right or wrong, provided that one fights well and cleanly'.[83] Not everyone agrees that it is right to fight, and kill, for one's country 'right or wrong'. Jonathan Glover identifies patriot justification for war as located on a spectrum, with 'my country right or wrong' at the strong end and at the mild end: 'the belief that one ought to fight for one's country, subject to some condition such as that the war be a just one or, perhaps more stringently, a defensive one'.[84] This, however, returns us once more to issues of the legality and morality of a state's entry into war and, as discussed above, this does not affect the ethical justification, if there be one, for the death of an individual.

An issue that should be considered alongside the issue of the ethical justification for killing in wartime is the issue of legal and ethical restraints upon such killing. The principle of distinction between civilian and soldier was discussed above. Alongside that principle in contemporary *jus in bello* are the principles of military necessity and proportionality. These are important restraints upon the deaths that are permissible. Indeed, Walzer argues that many deaths in war, of soldiers as well as civilians, are not necessary or proportionate:

These deaths are nothing more than the inevitable consequence of putting deadly weapons into the hands of undisciplined soldiers, and armed men into the hands of stupid or fanatical generals. Every military history is a tale of violence and destruction out of all relation to the requirements of combat: massacres on the one hand and, on the other, ill-planned and wasteful battles that are little better than massacres.[85]

The principles of necessity and proportionality (together with non-combatant immunity) are core aspects of the enduring just war tradition. Coates succinctly explains their meaning: 'Economy or restraint is the basic imperative, and combatants are required to employ only as much force as is necessary to achieve legitimate military objectives and as is proportionate to the importance of those targets. In other words, the use of force and the consequent infliction of suffering must be neither gratuitous nor excessive.'[86] In the view of May, these principles are grounded in the more fundamental principle of humane treatment. This idea connects well with the human rights perspective of the right to life. May explains that 'humane treatment is related to the principle of humanity that involves

---

[83] Lackey, n. 73 above, p. 18.
[84] J. Glover, *Causing Death and Saving Lives* (London: Penguin, 1977), p. 253. Glover argues in favour of 'contingent pacifism': the idea that there may be a justification for war but it is so unlikely that in practice there appears to be an almost absolute prohibition.
[85] Walzer, n. 74 above, p. 130.   [86] Coates, n. 69 above, p. 209.

treating another person as a fellow human, as a member of the same group, the human race, rather than in any number of other ways that take account of his or her otherness'.[87] This is a basic starting point for the protection of a human right, such as the right to life, and it is therefore fitting that it should be seen to underlie the principles of necessity and proportionality in IHL.

One of the best (or worst) examples of disproportionate loss of life are the World War One battles such as the Somme in which there was a huge loss of life for no apparent gain (and in circumstances in which that outcome was well known in advance). Both sides had the goal of attrition rather than territory and, as Coates points out, this is 'a method of warfare that has as its deliberate aim the mass expenditure of men and material'.[88] A war of attrition presents, in the words of Coates, 'a dehumanized view of war according to which war is seen as an industrial and mechanical process in which the distinction between the human and the material element is systematically suppressed'.[89] Such an approach is not consistent with the principles of dignity and equality of human beings, nor is it consistent with the ultimate value accorded to human life throughout all states of the world. The principles of necessity and proportionality send a strong message that each human life is something of value, even if some of those lives may, by necessity, be destroyed in order to bring the war to a speedy close. In that sense, necessity and proportionality could be justified on utilitarian grounds: human life may only be sacrificed if a greater good for mankind will be made possible by that loss. The classic example often given here is World War Two. If any war was justified, many would argue it was this one. The greater good of saving Europe from Hitler justified, it is said, the massive loss of human life entailed in achieving that goal. Similarly, Lackey gives the example of the use of the atomic bomb on Hiroshima and Nagasaki. This is often justified as for the greater good because it arguably saved lives that would have been lost with a land invasion and the continuation of the war. However, as Lackey notes, a land invasion was not imminent in August 1945 when the bomb was used and the genuine alternatives—negotiated peace, or a demonstration of the bomb—would have resulted in considerably fewer deaths. He concludes that the use of the atomic bomb was probably not necessary or proportionate, and it certainly failed to discriminate between combatants and civilians.[90] It is important to bear in mind here that

---

[87] May, n. 68 above, p. 67. May further explains that human treatment is a duty only 'when humans have rendered other humans vulnerable' as in wartime (p. 89).

[88] Coates, n. 69 above, p. 220.   [89] ibid.

[90] Lackey, n. 73 above, p. 77. Estimates of the combined dead at Hiroshima and Nagasaki range between 130,000–170,000. By contrast, Coates raises the example of the sinking of the *Belgrano* in the Falklands conflict and argues, contrary to widespread opinion, that this was justified as a necessary and proportionate loss of life (Coates, n. 69 above, pp. 209–13). The *Belgrano* was an Argentinean warship which was sunk by a British submarine as it apparently retreated, with the loss of 368 lives. Coates argues that in context, given the threat posed to British forces by the ship, this force was proportionate: 'Though in isolation from the context of the war as a whole a particular use of force may well appear cruel and excessive, it may still be judged proportionate and

proportionality has a 'bilateral interpretation':[91] it applies not only to the lives of a state's own troops but also to those of its enemy. Even if victory could be guaranteed as a result of a particularly vicious attack on enemy forces, it must still be assessed whether the loss of (enemy) lives will be proportionate to the victory achieved. This is a demanding test for military leaders, and one that may not come intuitively to them.

The vital role of the principles of military necessity and, particularly, proportionality in regulating the use of lethal force in wartime helps to secure some continued protection for the right to life when it is most threatened. The ICCPR's approach of prohibiting only arbitrary deprivations of life fits well with IHL's approach of prohibiting disproportionate loss of life.[92] Deaths that are not proportionate to the legitimate military goal sought (or that were not necessary to achieve the goal) are likely to be regarded as not only unlawful under IHL but also arbitrary under international human rights law, and thus a violation of the right to life. Of course, as discussed in the first section of this chapter, there remain issues of jurisdiction to be overcome before a state can be held liable under a human rights treaty for deprivations of life in another state. For this reason, IHL may in practice provide more effective protection for the right to life in this context than human rights law. There is an increasing recognition of the need for war criminals (whether individual soldiers or state leaders) to be held accountable for their actions. Intentional direct attacks on civilians, causing excessive loss of life to civilians in otherwise legitimate military attacks, and killing a combatant who has surrendered are recognized as war crimes under the Rome Statute of the International Criminal Court 1998. The protection offered by this criminalization of conduct during hostilities arguably goes further than the human rights treaties which, only under exceptional circumstances, will ensure protection for the lives of the individuals of one state against the armed forces of another.

D. Conclusion

The difficulty in discussing the application of the right to life in times of war or armed conflict arises from the apparent mismatch of the right with the reality of such conflict where life is treated cheaply. The death of civilians becomes collateral damage and young men and women in uniform become legitimate military targets. Glover has argued against the compartmentalism that causes us to regard killings in war as immune from the moral criticism that surrounds other

---

therefore morally justifiable in relation to the overall objective of destroying the military capacity of the enemy and winning the war' (Coates, p. 219).

[91] Coates, n. 69 above, p. 221.

[92] The relationship, and fundamental differences, between IHL and human rights law in the context of the right to life are well explained in J.J. Paust, 'The Right to Life in Human Rights Law and the Laws of War' (2002) 65 Saskatchewan Law Review 411.

killings: 'The circumstances seem so exceptional that we feel the general taboo on killing is unaffected by its suspension in the context of war.'[93] In Glover's view, this leads us both to regard killing in war as less serious than other state killings, but also to regard deaths in wartime with greater revulsion.[94] This inconsistency, and the general compartmentalization, is understandable but should be resisted. A life is of no less value in times of war than in times of peace, nor is the life of an enemy of less value than the life of a friend, although it may seem that way to us. Each life has the same value but not each life can be protected by or from the state. Even in peacetime, there are deaths that are justified (as we will see throughout this book) in self-defence, for example, or at the deceased's own request, or to save the lives of others. Likewise, in times of armed conflict, not all life can be protected and some deaths are necessary for the greater good of the collective. But these deaths should always be a last resort: they occur when a military goal cannot be achieved by any other means, and only where the deaths caused are proportionate to the goal sought, and not excessive. The balancing exercise, inherent in tests of proportionality and necessity, should occur in both war and peace, but it is harder to outweigh the value of human life in peacetime as compared to times of conflict where the survival of large numbers of the population, and perhaps even the state itself, is at stake.

[93] Glover, n. 84 above, p. 251.
[94] As Glover points out, World War One is viewed with greater revulsion than the flu epidemic of the same time even though it involved less fatalities (ibid, pp. 251–2).

5

The Right to Life and Prevention of Crime: Killing by the State as Punishment and/or Deterrence

This chapter will consider two very different circumstances in which the state may take a human life in the context of crime prevention. The first involves death as a punishment; the second death as a law enforcement measure.[1] Both may be defended on the basis that they prevent crime, and thus ultimately may save more lives than they take. There are considerable problems in this justification, however, both in practical and moral terms: how is the state to determine the future consequences of a killing or assess the merits of any alternatives; and should one life be taken to save another? Does it matter whether one life will save many? Or if the life taken is far from innocent? In addition to these difficulties, death as a punishment introduces a further problematic issue of death as a retributive measure: can an individual lose his or her entitlement to a right to life by pursuing criminal actions? The issues raised in this chapter are closely linked to many that follow in subsequent chapters, including, particularly, the balancing of a right to life with the rights of others. The distinguishing factor of the situations dealt with in this chapter, however, is that they involve the death of an individual who is perceived as posing a threat to society through actions for which that individual carries (or is perceived to carry) at least an element of moral guilt.[2] The situation where an entirely innocent bystander threatens other members of society (such as the life of a fetus threatening its mother; or the life of a disabled baby threatening its conjoined twin; or the lives of passengers of a hijacked aeroplane threatening hundreds of people on the ground) will be better dealt with in the next chapter. The lessons learnt here may well be of value there as well.

---

[1] This chapter will also consider how the state should respond to the taking of a life by another citizen in self-defence or the defence of others, in order to prevent unlawful violence.

[2] The extra difficulties posed by innocents on death row, and mistaken identities in the London underground, will be discussed later in this chapter.

A. The death penalty

We will start our discussion in this chapter with the death penalty: the imposition of death as a punishment for past crime(s). The discussion will begin by ascertaining current international practice and standards, before proceeding to investigate the collateral human rights abuses which often stem from the imposition of the death penalty. Having established that the death penalty raises human rights concerns above and beyond the right to life, the discussion will then focus on the relationship between this ultimate penalty and legal protection for the right to life.

(1) The death penalty in law and practice

(a) Current state practice and international standards

There is a widely recognized trend in international law towards the abolition of the death penalty. As of January 2008, ninety-two states have abolished the penalty, plus ten further states are abolitionist for ordinary crimes in peacetime. A further forty-four states, although retaining the death penalty in law, have not executed anyone for over ten years. Fifty states have held executions within the last ten years.[3] Prominent among them are many Asian states, including China, which executes more people than the rest of the world combined, and Singapore, which makes the greatest use of the death penalty per capita. Notwithstanding frequent attempts to seek to justify capital punishment on the basis of Muslim or Asian values, the Asian Charter of Human Rights urges all states to abolish the death penalty.[4] Other regions to retain the death penalty include Africa and the Caribbean, where some states are de facto abolitionist due to the Privy Council's judgments.[5] Perhaps most infamously, the United States is an anomaly, alone amongst western states in retaining capital punishment at both federal and, in many states, state level. The Fifth and Fourteenth Amendments to the US Constitution expressly permit the deprivation of life with 'due process of law'. While the US Supreme Court has sought to limit the ambit of capital punishment—under the Eighth Amendment's prohibition of cruel and unusual punishment—in respect of arbitrary and discriminatory imposition of the penalty and its imposition on juveniles, the insane, and the mentally retarded, a majority

---

[3] R. Hood & C. Hoyle, *The Death Penalty: A Worldwide Perspective* (Oxford: Oxford University Press, 2008, 4th edn.).

[4] Article 3(7) Asian Human Rights Charter (<http://www.material.ahrchk.net/charter/>). For a recent discussion of the death penalty in Asia, see D.T. Johnson & F.E. Zimrig, *The Next Frontier: National Development, Political Change and the Death Penalty in Asia* (Oxford: Oxford University Press, 2009).

[5] See, for example, *Pratt & Morgan v Attorney General of Jamaica* [1993] 4 All ER 769. This may soon change with the creation of a new Caribbean Court of Justice which will replace the Privy Council's jurisdiction on this issue.

of Supreme Court Justices have remained willing to classify the death penalty as constitutional. This stands in stark contrast to states such as South Africa, which shares with the US a high crime rate, but whose Constitutional Court has held the death penalty to be unconstitutional.[6]

As this list demonstrates, notwithstanding an international trend towards abolition, a large majority of the world's population remains subject to the death penalty. Furthermore, while some commentators identify an abolition-ist trend,[7] international law does not, as of today, prohibit the death penalty (although it may prohibit its application to certain persons).[8] Indeed, the main treaty protections for the right to life expressly recognize the death penalty as an exception to the right. The exception is, as Schabas engagingly describes it, an 'awkward and inconsistent appendage' to the right to life.[9] Absent from the Universal Declaration of Human Rights,[10] an aspirational and non-legally bind-ing document, the death penalty exception can be found, in various terms, in the International Covenant of Civil and Political Rights (ICCPR), the European Convention of Human Rights (ECHR) and the American Convention of Human Rights (ACHR). There is little doubt that these three human rights documents include the exception as a means of compromise, in order to avoid alienating retentionist states. The ECHR is perhaps most blatant in this, declaring merely that 'No one shall be deprived of his life intentionally save in the execution of a sentence of a court following his conviction of a crime for which this penalty is provided by law.'[11] Thus, in the very same breath, the right to life is given to all, yet taken back from those sentenced to death. There are none of the conditions and limitations evident in later treaties. Here the message is simple: we have a

---

[6] *State v Makwanyane & Mchunu* (Case no. CCT/3/94 (1995)). The South African Constitutional Court based its finding on the fact that the new South Africa was founded on the recognition of rights such as the right to life and the right to dignity, and therefore these values must be placed above all others: 'And this must be demonstrated by the State in everything that it does, including the way it punishes criminals. This is not achieved by objectifying murderers and putting them to death to serve as an example to others in the expectation that they might possibly be deterred thereby' (para. 144).

[7] William Schabas, for example, argues that 'The day when abolition of the death penalty becomes a universal norm, entrenched not only by convention but also by custom and qualified as a peremptory rule of jus cogens, is undeniably in the foreseeable future.' (W.A. Schabas, *The Abolition of the Death Penalty in International Law* (Cambridge: Cambridge University Press, 2002, 3rd edn.), p. 3.)

[8] Persons under the age of 18 at the time of the offence are expressly excluded from the death penalty under Article 6(5) ICCPR, Article 4(5) ACHR and Article 37(a) International Covenant on Rights of Child.   [9] Schabas, n. 7 above, p. 366.

[10] Schabas identifies that the drafters of the UDHR considered including either an express exception to the right to life in respect of the death penalty or a proclamation of its abolition, but eventually favoured a compromise, making no mention of either abolition or retention of the death penalty and thus adopting an 'ambiguous and equivocating' (p. 24) stance that Schabas regards positively: 'By its silence on the matter of the death penalty, it envisages the abolition of capital punishment and, at the same time, admits its existence as a necessary evil, a relatively fine line which in hindsight appears to have been rather astutely drawn' (pp. 42–3).

[11] Article 2(1) ECHR.

right to life except when the state legitimately plans to execute us. It is a message long since forgotten in Europe due to the later enactments of Protocols 6 and 13. The former has almost universal ratification (with Russia as the only exception) and prohibits the death penalty in peacetime, while the latter's prohibition in all circumstances remains only partially accepted. In practice, all European states except Russia have abolished the death penalty, and even Russia has had a moratorium on executions since 1996. It is significant, however, that the additional Protocols are not reflections of the right to life but distinct from it. They represent a limitation of (state) sovereignty for ratifying parties in respect of the death penalty, but this does not stem from an individual's right not to be deprived of his or her life. The death penalty has been practically eradicated from Europe but in a movement that is independent from the region's protection for the right to life. The European experience tells us little, therefore, of the relationship between the right to life and capital punishment, except perhaps that it is possible (or, at least, was possible in the 1940s) to draft protection for the right to life that encompassed a blatant exception for capital punishment. For the moral justification for such an approach, and the practicalities of restricting the death penalty while accepting the legitimacy of its continued existence, we must turn elsewhere.

The practicalities of this dual approach have been unavoidable under the ICCPR. The mixed message of Article 6 ICCPR's protection for the right to life is obvious: the death penalty is a necessary, and residual, evil. Article 6(2) contains the essence of this approach when it states that 'In countries which have not abolished the death penalty, sentence of death may be imposed only for the most serious crimes...' Further restrictions are included in Article 6(2–6), including the need to comply with other provisions of the Covenant and the Genocide Convention; the requirement of a 'final judgment rendered by a competent court'; the right to seek pardon or commutation of the sentence; and the exclusion from the scope of capital punishment of pregnant women and persons below the age of 18 when the crime was committed. The abolitionist flavour of Article 6 has become evident through the HRC's decisions, particularly through its decision in *Judge v Canada*[12] that the death penalty exception authorizes the imposition of the penalty only for retentionist states. This means not only that state parties cannot reintroduce the death penalty once it has been abolished, but also that abolitionist states cannot extradite an individual to a retentionist state unless there is a guarantee that the extradited person will not receive the death penalty. The HRC reasoned that paragraphs 2 to 6 in Article 6 'have the dual function of creating an exception to the right to life in respect of the death penalty and laying down limits on the scope of that exception'.[13] One such limitation is that only state parties that 'have not abolished the death penalty' (as stated in Article 6(2)) can avail themselves of the exception.[14] Article 6(1)'s protection for the right to life binds all states and, thus, for countries that have abolished the death penalty, there

---

[12] *Judge v Canada* (Communication No. 829/1998).   [13] ibid, para. 10.4.   [14] ibid.

is an obligation not to expose a person to the real risk of its imposition.[15] The disparity in treatment between abolitionist and retentionist states is said by the HRC to reflect the compromise inherent in Article 6 which seeks to 'appease very divergent views on the issue of the death penalty',[16] while the HRC's willingness to depart from its previous approach in this case was explicitly justified on the basis of a 'broadening international consensus in favour of abolition of the death penalty, and in states which have retained the death penalty, a broadening consensus not to carry it out'.[17] Thus, Article 6 reflects the need to appease different views on the death penalty but is now interpreted in a manner that recognizes an abolitionist trend among state parties. The result of this somewhat schizophrenic approach is that individuals in abolitionist countries can expect a higher level of protection for their right to life, from both the state bodies and the international treaty bodies, than their counterparts in retentionist states, who must live, and die, by the compromise written into the Covenant.

Some comfort for the latter group may be provided by the HRC's approach to the 'most serious crime' restriction in Article 6(2). It is through this mechanism that the HRC, and indeed other international and national bodies, have sought to confine, in an increasingly restrictive manner, the imposition of the death penalty. This is an important battlefront for the abolitionist movement because while some states, such as the US, have generally reserved this most serious punishment for the most serious crimes (usually forms of aggravated, intentional murder),[18] other states have executed for a disparate range of offences, including drug offences;[19] economic offences;[20] sexual offences;[21] and religious dissent.[22] The HRC has stated that the phrase 'most serious crimes' must be 'read restrictively to mean that the death penalty should be a quite exceptional measure'[23] and, together with other human rights bodies such as the Commission on Human Rights, has sought to exclude many such offences from the phrase. In *Lubuto v Zambia*, a violation of

---

[15] ibid.   [16] ibid, para. 10.5.   [17] ibid, para. 10.3.

[18] The US Supreme Court has recently struck down a Louisiana law permitting the imposition of the death penalty for the rape of a child (*Kennedy v Louisiana* 128 S. Ct. 2641; 171 L. Ed. 2d 525 (US, 2008).

[19] Under the Malaysian Dangerous Drugs Act 1952, anyone in possession of 15g of heroin/morphine, 1000g of opium or 200g of cannabis is presumed, until the contrary is proven, to be a drug trafficker and sentenced to death (Hood & Hoyle, n. 3 above, discuss this example at p. 138).

[20] In China, Iran and Thailand, for example, individuals have been sentenced to death for bribery or corruption of public officials, while in Libya and the Democratic Republic of Congo, currency speculation has led to death sentences (Hood & Hoyle, ibid, p. 139).

[21] Hood & Hoyle report that 28 countries retain the death penalty for sexual offences, most commonly aggravated rape (for example, rape of a child). As mentioned in fn 18 above, the US Supreme Court has recently found the imposition of a death sentence in respect of the rape of a child to be unconstitutional. Many states, particularly those influenced by Islamic law, also retain the death penalty for adultery, sodomy and prostitution. In Saudi Arabia, for example, three men were publicly beheaded in 2002 for homosexual acts (Hood & Hoyle, ibid, p. 141).

[22] Blasphemy and apostasy are punishable by death in at least seven Muslim countries, including Egypt, Pakistan and Sudan (Hood & Hoyle, ibid, pp. 142–3).

[23] General Comment No. 6, para. 7.

the right to life was found in the context of a death sentence imposed for an aggravated robbery in which firearms were used but did not result in any injuries.[24] The HRC's views in this case suggest that the death penalty should not be imposed for crimes such as this one where 'firearms did not produce the death or wounding of any person'.[25] The crimes for which the death penalty should (or could) be available is a significant issue because it is relevant to the core question of why the death penalty is permitted as an exception to the right to life. If (and this will be discussed fully below) the death penalty is an effective deterrent, why should it be restricted to the most serious crimes? If the penalty is (at least partly) justified on the basis of a retributive life-for-a-life basis (and again this will be discussed fully below), does any taking of a life justify a punishment of death? Or is it only the most serious examples of the most serious crime of murder that will suffice? Is it the consequence of the prisoner's actions that matters (for example, the death of another) or is it his culpability? If it is the former, an intentional homicide may be grouped together with manslaughter or felony murder, where the death is unintentional. Both retributive and deterrent justifications for the death penalty may suggest that it is a prisoner's culpability that matters when determining the 'most serious crimes' rather than the consequence of his actions. While the death penalty is framed as a protection for society, therefore, it is not necessarily responsive to the effects on society of the prisoner's crime.

The significance of the prisoner's culpability is also evident in the categories of persons protected from the possibility of execution under international law. Persons under the age of 18 at the time of the offence are expressly excluded under Article 6(5) (and also under Article 4(5) ACHR and Article 37(a) International Covenant on Rights of Child). The restriction was enforced by the HRC in *Johnson v Jamaica*[26] in which a violation of Article 6(5) was found in respect of a death sentence imposed on an applicant who was only seventeen when he committed the crime. Furthermore, both the UN Sub-Committee on Promotion and Protection of Human Rights and the Inter-American Commission on Human Rights have declared the juvenile exception to be customary international law.[27] Notwithstanding this apparent international consensus on the inappropriateness of executing an adult for a crime committed as a juvenile, seven countries are known to have executed juvenile offenders since 1990: Democratic Republic of Congo; Iran; Nigeria; Pakistan; Saudi Arabia; United States; and Yemen. The United States' rejection of the consensus was particularly blatant: it entered a reservation to Article 6(5) ICCPR, refused to sign the Child Convention and continued to execute juvenile offenders. However, in *Roper v Simmons*,[28] the US Supreme Court finally held that it would be unconstitutional under the Eighth and Fourteenth Amendments to execute such persons due to their diminished

---

[24] Communication 390/1990.   [25] ibid, para. 7.2.
[26] Communication 592/ 1994.   [27] See Hood & Hoyle, n. 3 above, p. 188.
[28] (2005) 543 US 551.

culpability and the international consensus now seems secure on this point. Similar reasoning has led to exemption on mental competence grounds where, as with juvenile offenders, the death penalty is hard to justify on either deterrent or retributive arguments. The HRC's stance on this issue became clear in *R.S. v Trinidad and Tobago*[29] when it found that the imposition of the death penalty on an individual who is mentally incompetent would breach Article 6(1) and further when it used its concluding observations to a report from the US to signify its regret about the state's failure to protect mentally incompetent persons from the death penalty.[30] The United States was again one of the last states to execute such offenders but on this issue also the US Supreme Court has recently extended its protection. In *Atkins v Virginia*,[31] a majority of the Court found that death is not a suitable punishment for mentally retarded offenders and is thus an excessive punishment under the Eight Amendment (although the means of implementing this decision, and of defining mental retardation, was expressly left to states to determine). Justice Stevens, giving the opinion of the Court, found that such offenders are less likely to be deterred by the death penalty (and their exemption will not cease to deter others), plus their reduced culpability for the offence removes them from the category of most serious offenders subject to the death penalty.[32] The increased risk of a miscarriage of justice was also recognized by the Court due to factors such as the increased possibility of a false confession, the defendant's potentially limited ability to assist counsel in preparing a defence, and the possibility of a poor performance as a witness.[33] In dissent, Justice Rehnquist (joined by Justices Scalia and Thomas) criticized the majority for giving weight to international opinion against the execution of mentally retarded individuals.[34] It is becoming increasingly obvious, however, that international disapproval of certain practices cannot be ignored. Part of the compromise inherent in the human rights treaties' treatment of the death penalty is to limit its application, while conceding its legitimacy. The exemption of those prisoners with clearly reduced culpability, as a class, is an important aspect of this.[35]

International law is ambiguous about the application of the right to life in situations where an individual has been sentenced to death by the state. Abolition of the death penalty is urged by most international bodies, most notably the HRC which has made clear its view that 'all measures of abolition should be considered

---

[29] Communication 684/1996.   [30] UN Doc. CCPR/C/79/Add. 50, para. 16.
[31] (2002) 56 US 304.   [32] ibid, pp. 319–20.   [33] ibid, pp. 320–1.
[34] ibid, pp. 321–8.
[35] Article 6(5) also exempts pregnant women from execution. Hood & Hoyle identify that the last reported instance of a pregnant woman being executed was in the Democratic Republic of Congo in 1998 (Hood & Hoyle, n. 3 above, p. 195). The exemption does not extend to mothers post-birth, although new mothers are given stays, of varying lengths, in some countries. It appears that the pregnancy exemption can also be explained on the basis of culpability: while the convicted prisoner may be culpable for her crime and 'deserve' death as a punishment, her unborn child is not culpable and so should not face death. Once it becomes possible to execute the mother without also of necessity killing the child, then the exemption wanes.

as progress in the enjoyment of the right to life'[36] and optional international agreements, such as Additional Protocols 6 and 13 to the ECHR, and the Second Optional Protocol of the ICCPR, indicate a widespread willingness on the parts of states to commit themselves by international law to abolish and not reintroduce capital punishment. And yet, these optional protocols are not framed in terms of the right to life; the ECHR perceives the death penalty as a legitimate exception to the right to life; and the ICCPR, while seeking in its terms to restrict the applicability of capital punishment, also implies a reconciliation between enforcement of the right to life and judicial executions. The possible justifications for such a purported reconciliation will be considered below, but first it is important to consider the almost inevitable infringement of other human rights in the imposition of the penalty.[37] It will be argued that the death penalty is not completely, or even primarily, about death. And this argument, if accepted, will have implications for the reconciliation of the penalty with the right to life.

(b) Other human rights abuses inherent in the imposition of the death penalty

Perhaps the most obvious human right of relevance to the death penalty (other than the right to life) is the prohibition on cruel, inhuman or degrading treatment or punishment.[38] In its General Comment No. 20, the HRC has declared that when the death penalty is imposed, 'it must be carried out in such a way as to cause the least possible physical pain and mental suffering'.[39] In terms of the means of execution, the HRC has held that the use of a gas chamber is a violation of Article 7 ICCPR's prohibition on cruel, inhuman and degrading treatment or punishment,[40] while the use of a lethal injection to bring about death was not a violation.[41] The US Supreme Court has also recently held that Kentucky's lethal injection protocol is not a violation of the Eighth Amendment's prohibition on cruel and unusual punishment.[42] Is such a comparison between different methods of killing a sensible venture? In terms of the right to life, it may be no more than a subsidiary issue, but it goes to the heart of the collateral human rights abuses issue. Methods of execution around the world vary from hanging (still performed in many countries, including Egypt, Japan and Singapore); shooting (as, for example, in Belarus, Vietnam and China); stoning (used in Sudan, Iran and Nigeria); lethal injection and the electric chair (both used in the US).[43] Most

---

[36] General Comment No. 6, para. 6.

[37] Hood & Hoyle argue that 'whatever justifications might be put forward for capital punishment, the process of inflicting it inevitably involves collateral abuses of human rights' (n. 3 above, p. 186).

[38] The prohibition is protected in these terms in Article 7 ICCPR, while Article 3 ECHR omits the word 'cruel'.   [39] General Comment No. 20, para. 6.

[40] *Ng v Canada* (Communication 469/1991).

[41] *Kindler v Canada* (Communication 470/1991).   [42] *Baze v Rees* 553 US 35 (2008).

[43] These examples are drawn from Hood & Hoyle, n. 3 above, pp. 156–7.

states retain more than one method of performing judicial executions. Some are patently more likely to cause suffering than others: indeed, that may be the point of them, as, for example, in respect of stoning. The Royal Commission on Capital Punishment, which reported in 1953 prior to the UK's abolition of the death penalty for homicide, helpfully identified three requirements in respect of methods of execution: humanity, certainty and decency.[44] The concept of humanity was regarded as requiring quick and simple preliminaries so as not to 'unnecessarily sharpen the poignancy of the prisoner's apprehension', as well as requiring a method of execution that would produce 'immediate unconsciousness passing quickly into death'.[45] The principle of certainty was regarded by the Royal Commission as demanding the method of execution most likely to avoid mishaps,[46] while the principle of decency required that the execution be conducted with 'decorum' and 'performed without brutality, that it should avoid gross physical violence and should not mutilate or distort the body'.[47] These principles are sound guidelines, once the general acceptability of judicial killings has been presumed, but even those states that seek the most painless and rapid method of killing cannot avoid the causation of physical and mental suffering before death. Borg and Radelet's investigation into 'botched executions' in the US reveals that they occur 'with regular frequency'.[48] In the study of the 749 executions between 1977 and 2001, the authors identify 'thirty four examples of executions involving unanticipated problems or delays that caused, or could have caused, unnecessary agony for the prisoner'.[49] Significantly, these instances were not drawn from any single execution method. Borg and Radelet conclude that the examples of botched executions 'in different jurisdictions, at different times, and regardless of execution method indicates that they are endemic to the modern practice of capital punishment, and they will continue to be for as long as the punishment remains in use'.[50] This is a significant argument, for it suggests that, regardless of the method of execution (and irrespective of other concerns such as the death row phenomenon, discussed below), the death penalty cannot be implemented without the risk of causing unnecessary suffering for the condemned prisoner. This is our first hint that the death penalty is not (just) about death. Borg and Radelet object to the death penalty on the basis that it 'involves making godlike decisions and taking godlike actions without godlike wisdom or skills'.[51] This argument reflects the philosophical underpinnings of the right to life, discussed in chapter 2, in which life is often regarded as a gift from God, which can only be taken back by its giver. In the context of botched executions,

---

[44] Report of the Royal Commission on Capital Punishment 1949–1953 Cmnd. 8932 (1953), para. 707.   [45] ibid, para. 724.
[46] ibid, para. 729.   [47] ibid, para. 732.
[48] M.J. Borg & M.L. Radelet, 'On Botched Executions' in P. Hodgkinson & W.A. Schabas (eds), *Capital Punishment: Strategies for Abolition* (Cambridge: Cambridge University Press, 2004).
[49] ibid, p. 147.   [50] ibid, pp. 157–8.   [51] ibid, p. 158.

it also indicates that while life is a precious and vulnerable element, all too easily lost, death too can be elusive and hard won.

Another aspect of the need to avoid unnecessary suffering when imposing the death penalty is the so-called death row phenomenon. This is a concept developed under the ECHR, seemingly for the very pragmatic reason of signifying the European Court of Human Rights' disapproval of capital punishment within the confines of enforcing a Convention that expressly permits it. In *Soering v United Kingdom*,[52] the Court first considered whether, despite Article 2(2), evolving standards in respect of the death penalty in Western Europe may have rendered it contrary to Article 3's prohibition of inhuman and degrading punishment. However, although the ECHR is a 'living instrument' and thus susceptible to evolving moral standards, it must also be read as a whole. Therefore, the death penalty cannot be expressly permitted in Article 2 and simultaneously be a violation of Article 3. This is a logical conclusion, although the Court was on less firm ground when it declared that the existence of Protocol 6 (which prohibits the death penalty in peacetime) signified the contracting parties' intention 'to adopt the normal method of amendment of the text in order to introduce a new obligation to abolish capital punishment'.[53] This argument suggests that, while Protocol 6 reveals the evolving trend in Europe to abolish the death penalty, it also reveals the contracting parties' intention to progress towards abolition by means of optional undertakings and thus sends an implicit instruction to the Court not to read this trend into the terms of Article 2 itself. This even suggests that without Protocol 6, the Court might have been inclined to read Article 2 in light of evolving standards as no longer exempting the death penalty from its protection against intentional deprivations of life. Such a conclusion is counter-intuitive, hinting that Protocol 6 has had the effect of halting progress towards abolition in the terms of the right to life itself. Perhaps one way to interpret the Court's views on this issue is to recall that the optional protocols are not framed in terms of the right to life. Therefore, a possible view would be that, while abolition of the death penalty is regarded as a positive move within Europe (perhaps even encouraged by international law), the contracting parties remain wedded to the view that the imposition of the death penalty is not, in itself, a violation of the right to life.

Given the Court's reluctance to regard the death penalty as a violation of Article 3, it moved on to consider whether a combination of circumstances to which the applicant would be exposed if sentenced to death (the 'death row phenomenon') might amount to a violation instead. This ingenious solution enabled the Court to express its dislike of the way in which the death penalty was enforced in the US and by implication the penalty itself. The types of surrounding circumstances regarded as relevant by the Court were broad:

The manner in which it [the death penalty] is imposed or executed, the personal circumstances of the condemned person and a disproportionality to the gravity of the crime

---

[52] (1989) 11 E.H.R.R. 439.   [53] ibid, para. 103.

committed, as well as the conditions of detention awaiting execution, are examples of factors capable of bringing the treatment or punishment received by the condemned person within the proscription under Article 3.[54]

Significantly, the Court was willing to take into account the contemporary attitudes of the contracting parties to capital punishment when assessing the 'acceptable threshold of suffering or degradation'.[55] It is well established under Article 3 that a minimum level of severity must be met before mistreatment becomes a violation of the Article, but it remains noteworthy that the Court is applying this acceptable level of mistreatment to the context of capital punishment, indicating once more that the death penalty is not (just) about death, but will also involve mistreatment of the living prisoner before death, at a level that may or may not surpass the 'acceptable threshold' of suffering. In addition, it is curious that the evolving standards of the contracting parties are relevant in this context but not in the context of whether the death penalty itself has surpassed a morally acceptable contemporary standard.

On the facts of the case, the Court was influenced by the fact that the applicant could have been extradited to Germany rather than the US and so could have been held liable for any crimes committed without facing the penalty of death. The Court regarded this possibility as relevant because 'it goes to the search for the requisite fair balance of interests and to the proportionality of the contested extradition decision'.[56] This is unsatisfactory reasoning, however, because Article 3 is not concerned with balancing interests or with proportionality. Indeed, it is almost alone in Convention articles in not being concerned with such issues. Torture, or inhuman or degrading treatment or punishment is prohibited in all circumstances, regardless of any conflicting interests, and regardless of whether the mistreatment may be proportionate to some conflicting aim. If the circumstances of the applicant facing the death penalty in the US would amount to degrading punishment, then it is prohibited by Article 3. This will hold true even if the result will be a guilty person going free. The possibility of the applicant facing more legitimate punishment elsewhere should be entirely irrelevant to the question of whether he should be extradited to a state where he will face degrading punishment.

The average time spent on death row in Virginia was identified as between six and eight years, largely due to prisoners making use of every possible optional avenue of appeal. The Court refused to place the blame for this delay on the prisoners, however, recognizing that it is 'part of human nature that the person will cling to life by exploiting those safeguards to the full'.[57] The existence of such safeguards is crucial as they help to ensure that 'the ultimate sanction of death is not unlawfully or arbitrarily imposed', but the Court was adamant that, however well-intentioned these procedures are, their consequence is to require condemned prisoners to face years on death row in extremely severe conditions

---

[54] ibid, para. 104.   [55] ibid.   [56] ibid, para. 110.   [57] ibid, para. 106.

with 'the anguish and mounting tension of living in the ever-present shadow of death'.[58] While it might perhaps be argued that we all live in this shadow from the moment we are born, the Court regarded the combination of the mental anguish of being sentenced to death, the strict security conditions on death row, and the personal characteristics of the applicant to amount to a real risk of treatment going beyond the minimum severity threshold of Article 3. In particular, the applicant's age (seventeen at the time of the offence) and mental state influenced the Court in determining a potential violation of Article 3. The Court was quick to acknowledge, however, that the machinery of justice to which the applicant would be subject if extradited to the US 'is in itself neither arbitrary nor unreasonable'.[59]

The focus on the particular characteristics of the applicant, an entirely legitimate, and common, consideration under Article 3, has allowed other courts to avoid reaching the same conclusion upon the death row phenomenon.[60] The HRC in *Kindler v Canada* expressly declined to follow the *Soering* approach by distinguishing *Soering* on the basis of the age and mental state of the offender, as well as the different prison conditions in Pennsylvania.[61] Despite the HRC's demand that the death penalty, when imposed, be carried out 'in such a way as to cause the least possible physical pain and mental suffering',[62] the Committee has repeatedly refused to interpret Article 7 as encompassing a prohibition on lengthy detention prior to execution. In *Errol Johnson v Jamaica*, the HRC emphasized that it did not wish to send the message that executions should be carried out as expeditiously as possible: 'Life on death row, harsh as it may be, is preferable to death . . . The Committee would wish to avoid adopting a line of jurisprudence which weakens the influence of factors that may well lessen the number of prisoners actually executed.'[63] Such subsidiary considerations should not really be taken into account in determining whether a condemned prisoner is being subjected to cruel, inhuman or degrading punishment. If the level of treatment meets that threshold, then a violation of Article 7 should be found, regardless of the strange message that such a finding sends. While Article 6 ICCPR (and Article 2 ECHR) expressly accept the death penalty as a legitimate exception to the right to life, and therefore puts that issue out of bounds for the treaty bodies, they must turn their attention instead to the state's treatment of the living prisoner condemned to death. If such treatment causes unnecessary mental anguish, then the state should be held liable for that. It is an aspect of the argument that the death penalty is not (just) about death, but also about how

---

[58] ibid.   [59] ibid, para. 111.

[60] The European Commission of Human Rights in *Çinar v Turkey* ((1994) 79A DR 5) interpreted *Soering* as not requiring extenuating factors such as age or mental instability in order for a long wait on death row to amount to a violation of Article 3, although no violation was found in this case.   [61] See n. 41 above.

[62] General Comment No. 20, para. 6.

[63] No. 588/1994, para. 8.4. The assumption that life on death row is better than death will be discussed further below.

the state treats the citizen it condemns to death. Notwithstanding this point, it has to be said that the HRC's view on this issue is more intuitive than that of the European Court of Human Rights which seems to be sending a message that executing a prisoner is not a violation of his human rights, but making him wait a long time before being executed is. As sound a line of argument as that may be under the ECHR (and arguably the ICCPR), it is hard to defend on common-sense grounds.

By contrast with the HRC, the Privy Council has applied and developed the *Soering* approach to the death row phenomenon.[64] In *Pratt & Morgan v AG of Jamaica*, the court recognized an 'instinctive revulsion' against hanging a man many years after he has been sentenced to death and regarded that revulsion as based upon our humanity: 'we regard it as an inhuman act to keep a man facing the agony of execution over a long extended period of time'.[65] This conclusion seems debatable. While many would regard it as contrary to our humanity to execute a man, it seems unlikely that those who regard this as acceptable would be repulsed by the thought of doing so some years after the sentence is imposed. The 'instinctive revulsion' will surely arise in respect of the core of the issue—the idea of legitimized state killing—if it is to arise at all. Nevertheless, the Privy Council felt justified in utilizing this perceived reaction to impose a rigid five-year period after the imposition of a death sentence in which an execution must take place. If an execution takes place after the five-year period, the Privy Council held there would be strong grounds for regarding the delay as constituting inhuman or degrading punishment.[66]

While the right to be free from cruel, inhuman or degrading punishment is the most obvious collateral human rights abuse in the context of capital punishment, international treaties and national legal systems also emphasize the need to ensure full protection of the prisoner's right to a fair trial. A death sentence imposed without a fair trial is likely to amount to an arbitrary deprivation of life, despite the general death penalty exceptions in right to life provisions. Given the importance of this issue, it is perhaps surprising that the requirement is implicit rather than explicit in the main treaties. Article 6(2) ICCPR states only that the imposition of a death sentence must not be contrary to the provisions of the Covenant. This has the effect of incorporating all of Article 14 ICCPR's procedural guarantees into Article 6. Thus, in *Mbenge v Zaire*, for example, a sentence of death which was imposed in circumstances breaching the fair trial requirements

---

[64] For discussion of these two contrasting reactions to *Soering*, see W.A. Schabas, '*Soering's* Legacy: The Human Rights Committee and the Judicial Committee of the Privy Council Take a Walk Down Death Row' (1994) 43 I.C.L.Q. 913.   [65] [1993] 4 All ER 769, at p. 783.

[66] ibid, pp. 788–9. The response to this approach in Caribbean states has been negative. See Hood & Hoyle, n. 3 above, pp. 106–7, quoting the Jamaican Justice Minister in 2006 saying that 'the processes cannot be completed in five years'.

of Article 14 ICCPR was held to also be a violation of the right to life.[67] The African Commission on Human and Peoples' Rights has also found a violation of the right to life in respect of a death penalty imposed in circumstances breaching the fair trial provisions of the Charter.[68] Similarly, while Article 2 ECHR imposes no explicit restrictions on the death penalty, it does expressly require that a sentence of death be handed down by a 'court' and that the penalty is 'provided by law'. These are not extensive procedural rights but they do impose a requirement that a death sentence be imposed in a non-arbitrary manner in order to qualify as a legitimate exception to the right to life. Furthermore, in *Ocalan v Turkey*, a Grand Chamber of the European Court of Human Rights confirmed that the implementation of a death sentence following an unfair trial will amount to a violation of both Articles 2 and 3.[69]

The requirement that a sentence of death be imposed only after a fair trial offers vital protection from arbitrary state power over life and death. It should be relatively easy for a state to ensure that the fair trial requirements are satisfied, at least in capital cases. (Although the US's continued difficulties in this context, especially in relation to inadequate legal representation, suggest that no state can eliminate such problems entirely.) While collateral violations of the right to a fair trial may be less significant in undermining the continued legitimacy of the death penalty than violations in respect of cruel, inhuman or degrading punishment, it may be far harder for a state to eliminate all aspects of unfairness and arbitrariness in the context of capital punishment. This is an issue that dominates the death penalty debate in the US, following the US Supreme Court's decision in *Furman v Georgia*[70] that the imposition of the death penalty was unconstitutional (and its rapid reversal of that decision in *Gregg v Georgia* four years later).[71] The main issue raised in *Furman v Georgia* was whether the death penalty was fairly imposed in the US given its disproportionate implementation against poor and/or black prisoners. Justice Douglas made clear that it was impossible to assert that the defendants in this case, both black, were sentenced to death because of their race. However, he argued that if a law expressly stated that the rich were exempt from the death penalty, or that it was restricted to black, uneducated and poor defendants, it would be held to be unconstitutional and a law which reaches the same result in practice should be treated the same way.[72] The problem with the law in this case was that 'no

---

[67] Communication 16/1977. Many cases involving Caribbean states under the ICCPR have reached similar conclusions. However, not all violations of the fair trial provisions in capital trials will result in violations of the right to life. An unreasonable delay, for example, may not indicate that the substance of the trial has been unjust. (See *Brown and Parish v Jamaica* (Communication 665/1995).)

[68] *International Pen, Constitutional Rights Project, Interights on behalf of Ken Saro-Wiwa Jr and Civil Liberties Organisation v Nigeria* (137/94, 139/94, 154/96, 161/97).   [69] 2005-IV.

[70] (1972) 408 US 238.   [71] (1976) 428 US 153.

[72] *Furman v Georgia*, n. 70 above, p. 256.

standards govern the selection of the penalty. People live or die, dependent on the whim of one man or of twelve.'[73] The aspect of this which most concerned the Supreme Court was the rarity of the imposition of the death penalty and the lack of any meaningful basis for distinguishing between those few prisoners subjected to it and the many who, despite committing apparently equally heinous crimes, were not so subjected. Justice Brennan argued that 'When a country of over 200 million people inflicts an unusually severe punishment no more than 50 times a year, the inference is strong that the punishment is not being regularly and fairly applied.'[74] In the words of Justice Stewart, the death penalty could be 'so wantonly and so freakishly imposed' that the few prisoners sentenced to death amounted to a 'capriciously selected random few'; a death sentence was equivalent to being struck by lightning.[75] It is easy to see the potential objection to a line of reasoning which seems to suggest that too few people are being executed. Would more deaths be better? (In a similar way, perhaps, to how sooner deaths are preferred under the *Soering* legacy?) The dissenting Justices in this case developed this point, arguing that the very infrequency of death sentences imposed by jurors 'attests their cautious and discriminating reservation of that penalty for the most extreme cases'.[76] Justice Burger noted the irony in the majority's apparent conclusion that the flexible sentencing system 'has yielded more mercy than the Eighth Amendment can stand'.[77] The majority's finding of an Eighth Amendment violation in respect of the death penalty did not endure for long. The violation was connected to the arbitrary imposition of the penalty, rather than the penalty itself, and so revised state laws were soon enacted to attempt to remove the arbitrariness and capriciousness from the decision to impose a death sentence. A total of thirty-five states enacted new statutes following *Furman* and in *Gregg v Georgia* the Supreme Court acknowledged that the concerns expressed in *Furman* could be met 'by a carefully drafted statute that ensures that the sentencing authority is given adequate information and guidance'.[78] The revised Georgia statutes achieved this by requiring the jury to consider the specific circumstances of the crime and the criminal before it hands down a death sentence: 'No longer can a Georgia jury do as Furman's jury did: reach a finding of the defendant's guilt and then without guidance or direction, decide whether he should live or die.'[79]

The need for full consideration of aggravating and mitigating circumstances before the imposition of a death penalty is an important step towards avoiding an arbitrary deprivation of life, particularly when coupled with proportionality review, as in the Georgian procedure, but it does not go to the crux of the problem alluded to in *Furman*, namely that poor, black, male Americans are disproportionality likely to face the death penalty. The inherent problem in this most

[73] ibid, p. 253.   [74] ibid, p. 293.   [75] ibid, pp. 309–10.
[76] ibid, p. 402 (per Justice Burger).   [77] ibid, p. 398.
[78] *Gregg v Georgia*, n. 71 above, p. 195.   [79] ibid, p. 197.

extreme of legal punishments is that its mandatory imposition must be avoided but, as soon as discretion is introduced, we are entrusting a judge or jury with the power of life and death. We must trust that the discretionary power to sentence an individual to death will not be used in an arbitrary or discriminatory manner, and stricter guidance certainly helps with that leap of faith, but in an imperfect and unequal society the possibility of conscious, or unconscious, misuse of such a vital discretion cannot be ruled out. Thus, we have discovered another collateral problem with the death penalty, one that threatens to overwhelm its legitimacy. Justice Blackman, formerly a supporter of the death penalty, changed his mind due to this very issue:

Experience has taught us that the constitutional goal of eliminating arbitrariness and discrimination from the administration of death...can never be achieved without compromising an equally essential component of fundamental fairness—individualized sentencing... It is virtually self-evident to me that no combination of procedural rules or substantive regulations can ever save the death penalty from its inherent constitutional deficiencies.[80]

If Justice Blackman is correct that arbitrariness and discrimination can never be eradicated from the imposition of the death penalty, and the evidence so far suggests that its eradication has not been possible, we must either agree with him that this defeats all arguments for the constitutional legitimacy of the penalty, or take a more pragmatic view, proposed by Pojman, that 'unequal justice is no less justice, however uneven its application'.[81] Pojman's view is that, while legal practices should be reformed as much as possible in an attempt to eradicate unjust discrimination, we should not despair if we cannot achieve equality in the imposition of the death penalty: 'if we are not allowed to have a law without perfect application, we will be forced to have no laws at all.' While it is undoubtedly true that laws are often applied in imperfect manners, we should not overlook the fact that the imposition of a death sentence is a life and death decision which is ultimately irreversible. 'Unequal justice' in this context is just not good enough.

In this section, we have encountered a number of collateral human rights abuses which frequently, perhaps even inevitably, accompany capital punishment. These abuses vary from the imposition of degrading punishment prior to, and/or during, the execution; due process failures; and arbitrariness or discrimination in the exercise of a discretionary power to impose a death sentence. These worrisome issues contribute to an argument that the death penalty is not (just) about death. The problems inherent in the imposition of capital punishment are not limited to the intentional deprivation of life by the state but rather extend to concerns about mental anguish, conditions on death row, unfair trials and racial

[80] *Collins v Collins* (1994) 510 US 1141.
[81] L.P. Pojman, 'Why the Death Penalty is Morally Permissible' in H.A. Bedau (ed.), *Debating the Death Penalty: Should America have Capital Punishment? The Experts on Both Sides make their Best Case* (Oxford: Oxford University Press, 2004), pp. 70–1.

discrimination. Setting to one side the question of whether the death penalty is truly reconcilable with the right to life, it is inconsistent with the array of other human rights owed to individuals. It is a violation of human rights, irrespective of the actual taking of life.

The argument that the death penalty is not (just) about death also has a further string to it. If the ending of life was the crucial element in a judicial execution, then prisoners on death row would not need to be on suicide watch. The fact that death row prisoners are actively prevented from taking their own lives (and that many wish to do so) suggests that the death penalty contains an additional punishment beyond mere death. This additional punishment may stem from the method of execution, or from its public nature or, perhaps most significantly, from its nature as a killing by the state, signifying as it does that the prisoner's own community has rejected his very existence. Jonathan Glover engages with this issue when he argues that a person sentenced to death faces the additional fear of knowing that his death 'will be in a ritualized killing by other people, symbolising his ultimate rejection by members of his community'.[82] The Royal Commission also alluded to this issue when it considered, and rejected, the idea of offering a prisoner a lethal dose enabling him to commit suicide should he wish to do so the night before the execution: 'The purpose of capital punishment is not just to rid the community of an unwanted member; it is to mark the community's denunciation of the gravest of all crimes by subjecting the perpetrator, by due forms of law, to the severest of all punishments.'[83] It appears, therefore, that not only does the death penalty carry with it frequent (perhaps inevitable) collateral human rights violations, but it also encompasses an additional punishment beyond that of death. Some supporters of the death penalty argue that life imprisonment without the possibility of parole is a worse punishment than death but, as Bedau has pointed out, 'those in the best position to know behave in a manner that suggests otherwise',[84] clinging to life until there is no hope left. The death penalty is not (just) about death but, because it includes death as part of its punishment, it is the most extreme and severe punishment that exists, and this is its very point: 'This is why its opponents want to abolish it—and why its supporters want to keep it.'[85] Let us now investigate why its supporters want to retain the death penalty, and why it is regarded as a legitimate exception to the right to life, while bearing in mind that the deprivation of life at the heart of the death penalty is only the starting point, both for the punishment

---

[82] J. Glover, *Causing Death and Saving Lives* (London: Penguin, 1977), p. 232.

[83] Royal Commission Report, n. 44 above, para. 769. This Commission's conclusion on this point was influenced by the fact that suicide was both a crime and (according to the Archbishop of Canterbury) a sin. Suicide is no longer a crime in the UK, and not all members of society will be influenced by the religious argument that it is a sin, so the question arises: if it is neither a crime nor a sin for the prisoner to commit suicide the night before his scheduled execution, does the Royal Commission's objection still stand?

[84] H.A. Bedau, 'An Abolitionist's Survey of the Death Penalty in America Today' in Bedau, n. 81 above, p. 35.   [85] ibid.

that it encompasses and the limitation of the condemned prisoner's rights that it entails.

(2) The death penalty as an exception to the right to life

As the pages of this book make clear, there are a number of claimed exceptions to the right to life, some easier to justify than others, but none more counter-intuitive than the death penalty. As Schabas has argued, 'while the other exceptions are logical and self-evident, there is something contradictory and incompatible about recognising a right to life and at the same time permitting capital punishment'.[86] The following section will consider whether there are sufficiently weighty reasons for recognizing the death penalty as a legitimate exception to the right to life.

(a) Retributive arguments: death is what the prisoner deserves

There is an ancient tradition that execution is a fitting punishment for murder which can be traced back to biblical pronouncements such as 'who so sheddeth man's blood, by man shall his blood be shed',[87] and beyond. In later centuries, deontological theorists argued that rational agents who kill deserve to die. Kant, for example, argued that only death could suffice as a just punishment for murder: 'In this case, no possible substitute can satisfy justice. For there is no parallel between death and even the most miserable life, so that there is no equality of crime and retribution unless the perpetuator is judicially put to death.'[88] Retributive theory declares that a criminal deserves a punishment that fits the gravity of his crime. For the most extreme crime, the most extreme punishment is only fitting. Or, in other words, 'a life for a life'.[89] One of the difficulties with this simplistic approach is that if a murderer deserves death, then surely a rapist deserves to be raped as punishment, and a torturer tortured? And yet society shirks from such results. There are further logical difficulties with the just desert argument. For example, how do we satisfactorily punish a serial murderer? The state only kills him once. Should it repeatedly kill and then revive and then kill again? At the other end of the scale, many relatively minor crimes are currently punished far more severely than would be proportionate with the harm caused. A thief is not deprived of his property but is rather deprived of his liberty: a far more precious commodity.[90] Society does not, it seems, always feel that the

---

[86] Schabas, n. 7 above, pp. 7–8.   [87] Genesis 9:6.

[88] I. Kant, *Groundwork of the Metaphysics of Morals* (ed. L. Pasternack, London: Routledge, 2002), p. 156.

[89] Exodus 21:23–24. The famous pronouncement of 'life for life, eye for eye, tooth for tooth', etc. could actually be regarded as an argument for restraint: taking a life is not a fitting punishment for the loss of an eye.

[90] The reason for this relatively severe punishment may be based upon the fact that the chances of getting caught are fairly slim and so a punishment that was equal to the harm caused would be highly unlikely to act as a deterrent. See J. Reiman, 'Why the Death Penalty should be Abolished

punishment should mirror the crime; but rather that the punishment should be proportionate to the crime. A thief should be punished less severely than a rapist who should be punished less severely than a murderer who should be punished less severely than a multiple murderer. The state punishes not in a manner equal to crime but in a manner proportionate to it.[91] But why does it do this? Is the *lex talionis* argument—that a criminal should receive a punishment matching his crime—inherently flawed? Or do civilized states merely choose to exercise mercy by not extracting the fitting punishment? Reiman has argued, convincingly, that 'even though it would be just to rape rapists and torture torturers, other moral considerations weigh against doing so'.[92] If this is true, then we can easily extend this moral prohibition to killing a murderer. The convicted murderer may deserve to die as punishment for his crime, but for the state to kill him would violate his right to life. It may also send a mixed message on the importance of preserving human life within that society. The latter point is arguable because it remains unclear how the lesson that taking human life is wrong is best taught. Does society best teach this lesson by subjecting murderers to the ultimate penalty or by refusing to let a further human life be taken in its name? Opponents of the death penalty, such as Reiman, take the view that a refusal to execute even those who deserve it has a civilizing effect and teaches a lesson about the wrongfulness of murder.[93] He argues that 'refusing to execute murderers though they deserve it both reflects and continues that taming of the human species that we call civilization—and it should, over time, contribute to reducing the incidence of murder'.[94]

An alternative conflicting moral consideration mentioned above, which may weigh against executing a murderer, even if that is what he deserves, is his right to life. It seems axiomatic that capital punishment violates the right of every human being not to be arbitrarily deprived of his life. However, as we have seen in the discussion above, various international treaties proclaiming this right perceive the death penalty as an exception to it. How is this exception justified? One retributive argument in favour of the death penalty which directly engages the right to life is the forfeiture argument. This is the view that the right to life, rather than being overridden by another's right or by a societal interest, is forfeited by some criminals.[95] The argument is based on the idea that by violating another's right to life, a murderer forfeits his own. This is flawed reasoning, however, because a murderer does not violate another human being's right to life; only the state can do that. There is no direct horizontal effect in respect of the right to life. The murderer takes a life; the state punishes him. There is no violation of the victim's right to life, despite the tragic destruction of a human life by another citizen. Only if the state

in America' in L.P. Pojman & J. Reiman, *The Death Penalty: For and Against* (Lanham: Rowman & Littlefield Publishers, 1998), p. 73.

[91] See L.P. Pojman, 'For the Death Penalty' in Pojman & Reiman, ibid, p. 12.
[92] Reiman, in Pojman & Reiman, ibid, p. 95.   [93] ibid, p. 106.   [94] ibid, p. 116.
[95] See, for example, Pojman in Pojman & Reiman, ibid, p. 30.

inadequately protected the victim, or fails to punish the murderer, will the right to life be engaged. It is not possible, therefore, to regard capital punishment as a like-for-like response to a murder. The executed prisoner's right to life is violated by the state (subject to the recognition of a legitimate exception to the right) but there has been no prior right to life violation initiated by the prisoner. This illustrates once more the fact that the death penalty is not (just) about death: a prisoner killed by the state has his right to life (prima facie) violated; the unfortunate victim of his crimes does not. Two deaths; one violation of the right to life, because the state, and the state alone, is responsible for protecting and respecting this right.[96]

The background to the forfeiture argument is a willingness to accord different values to different human lives. This can be seen clearly in Pojman's writing on the death penalty. He considers two possible bases for the value of human life: religious and secular. This reflects, to some extent, the discussion in chapter 2 on the philosophical background to the right to life. It will be recalled that the concept of the sanctity of human life developed from a religious perspective but was later consolidated through secular reasoning. Pojman argues that, if human life is valued because of a religious view that human beings 'have a dignity that is based on a transcendent trait, then the fact that we have freely killed a child of God leads to the judgment that we deserve to be executed for our malicious act'.[97] In Pojman's view, the secular justification for the value of life is based on the idea that 'we have no value apart from our moral character and social function', and thus, again, the execution of a murderer can be justified, this time because the criminal manifests a corrupt soul 'so destroying them is good riddance to bad rubbish'.[98] The problem with Pojman's reasoning is that in both instances he misunderstands the *reason* for valuing life. This can most clearly be seen in his reasoning from a secular point of view. Pojman argues that, from a secular viewpoint (and thus disregarding any 'transcendent trait' bestowed by God), what gives us worth is 'some quality like moral integrity or contribution to the community'.[99] But this is a very misleading explanation of the secular justification for the value of life. It focuses entirely on the instrumental value of a right to life while excluding all inherent value. This is not the secular viewpoint; it is an aspect of the secular viewpoint. If we refer, for example, to Dworkin's famous discussion of the value of life, we can see that there is both a natural (whether God-given or otherwise) and a human investment in human life, that both contribute to its inherent value.[100] Excluding all consideration of religion, we can still find value in human life due to its representation of the culmination of millennia of evolution, human

---

[96] This is perhaps an overly simplistic conclusion because there are circumstances in which the state may be liable for a violation of the victim's right to life: for example, due to inadequate policing or even a failure to punish adequately so as to deter other potential murderers. But crucially it is the state and not the murderer who will be so liable.

[97] Pojman in Pojman & Reiman, n. 90 above, at pp. 36–7.   [98] ibid.

[99] ibid, p. 44.

[100] R. Dworkin, *Life's Dominion: An Argument about Abortion and Euthanasia* (London: HarperCollins, 1993), pp. 82–4.

culture and development, as well as its reflection of internal personal creation. We are of value partly because of the investment, through choices, values and priorities, that we each put into our own lives, as well as the investments that others put into those lives. We are not just of value because either we are created by God or we are useful to the community. The danger in such a view can be seen by Pojman's willingness to accord differing values to different human beings, based upon their (perceived) morality. Pojman even goes so far as to estimate 'the utility value of a murderer's life', which he puts at 5, in contrast to the value of 'an innocent's life', which he puts at 10 (although he later states his preferred equation of 1,000 to 1).[101] While acknowledging that 'we cannot give lives exact numerical values', he nevertheless proceeds to 'make rough comparative estimates of value'.[102] The latter is no less objectionable than the former. It is this comparative exercise that facilitates arguments that a criminal forfeits his right to life, for his life no longer has as much (if any) value as that of other members of society. Pojman makes this assumption explicit, while many other supporters of the death penalty rely on it in a more implicit manner. It enables supporters of the death penalty to claim that it is because they value human life, rather than because they disvalue it, that they support the state taking the lives of those who have forfeited the right to live. Whether express or implied, this reasoning depends upon a very special, and controversial, concept of the value of life. It requires us to accept that our lives are of value, primarily, because of the good to which we put those lives, but it overlooks inherent value and misconceives the human investments in life, which do not depend upon our good to society but upon our effort in creating a unique entity. Some of those unique entities may be evil; they may do more harm than good; and they may deserve to be punished for the harm they have done. But as human lives, they have value, and a value no less than any other. That value cannot be forfeited, and neither can the right to life that it underlies.

(b) Deterrent arguments: take one life to save others

Distinct from the forfeiture argument, is the argument that some lives have to be destroyed by the state in order to protect others in society, not (just) as punishment for the individual for past crimes, but as a deterrent to others. In other words, there is an argument that the death penalty may be justified not on retributive grounds but as the best means of protecting society from future crimes which may endanger their lives. This argument is based upon a recognition that the state is liable for protecting all lives, not just the lives of those in its custody. While an execution will violate the condemned prisoner's right to life, it is possible that a failure to execute (if this will entail a failure to present an effective deterrent) may put other members of society at risk of murder and thus infringe their rights to life also.

---

[101] Pojman in Pojman & Reiman, n. 90 above, p. 40.   [102] ibid.

The background to arguments on deterrent effect is a utilitarian argument. If the execution of a murderer deters more people from murdering than other lesser punishments, it has a utilitarian value. Sorrell explains this justification as follows: 'If capital punishment deters violent criminals and the benefit to members of the general public exceeds the distress of the executed criminals and others affected by their deaths, then the execution of those criminals is right or at least morally permissible.'[103] Such a balancing suffers somewhat from a failure to regard each individual human life as something of value regardless of potential costs and benefits to society in preserving that life. Sorrell recognizes this potential criticism that utilitarianism 'does not recognise the separateness of persons'.[104] This is an old and tried issue, however,[105] and perhaps a more pressing problem with a utilitarian justification for the death penalty is that it depends entirely upon evidence as to deterrent effect. And the evidence of this is far from satisfactory. While some studies report a strong deterrent effect, and one that cannot be equalled by other punishments,[106] other studies negate these conclusions,[107] leaving one inclined to agree with Hodgkinson that the deterrence justification 'provides more heat than light'.[108] Even though there is wide acknowledgement of the ambiguous research findings on deterrence, some supporters of the death penalty resort to making so-called common-sense cases for deterrence.[109] A better view is that of Hood and Hoyle who conclude that it is not 'prudent' to accept a stronger deterrent effect for capital punishment without stronger evidence to support it.[110]

Even if we put to one side the argument over proof of deterrence, we can still pursue the issue of whether a proven deterrent effect would justify an exception to the right to life for the death penalty. This is exactly the path adopted by Sunstein and Vermeule, who, for the purposes of their argument, assume a deterrent effect for capital punishment. The question is whether, even if capital punishment deters other potential murderers, it is an acceptable violation of an individual's right to life. Sunstein and Vermeule conclude that it is and they even go further, arguing that in such circumstances capital punishment may be morally required.[111] Their

[103] T. Sorell, *Moral Theory and Capital Punishment* (Oxford: Basil Blackwell, 1987), p. 57.
[104] ibid, p. 67.
[105] See, for example, J. Rawls' critique of utilitarianism in *A Theory of Justice* (Cambridge: Harvard University Press, 1971).
[106] See, for example, I. Ehrlich, 'The Deterrent Effect of Capital Punishment: A Question of Life and Death' (1975) American Economic Review 397.
[107] For a response to the above cited article, see W.L. Bowers & G.L. Pierce, 'The Illusion of Deterrence in Isaac Ehrlich's Research on Capital Punishment' (1975) 85 Yale Law Journal 187.
[108] P. Hodgkinson, 'Capital Punishment: Improve it or Remove it?' in Hodgkinson & Schabas, n. 48 above, p. 8.
[109] See, for example, L.P. Pojman, 'Why the Death Penalty is Morally Permissible' in Bedau, n. 81 above, who bases his conclusions on comparison with a hypothetical cosmic punishment of being struck by lightning immediately after killing. He argues that this would have a strong deterrent effect and thus by analogy so does the less immediate and less consistent judicially imposed death sentence (pp. 58–9.)   [110] Hood & Hoyle, n. 3 above, p. 347, and generally chapter 9.
[111] C.R. Sunstein & A. Vermeule, 'Is Capital Punishment Morally Required? Acts, Omissions, and Life-Life Tradeoffs' (2005–06) 58 Stan.L.Rev. 703.

argument is based on the proposition that, for governments, acts are not morally different from omissions. Thus, a failure to execute murderers which costs lives (of future victims of future murderers undeterred by a lesser punishment) is equally culpable as an execution. The act/omission distinction which is ingrained in many states' domestic laws, including that of the UK, generally provides culpability for an omission only in circumstances where there is a duty to act. If applied superficially to the issue of state killing by means of the imposition of a death sentence, the act/omission distinction would hold the state liable for the death of the executed prisoner but not for any deaths stemming from a failure to deter potential murderers by declining to execute a convicted murderer. Sunstein and Vermeule, however, argue that the act/omission distinction is not applicable in the context of government regulation: 'The only interesting question or even meaningful question government ever faces is not whether to act, but what action should be taken—what mix of criminal justice policies government ought to pursue. The policy mix that does not include capital punishment is not an "omission" or a "failure to act" in any meaningful sense.'[112] If this is true, and assuming a deterrent effect to capital punishment greater than that stemming from life imprisonment can be proven, then a government must make a choice between saving the life of the convicted murderer or saving the lives of future victims of other murderers. Thus, the government would be concerned in balancing conflicting rights to life, rather than finding a societal interest that overrode a single right to life, and in this balance, even without accepting the reduced value of life argument outlined above, a reasoned answer is likely to favour the saving of many lives over that of one.[113] The failure of most governments, and citizens, to see the issue in these terms may be explained by the reduced significance often accorded to 'statistical lives', such as potential future homicide victims, which Sunstein and Vermeule claim are 'pervasively neglected in policy, in part for cognitive reasons'.[114] The rejection of the act/omission distinction for governments has some merit to it, as will be seen in chapter 9. However, Steiker, in response to Sunstein and Vermeule, argues that a distinction can be made between the regulatory context and the criminal justice context on the basis that in the former, government acts and omissions are not done with the purpose of taking human life, whereas when the state executes a prisoner, it is purposefully taking life.[115] These are not, in Steiker's view, morally equivalent choices. Related to this point, is the argument that capital punishment is not merely killing but is also an unjust punishment. This is another instance of the argument that the death penalty is not (just) about death. When the state kills its citizen following the imposition of a death sentence, it is enacting a judicial punishment. If that punishment is disproportionate or undignified or cruel or applied

---

[112] ibid, p. 722.
[113] This is not necessarily true but the issue will be discussed further in the next chapter.
[114] Sunstein & Vermeule, n. 111 above, p. 740.
[115] C.S. Steiker, 'No, Capital Punishment is Not Morally Required: Deterrence, Deontology, and the Death Penalty' (2006) 58 Stan.L.Rev. 751, at p. 757.

in a discriminatory manner, then it is an unjust punishment. Therefore, 'executions, as punishments, have the capacity to be morally problematic in ways that go beyond their wrongness as "killing".[116] This is one of the factors that distinguish capital punishment from the use of lethal force to prevent a crime. The latter is not a punishment for criminal action, but (when justified) a necessary preventative measure. An execution, even if proven to have some deterrent effect and thus serve to some extent as a preventative measure to save future lives, is also a punishment for past behaviour, and must be justly imposed. Sunstein and Vermeule query why the death penalty is any different from killing a hostage-taker to save the hostages: 'police officers are permitted to kill (execute) those who have taken hostages if this step is reasonably deemed necessary to save those who have been taken hostage. If the evidence of deterrence is convincing, why is capital punishment so different in principle?'[117] There are numerous convincing answers to this: the risk to the hostages is real and immediate, unlike that of potential future murder victims; lethal force is directed at the cause of the risk, rather than at someone who is safely confined in prison;[118] and the killing is solely a deprivation of life, without the collateral abuses inherent in a judicial execution. We will shortly see that the use of lethal force to prevent crime must always be restricted to situations where there is no viable alternative, but that is never true in respect of the death penalty. There is always an alternative. Even if the state sometimes has to kill, to save others, it does not have to kill as a punishment, and neither retributive nor deterrent arguments can provide a strong enough case for doing so.

B. The use of lethal force to prevent crime

Three examples of the use of lethal force (purportedly) to prevent crime will illustrate the breadth of cases included in this section. In March 1988, three members of the IRA, Daniel McCann, Mairead Farrell and Sean Savage, were shot dead on the streets of Gibraltar. They were suspected of planning to detonate a car bomb on the island and were killed by members of the SAS who fired a total of twenty-seven shots at close range into these three individuals. None of the suspects were armed. In August 1999, a Norfolk farmer, Tony Martin, shot dead a 16-year-old burglar who broke into his home. In July 2005 Jean Charles de Menezes, a Brazilian national, was shot dead on the London underground by members of the

---

[116] ibid, p. 774.   [117] Sunstein & Vermeule, n. 111 above, p. 719.
[118] The Constitutional Court of South Africa's judgment in *State v Makwanyane* recognized the important distinction between killing in self-defence and capital punishment: 'Self-defence takes place at the time of the threat to the victim's life, at the moment of the emergency which gave rise to the necessity and, traditionally, under circumstances in which no less-severe alternative is readily available to the potential victim. Killing by the State takes place long after the crime was committed, at a time when there is no emergency and under circumstances which permit the careful consideration of alternative punishment' (n. 6 above, para. 138).

Metropolitan Police. He was mistakenly identified as a suspected suicide bomber. A total of eleven shots were fired by the armed police at close range. The legal outcome in each of these three cases has been extremely controversial. The Gibraltar operation was regarded as amounting to a violation of the right to life by the European Court of Human Rights by a narrow majority, a decision criticized by the British government. Tony Martin was initially convicted of murder by a jury but had the conviction reduced to manslaughter on the basis of diminished responsibility. No criminal charges have been brought against any member of the Metropolitan Police for the de Menezes shooting, but the Metropolitan Police service was found guilty under the health and safety laws for its actions that day and an inquest jury (denied the opportunity to make a finding of unlawful killing by the judge) has recently returned an open verdict. Five lives were lost in these three cases. One of the lives lost (that of de Menezes) was entirely innocent, the others were engaged in or planning a criminal offence, but death is not usually regarded as a just punishment for a burglary, and even those planning to detonate a bomb are entitled to due process. Does an individual lose his right to life when he engages in a criminal enterprise (or is suspected of doing so)? What is the justification for the taking of human life in this context?

(1) The use of lethal force to prevent crime

All three cases above arose under English law, which provides a clear authority for the use of force, even lethal force, in order to prevent crime. Section 3 of the Criminal Law Act 1967 states that 'Any person may use such force as is reasonable in the circumstances in the prevention of crime, or in effecting or assisting in the lawful arrest of offenders or suspected offenders or of persons unlawfully at large.' It is obvious that the key word in this provision is 'reasonable'. Force is authorized provided that it is a reasonable response to the situation. In some circumstances, lethal force may, therefore, be justified but only if it can be regarded as reasonable in the circumstances. There is also a common law defence of self-defence but it is likely that force used to defend oneself against an attack is likely also to be force used to prevent crime and thus most cases can be subsumed into the 1967 Act. While the authorization of such force as is reasonable in the circumstances may seem straightforward, section 3 hides a hidden complexity: is the reasonableness of the force used to be judged on an objective basis or judged subjectively in the view of the defendant? Caselaw, and now the Criminal Justice and Immigration Act 2008, has determined that the defendant is to be judged on the reasonableness of the force in the circumstances as he believed them to be (regardless of whether that belief was reasonable or not).[119] It is thus an objective test on that issue. However, the 2008 Act, which is described as 'intended to clarify the operation of the existing defences',[120] declares that evidence that a defendant used force that he 'honestly and instinctively thought was necessary' will be strong evidence that such

---

[119] *R v Gladstone Williams* (1984) 78 Cr App R 276 (CA); section 76(3) Criminal Justice and Immigration Act 2008.   [120] Section 76(9).

force was objectively reasonable.[121] The Act also requires the courts to take into account the fact that a person acting for a legitimate purpose 'may not be able to weigh to a nicety the exact measure of any necessary action'.[122] This is an important consideration because it is all too easy to be guided by hindsight in determining whether the force used was reasonable and to permit this may be unduly harsh for a defendant who acted instinctively while in perceived danger. Section 76 of the Criminal Justice and Immigration Act 2008 was a direct response to the Tony Martin case mentioned above. The conviction of Martin was greeted by some public outcry and various proposals for new legislation to protect the rights of householders.[123] The government took the view, quite rightly, that the existing law already provides adequate legal protection for householders, and others, who use reasonable force in response to a criminal threat. However, section 76 enabled this position to be clarified and for the courts to be encouraged to give due regard to the fear and panic which may give rise to the use of greater force than was strictly necessary to avert a threat of unlawful violence. It should be noted that, in contrast with the English test of reasonableness of force, Article 2 ECHR permits lethal force only when it is 'absolutely necessary' for one of a specified number of reasons. It seems clear that a test of necessity of force goes beyond a reasonableness test and may cause problems for English law's compatibility with Article 2.[124]

It is worth noting that section 3 Criminal Law Act 1967 does not only authorize the use of force against a threat of unlawful violence but whenever it is reasonable in order to prevent crime. This suggests that in principle lethal force might be justified in order to protect property, but the question is whether such force could ever be reasonable. In England, such a question will be left to a jury to decide. Other legal systems take varying views. In Canada, the Supreme Court has expressly ruled out the possibility of a legitimate use of lethal force to protect property,[125] and the possibility also seems to be excluded in Scotland.[126] In France, there is a general defence in respect of force used to interrupt the commission of a crime against property provided that the force used was 'strictly necessary for the intended objective and the means used are proportionate to the gravity of the offence'.[127] However, while force is justified in such circumstances, this defence does not apply to 'wilful murder' and therefore lethal force will not be regarded as acceptable by French law to defend property.[128] In German law, it

---

[121] Section 76(7)(b).

[122] Section 76(7)(a). Both points in section 76(7) are drawn from Lord Morris in *Palmer v R* [1971] 1 All ER 1077 at 1078 (PC).

[123] David Ormerod describes the 'considerable public concern, fuelled by misinformed newspaper reports, and a resulting clamour for a new law to protect the rights of householders' which led to section 76, a provision that Ormerod regards as 'a very strange provision, seeming merely to restate the common law' (Smith & Hogan, *Criminal Law* (12th edn., ed. D. Ormerod, Oxford: Oxford University Press, 2008), p. 372).

[124] The position under the ECHR will be considered in greater detail below.

[125] *R v Gunning* [2005] 1 SCR 627.   [126] *McCluskey v HM Advocate* (1959) JC 39.

[127] Article 122–5 *Code Pénal*.

[128] See J.R. Spencer, 'Intended Killings in French Law' in J. Horder (ed.), *Homicide Law in Comparative Perspective* (Oxford: Hart Publishing, 2007), p. 47.

is possible that lethal force to protect property may be justified as German law's consequentalist approach would weigh the aggressor's life against both the property interest and the wider public interest in defending the legal order.[129] This latter point is also clearly expressed in the 1967 South African case of *In re S Van Wyk*: 'One who invades another's rights, who defiantly ignores the prohibition, warning and resistance of the defender so that he can only be prevented by the most extreme measures can with good reasons be seen as the author of his own misfortune.'[130] Leverick rejects this view on the basis that 'human life is always worth more than property' and this seems a preferable approach. While some degree of reasonable force may be justified in order to prevent a crime against property, it can never be reasonable to take a human life in order to protect property, regardless of the rights and wrongs of the situation. If the threat to property evolves into a threat to life, as for example in the cases of violent intruders into homes, then lethal force may potentially be justified but in order to save life, not property.

A more difficult scenario is the use of lethal force to prevent a rape in which there is known to be no threat to life. Rape is a more serious threat than a property offence but, if the potential rape victim's life is not in danger, is he or she justified in killing the attacker if that is known to be the only way to prevent the rape? In English law, this issue would again be left to a jury on the basis of the reasonableness of such a use of force, but in Scots law the issue is complicated by the fact that rape remains a gender-specific crime, thus a woman might be entitled to use lethal force to prevent a rape, but a man would not be so entitled. This point was made clear in *McCluskey v HM Advocate* where it was held that a man can only kill in self-defence in order to save his life.[131] In Canada, self-defence requires a reasonable apprehension of death or grievous bodily harm.[132] Whether rape would always, sometimes or never be regarded as such harm remains open to question.[133] The US Model Penal Code, as well as the penal codes of some US states, provides that deadly force may be justifiable where there is a threat of, inter alia, sexual intercourse compelled by force or threat.[134] Any extension beyond self-defence in order to save life is problematic, however. There may be adequate justification for lethal force against an aggressor threatening one's own life or the life of another person, but if the threat is of some bodily harm less than death, how can we possibly justify taking the aggressor's life? As Leverick argues, 'the life of even a terrorist or kidnapper is worth more than the bodily integrity of another person'.[135] This argument is based on an assumption that a deprivation of life is worse than any other attack on bodily integrity (although Leverick does leave open the question of whether prolonged and painful torture might be as ser-

[129] See F. Leverick, *Killing in Self-defence* (Oxford: Oxford University Press, 2006), p. 135.
[130] (1967) 1 SA 488, quoted in Leverick, ibid, p. 134.   [131] (1959) JC 39.
[132] Section 34(2)(a) Canadian Criminal Code.   [133] See Leverick, n. 129 above, p. 146.
[134] Section 3.04(2)(b) US Model Penal Code. See Leverick, ibid, p. 145.
[135] Leverick, ibid, p. 152.

ious a harm as a deprivation of life). The broader issues raised by such a comparison of bodily harms will be better dealt with in a later chapter on quality of life as
a potential conflicting interest to the right to life. In the context of self-defence,
it is worth bearing in mind that any threat of serious bodily harm is likely to be
accompanied by reasonable fear as to a threat to life. In such circumstances, lethal
force may be justifiable against the aggressor on the basis of a perceived threat to
life, rather than the prevention of bodily harm. It is also in this context in which
it is vital to judge the defendant's actions without the benefit of hindsight. An
honest belief in a threat to life, in circumstances such as an intruder into the
home at night-time, or a rape, is likely to be given the benefit of the doubt, even
if objectively and in hindsight the threat was of a lesser form of bodily harm. But
a genuine belief that there is a threat to life that can only be repelled by the use of
lethal force is essential if such extreme force is to be justifiable. A threat to bodily
harm less than a deprivation of life will not suffice to take the life of a criminal
without the usual due process protections of a fair trial. Leverick regards rape as
a special case, however, and sees this as an exception to the general principle that
only a threat to life will suffice for the use of lethal force. What distinguishes
rape in her view is that it denies the victim's humanity and thus 'approaches the
standard of a wrong equivalent to a deprivation of life itself'.[136] This view of rape
is based on one developed by Gardner and Shute which Leverick describes as
follows: 'the wrongness of rape lies not in the harm that it causes, but in the fact
that the rapist uses the rape victim as an object and in doing so dehumanizes
her'.[137] This seems a convincing view of the wrongness of rape but even if this
crime is unique in dehumanizing its victim (and this seems doubtful, as many
forms of physical violence, of both a sexualized and non-sexualized form seem
capable of doing the same), this does not mean that it should thereby be regarded
as approaching a wrong equivalent to death. It is a different type of wrong entirely—perhaps even one that is worse than death in some circumstances for some
victims—but it is not equivalent in any manner. An unlawful killing deprives an
individual of the very essence of his or her being—it takes every element of that
human life and destroys it irrevocably. The harm in death is not in dehumanizing
or causing pain—although of course some killings may cause those additional
harms as well—but in the mere ending of the precious commodity of human life
itself. Rape is a terrible crime and represents a fundamental wrong, but it is not
equivalent to a deprivation of life and thus cannot be regarded as an exception to
a general principle that lethal force should only be used where there is a perceived
threat to life.[138]

---

[136] ibid, p. 157.
[137] ibid, p. 156. See J. Gardner & S. Shute, 'The Wrongness of Rape' in J. Horder (ed.), *Oxford
Essays in Jurisprudence, 4th Series* (Oxford: Oxford University Press, 2000) pp. 193–217.
[138] Of course it should be borne in mind that in many cases of rape there will be a perceived
threat to life evident as well.

(2) The justification for killing in self-defence

The section above has argued against the use of lethal force in order to prevent any crime except in circumstances where there is a perceived threat to life. It may seem obvious that any individual (private citizen or law enforcement officer) has the right to kill another who is threatening his life (perhaps with the proviso that this would only be permitted if there is no other way to prevent the risk to life). Why is such a killing justified? As Wasserman has identified, self-defence 'seems to express a preference for one life over another in a system of law supposedly premised on the equality or incommensurability of lives'.[139] A killing in self-defence is a deprivation of human life and one that is likely to be both intended and self-interested.[140] Why should criminal liability not ensue?

One common approach to answering that question is a consequentalist approach which focuses on the consequences which are likely to flow from a choice between the death of an aggressor and the death of his intended victim. The death of the aggressor is seen to be the preferred consequence but this only leads us to ask why this is so. One answer would be that the aggressor's life is of lesser value than the victim's life because the aggressor carries the moral blame for the attack. However, it was argued earlier in this chapter in relation to the death penalty that all lives should be regarded as being of equal value, even the lives of convicted murderers. This was said in the context of the death penalty, however, and it is conceivable that while a murderer has an equal value of life when sitting on death row, an attempted murderer in the midst of his attack has a life of lesser value than his innocent victim. The problem with any attempt to distinguish between the two individuals on the basis of the values of their respective lives, however, is that it opens the door to more widespread comparisons in other situations, as well as to issues of the moral blameworthiness of the victim. What if the aggressor is a man of previously good character and he is threatening a multiple murderer? Does the aggressor's current moral guilt outweigh the accumulated moral guilt of his victim? We are opening Pandora's box as soon as we begin to compare the value of respective lives and then proceed to use that information to choose between them. As was quoted in the context of the death penalty, we would be attempting to make godlike decisions without godlike wisdom. A more refined variant of consequentalism is 'rule consequentalism' which similarly regards the loss of the aggressor's life as a lesser evil than the loss of the victim's life but does so on the basis of the deterrent effect rather than by devaluing the aggressor's life. A rule permitting killing in self-defence will, the argument goes, tend to deter aggression and save lives. This point is arguable, for it may be that a rule permitting such killing in itself encourages rash aggression in self-defence, plus, as in the death penalty context, a deterrent justification is inappropriate as

---

[139] D. Wasserman, 'Justifying Self-Defence' (1987) 16 Philosophy and Public Affairs 356, at p. 356.   [140] Leverick, n. 129 above, p. 43.

a sole justification for killing because the strongest deterrent effect may require behaviour that society would find repulsive such as the use of force in self-defence that goes far beyond what is reasonable in the circumstances. The problem with all forms of consequentialist justifications for killing in self-defence is that they fail to pay adequate regard to the fundamental nature of the right to life which is owed to all human beings, regardless of conduct.

An alternative approach is the personal parity approach, under which an individual is entitled to give preference to his or her own life in situations where a choice must be made between lives. This approach avoids the difficulties inherent in objectively devaluing certain lives and focuses instead on a recognition that most individuals will value their own lives above that of an aggressor. Leverick is critical of the personal parity approach as a justification for killing in self-defence because, as with consequentialist approaches, it fails to pay adequate regard to the right to life of the aggressor and also fails to sufficiently explain why an individual is entitled to favour his or her own life over that of another person with a supposedly equal right to life. Leverick is more sympathetic, however, to the idea of the personal parity approach excusing, rather than justifying, a killing in self-defence. While it may be hard to explain why an individual being unjustly attacked is entitled to favour his or her own life, it is far easier to excuse them for doing so, especially if they act in fear for their life.[141]

Leverick's preferred option, and the one that is favoured here, is a right to life approach. This approach has been developed by Uniacke and holds that we all possess a right to life 'only so far as we are not an unjust immediate threat to another person's life or proportionate interest'.[142] On this reasoning, the victim of an unjust attack has a right to life but the attacker does not, thus enabling a killing in self-defence by the victim (or by another acting in defence of the victim). In Uniacke's view, the right to life depends not just on our rights as humans but also on our conduct.[143] This view is supported by the protection of the right to life in, for example, the ECHR where Article 2(1) recognizes that everyone has the right to life but Article 2(2) recognizes that a deprivation of life in certain specified circumstances is not contrary to that right. The HRC's interpretation of ICCPR suggests a similar approach applies under that document.[144] While there is a danger in making the right to life dependent on satisfactory conduct, such an approach seems inevitable within democratic societies where other societal interests, and the rights of others, may be inconsistent with an individual's right to life. What is essential, however, is that the conduct requirement is interpreted restrictively. Uniacke's approach of requiring an unjust immediate threat to life is adequately restrictive so as to strictly limit the circumstances in which an individual may lose his or her right to life due to conduct. Even Uniacke arguably

---

[141] ibid, pp. 52–3.
[142] S. Uniacke, *Permissible Killing: The Self-defence Justification of Homicide* (Cambridge: Cambridge University Press, 1996), p. 196.   [143] ibid, p. 201.
[144] *Suarez de Guerrero v Colombia* (Communication 45/1979).

goes too far in including unjust immediate threats to other proportionate interests beyond life. While an unjust immediate threat to another's life may justify the loss of one's own life (subject to what will be said below), a similar threat to another's bodily integrity or freedom should not do so. Conduct must be extreme before it will result in the loss of the protection owed under a fundamental right to life. Conduct that undermines the right to life of another individual is a necessary condition. It is not, however, a sufficient one. The mere existence of an unjust immediate threat to life should not justify a killing in self-defence unless and until that is the only reasonable means of averting the threat. The favoured option will always be one that preserves both lives and ensures continued protection for this most fundamental of rights. But where that favoured option is no longer a possibility, then the victim of the unjust attack can be justified in killing as a last resort in order to save his or her own life. Thus, the right to life approach to justifying killing in self-defence necessarily incorporates considerations of proportionality and necessity: lethal force will not be justified to protect bodily integrity or privacy interests or property rights, and neither will it be justified to protect life if there are other means of doing so which will also preserve the right to life of the attacker. The vital point that underlies this approach is that the unjust aggressor loses the protection of his or her right to life based on conduct that poses an immediate threat to another's life, in circumstances that preclude any other reasonable means of averting the threat. The aggressor does not lose the right to life due to moral fault and its loss it not a punishment.

Does this right to life approach to killing in self-defence represent a forfeiture of the right for the aggressor? It will be recalled that the concept of an individual forfeiting his or her right to life due to criminal conduct has been rejected previously in this chapter. Uniacke argues that the labelling is not important in this context. On her view, the aggressor 'sacrifices something morally very weighty, when he becomes an unjust immediate threat; and if he does not forfeit the right to life itself, then he forfeits moral parity in respect of that right'.[145] This much cannot be denied because the lack of legal liability for the aggressor's death clearly means that the aggressor's right to life, should it in principle still exist, lacks the moral weight of the victim's. While Leverick rejects Uniacke's attempt to avoid the nomenclature of forfeiture, on the basis that forfeiture is exactly what she is describing regardless of her rejection of the terminology,[146] it does seem preferable to avoid the concept of an individual forfeiting his rights. A better approach is to regard the aggressor as unable to enforce his right to life against his victim (or the victim's defender) in circumstances where only his death can avert the unjust and immediate threat to the life of the victim. As explained above, this is not a punishment for the aggressor and he is not forfeiting his right to life because he deserves to die, and thus the forfeiture terminology does not assist us in this context.

[145] Uniacke, n. 142 above, p. 198.   [146] Leverick, n. 129 above, p. 62.

It is worth adding here a brief discussion of the concept of rights necessary for the application of a right to life justification for killing in self-defence. This right to life approach seems to be based on a Hohfeldian concept of rights: i.e. if X has a claim-right to life, then Y has a corresponding duty to refrain from violating it. This approach does not, at first glance, appear to sit easily with the positive enactments of the right to life in human rights treaties and national constitutions because these documents tend to frame the right to life (and other human rights) as a right against the state only. If X has a right to life under the ECHR, he holds that right against the state, not against Y. Indeed, the entire purpose of treaties such as the ECHR is to subject the contracting states to binding legal obligations. Y will face no liability under the ECHR, nor under comparable treaties nor most domestic legal systems' versions of the right to life, by failing in his duty not to kill X. However, the protection of the right to life in documents such as the ECHR does nothing more than recognize a pre-existing right. Article 2 states that everyone's right to life shall be protected by law; it does not create the right. It is possible, therefore, that X does hold a right to life as against Y. This would suggest that the obligation on the contracting states of the ECHR is to recognize that corresponding duty and to enforce it in domestic law. If Y fails in his duty not to kill X, the state is expected under the ECHR and other treaty provisions, to hold Y liable for this. The ECHR manifestation of the right to life also imposes a newly enforceable duty on the state to similarly refrain from killing X (or violating his right to life in any other manner). The right to life approach to justifying killing in self-defence is, therefore, a viable approach even in the context of international treaty protection for the right. All members of society have a duty not to kill any other member of society and they have that duty because it co-exists with our individual rights to life. Only when we pose an unjust and immediate threat to the life of another do we lose the usual protection for our lives afforded by our fellow citizens' duties to refrain from killing us, which are, in normal circumstances, enforced by the state. When we are the unjust aggressor, and our death is the only means of preventing us from violating our duty to refrain from killing, then we are no longer able to rely upon our right to life to require others to refrain from killing us.

(3) Mistakes as to a threat to life and necessary force

The above section has outlined a possible justification for the use of lethal force to prevent an unjust immediate threat to life. The justification assumes that threats to life can be reliably identified and that the necessary force needed to avert such a threat is similarly easily ascertainable. In the real world, and especially in the circumstances in which perceived threats to life may occur, the issues are far from simple. Mistakes are frequently made resulting in innocent people being subjected to the use of deadly force or unjust aggressors killed in acts of excessive force. Where does the right to life stand in these such cases?

There are two possible types of mistake relevant here: (a) a mistake in relation to the perception of the attack and (b) a mistake in relation to the force necessary to avert the attack. Most jurisdictions have sympathetic rules in place to deal with reasonable mistakes pertaining to the attack. This is because of a widespread recognition that perceptions of an attack may easily be influenced by fear, panic or distress. Thus no common law jurisdiction permits a reasonable mistake as to the attack to defeat a claim of self-defence.[147] However, the key issue is whether the mistake is reasonable. If it is not, then a claim of self-defence may not be permitted to succeed. In Canada,[148] Australia[149] and Scotland,[150] for example, a mistake as to the attack must be reasonable in order for the self-defence (or defence of others) claim to stand. The reason for this strict approach relates back to the justification of such killings, discussed above. If the victim makes an unreasonable mistake that leads him to kill a perceived aggressor who was not in fact posing any threat to the victim's life (and no reasonable person would have thought that he was doing so), then the aggressor remains entitled to rely upon his right to life and as a consequence there should be a good reason for his death.[151] While this reasonableness requirement is an important protection for the right to life of someone unreasonably mistaken as a threat to life, it does mean that an individual who honestly, albeit unreasonably, believed that his life was in immediate threat will be unable to rely upon a defence of self-defence. Does the honestly, but unreasonably, mistaken killer deserve to be convicted of murder? This may depend largely upon the circumstances of the killing and perceived attack. When the consequence of a mistake is the death of a human being, however, it may be argued that those who act unreasonably in assessing the need for that death are deserving of punishment.[152] A failure to so punish may be seen as undermining the value of the protection offered for the right to life.

English law is unusual in this respect as it does not require a mistake as to the attack to be reasonable, merely that it be honestly held. In *R v Gladstone Williams*,[153] it was held that in order to be guilty of assault, the defendant must intend to use or threaten force unlawfully. A defendant who honestly believed

---

[147] The New York Court of Appeals upheld a conviction for assault based on a reasonable mistake about the defence of others in *People v Young* (183 NE 2d 319 (1962)) but this approach has since been overruled by statute. See Leverick, n. 129 above, p. 160, for discussion.

[148] *R v Reilly* [1984] 2 SCR 396.   [149] *Zecevic v DPP* (1987) 162 CLR 645.

[150] *Owens v HM Advocate* (1946) JC 119. More recently, *Drury v HM Advocate*, a case on provocation, defined murder as requiring a 'wicked' intention to kill. As Leverick points out, if such an approach was followed in the context of self-defence, then an honest but unreasonable belief would suffice, as the mens rea for murder would not be satisfied (see Leverick, n. 129 above, p. 163).

[151] See Leverick, ibid, pp. 165–6.

[152] Leverick takes a similar view, arguing that such punishment sends a message that 'we should all take reasonable care to check the accuracy of our beliefs before acting rashly in self-defence. Where the consequences of a mistake are as serious as the death of a human being who was posing no threat, it does not seem unreasonable to conclude that we are all under an obligation, as responsible citizens in society, to control our behaviour in this way.' (ibid, p. 168.)

[153] *R v Williams* [1987] 3 All ER 411.

that he was acting in self-defence (even if it was unreasonable to hold this belief) does not have an unlawful intention and thus cannot possess the necessary mens rea for the offence. The Privy Council has confirmed that this principle also applies to murder.[154] In practice, it means that the most unreasonable of mistakes can suffice as justification for the use of even lethal force. In 1999, for example, Harry Stanley was shot dead by police officers in the belief that he was an armed terrorist. He was carrying something that appeared to be a gun but was, in fact, a table leg. He was also believed to be speaking with an Irish accent although he was actually Scottish. The CPS declined to prosecute the police officers because their apparently genuine belief that Stanley was about to shoot them would be sufficient to establish a defence.[155] Such a generous approach in respect of unreasonable mistakes undoubtedly presents problems for the right to life of the victim of the mistake. While English law is content to require only an honestly held belief, there is considerable doubt about whether that is sufficient to satisfy the requirements of Article 2 ECHR.

Article 2 does not expressly mention mistakes in respect of the use of lethal force. It does, however, require that the use of lethal force be 'absolutely necessary' for one of three specified reasons if it is to be compatible with the victim's right to life. A mistake that it was not reasonable for the defender to make cannot satisfy such a strict test. It cannot be absolutely necessary to kill a person who does not present any risk of unlawful violence merely because the killer honestly believed that he did present such a risk. It is important to give some weight to the difficulties of making split second decisions in times of panic, and thus we should not require the actual presence of a threat, merely a perception of a threat that was mistaken but reasonable in the circumstances, but to permit the death of a human being merely because somebody unreasonably perceives a threat is to go too far. The European Court of Human Rights caselaw, while not explicitly using the reasonableness test, does establish that the Court will require good reasons for an honest, but mistaken, belief. Thus far this has not led to a finding of a violation in respect of English law's entirely subjective test but this may be because the mistaken beliefs that have been considered before the Strasbourg Court have, arguably, been based upon good reason. The Court has, therefore, been happy to give the benefit of the doubt to those who have used lethal force against a perceived threat, for even if not an objectively reasonable perception, it has been both honestly held and based on good reasons. It will be interesting to see the Court's approach to a mistaken belief that lacks such a foundation. The lack of any requirement of objective justification for a mistaken belief is a serious shortcoming in English law's protection of the right to life and should be rectified as soon as possible in a manner that continues to protect the individual who forms

---

[154] *Beckford v R* [1988] AC 130.

[155] Leverick, n. 129 above, p. 347. For discussion of this case, and a number of others, see N. Davies, 'Armed and Dangerous: The Police with their Fingers on the Trigger' *The Guardian*, 23 May 2001.

an erroneous perception of the situation due to fear and panic but also ensures that the victim of such a mistaken perception is not legitimately killed in the absence of any good reason.

So far the discussion on mistake has focused on a mistake as to the perception of a threat and it has been argued that the ECHR approach of requiring a good reason for such a mistake is preferable in right to life terms to English law's approach of protecting even unreasonable mistakes. A more common mistake, however, is in relation to the amount of force necessary to repel a genuine attack. In the context of the right to life, this issue may arise where the victim of an unjust immediate threat to his or her life responds by killing the aggressor when objectively the use of a lesser degree of force may have sufficed to avert the attack. Most jurisdictions, even England, require such a mistake to be reasonable before the defender can be acquitted. In English law, *R v Owino*[156] established that the force used must be reasonable in the circumstances as the defendant believed them to be. This is, in effect, a requirement of proportionality:[157] the minimum force necessary to prevent the attack should be used and lethal force will only be justified in the most extreme situations. This represents vital protection for the right to life. It could be argued that it goes too far in doing so because in circumstances where there is a genuine threat but the defendant uses an excessive amount of force to seek to repel the attack, there will be no defence to a murder charge if the aggressor dies. In *R v Clegg*,[158] for example, a soldier in Northern Ireland was held to have acted reasonably in firing shots at a car that approached a checkpoint without stopping—and thus his perception of a threat was reasonable—but the fourth shot, which was fired after the car had passed the checkpoint and was 50 feet along the road, was held to be excessive. As it was the fourth shot that proved fatal, the soldier's conviction for murder was upheld by the House of Lords. This may seem a harsh result. It provides strong protection for the deceased's right to life by holding his killer liable for the most serious of all crimes despite the reasonable perception of a threat but arguably punishes the soldier more strictly than is really justified in the circumstances. One solution to this type of situation, that would preserve the strong protection for the right to life, would be to regard an excessive use of force in self-defence as amounting to a partial defence. This would work in a similar way to a partial defence such as provocation or diminished responsibility, and would reduce a charge of murder to one of manslaughter (which in the UK has the added benefit of opening the door to sentencing discretion). Such a partial defence exists

[156] [1996] 2 Cr App R 128, affirmed by the Privy Council in *R v Shaw* ([2001] UKPC 26) and by the Court of Appeal in *R v Martin* ([2001] EWCA Crim 2245).
[157] This is now made explicit in section 76(6) Criminal Justice and Immigration Act 2008: the force used is not reasonable if it is disproportionate.   [158] [1995] 1 All ER 334.

in India,[159] Singapore[160] and some Australian jurisdictions.[161] It has the advantage of avoiding the harshness of a murder conviction in circumstances where the defendant honestly believed that he was using only the force necessary to repel the attack, but avoids a complete acquittal for behaviour that remains morally blameworthy due to the lack of care exercised by the defendant in determining the reality of the situation before resorting to unnecessary lethal force.

As we have seen, there is a complex approach to the issue of mistake in self-defence in English law: a mistake as to the existence of an attack need only be honestly held but a mistake as to the amount of force necessary to repel that perceived attack must be objectively reasonable. As Leverick points out, either type of mistake may 'result in the death of a human being who, if the defendant had taken more care to evaluate the situation, would still be alive'.[162] When applying the law on self-defence to private individuals, it must always be borne in mind that the individual is likely to be in a state of panic due to either a perceived or an actual unjustified attack. The law should require due care to be taken before resort to lethal force but should also be forgiving of actions based on erroneous, but reasonable, conclusions. When the law on self-defence and prevention of crime is applied to law enforcement officers or other agents of the state, the situation is arguably very different.

(4) The use of lethal force by agents of the state

A requirement of due care becomes an absolutely essential component and the expectations of reasonable conclusions should be higher when lethal force is used by an agent of the state. State agents such as police officers and members of the armed forces have been trained to act reasonably in times of attack; the consequences of fear and panic should be reduced through training and experience; and their assessment of the need for force should be grounded in specific training. Is it appropriate therefore to hold state agents to the same standards as members of the public who lack the training, experience and ability (not to mention the

---

[159] Section 300 Indian Penal Code.

[160] Exception 2 to section 300 Singaporean Penal Code: 'Culpable homicide is not murder if the offender, in the exercise in good faith of the right of private defence of person or property, exceeds the power given to him by law, and causes the death of the person against whom he is exercising such right of defence, without premeditation and without any intention of doing more harm than is necessary for the purpose of such defence.' See S. Yeo, 'Fault for Homicide in Singapore' in Holder, n. 128 above.

[161] Partial defence applied by High Court in *Viro v R* ((1978) 141 CLR 88) but overturned by the same court in *Zecevic v DPP* ((1987) 162 CLR 645) on basis that it was too complex for juries to understand. The partial defence has since been reintroduced in New South Wales (section 421 Crimes Act 1900, as amended by Crimes Amendment (Self-defence) Act 2001) and South Australia (section 15(2) Criminal Law Consolidation Act 1935, as amended by Criminal Law Consolidation (Self-defence) Amendment Act 1997). See Leverick, n. 129 above, p. 173.

[162] Leverick, ibid, p. 72.

firepower) of the former? Skinner has investigated the 'citizen in uniform' doctrine which means that police officers and soldiers rely on the same powers and are subject to the same rules as the private citizen under English law. The authorization of the use of reasonable force in section 3 Criminal Law Act 1967, discussed above (as well as the common law rules on self-defence), provides justification for the use of lethal force to state agent and private citizen alike. On the one hand, when coupled with a mandatory sentence for murder, this may operate harshly against a police officer or soldier performing his duties, as for example in the case of *Clegg*. On the other hand, it provides inadequate protection for the individual against the use of force by the state. The state will train its law enforcement officers in the use of force and the public is entitled to have higher expectations of these officers than of their fellow citizens. Not only do the state agents have the training to make reasoned judgements in times of threat, as well as experience of doing so, but they can also be distinguished from the private citizen in terms of the provision of armaments. As Skinner points out, 'Firearms, riot guns, batons and CS gas are legitimate tools for the soldier and police officer but illegal for the citizen.'[163] This contributes to a 'real disparity between ordinary citizens and state agents who use force'.[164] This disparity should be recognized by the law in terms of the right to life. While the state may be entitled to be tolerant of mistakes by members of the public who kill in the belief that they are doing so to save another life, it should be held fully responsible for similar misjudgements by its own agents that result in the unnecessary death of one of its citizens. The different status of the individuals involved when a state agent uses lethal force against a citizen is ignored in English law's citizens in uniform doctrine. As Skinner points out, in this context the different status of the actors involved amounts to one of them, the state, 'being judged in the context of a legal regime of rights that exists entirely to protect the other (the citizen)'.[165] The citizens in uniform doctrine, which ignores the status of the actors involved, 'obscures and seems to conflict with the rationale on which human rights law rests'.[166] This problem extends beyond the issue of mistake. While, a reasonableness requirement may be satisfactory for the use of force by private citizens, the absolutely necessary requirement in Article 2 ECHR is far more appropriate for the use of lethal force by state agents. Judging all killings to prevent crime by the same standard provides inadequate protection for the individual against the state.

The protection afforded to the right to life in Article 2 ECHR, namely that everyone's right to life shall be protected by law and that no one should be intentionally deprived of his or her life, is expressly limited by the recognition that lethal force may be absolutely necessary in order to prevent unlawful violence, quell a riot or effect a lawful arrest or prevent an escape. Article 2 is, therefore,

---

[163] S. Skinner, 'Citizens in Uniform: Public Defence, Reasonableness and Human Rights' [2000] P.L. 266, at p. 278.   [164] ibid.

[165] ibid, p. 281.   [166] ibid.

broad in its identification of situations which potentially may merit the use of lethal force, going beyond the unjust and immediate threat to life requirement proposed above, although stopping short of English law's wide prevention of crime justification. Article 2 complements its breadth in this regard, however, with strictness in relation to when resort to lethal force is justified, requiring it to be 'absolutely necessary' in order to achieve the specified objective. As this incorporates a proportionality requirement,[167] it may be assumed that it would only be absolutely necessary to use lethal force in respect of unlawful violence and riots when a threat to life has emerged. Certainly, in respect of effecting an arrest, the European Court of Human Rights has made clear that it will never be absolutely necessary to use lethal force to arrest a non-violent suspect if he is posing no threat to life or limb, even if the failure to use lethal force will result in the suspect's escape.[168] Arguably even this goes too far in justifying a use of lethal force by the state against an individual suspected of posing a threat short of death.

In determining the absolute necessity of the use of lethal force by state agents, the European Court of Human Rights has held that 'a stricter and more compelling test' of necessity must be used in Article 2 as compared to the other Convention Articles that refer to limitations to rights that are 'necessary in a democratic society' and also that the force must be 'strictly proportionate' to the aim pursued.[169] It has also determined that it will 'subject deprivations of life to the most careful scrutiny, particularly where deliberate lethal force is used'.[170] In *McCann*, in which the four soldiers admitted that they shot to kill the three suspects, the Court accepted that the soldiers had honestly believed, in light of the information they had received, that this was necessary in order to prevent the detonation of a bomb and a serious loss of life.[171] This honest belief (which it would be hard to dispute when agents of the state are acting in pursuance of their official duties without established personal motivation) was held to be sufficient to prevent a violation of Article 2, despite the fact that it was mistaken. The suspects, although they may have been planning a terrorist attack on Gibraltar, were not about to detonate a bomb at the time they were shot and were therefore not posing any immediate threat to life. They could have been arrested with minimal, or at least less, force. The Court held, however, that the honest belief of the soldiers was 'perceived, for good reasons, to be valid at the time'.[172] This introduces an element of objectivity to the equation for it is entirely possible that some honest but mistaken beliefs may not be founded on objectively 'good reasons' and thus may not suffice to excuse state liability for deaths under Article 2. This

---

[167] See *McCann v United Kingdom* (1995) Series A No. 324; 21 E.H.R.R. 97, at para. 149: 'the force used must be strictly proportionate to the achievement of the aims set out in sun-paragraphs 2(a)(b) and(c) of Article 2.'

[168] *Nachova v Bulgaria* (ECHR 2005—VII (Judgment of 6 July 2005)).

[169] *McCann*, n. 167 above, para. 149.   [170] ibid, para. 150.   [171] ibid, para. 200.

[172] ibid.

is a vital protection for the right to life against incompetence or dishonesty by state agents using lethal force. The Court was not willing to go further, however, and require the lethal force to be objectively absolutely necessary. It held that this would impose 'an unrealistic burden on the State and its law-enforcement personnel in the execution of their duty, perhaps to the detriment of their lives and the lives of others'.[173] In this way, the Strasbourg Court permits agents of the state to kill citizens when to do so was not absolutely necessary. This is a dangerous precedent and does not adequately recognize the disparity between state and citizen discussed above. While individuals may be forgiven for (reasonable) errors in judgement that lead to unnecessary deaths, the standard imposed on the state should be far stricter. An honest mistake should not excuse the state from liability for unnecessary killings, and it is vital that the requirement of good reasons for such a mistake is more strictly enforced than it was in *McCann* in order to impose a genuine objective standard upon the actions of state agents who hold the power of life and death over members of the public.

The key principles upheld by the European Court of Human Rights in *McCann*, such as the need for careful scrutiny and proportionality had previously been applied by the Human Rights Committee when interpreting Article 6 ICCPR in *Suarez de Guerrero v Colombia*.[174] The HRC recognized that state killings are matters of 'utmost gravity' and that 'the law must strictly control and limit the circumstances in which a person may be deprived of his life by the authorities of a state'.[175] Furthermore, even though the ICCPR prohibits all arbitrary deprivations of life, with no explicit exceptions in the prevention of crime context, the HRC was willing to read these into the terms of Article 6. Thus the shooting of seven suspects at close range without warning was held to be a violation of Article 6 because the deprivation of life was clearly intentional and was not necessary in the officers' own defence or the defence of others, or to effect the arrest or prevent the escape of the suspects.[176] In taking this approach, the HRC used the term 'arbitrarily' to ensure that Article 6's protection for the right to life contains similar requirements to that of Article 2. The use of lethal force that is necessary in order to achieve one of these aims may well be consistent with Article 6. The HRC pointed out that, while the death penalty is permitted under Article 6, it can only be imposed for the most serious crimes. This signifies the gravity of deprivations of life by the state. The HRC also recognized that the police killings deprived the suspects of the due process protections laid down in the Covenant.[177] The use of lethal force by the state in the crime prevention context circumvents both the strict limitations upon the imposition of the death penalty and the stringent protection for due process rights, such as a right to a fair trial, and this further supports the argument that the use of such force should only be permitted in extreme circumstances, when absolutely necessary. It

---

[173] ibid.   [174] Communication 45/1979.   [175] ibid, para. 13.1.
[176] ibid, para. 13.2.   [177] ibid.

also explains why it is essential that deprivations of life by the state are subjected to such close scrutiny by both the HRC and the European Court of Human Rights.

The standard set in *McCann* has been applied in subsequent cases under the ECHR. In *Andronicou and Constantinou v Cyprus*[178] both a hostage-taker and his hostage were killed by police fire after the hostage-taker fired at a police officer. The Court accepted that the police officers had honestly believed in the circumstances that it was necessary to kill Andronicou in order to save the life of Constantinou and their own lives. The officers fired a total of twenty-nine shots at Andronicou while Constantinou was held in front of him, killing them both. The Court found it 'clearly regrettable that so much fire power was used in the circumstances' but refused to substitute its own assessment of the situation, made with 'detached reflection', with that of the officers who 'were required to react in the heat of the moment in what was for them a unique and unprecedented operation to save life'.[179] The Court explained that the officers were entitled to take all measures which they honestly and reasonably believed were necessary to eliminate the risk to life to the hostage or themselves. The inclusion of a reasonableness requirement here is interesting, although the Court did not go to any lengths to assess the reasonableness of the police action. It was held that the use of lethal force 'however regrettable it may have been, did not exceed what was "absolutely necessary"'.[180] Four out of the nine judges dissented on this point and concluded that the force used was not proportionate. Judge Pekkanen made the reasonable point that the use of machine guns in a small room where the operation's main purpose was to save the life of a hostage was an excessive use of force that was not strictly proportionate to that aim and which unnecessarily endangered both persons' lives.[181] Judge Jungwiert, also dissenting, made a similar point: 'Using machine guns in a small confined space without proper lighting and knowing that the very person to be rescued was next to or in front of the person being aimed at...seems to me more than irresponsible.'[182] These are good points, although they are somewhat undermined by the suggestion by Judge Pekkanen that the police action was not proportionate partly because 'the crisis did not concern hardened criminals but a quarrel between two young lovers'.[183] Regardless of the relationship between Andronicou and Constantinou, to regard the situation that developed, in which Andronicou was armed and threatened to kill Constantinou, as merely a lovers' quarrel gives insufficient weight to the very real threat to the life of an innocent party.

The Court's sympathy for honest assessments as to necessary force made under pressure in emergency situations has meant that very few cases under Article 2 have resulted in the finding of a violation in respect of the use of lethal force

---

[178] (1997) 25 E.H.R.R. 491; 1997-VI.   [179] ibid, para. 192.   [180] ibid, para. 193.
[181] ibid, Partly Concurring, Partly Dissenting Opinion of Judge Pekkanen.
[182] ibid, Partly Concurring, Partly Dissenting Opinion of Judge Jungwiert.
[183] Judge Pekkanen, para. 4.

(although the court has been more willing to criticize the planning and control of police operations for failing to respect life, as we shall shortly see). In *Gül v Turkey*,[184] however, the state was no longer able to hide behind the honest mistake of its agents. Mehmet Gül was killed while he was unlocking his front door in the early hours of the morning by three police officers opening fire through the door. The European Commission of Human Rights' findings of fact concluded that the police's assertion that Gül had fired a pistol shot at them lacked credibility and was unsupported by any other evidence. The European Court of Human Rights, accepting the Commission's findings of fact, held that the firing of fifty to fifty-five shots at the door 'was not justified by any reasonable belief of the officers that their lives were at risk from the occupants of the flat'.[185] While it was possible that the officers had mistaken the sound of the door bolt being drawn back for the sound of the occupant of the flat opening fire at them, their reaction of 'opening fire with automatic weapons on an unseen target in a residential block inhabited by innocent civilians, women and children' was, in the Court's view 'grossly disproportionate'.[186] The Court unanimously found a violation of Article 2 in relation to the police officers' disproportionate reaction. It distinguished this case from that of *Andronicou* on the basis that in the earlier case it was not disproportionate for the police to open fire at an identified hostage-taker who was in known possession of a gun and had already fired at an officer. It appears, therefore, that a crucial factor in determining the proportionality of lethal force, and thus whether it is absolutely necessary, is the information known about the person killed. In *Gül* the person killed had not been previously identified as a threat (the police were searching all apartments in the building) and the police opened fire first at an unknown person. In *Andronicou* the person killed was clearly posing a threat to life, although different views might be taken on how best to counter that threat. Even in *McCann*, although the imminence of the threat to life was mistaken, the suspects had at least been clearly identified as suspected terrorists. *Gül* thus stands apart from cases in which an honest mistake is made about the imminent threat posed by a suspect and the force necessary to save life. The shocking events at Stockwell underground station in 2007, in which an innocent man was killed by the police, seem closer to the *Gül* situation than that of *McCann* and this may be crucial in determining the compatibility of the shooting with Article 2. It is worth querying before moving on to the de Menezes case, however, whether the distinction between *Gül* and *McCann* is justifiable. What must be avoided is an impression that the life of an innocent person such as Gül or de Menezes receives a greater degree of protection from the right to life than a known threat such as Andronicou or reasonably suspected threats such as McCann, Farrell and Savage. It is not the individuals' past actions or current status that should matter under Article 2, but rather the immediate threat to life reasonably believed to be posed by

---

[184] Case no. 22676/93 (Judgment of 14 December 2000).   [185] ibid, para. 82.
[186] ibid.

them. Honest mistakes as to the level of threat posed and the best course of action to counter the threat are more likely to be based on good reasons if there is convincing evidence of their criminal intentions and ability and willingness to take life. This might be evidenced by the suspect opening fire, or appearing to move to do so, or to detonate an explosive. In *Huohvanainen v Finland*,[187] for example, an armed man was shot dead while crawling out of a burning building after a two-day siege. Whether he currently posed an immediate threat to life is debatable, but the police officers' honest belief that the lethal force was necessary to protect their colleagues was accepted by the Court because of the genuine threat posed by the man during the siege as evidenced by his previous willingness to fire at the police. The use of lethal force was, therefore, held not to be a disproportionate response in the circumstances.[188] Similarly, in *Bubbins v United Kingdom*,[189] the Court found no reason to doubt the evidence of a police officer that he honestly believed his life was in danger from a suspected armed criminal. The Court described how the officer 'found himself confronted by a man pointing a gun at him. That man had ignored previous warnings to give himself up and, in defiance of these warnings, conveyed on occasions a clear impression that he would open fire.'[190] In these circumstances, while the Court found the used of lethal force regrettable, it was not prepared to find it to be disproportionate. In cases such as *Gül*, however, it is harder for the state to rely upon an honest mistake because it is difficult to establish the foundational reasoning for the choice to use lethal force: the individual is not identified; there is no convincing evidence of his or her being armed or intending to take life. The mistake made by the officers in that case, even if it was an honest mistake, was a mistake as to the very existence of a threat to life, rather than a mistake as to the level of threat or the best way to counter it, and therefore very convincing reasons should exist for the mistake before it can be regarded as justifying a state killing of an innocent man posing no threat to life. Did such reasons exist in relation to the shooting of de Menezes?

When two armed police officers shot and killed Jean Charles de Menezes at close range on a London underground train, they believed that he had been identified as Hussain Osman, a suspected suicide bomber. In reality, he had not been positively identified. When the armed officers entered the train on which de Menezes was seated and saw him stand up, they believed that he was a suicide bomber who was about to detonate a bomb that would cause massive loss of life. Acting on this mistaken belief, they opened fire with the intention of killing the suspect. There seems little doubt that these police officers acted on a genuine belief that lethal force was

---

[187] Case no. 57389/00 (Judgment of 13 March 2007).

[188] It is perhaps significant that the Court focused upon whether the lethal force was proportionate to the aim of protecting the lives of other police officers, rather than whether it was proportionate to the aim of preventing an escape. Article 2(2)(b) permits the use of lethal force when it is absolutely necessary to prevent an escape, but it may have been harder to establish proportionality in this context.   [189] ECHR 2005—II.

[190] ibid, para. 139.

absolutely necessary in order to save life. Their orders to stop the suspect from boarding a train, following a briefing earlier in the day emphasizing the serious threat posed by the genuine suspects, and the fact that this event took place the day after the failed London bombings (and two weeks after successful bombings) lend support to the suggestion that their belief was not only honestly held, but also based on good reasons. The only factor that raises doubt is the officers' action immediately preceding opening fire and their subsequent attempt to lie about this. All the police officers on the train (including a number of (armed) surveillance officers as well as the armed response unit officers who opened fire) claimed that the firing officers had shouted a warning of 'armed police' on the train before firing any shots. This evidence is problematic for two reasons. First, it suggests that the police did not fire immediately on the suspect despite being convinced that he was a suicide bomber about to detonate a bomb. The only justification for the use of lethal force, rather than an attempt to arrest the suspect, was that he presented an immediate threat to life and had to be stopped urgently by shots to the head to prevent any further movement. If these shots were not fired at the first opportunity, but only following a warning, giving the suspect plenty of time to detonate the bomb, this undermines the argument about the necessity of lethal force. Secondly, it appears that the police officers did not actually shout a warning. Witnesses on the train did not hear it, and an inquest jury has recently concluded that no warning was given. While this counters the first concern, it raises an entirely new one: the officers, in collusion, were lying about this. The fact that collusion takes place is perhaps not surprising. The police officers involved, following standard procedure at the time, were not required to write their notes about the incident until twenty-eight hours later and were permitted to do so together.[191] It is noteworthy that in *Ramsahai v Netherlands*,[192] a Grand Chamber of the European Court of Human Rights was critical of the fact that the two officers involved in a shooting in that case were not separated after the incident and not questioned until nearly three days later. The Court held that regardless of whether there was actual collusion between the officers, 'the mere fact that appropriate steps were not taken to reduce the risk of such collusion amounts to a significant shortcoming in the adequacy of the investigation'.[193] This finding contributed to the Court's conclusion that Article 2 had been violated in its procedural aspect.

Notwithstanding the significant concerns about the circumstances in which the evidence of the officers was taken, and its veracity, there are, as explained above, some good reasons for the officers' belief that lethal force was absolutely necessary at Stockwell that day. The real failure of the Metropolitan Police was not in the regrettable response of the armed officers, but in the planning and control of the surveillance operation that led to the officers' response and made

---

[191] See IPCC, Stockwell One: Investigation into the Shooting of Jean Charles de Menezes at Stockwell underground station on 22 July 2005, paras 17.15–17.19.
[192] Case no. 52391/99, ECHR 2007.   [193] ibid, para. 330.

almost inevitable a loss of human life that day. It is now necessary, therefore, to investigate the surrounding circumstances of the police operations that led to the killing of de Menezes, as well as to the other suspects discussed above. While the last-minute decision of whether to shoot or not may be difficult to criticize when innocent lives are honestly and reasonably believed to be at stake, the state is likely to be given far less discretion in respect of the operation that led to officers being faced with that difficult decision. This is in some ways comparable to the discussion above about the circumstances surrounding the imposition of the death penalty. While death is the inevitable result of the actions of the executioner and the armed officer's choice to use lethal force, those deaths do not occur in a vacuum. The punishment or the deterrent measure is the final step in an often lengthy road, and that road will frequently be littered with further human rights abuses. In the context of the death penalty, the subsidiary abuses were identified as abuses of rights other than the right to life, but in the context of the use of lethal force, the earlier abuses are regarded as elements of the right to life. Violations of the right to life can be identified, therefore, even if the armed officers' final choice to use lethal force can be excused.

(5) The circumstances that surround the use of lethal force: planning and control of the police operation

In *McCann*, the European Court of Human Rights established that Article 2's protection for the right to life requires 'most careful scrutiny' not only of the actions of the state agents who administer lethal force but also of 'all the surrounding circumstances including such matters as the planning and control of the actions under examination'.[194] It was on this element of Article 2 that the Court found a violation because, as we have seen, the honest belief of the soldiers who actually killed the suspects was sufficient to preclude a violation in respect of the actual use of lethal force. The Court found, however, that because the soldiers were trained to shoot to kill, the greatest of care must be taken in evaluating all information provided to those trained killers.[195] The definite reporting to the armed soldiers that a car bomb had been found which could be detonated at the press of a button, without any allowance for the possibility of error, made the use of lethal force by these soldiers who had been trained to shoot to kill, 'almost unavoidable'.[196] The Court was also critical of the shoot to kill policy, saying that the soldiers' 'reflex action in this vital respect lacks the degree of caution in the use of firearms to be expected from law enforcement personnel in a democratic society, even when dealing with dangerous terrorist suspects'.[197] The existence of a shoot to kill policy in order to prevent the detonation of a bomb was also evident more recently in the de Menezes shooting. Is such a policy inherently flawed

---

[194] *McCann*, n. 167 above, para. 150.   [195] ibid, para. 211.   [196] ibid, para. 210.
[197] ibid, para. 212.

in human rights terms? It has to be borne in mind that the state is responsible for protecting the lives of all within its jurisdiction, not only those it perceives as a threat, and thus if a serious threat to life has been identified it will be vital for the state agents to repel that threat, using lethal force if that is the only means of effectively doing so. As was argued above, when an individual poses an immediate and unjust threat to the lives of others he will lose the usual protection for his life afforded by the right to life. This does not mean that his death will always be justifiable but that it may be so if his death is absolutely necessary in order to repel the threat to others. It is sometimes argued that a shoot to wound policy would not reduce the threat of death and serious injury but would rather increase them for a variety of reasons. Waddington argues that shots intended to wound are more likely to miss, creating a danger of the bullet hitting someone else or enabling the target to carry out his threat.[198] In addition, he argues that a wounded person is unlikely to be totally or immediately incapacitated and may thus still be able to carry out his threat and that the knowledge of this possibility will encourage the police to open fire sooner when the level of threat is at a lower level than would be required under a shoot to kill policy.[199] Waddington concludes that it is preferable for state agents to have recourse to firearms only in extreme situations but that when shots are fired they should be intended to inflict sufficient injury to incapacitate the threat immediately.[200] This need for immediate incapacitation requires, in Waddington's view, that officers keep firing until all threat posed by the suspect has been eliminated:[201] 'in some circumstances it may be wholly justifiable under the principle of "minimum force" to inflict the most devastating injury upon an adversary by firing a fusillade of shots possibly at the head'.[202] Such an approach is common in the type of cases that raise arguable issues under the right to life. In *McCann, Andronicou, Gül* and the Stockwell incident the use of firepower by the state agent was overwhelming, and clearly intended to totally and immediately incapacitate the threat. Only in *Gül* was the police response regarded as contrary to Article 2 (although the de Menezes shooting has yet to be evaluated on this ground). The criticism of the shoot to kill policy by the European Court of Human Rights in *McCann*, however, contributed to the finding of a violation in that case in respect of the planning and control of the operation.[203] The automatic recourse to lethal force may be justifiable in some

---

[198] P.A.J. Waddington, 'Overkill or Minimum Force?' [1990] Crim.L.R. 695, at p. 698.

[199] ibid.

[200] ibid, p. 699. Waddington uses this conclusion to argue that ammunition forbidden by the Hague Conventions in times of war, such as so-called dum-dum bullets, should be used by state agents (pp. 703–4). The use of such ammunition in the de Menezes shooting remains controversial.   [201] ibid, p. 705.

[202] ibid, p. 706.

[203] In *Andronicou*, the use of armed officers who had been trained to shoot to kill if fired at was not incompatible with Article 2 because the officers were 'issued with clear instructions as to when to use their weapons. They were told to use only proportionate force and to fire only if Elsie Constantinou's life or their own lives were in danger.' (n. 178 above, para. 185.) When the officers entered the flat, no prior decision had been taken to use weapons and 'the authorities were deeply

extreme circumstances but it carries with it a great responsibility on the part of the state. If the state is to send out agents trained to shoot to kill individuals suspected of posing a serious and immediate threat to the lives of others, then it must ensure that the suspicion on which it bases its actions is extremely well founded. The state cannot be given a discretion to make honest mistakes on this issue, and even apparently reasonable mistakes must be subjected to close scrutiny. This is because, while the right to life may justify the state using lethal force when absolutely necessary to do so to save innocent life, it can never establish that necessity if it resorts frequently and automatically to a shoot to kill policy. The need for lethal force must be individually assessed in each case and, because it may be unrealistic to expect a genuine assessment by the officers on the ground who must act quickly and assuredly if they are to perform their obligation of saving lives, this careful assessment must be undertaken by those in control of the planning and control of the operation. In *McCann* it was the failure of those in control to make sufficient allowances for the possibility that their intelligence assessments might be erroneous (as well as the failure to stop the threat at an earlier stage before any immediate threat to life could be perceived to exist)[204] that led the UK into actions incompatible with the right to life. It is likely that similar failings in the de Menezes incident were similarly incompatible with the right to life.

As in *McCann*, armed officers trained in accordance with a shoot to kill policy were given information about which those in control of the operation should have known there was some doubt. In contrast to the *Andronicou* case, the armed officers who killed de Menezes were not briefed along the lines that lethal force should be used only as a last resort. The Independent Police Complaints Commission's investigation into the shooting was critical of the fact that, in respect of the shoot to kill policy, the officers 'were not told that it should only be used as a matter of last resort when they were sure of the identity of the person in relation to whom the policy was to be applied'.[205] Instead, a stop order was conveyed to the officers without it being made clear that this was a usual stop and detain order on a suspect, rather than an authorization to use lethal force. In addition, it was not conveyed to the officers (and seems not to have been fully understood by those in command of the operation) that no positive identification of the suspect had been obtained. The problem initially arose because the original strategy to stop and determine the identity of anyone leaving the suspect's address was not given effect, due to inadequate police resources at the address. While the specialist

---

anxious to avoid any harm to the couple'. In line with this approach, the police did not fire until they had first been fired upon. In the view of the Court, therefore, the planning and control of this operation could be distinguished from that in *McCann* and in this case it was not established that the rescue operation was not planned and controlled in a way that minimized, to the greatest extent possible, the risk to life.

[204] The Court was critical of the failure to prevent the suspects from travelling to Gibraltar as to do so would have prevented the need to choose between the lives of the suspects and the lives of others that ultimately manifested itself.

[205] IPCC, Stockwell One, n. 191 above, para. 20.8.

armed officers were still being briefed, an observation team was at the suspect address and a number of people were leaving without being stopped.[206] As the IPCC investigation found: 'None of the eight people who left the flats before Mr de Menezes left were stopped in accordance with the strategy and when he left he was simply followed while ineffective attempts were made during the course of half an hour to determine whether he was [the suspect].'[207] Those ineffective attempts never culminated in a positive identification and indeed some of the surveillance officers expressed the view that the man they were following was not the suspect. And yet the armed officers sent into Stockwell tube station were left with the impression that they had to stop a dangerous suicide bomber from detonating a bomb. Perhaps most significantly, during the ineffective attempts to identify de Menezes, he was followed by surveillance officers (some of whom were armed) onto two buses, into an underground station, and onto a train. As the IPCC pointed out, 'Had this been a terrorist followed to Stockwell, the failure to apprehend him sooner could have resulted in an even more catastrophic outcome resulting in many deaths.'[208] Therefore, the failure of the planning and control of the police operation that day was not only in relation to the right to life of de Menezes, but also to the rights to life of members of the public. The operation was not planned and controlled in a manner that reduced the risk to life of either de Menezes or the public. The tragic outcome of one innocent death could easily have been many more innocent deaths if the failings that day had related to the actual suspected suicide bomber rather than an innocent man living in the same block of flats.

In an earlier section, it was acknowledged that the state, or its citizens, may on occasion have to resort to lethal force in order to avert an unjust and immediate threat to life. The fact that such choices are likely to arise in circumstances of fear and danger requires that bodies enforcing the right to life take a forgiving view of honest mistakes based on good reasons. This will be particularly appropriate where the person using lethal force is a member of the public with no training or experience in either using force or assessing risks to life. When the lethal force is employed by agents of the state, however, a far more stringent view must be taken in order to provide adequate protection for the right to life. This will manifest itself both in terms of a strict requirement of necessity and proportionality of force, and in terms of a need for the armed operation as a whole to be planned, controlled and conducted in a manner that reduces the risk to life, so far as possible, of both the suspect and the public. When an individual kills another individual to save his own life or that of others, he is likely to have little control over how that threat has developed and the key responsibility for the person using defensive force will be to act on reasonable grounds in determining the existence of the threat and what is necessary in order to repel it. In contrast, when an individual is killed by an armed officer of the state, it rarely happens in isolation.

---

[206] ibid, para. 20.26.   [207] ibid, para. 20.15.   [208] ibid, para. 20.76.

The officer will usually have an entire police operation backing him up and often that operation may be a lengthy one that observes the threat to life as it develops and potentially escalates. There is not only one relevant choice in this context. The armed officers' choice as to whether to use lethal force is merely the last in a long line of choices taken by the authorities that have led to this final moment. In *McCann*, for example, there was a choice made to permit the suspected terrorists to enter Gibraltar despite evidence that they were planning to detonate a bomb there. In de Menezes, a choice was made to permit the suspect to enter an underground station. The state must be held responsible not only for its agents' last-minute decision to kill or not to kill, but also for the decisions that may have contributed to the need for such a choice. The state, and not the individual acting in self-defence, often has the power to influence the development of the threat. It must do all that it reasonably can to prevent the threat developing to the stage where only the death of the suspect can repel it. And it must take far greater care than did the Metropolitan Police in relation to the Stockwell incident, to ensure that when the ultimate decision is taken to kill a suspect, it is a clear and unambiguous decision taken in respect of the correct person.

C. Conclusion

The only situation in which the prevention of crime can justify the killing of an individual by the state is when this is absolutely necessary in order to save another innocent life that is immediately under threat. The death is justified in those circumstances because, and only because, it is the only means of saving the lives threatened by the aggressor. Killing by the state is never justified in order to punish an individual, no matter how heinous his crimes, nor to prevent future crime in an intangible manner or that falls short of a risk to life, nor where other means might equally repel the risk to life. Lethal force is a last resort, available to agents of the state (as well as private individuals) when no other means exist in order to prevent an aggressor from taking an innocent life or lives, and because of this, any police operation leading to the use of lethal force must be planned and controlled in a manner that genuinely treats the death of any person as a last regrettable resort. This emphasis on death as a last resort is part of the reason why the death penalty can never be a legitimate exception to the right to life, for it is never a means of last resort to save lives. It was argued above that an important feature of the death penalty is that it is not just about death and the other human rights abuses and additional punishment inherent in the penalty also serve to negate its legitimacy. By contrast, the use of lethal force by the state in order to save lives immediately and directly threatened by the person killed is ultimately about death: death as the only realistic means of saving innocent lives. The aggressor in this situation is not punished by means of being killed; but prevented from killing others. His right to life is not forfeited but overridden, and not by general societal interests, such as the prevention of crime, but by, and only by, the right to life of the person currently being threatened which includes protection against unjust threats to life. Part of the underlying justification for this overriding of the unjust aggressor's right to life is that he knowingly risks his right to life by threatening that of another. There are other situations, however, where one person poses a threat to the life of another but does not do so knowingly or willingly. In these situations, as we will now see in the next chapter, it may be far harder to justify the choosing of one life over another.

6

The Right to Life and Conflicting Rights of Others

The right to life, like all other human rights, has to apply within the context of a civil society in which it may confront the conflicting rights of other members of that society. In the previous chapter, we saw one potential conflict: where the death of a criminal may save other innocent lives. It was concluded, however, that any restriction on the right to life in the prevention of crime context must be narrowly drawn, with lethal force used as a last resort only in circumstances where the person to be killed is imminently threatening another life. Within a complex modern society, potential conflicts of rights to life may arise in other situations, such as between conjoined twins, or between a pregnant woman and a viable fetus, or in the context of a hijacked plane being used as a weapon. In situations such as these, there is no relevant moral guilt to tip the balance away from one right to life and in favour of another. Instead, we may be drawn towards a utilitarian solution: saving the greater number of lives. Unchecked, however, such an approach may cause considerable difficulties for the right to life, rendering it vulnerable to considerations of the greater good, and undermining the inherent value in each human life. This chapter will, therefore, seek to identify the limited circumstances in which an innocent human life may be terminated in order to protect the rights of others. The acknowledgment that there are any such circumstances is based on a recognition that sometimes hard choices between lives should not be avoided, for to do so is merely to make an implicit, rather than explicit, choice and to do so without the need for justification or accountability.

A. Of trolley buses and hijacked planes

In the previous chapter, it was argued that lethal force could be used, by an agent of the state or a private individual, to prevent an aggressor taking innocent life. An important restriction upon that proposition was that the lethal force must be a measure of last resort. The types of situations considered in the previous chapter related to what may be termed villainous aggressors because the discussion was in the context of the prevention of crime. The aggressor's imminent violation of an innocent person's right not to be killed provided the ethical justification for the overriding of the aggressor's own right to life. We might be inclined, therefore, to perceive moral guilt as a necessary condition for the overriding of an individual's right to life. However, it was emphasized in the previous chapter that the individual's right is not forfeited, and there exists sound ethical reasoning for the extension of this principle to so-called innocent aggressors and innocent threats. Judith Thomson argues that neither moral fault nor agency is required in order for lethal force to be justified in self-defence (or the defence of others).[1] The only requirement, she argues, is that the person is about to violate another's right to life and there is no other means of preventing this violation.[2] Not all commentators agree with this approach. Otsuka, for example, disputes that an innocent threat, such as a falling body about to crush you to death, is capable of violating your right to life (and thus losing the protection of his own).[3] Instead, he regards an innocent threat as a mere bystander 'in the morally relevant sense because...that which endangers another's life is neither an action of hers nor the consequence of any action of hers'.[4] Otsuka then proceeds to argue that no moral asymmetry can be found to distinguish an innocent threat from an innocent aggressor because both lack morally responsible agency for their actions which endanger life.[5] This view, that morally responsible agency is required before an individual's right to life can be overridden in order to save another's innocent life, is unconvincing because the right to life must encompass a right not to be killed by anyone, not merely by those who are morally responsible for the killing. In protecting the right to life, the state may provide excuses, and even justifications, for killers but the very fact that it does so, rather than merely assuming that such a death requires no legal action, suggests that the victim's right to life is in play here.

On the other hand, an innocent bystander is immediately distinguishable from aggressors or threats because he or she does not present any threat to your right to life. If A is an innocent bystander to a threat to B's life, both A and B retain their rights to life and B is not justified in killing A in order to save his own life because A's right to life is just as strong as B's own right. As was recognized in both chapters 4 and 5, it is not generally ethically justified to kill another person merely to avoid being killed oneself, for a life is still lost and if all lives are equal then mere substitution of one death for another is hard to justify. As Otsuka correctly recognizes, 'All moral bets are not off when one's life is endangered.'[6] Instead, some extra element must be present to justify the killing, such as the imminent violation of your own right to life by the other, or a net gain in human life. This latter extra element can be seen when killing one bystander will save two others. The classic statement of this ethical dilemma is the trolley problem.[7] At its most basic,

---

[1] J. Thomson, 'Self-Defence' (1991) Philosophy and Public Affairs 283, p. 302.

[2] ibid, p. 303.

[3] M. Otsuka, 'Killing the Innocent in Self-Defense' (1994) 23 Philosophy and Public Affairs 74.   [4] ibid, pp. 84–5.

[5] ibid, p. 90.   [6] ibid, p. 94.

[7] P. Foot, 'Abortion and the Doctrine of Double Effect' (1967) Oxford Review 5.

this consists of the simple dilemma facing the driver of a trolley. The trolley's brakes have failed and there are five people on the track in front of the trolley who will be killed unless the driver takes some action. The only action available to him is to divert the trolley onto another track. By doing this, the driver will save the life of the five people on the original track but will kill the one person standing on the second track. In this form, most people will feel that he is justified in diverting the trolley. A death will still result but there will be a net gain in human life of four. When we start to analyse why this action is justifiable, our instincts become somewhat hard to define. All things being equal, we often feel that killing is worse than letting die. In the trolley problem, if the driver takes no action, then he is merely letting the people on the track die, but if he diverts the trolley, and in effect aims it at a different person, then it could be argued that he is killing rather than letting die. Why does this not seem to bother us in this situation? What about if we disregard the trolley entirely and instead imagine a patient who is terminally ill and whose organs could save the lives of five other patients. Most people would instinctively regard it as morally abhorrent for a doctor to kill the one patient in order to distribute his organs to the others. And yet, is this not the trolley problem in disguise? One life could be sacrificed in order to save five other lives. Thomson sees the distinction between these two scenarios as relating to the threat posed. So, 'deflecting a threat from a larger group onto a smaller group', as in the trolley problem, may be justified (subject to what is said below) but 'bringing a different threat to bear on the smaller group', as in the transplant example, is not justified.[8] In other words, where there is a single threat that will inevitably kill, such as a trolley with failed brakes, it is justifiable to divert that threat so that the least number of people possible lose their lives from it. But where one threat to life can only be removed by introducing a new threat to the lives of others, such as when imminent organ failure can only be remedied by a doctor's knife into another patient, the taking of human life is not justifiable. We need to spend a little time reasoning why this is so.

Thomson explains that by deflecting a threat, a bystander 'minimises the number of deaths which get caused by something that already threatens people, and that will cause deaths whatever the bystander does'.[9] This approach is similar to, although distinct from, the concept of 'designated for death' which has arisen in caselaw and commentary on the possible murder defence of necessity. For example, in the conjoined twins case,[10] which will be considered below, the judges regarded the weaker twin as designated for death, regardless of the doctors' actions and were therefore willing to permit a separation operation which would inevitably kill this twin in order to save the other, stronger, twin. In both the 'deflecting an existing threat' argument and the 'designated for death' argument,

---

[8] J.J. Thomson, *Rights, Restitution and Risk: Essays in Moral Theory* (ed. W. Parent) (Cambridge: Harvard University Press, 1986), p. 83.   [9] ibid, p. 108.
[10] *Re A (children)(conjoined twins: surgical separation)* [2000] 4 All ER 961.

there already exists a lethal threat to human life which will unavoidably kill someone. Where the two arguments differ, and why the former is to be preferred, is in respect of the lessons to be drawn from the pre-determined death. Under the designated for death argument, the person currently facing death, such as the weaker twin, is treated in a manner that reduces the protection afforded by the right to life. The existing threat is treated as an excuse for prioritizing the rights of another person who can avoid the threat to life. By contrast, the deflecting argument does not use the existing threat and its apparent victim as a means of writing-off that person's rights but rather to justify a killing that will result in a net gain in human life. (It is worth noting here that the killing of the weaker conjoined twin may also have satisfied this stricter test because only her death could prevent both twins dying, as we shall see below.) Nobody is designated for death but, if human life will be lost regardless of any intervening action, then an intervention to limit that loss of life to the minimum possible may be justifiable. It might be argued that the result for the unfortunate individual killed—the person standing alone on the second track, for example—is no less tragic than if he were identified as designated for death and his life sacrificed on that basis. However, in terms of the right to life, it is important that an individual's rights are not ignored merely due to a pre-determined status of designated for death. Ultimately, every human being ever born has been designated for death and the imminence of an expected death is not good reason for abandoning all legal and ethical protection for that life. (This point will be considered in greater detail in chapter 8 in the context of quality of life concerns.) Subject to what is said below, however, tragic choices must sometimes be made in order to save the greatest number of lives possible from an unavoidable threat of death.

A variation on the trolley problem creates a different solution to save the five lives: here the only person who can stop the trolley killing these five people is a bystander on a bridge overlooking the track who can only stop it by throwing a heavy object onto the track in front of the trolley. The only heavy object available is a fat man. In this scenario, most people instinctively feel it would not be ethically justifiable to push the fat man onto the track even though there would still be a net gain in human life. Why is killing this man not a reasonable price to pay in order to save five lives, whereas killing the man on the other track is widely regarded as acceptable? Thomson identifies a crucial distinction between the two scenarios. Diverting the trolley involves an intervening action upon an object, whereas pushing a man off a bridge involves an act upon a person. The latter has the potential to amount to an infringement of the individual's rights. As Thomson explains, 'It is not morally required of us that we let a burden descend out of the blue onto five when we can make it instead descend onto one if we can make it descend onto the one by means which do not themselves constitute infringements of rights of the one.'[11] This is a further distinguishing factor

---

[11] See Thomson, n. 8 above, p. 108.

between diverting the trolley to save five people on the track and killing a poten-tial organ donor in order to save five patients. Part of the ethical justification for this distinction is Kant's idea of not using a person as a means to an end.[12] To cut up a patient in order to save other lives, or to throw a man off a bridge onto the trolley track below, is to use them as means to an end, rather than as ends in themselves. Diverting a trolley towards one person rather than five does not use that one person as a means to an end. Indeed, it would be preferable to everyone if that one person on the track could somehow vanish, leaving an empty track onto which the trolley could be diverted. However, if the fat man on the bridge or the potential organ donor suddenly vanished, the controversial plans to save other lives could not proceed. The man on the bridge and the organ donor are them-selves integral to the plan. It is their lives that must be sacrificed in order to save the lives of others. The infringement of their rights is an unavoidable aspect of the intervening action, and therefore such an intervention is not ethically justified, no matter the net gain in human life that could result from it.

The ethical discussion so far has identified a number of propositions of rele-vance to a conflict of rights to life. In general, as established in the previous chap-ters, one person's right to life cannot be legitimately violated simply because it is necessary to save another person's life. If, however, there would be a net gain in human life from this violation—for example, if five lives could be saved in return for only one lost—then this may be justified but only if the following two condi-tions are met. First, the only intervening action that can be taken is to divert an existing threat, not to introduce a new threat to an individual's life. Secondly, the intervening action must not entail an infringement of a person's rights and thus treat that person as a means to an end. These two conditions will often go hand in hand because the introduction of a new threat is likely to involve a violation of the rights of the person so threatened. These conditions provide meaningful protection for an individual's right to life and avoid the categorization of anyone as designated for death, while also permitting action for the greater good, specifi-cally a net gain in human life, if the conditions are met. It should go without say-ing that, as in the previous chapter, any action to kill must be a last resort. It will now be useful to consider how these principles might apply in a real-life situation, such as a hijacked plane.

The tragic events of 11 September 2001 in the US have led to widespread con-templation of how states might deal with similar events in the future. The possibil-ity of a passenger plane hijacked by terrorists and used as a weapon against people and buildings on the ground presents a challenging dilemma for governments. Should the plane be shot down, killing all passengers on board, in order to save a greater number of lives at the intended target on the ground? Unlike most states, in which the possibility of such executive action is shrouded in secrecy, Germany enacted a piece of federal legislation to deal with this very issue. Section 14(3) of

---

[12] ibid, pp. 100–1.

the Air-Transport Security Act, which entered into force in 2005, expressly permits the use of armed force 'where it must be assumed under the circumstances that the aircraft is intended to be used against human lives, and where this is the only means to avert the imminent danger'. Section 14(2) further requires that any measure taken against the aircraft must be proportionate and section 15(1) requires that, before any direct action is taken, an attempt is first made to warn and divert the aircraft. Despite the requirements of warning, proportionality and last resort, this provision is highly unusual in expressly authorizing the use of (lethal) armed force against a plane full of innocent passengers. For the German Constitutional Court this was a step too far. The German Constitution, or Basic Law, guarantees the right to life in Article 2(2), but it also enshrines human dignity in Article 1(1) and it was the latter value that was key to the Court's striking down of Article 14(3). The Court adopted a Kantian approach by emphasizing that the constitutional value of human dignity 'generally precludes making a human being a mere object of the state. What is thus absolutely prohibited is any treatment of a human being by public authority which fundamentally calls into question his or her quality as a subject, his or her status as a legal entity, by its lack of respect of the value which is due to every human being for his or her own sake, by virtue of his or her being a person.'[13] In the German Court's view, the state would be treating the passengers on the hijacked plane as mere objects, or means to an end, if it resorted to the use of armed force against the plane:

> By their killing being used as a means to save others, they are treated as objects and at the same time deprived of their rights; with their lives being disposed of unilaterally by the state, the persons on board the aircraft, who, as victims, are themselves in need of protection, are denied the value which is due to a human being for his or her own sake.[14]

It is central to the Court's view that the passengers are being used as means to an end rather than as ends in themselves.[15] However, this is arguable because, applying the test mentioned above in respect of the trolley problem, if the passengers suddenly vanished from the plane, the intervening act would still save the lives on the ground and, indeed, this would be a preferable situation. It is not, therefore, the lives of the passengers themselves that are being used to save the lives of others but rather they are incidentally positioned, as was the person in front of the diverted trolley, in harm's way should the intervening act be

---

[13] BVerfG, 1 BvR 357/05 (Judgment of 15 February 2006), para. 119 (references omitted).
[14] ibid, para. 122.
[15] Bohlander has queried whether a decision not to shoot down the plane might similarly result in the intended targets on the ground being 'turned into objects for the purpose of giving the passengers the benefit of a short extension of their doomed lives?' (M. Bohlander, 'In Extremis: Hijacked Airplanes, "Collateral Damage" and the Limits of the Criminal Law' [2006] Crim.L.R. 579, at p. 590). In addition to the points mentioned below about the uncertainty of any conclusion that the passengers' lives are doomed, this argument also fails because the intended targets are not treated as means to any other end simply because the state fails to take any particular action to save them.

initiated. Unlike the person in front of the trolley, however, the passengers are unlikely to avoid death even if the intervention does not occur. Diverting the trolley endangers the single person on the track for the first time, whereas the passengers on a hijacked plane are already likely to lose their lives in the near future. The German Court was correct to reject the designated for death argument, however. The Court was unconvinced of the relevance of an argument that the passengers' lives were already doomed, and emphasized that both human life and human dignity enjoys the same protection regardless of life expectancy.[16] This issue also raised a more general concern of the Court, and one that is far more practical. The Court was unconvinced that the factual situation would ever be fully known or assessed correctly by the authorities on the ground.[17] Terrorists are unlikely to inform the authorities of their exact plans, not to mention that events are likely to unfold rapidly and unexpectedly. Not only does this negate any concept of the passengers being designated for death,[18] but it also means that a decision to shoot down a hijacked plane is unlikely ever to be proportionate for it will always be taken in a state of uncertainty. As Oliver Lepsius explains, 'The downing order, then, inevitably, will be based on a presumption. Conjecture, however, does not suffice as a rationale for the most severe infringement of civil rights, namely death.'[19]

The 'gap between the factual speculation on the one hand and the determination to sacrifice the lives of innocent people on the other hand'[20] is a sound reason for the German Court's conclusion that the use of lethal armed force against a hijacked plane is unconstitutional. The Court's emphasis on human dignity, rather than human life, is somewhat more controversial, however. The principle of human dignity is fundamental to the German Constitution. It is given absolute protection and is regarded as the most important underlying principle of the Constitution. Given the events of history, it is not difficult to understand why human dignity is treated with such sanctity in Germany. The Constitutional Court has developed a practice, however, of utilizing the principle in conjunction with other fundamental rights provisions, including the right to life, which are not protected in absolute terms but are rather subject to proportionality limitations. While this approach has the positive effect of strengthening the core elements of rights such as the right to life, by coupling it with the fundamental principle of dignity, it can also conflict with the absolute character of the human dignity clause.[21] The coupling of the rights to life and dignity has been subject to some criticism from German commentators but Lepsius argues that, in this case, the Court departed from that tendency and focused instead on dignity itself,

[16] BVerfG Judgment, n. 13 above, para. 130.   [17] ibid, para. 123.
[18] ibid, para. 131.
[19] O. Lepsius, 'Human Dignity and the Downing of Aircraft: The German Federal Constitutional Court Strikes Down a Prominent Anti-terrorism Provision in the New Air-transport Security Act' (2006) 7 German Law Journal 761, at p. 775.   [20] ibid.
[21] See Lepsius, ibid, p. 769.

rather than in conjunction with the right to life.[22] The key issue for the Court was not the loss of life of either the passengers or the intended victims on the ground, but rather the treatment of the passengers as mere objects, which was regarded as contrary to the absolute constitutional protection of human dignity. This conclusion has some supporters. Lepsius, for example, is grateful that the Court did not permit the law to 'give an easy answer in advance' to such an ethically complex dilemma. He says that the Court 'denied the parliament the right to make tragic choices. When such decisions must be made, those who have to act at least cannot rest upon the authorisation of the law.'[23] This is little comfort, however. It is undeniable that tragic choices must sometimes be made and when such a decision is unavoidable, it would be preferable for the law to provide at least some guidance. As Bohlander recognizes, while we may all normally subscribe to the idea that one life cannot be set off against another, 'in some situations there may be no other way than to start counting lives'.[24] This is the essence of the trolley problem discussed above: sometimes, when it is inevitable that there will be a loss of human life, tragic choices must be made as to the best way of saving the most individual lives. It was noted above that the scope for infringing an individual's right to life while making such choices must be strictly confined, but there are some situations where not to intervene to save the greatest number of lives can in itself be a regrettable violation of the right to life of the greater number of people left to die. This assumes, of course, that the state owes a duty to take reasonable measures to preserve the life of its citizens. The German Constitutional Court faced a somewhat simplified, and one-sided, dilemma because they failed to refer to the 'duties to protect' that had been recognized in other cases. In the absence of a constitutional duty to protect the lives of the intended victims of the plane on the ground, the question of whether the state may intervene to kill the passengers becomes much easier to answer in the negative. It is clear, however, that under the international protection of the right to life, states face positive obligations to preserve life, as well as negative obligations not to take life. Although the latter are far more robust than the former (for reasons that will be considered in chapter 9), it is the conflict between these two obligations that presents us with the ethical challenges of the trolley problem and the hijacked plane dilemma.

In respect of the trolley problem, it was concluded above that it may be justifiable to violate an individual's right to life if the consequence will be a net gain in human life, provided that the intervening action diverts an existing threat to life, rather than creating a new one, and does not treat the person(s) killed as merely means to an end. All three of these requirements are debatable in the context of the hijacked plane dilemma. If the state shoots down the plane, is that the diversion of an existing threat—i.e. the plane crashing—or the introduction of a new threat—i.e. armed force by the state? Either view seems arguable. On the issue of whether the passengers are treated as means to an end, the German Court

[22] ibid, p. 771.   [23] ibid, p. 772.   [24] Bohlander, n. 15 above, p. 592.

concluded that they were, but a better view seems to be that they are merely incidental to the removal of the threat. As argued above, if the passengers suddenly vanished from the plane, the state action could continue and the lives of the intended victims on the ground could still be saved (and at a much reduced human cost). Given this, it is unconvincing to regard the passengers themselves as means to an end; their lives are not being used in order to save others, as they would be if thrown off a bridge to stop a trolley or cut open to remove their organs. Despite this, the violation of their right to life must result in a net gain in human life in order to be justifiable and, although a theoretical example involving a hijacked plane which satisfies this requirement can certainly be envisaged, the German Court is correct to doubt the existence of sufficient certainty in practice to justify such a violation. The impossibility of the state achieving any satisfactory degree of certainty as to the factual position means that it is unlikely ever to be a proportionate response to knowingly kill, for example, one hundred innocent passengers in the hope that one thousand other innocent lives may perhaps be saved. One additional factor that should not be overlooked, however, is that the hundred lives on the plane will be added to the thousand lives on the ground if the plane is ultimately used as a weapon by the terrorists. It is a choice, then, between killing one hundred people now in order to potentially save one thousand others, or letting eleven hundred potentially die at some point in the near future. On a much smaller scale, this dilemma can be seen in the conjoined twins case, where the tragic choice facing the court is not simply between two conflicting rights to life but between two deaths in the future or one death now.

B. Conflicting rights of conjoined twins

The conjoined twins' case of *Re A (children)(conjoined twins: surgical separation)*[25] presented an unusually stark dilemma for the British courts. The facts were as follows. Jodie and Mary[26] had been born conjoined. Mary was the weaker twin and she had a poorly developed brain, an abnormal heart and scarcely any functional lung tissue. The only reason she survived after birth was because her sister Jodie's heart was pumping blood through both of their bodies. Unfortunately, the extra effort required for this task by Jodie's heart would soon lead to Jodie suffering heart failure. When this happened, and the estimate was within three to six months, both twins would die. An operation to separate the twins would save Jodie's life but would simultaneously and inevitably cause Mary's death. The choice is comparable to that involving the hijacked plane: should Mary (the passengers) be immediately killed in order to save Jodie (the targets on the ground), or should the state fail to intervene and face the strong possibility that all will die within a relatively short time frame. The problem of factual uncertainty was less

---

[25] [2000] 4 All ER 961.   [26] These were not the twins' real names.

evident in *Re A* (although it can never be entirely eliminated) because the medical prognosis was unanimous and based on sound knowledge of the facts. Both twins could not survive long term, although their exact life expectancy in their natural state could only be estimated. Killing Mary, by means of the separation operation would give Jodie a good chance of a relatively normal life, both in terms of life expectancy and quality of life. The question facing the Court of Appeal judges in this case was whether they could, and should, authorize the separation operation, knowing as they did that to do so would be to authorize the killing of Mary.

All three judges regarded the key issue in this case as being a family law one, namely whether the operation was in the best interests of either or both of the twins. They did acknowledge, however, that their decision would have significant right to life implications. Having recognized that both Jodie and Mary enjoyed the protection of the right to life,[27] Ward LJ attempted to perform a balancing exercise. He began by putting both girls' right to life into a set of scales: 'The universality of the right to life demands that *the right* to life be treated as equal. The intrinsic value of their human life is equal. So the right of each goes into the scales and the scales remain in balance.'[28] It will be noted that Ward LJ felt the need to emphasize that it is the right to life of each twin which is equal, leaving scope for the development of an argument that the actual lives of each twin may not deserve equal protection. He acknowledged that, when deciding on the best interests of each twin, 'it is legitimate to have regard to the actual condition of each twin' and 'to bear in mind the actual quality of life each child enjoys and may be able to enjoy'.[29] So, despite declaring that the rights to life of Jodie and Mary are equal, it is regarded as legitimate to take into account their respective physical conditions and quality of life. The relevance of quality of life considerations in respect of the right to life will be considered further in chapter 8 but it is significant here that the opening of the door to such issues immediately placed Jodie at an advantage. This advantage was further strengthened once Ward LJ proceeded to take into account issues of life expectancy. In contrast to Jodie's prospects for a relatively normal life, Mary was said to be 'doomed for death': 'Mary is "designated for death" because her capacity to live her life is fatally compromised. The prospect of a full life for Jodie is counterbalanced by an acceleration of certain death for Mary. That balance is heavily in Jodie's favour.'[30] In general, the concept of an individual being designated for death, and thereby having a reduced right to life, has been rejected in the discussion above. There are a number of reasons for this: the lack of factual certainty about future death; the ethical difficulties in determining why a life that is soon to end is of less value than one which will continue; and the fact that we are all ultimately designated for death and an arbitrary line would have to be drawn to distinguish the cases in which this suddenly becomes a relevant factor. So, in general, the concept of a person being designated for death

---

[27] Not all commentators agree with this conclusion, as will be seen below.
[28] *Re A*, n. 25 above, p. 1010.   [29] ibid.   [30] ibid.

is rejected. However, in *Re A* (and perhaps in the hijacked plane scenario also) it may be relevant that Mary (or the passengers on the plane) will die as a result of the lethal threat regardless of whether other people are saved from it. There is no way in which Jodie's death can save Mary; indeed, Jodie's death will inevitably lead to Mary's death. (Similarly, there is no means by which the intended victims on the ground can die to save the passengers in the plane, and their death by means of the crashed plane will also almost inevitably lead to the passengers' death.)[31] In this way, the facts of *Re A* differ significantly from the hypothetical trolley problem, in which if the five people on the first track were killed by the trolley, the single person on the second track could be saved. The trolley problem is then truly a choice between (numbers of) lives, whereas the choice facing the Court in *Re A* is merely whether Mary should be killed to save Jodie. There is no possibility of choosing to save Mary rather than Jodie. There is not a choice between lives but between different deaths for Mary: one of which would save her sister; the other of which would be considerably postponed and thus give her a longer (albeit of limited quality) life. She is in that sense designated for death, and in a more meaningful way than most of us, but that does not in itself have any effect upon her entitlement to a right to life.

It will be apparent from the quotations above that Ward LJ appeared to be engaging in a comparison of Jodie's and Mary's lives, by regarding their condition, quality of life and life expectancy as relevant factors in balancing their respective rights to life. However, it should be noted that he categorically denied that this was happening. Twice within one paragraph, Ward LJ reiterates that he is not comparing the value of the twins' lives because 'the value of each life in the eyes of God and in the eyes of law is equal'.[32] So, why did he regard these factors as relevant to the choice to be made? He explained that it would be 'impossible not to put in the scales of each child the manner in which they are individually able to exercise their right to life'. He then justifies this by stating that 'Mary may have a right to life, but she has little right to be alive. She is alive because and only because, to put it bluntly, but none the less accurately, she sucks the lifeblood of Jodie and she sucks the lifeblood out of Jodie.'[33] There appear to be two elements to this argument: first, there is an implication that Mary is not entitled to a full right to life because she is not a full person; and secondly, and related to this, there is an implication that Mary is a threat (albeit an innocent threat) to Jodie and therefore has forfeited her right to life. Both proposals are problematic, as we shall now see.

As David Gurnham points out, while the dilemma presented by *Re A* seems at first to be insoluble, 'the possibility of identifying the weaker child as lacking the universal qualities of the person allows a judgement that is simultaneously principled and utilitarian, without there arising a contradiction'.[34] The Court

---

[31] As noted above, there is considerably less factual certainty about this scenario.

[32] *Re A*, n. 25 above, p. 1010.   [33] ibid.

[34] D. Gurnham, 'Kantian Principle and the Right to Life in Legal Judgement: The Case of the Conjoined Twins' (2003) 14 KCLJ 21, at p. 22.

of Appeal does not go so far as to expressly exclude Mary from personhood, and indeed the judges are at pains to deny any possibility of Mary being less than a human being. While many commentators emphasize the distinction between a human being and a person with rights,[35] the Court does not explicitly apply such a distinction. Instead, the judgments imply a moral distinction between Mary and Jodie that enables them to deny practical effect to Mary's right to life. Issues such as capacity to enjoy life and life expectancy are not relevant to the existence of a right to life but, by relying upon 'metaphors of threat, aggression and disaster',[36] the judges distinguish Mary's moral position from that of her sister. They are not treated as two individuals born into a dire situation, but rather as one individual threatening the life of another: 'by the judges' emphasis upon her brutal egocentricity in threatening the life of her sister Jodie, her lack of autonomy and her lack of rationality, Mary is seen to lack Kantian inherent value'.[37] Mary does not therefore need to be treated as an end in herself and her early death 'is justified by her failure to establish herself within the practical scope of the right to life'.[38] Gurnham is careful to note that the judges do not explicitly deny Mary a right to life in a theoretical sense, because they reiterate that Mary, as a separate, living human being has a right to life equal to that of her sister, but he argues that 'through their rhetoric of aggression, threat and dependence, they make it clear that she is beyond the right's practical limit'.[39] It cannot be denied that the Court adopts such a rhetoric. Ward LJ, for example, describes Mary's 'parasitic living' and claims that, if Jodie could speak, she would say: 'Stop it, Mary, you're killing me.'[40] Ward LJ says that Mary would have no answer to that, but it is entirely likely that Mary would respond by saying: 'Stop what? I'm not doing anything.' This implication that Mary is threatening her sister is regrettable. Both twins were born into the unfortunate situation in which they now find themselves; Mary has not attached herself to Jodie and she is not 'sucking the lifeblood' out of her. Rather, both twins are attached to each other and both are threatened by that attachment. Uniacke also makes this point: 'The configuration of the twins' conjoined bodies was not an interference with Jodie on Mary's part. Mary was not invading or interfering with Jodie's body, either actively (as an agent) or passively (as an involuntary human missile might).'[41] She explains that Mary and Jodie are comparable to two people adrift on a waterlogged raft: both are endangered by the other but it is impossible to identify one of them as a threat. By contrast, if one individual was safely on a raft and a second individual tried to climb aboard and thus endangered the safety of both, we could view the latter as a threat. (This might, perhaps, be regarded as comparable to a pregnancy, although this will be

---

[35] See, for example, J. Harris, *The Value of Life: An Introduction to Medical Ethics* (London: Routledge, 1985). For a more recent discussion of varying views on personhood against a medical ethics background, see M. Ford, 'The Personhood Paradox and the "Right to Die"' (2005) 13 Med.L.Rev. 80   [36] Gurnham, n. 34 above, p. 27.
[37] ibid, p. 28.   [38] ibid.   [39] ibid, p. 30.   [40] *Re A*, n. 25 above, p. 1010.
[41] S. Uniacke, 'Was Mary's Death Murder?' (2001) 9 Med.L.Rev. 208, at p. 212.

discussed more fully below.) Jodie was not originally in a safe position, which was then threatened by Mary conjoining with her. As Uniacke asserts, 'There was no interference by or involving Mary that undermined Jodie's prior position; the twins came into existence conjoined and thereby endangered.'[42]

We can now see, therefore, that both elements of the Court of Appeals' argument are flawed. Mary is neither an aggressor nor a threat to Jodie, and she should not thereby be excluded from the practical effect of her right to life, to which the Court unanimously agrees she is entitled. Any attempt to sidestep the consequences of killing Mary should be avoided. The choice facing the Court, as noted above, was between two different types of deaths for Mary: one would be immediate, caused by the state, and potentially save the life of her sister; the other would be postponed for a relatively short period of time, would occur without state interference, and would result from the death of her sister. State interference, by means of an operation to separate the twins, will prima facie be a violation of Mary's right to life.[43] It was argued above, however, that where there will be a net gain in human life, where an existing threat to life is merely diverted, and when this is achieved without violating the rights of the person who is to die, particularly by treating her as a mere object or means to an end, such an infringement may be justified. Here, if it is certain that both twins will die without an intervention and reasonably certain that one can be saved by such an intervention, these conditions appear to be satisfied. Jodie will be saved; the lethal threat posed by the twins' conjoined nature will be diverted from its current burden upon Jodie's heart to a new burden of lack of blood for Mary; and Mary is not treated as a means to an end. It is important that the separation of the twins is the cause of Mary's death, rather than any more direct means, and also that the separation take place at a time when both twins' deaths are imminent. Subject to what will be said in chapter 8 about whether Mary's quality of life requires her earlier death for her own interests, her right to life requires that her life not be sacrificed immediately because to do so would cast doubt upon the net gain in human life requirement: one twin would live where currently two are living. If both are about to die (and there would need to be some flexibility on the exact time frame here) then killing one to save the other will be justified. Mary's life must be given the same protection as that of any other living human being, but the right to life is not absolute and her life may be cut short if to do so is the only means, and a last resort, in order to save the life of another in circumstances where otherwise both would die and her death does not involve a violation of her

---

[42] ibid, p. 213.

[43] Robert Walker LJ attempted to argue that Mary's death would not be a violation of her right to life because it would not be an intentional deprivation of life, such as is prohibited under Article 2 ECHR. In this judge's view, because the separation operation would not be undertaken with the primary purpose of killing Mary, it is not an intentional deprivation of life. This attempt to avoid any conflict of rights, which is supplemented by Robert Walker LJ's belief that Mary's death would be in her own best interests, is a regrettable attempt to avoid making a difficult choice.

rights or the downgrading of her life to one of mere instrumental value to another person. And it is worth reiterating that Mary is neither an aggressor, nor a threat, and that her right to life is not forfeited by her behaviour because she is doing nothing other than living and an individual's life itself should never be treated as a justification for her death.

For these reasons, private defence can be ruled out as a criminal law justification for the killing of Mary. Ward LJ suggested the use of such a defence in *Re A* when he referred to the need to protect Jodie from the lethal threat posed by Mary.[44] Jonathan Rogers correctly recognizes that this potential defence is linked to the issue of the nature of Mary and the threat she poses:

The issues of private defence and that of Mary's humanity are indeed linked. If we cannot countenance Mary as being anything other than a human, albeit a grossly disabled one, then we are likely to recoil at the notion of private defence. If, on the other hand, we regard Mary's existence as an essentially parasitic one, as did Ward LJ, then we may accept that her existence is itself one of a threatening nature.[45]

The view of Mary as parasitic upon Jodie has already been dismissed in the preceding argument; the view that she is nothing but human is thus accepted. While Rogers also attempts to argue that even as a human being her mere existence may amount to 'unlawful violence' in the terms of Article 2 ECHR,[46] this is unconvincing. The mere fact of Mary's life cannot be regarded as amounting to violence upon Jodie, nor can it be regarded as unlawful. To so regard it would fail to pay due regard to the value of Mary's life as a human being.

A preferable means of categorizing the proposed exception to the right to life is by means of the legal doctrine of necessity. In the English legal system, necessity has traditionally not been available as a defence to murder, and nor has its close relation, duress.[47] In *Re A*, however, the Court of Appeal, and especially Brooke LJ, were prepared to extend necessity to the facts of the case in order to provide the doctors with a legal defence to a charge of the murder of Mary. The starting point for the application of this criminal defence was the Court's prior decision that the separation was the best course of action. Having established that Jodie's interests must be preferred over those of Mary, the judges were keen to avoid any conclusion that their preferred course of action would amount to murder. Previous caselaw, including *R v Dudley & Stephens* in which a defence of necessity was not available to sailors who killed and ate a cabin boy in order to save their own lives,[48] was distinguished on the basis that, unlike the cabin boy, Mary was designated for death and that a neutral decision-making process existed in

[44] *Re A*, n. 25 above, pp. 1016–17.
[45] J. Rogers, 'Necessity, Private Defence and the Killing of Mary' [2001] Crim.L.R. 515, at pp. 524–5. Walker LJ also rejected the notion of Mary as an 'unjust aggressor' (ibid, p. 1067) although Rogers claims that his 'repugnance is purely intuitive' (p. 524).	[46] ibid, p. 525.
[47] *R v Howe* [1987] AC 417 (duress); *R v Dudley & Stephens* (1884) 14 QBD 273 (necessity).
[48] ibid.

the current case. The concept of Mary being designated for death, and thereby having a lesser right to life, was rejected above, however. While the existence of a neutral decision-making process in *Re A* may provide a safeguard against the mob-rule danger of the strong killing the weak to save themselves, a better distinction between the two cases is that the starving sailors were introducing a new threat to the cabin boy, that of murder, and there are few clearer cases of treating a human being as a means to an end than killing him for food. The facts of *Dudley & Stephens* would not, therefore, satisfy the limited exception to the right to life being developed in this chapter. That is not to say that the sailors should have been convicted of murder. The availability of an excuse to the starving sailors, which would at least reduce their culpability would arguably be justified within the state's right to life obligations. Gardner makes the point, however, that one reason for the upholding of the murder convictions in that case was because, as much as an acquittal on the basis of excuse may have been desired by all, the danger that an acquittal would be viewed as a justification of the sailors' actions, and the implications of that in the close-knit sailing community, prevented the use of a necessity defence.[49]

The US case of *US v Holmes* is perhaps more comparable to the conjoined twins' situation.[50] In *Holmes*, a crewmember of a sinking ship threw overboard a number of passengers from an overloaded lifeboat. He was convicted of manslaughter with the judge emphasizing, in his address to the jury, that a defence of necessity would not exist 'unless all ordinary means of self preservation have been exhausted. The peril must be instant, overwhelming, leaving no alternative but to lose our own life, or to take the life of another person.'[51] While this, together with equal emphasis by Baldwin J on the existence of a duty of care on the part of a sailor for the passengers of his ship and the need for a random selection method as to who should die to save the others, may have justified the conviction in *Holmes*, it also cautions against the killing of Mary too soon. The threat to both Jodie's and Mary's life should be imminent before Mary's killing can be justified as necessary.

In *Re A*, Brooke LJ explained the three requirements for necessity and concluded that all were satisfied in this case. The three requirements are all based on the principle of proportionality: (a) the act is needed to avoid inevitable and irreparable evil; (b) no more is done that is reasonably necessary for the purpose; and (c) the evil inflicted is not disproportionate to the evil avoided.[52] The Court's

---

[49] S. Gardner, 'Necessity's Newest Inventions' (1991) 11 O.J.L.S. 125, at p. 127. Gardner's article provides the classic distinction between an excuse and a justification: 'With excuses, we should have preferred the law not to have been broken, so the conduct is accepted as unlawful, but given the situation in which the actor found herself we are prepared to condone the breach. With justifications, the idea is that we actually regard the conduct in question as right, preferable to the conduct apparently required by the relevant rule' (p. 126).   [50] (1842) 26 Fed.Cas. 360.

[51] ibid.

[52] *Re A*, n. 25 above, p. 1052. For a more detailed discussion of the necessity doctrine as applied in *Re A*, see E. Wicks, 'The Greater Good? Issues of Proportionality and Democracy in the Doctrine of Necessity as Applied in *Re A*' (2003) 32 C.L.W.R. 15.

approach of first deciding that the operation should take place, as in Jodie's best interests and consistent with the twins' rights to life, and then seeking a criminal law justification for it, meant that these conditions were easily satisfied. The issue of proportionality, however, depends upon the ethically problematic issues discussed above, including whether there is a net gain in human life and whether Mary's right to life prohibits the operation. The Court's unsatisfactory approach to those fundamental questions taints the entire judgment, even if the ultimate decision to authorize the operation is tragically the best choice in the circumstances.

C. Conflicting rights of a pregnant woman and fetus

In chapter 1, some preliminary conclusions were made about the beginning of life. It was proposed there that human life begins once a fetus develops organic integration. While the key to human life was argued to be the high level of consciousness enjoyed by members of the human species, the key to an individual organism's life was argued to be integrative function (governed by the brain and requiring sufficiently developed lungs to supply oxygen to the major organs). The stage in fetal development at which this occurs is viability which, in developed countries where neonatal intensive care is available, currently stands at about twenty-two weeks' gestation. When these issues were considered in the first chapter, no account was taken of any potentially conflicting rights of the pregnant woman carrying the fetus. Now, in the context of conflicting rights, is the place for that discussion. First, it should be noted that pre-viability, there is no question of conflicting rights. Following the argument in chapter 1, the pre-viable fetus does not possess a human life in the sense in which law and ethics seek to protect it. It is human; it is alive; but it is not yet an integrated human organism and thus does not possess a right to life. This does not mean that a pre-viability fetus should not have some degree of legal and ethical protection. Dworkin produces one possible argument for this when he draws a distinction between two different types of objections to abortion: (1) derivative objections, which are derived from the idea that a fetus has rights and interests, and (2) detached objections, where the fetus is not necessarily regarded as having any rights or interests but abortion is opposed because it disregards and insults the intrinsic value in human life.[53] He argues that 'Almost everyone who opposes abortion really objects to it, as they might realise after reflection, on the detached rather than derivative ground. They believe that a fetus is a living, growing human creature and that it is intrinsically a bad thing, a kind of cosmic shame, when human life at any stage is deliberately

---

[53] R. Dworkin, *Life's Dominion: An Argument about Abortion and Euthanasia* (London: HarperCollins, 1993), p. 11.

extinguished.'⁵⁴ This view recognizes that the destruction of any human life is regrettable, but is consistent with the argument that the fetus, pre-viability, does not possess a right to life that can conflict with the rights of the woman carrying it. Once viable, the fetus is a human life worthy of the law's protection, but so too is the woman carrying it, and thus the potential for conflict arises. This is not a conflict comparable to the others discussed in this chapter, however, for the woman and the fetus arguably do not possess moral symmetry.

If, for the sake of argument, we regard the fetus and the woman as of equal moral status, and assume that a termination of pregnancy is needed to save the woman's life but will end the fetus' life, we can ask whether the woman is entitled to end the fetus' life in order to save her own. Previous discussion in this chapter has required a number of conditions to be fulfilled before an innocent life can be taken in order to save another: there must be a net gain in human life; an existing lethal threat must be deflected; and the life taken must not be treated as a means to an end. These requirements will rarely be satisfied in the context of abortion, because there will rarely be a net gain in human life. It is possible, however, that a situation might exist, comparable to that of the conjoined twins discussed above, in which both woman and fetus will die imminently unless the pregnancy is terminated. Here there can be a net gain in human life from the termination, which will deflect the threat of the symbiotic relationship away from the woman and onto the fetus, and will not treat the fetus as a means to an end. As with the conjoined twins' case, in this situation the killing of one moral entity can be justified in order to save another, even if both have an equal right to life because one is not being favoured arbitrarily over the other. Jodie's death could not save Mary and thus could not result in a net gain in human life; neither can the death of the pregnant woman, but the death of Mary, and of the fetus, may do so. This is a rather narrow example, however. An alternative scenario, in which the fetus would benefit from being carried to full term but doing so would kill the mother, cannot justify an abortion even to save the life of the mother, because there is no net gain in human life, but rather the choosing of the woman's life over that of the fetus. More commonly, a woman may seek to have an abortion for a reason other than saving her life, perhaps to secure her physical or mental health; perhaps as an exercise of her autonomy without any health justification at all. We would not usually permit a violation of the right to life for such reasons. The exceptions to the right, as we will see throughout this book, are, and must be, narrowly drawn.

The pregnancy situation is distinct, however, from other conflicts of rights, and this is because the fetus' life is dependent upon a violation of the woman's bodily integrity. This situation can be distinguished from that of the conjoined twins discussed above. Contrary to the implication of the Court of Appeal judges, Mary did not threaten Jodie's bodily integrity, nor attack it; Mary and Jodie were both born conjoined to each other. A fetus is similarly born conjoined with its mother

---

⁵⁴ ibid, p. 13.

but, by contrast, the pregnant woman has not always been so conjoined. She has, in the past, enjoyed full bodily integrity. The fetus, innocently and inevitably, has breached that integrity. And that creates a moral asymmetry that is lacking from the case of conjoined twins. Judith Thomson's famous violinist example illuminates the implications of this approach.[55] She described a hypothetical case of a woman who awakes to find that a world-class violinist has been attached to her kidneys in order to preserve his life. Most people admit that there would be no obligation upon the woman to permit the violinist to stay attached to her, even on a temporary basis, despite the violinist having an equal right to life. There is no question of choosing to favour the woman's right to life over that of the violinist; instead the focus is upon what is required by the right to life. Thomson argues that it does not include a right to anything needed to preserve life if otherwise there would be no right to such a thing. For example, there is not generally a right to use another person's kidneys, and so Thomson argues that this right does not magically appear merely because it is necessary in order to preserve the violinist's life. Similarly, there is not generally a right to use another's body for sustenance and thus no reason why the fetus should acquire one merely because it is necessary for its survival. In Thomson's own words, 'having a right to life does not guarantee having either a right to be given the use of or a right to be allowed continued use of another person's body—even if one needs it for life itself.'[56] There is, in general, no obligation to be a Good Samaritan, especially at a cost to one's own rights and interests, including bodily integrity. Pregnancy is commonly seen as an exception to this, however. The reason can be traced to what is often referred to as the responsibility objection to Thomson's argument. This is the argument that 'ordinary, non-rape, pregnancies are crucially disanalagous'[57] to the violinist example because, so it is argued, the pregnant woman must take some responsibility for the joining of her body with that of the fetus. She did not, at least in non-rape cases, wake up to find a fetus had invaded her body; she partook of voluntary behaviour which she knew, or should have known, held a risk, however small, of resulting in pregnancy. The responsibility objection thus asserts that the woman has acquired some degree of responsibility for ensuring the survival of the fetus, given that it is (at least partly) her actions that have resulted in its current predicament. McMahan, although he has some sympathy with Thomson's argument, argues that, where the pregnancy is the result of voluntary sexual behaviour, 'it is hard to believe that it is permissible to kill one's own child in order to avoid the burden of providing the aid one has caused it to need'.[58] There are,

---

[55] J.J. Thomson, 'A Defence of Abortion' (1971) 1 Philosophy and Public Affairs 47.

[56] ibid, p. 32.

[57] H.S. Silverstein, 'On a Woman's "Responsibility" for the Fetus' (1987) 13 Social Theory and Practice 103, at p. 104.

[58] J. McMahan, *The Ethics of Killing: Problems at the Margins of Life* (Oxford: Oxford University Press, 2002), at p. 398. McMahan avoids this perceived problem by combining Thomson's argument with his own belief that the fetus is not of equal moral status.

however, a number of convincing arguments against the responsibility objection that suggest that the violinist example, and what it teaches us, is not disanalagous to pregnancy at all.

One problem with the responsibility objection is that it distinguishes so starkly between pregnancies resulting from rape and other pregnancies. From the pregnant woman's perspective, there is, undoubtedly, a clear distinction here: only in rape can it be said that the woman bears no responsibility at all for the pregnancy; in all other cases, the degree of responsibility may vary drastically (depending, for example, on whether contraceptives were used) but will not be completely eliminated. However, from the perspective of the fetus—and it is, after all, the fetus' right to life that is at issue here—whether it came into existence from rape should have no impact on its rights. We cannot sensibly argue that (viable) fetuses have a right not to be killed, except if their conception arose from rape, in which case they have no right to life. The entity is the same and has no responsibility for the acts of its father. Even if we can disregard the difficulty in the rape distinction, there remain other problems with the responsibility objection. Even accepting that the pregnant woman is at least partially responsible for the fact that the fetus exists, she is not responsible for the fact that, given that it exists, it needs the use of her body. As Silverstein points out, there is no alternative for the woman that would have avoided that outcome: the fetus could not both exist and not need her body.[59] Nothing the woman has done, or can bear responsibility for, has caused this reliance upon her body. Furthermore, we might even query whether we wish to accept this proposition that the woman who becomes pregnant by consensual intercourse is to be held responsible for the fetus inside her. Thomson compares this with a homeowner leaving a window open, through which a burglar enters. We would not then seek to claim that the burglar has a right to stay and make use of the home, despite his presence there being partly the responsibility of the homeowner.[60] By analogy, the fact that the woman's actions have contributed to the presence of a fetus inside her should not necessarily imply that she must now act to preserve the life of that fetus. (There is, however, an important distinction here because the burglar also holds (even greater) responsibility for his presence in the home, whereas the fetus is not responsible at all for its presence in the woman's womb.) It is also possible to argue that the concept, and implications, of a woman's responsibility for the creation of a fetus are not applied consistently. It is now possible to create embryos outside the body, and the woman whose eggs are used in IVF treatment bears partial responsibility for such a creation. It does not follow, however, that with that responsibility goes an obligation either to preserve the embryo or to have it implanted. Indeed, in English law, both parents

---

[59] Silverstein, n. 57 above, at p. 108.

[60] Thomson, n. 55 above, p. 34. Thomson gives an alternative example of a homeowner putting up bars at the window but the bars having a defect and thus permitting a burglar to enter. This analogy to defective contraceptives, as opposed to failing to use contraceptives, further highlights the difficulty in assigning responsibility for the existence of the fetus to all pregnant women.

will need to consent to the storage of the embryos and a woman endures no legal obligation to have the embryos implanted into her body. Why is the situation so different when the woman's responsibility is for the creation of an embryo inside her body rather than outside? In both cases, the embryo/fetus requires the woman's assistance if it is to be preserved and, although pre-viability there will be no issue of a right to life, it is not logically consistent for partial responsibility for creation to lead to onerous obligations in one case and not the other. In addition, once the child is born alive, parental responsibility can be relinquished by a mother (through adoption). Why can such responsibility not be relinquished pre-birth when the fetus can hardly have more (although perhaps it does not have less) rights?

The responsibility objection to Thomson's argument appears to be flawed in a number of respects and does not sufficiently counter the argument that a fetal right to life, by analogy with a post-birth right to life, does not entail a right to everything necessary to preserve life. We will see the broader implications of this limitation in chapter 9 in respect of positive obligations on the state to preserve life. We should not demand more of an individual in order to preserve the life of another than we would of the state. A fetal right to life does not, therefore, entail a right to remain within, and use, its mother's body. This does not necessarily mean, however, that a woman has the right to kill a fetus located within her body. Thomson recognizes that the question of the permissibility of an abortion is not the same as a right to secure the death of the fetus.[61] While there may be no obligation on the pregnant woman to permit the fetus to continue to use her body to preserve its life, the most that the woman can do is to ask for the fetus to be removed, as the woman in Thomson's example is entitled to ask for the violinist to be removed. Given that it was argued above that the fetus only acquires a right to life once it is viable (and an integrated human organism) then the woman's wish that the fetus be removed from her body may not result in the death of the fetus. The key here, however uncomfortable it may make us, is a distinction between killing and letting die. In practice, only so-called extractive abortions, during which the fetus is removed from the woman while alive and intact, can be regarded as satisfying the requirements above. It is important to bear in mind, however, that this restriction will only apply after viability. A fetus that is not viable outside the woman's body does not, based on the argument in chapter 1, have a right to life. Once viable, the fetus does have such a right and must not be killed but the woman is not obligated to continue the pregnancy until full term. The implications of this are worth noting. In many requested terminations after viability, the woman may wish the child to survive; it may be the pregnancy which must be terminated for the woman's health or life, and there may be no desire to terminate the life of the fetus. In this situation, the ethical position outlined in this section will be unproblematic and, indeed, will clearly reflect the reality of

---

[61] See Thomson, n. 55 above, pp. 40–1.

the situation. Other post-viability abortions will be more problematic, however, because one common reason for a late termination is the late discovery of a fetal abnormality. If the woman merely wishes to terminate her pregnancy as an exercise of her autonomy, frequently, and preferably, the abortion will be performed before the fetus becomes viable and is thus unproblematic in right to life terms. But if a fetal abnormality is discovered after viability, and with many abnormalities this is inevitable, the abortion will take place at a stage where the fetus has a right to life and should not, under the argument developed in this chapter, be killed. In some such cases it may be that the fetus will not survive after being extracted from the woman, even though it is past the stage of viability, because of its abnormalities. But what if the fetus can survive but it is thought, by the parents and perhaps the doctors, that survival is not in the child's own best interests? Does it still remain an infringement of the fetus' right to life to cause its death, either within the woman before extraction or later outside the woman's body? The answer to this question must be found in the context of quality of life considerations, which will be fully investigated in chapter 8. It is clear, however, that the viable fetus cannot be killed in the interests of its mother, although equally it cannot depend upon a continuation of its occupation of another human being. If it is viable, it has a right to life but that does not guarantee the fetus, any more than it guarantees the rest of us, that its life will be preserved. It must take its chances in the dangerous world outside its mother's body.

International manifestations of the right to life, at both regional and international levels, are ambiguous on the issues of maternal–fetal conflicts, due to a reluctance on the part of the drafters of these provisions to state categorically that a fetus is entitled to a right to life. Most of the right to life provisions leave the question open and even the American Convention on Human Rights, which explicitly protects the right to life from the moment of conception, only does so subject to the proviso 'in general'.[62] The reluctance to unambiguously clarify this issue, adopted by the bodies established to enforce these provisions as well as the documents themselves, and particularly evident in these pronouncements of the European Commission and Court of Human Rights, seems to be due to a reluctance to permit the widespread limitation of the rights of pregnant women. If, for example, a fetus is declared to have a full right to life under a provision such as Article 2 ECHR, the question arises of what happens if the mother's right to life can only be protected by means of terminating the fetus' right to life. The terms of Article 2 are far too crude to resolve such an issue. It is apparent, however, that by implication if not explicitly, institutions such as the European Court of Human Rights have adopted approaches consistent with the ethical approach outlined above. This can be seen in a number of ways. First, the treaty bodies have refused to exclude the possibility of the right to life extending to the fetus but have also declined to regard domestic laws permitting abortion as in violation of

---

[62] Article 4(1) ACHR.

this right. The implied message is clear: a fetal right to life does not preclude the possibility of legal terminations of pregnancy. This apparent reluctance to allow a fetal right to life to overrule the rights of the mother can be seen in cases such as *Paton v United Kingdom*,[63] *H v Norway*[64] and *Boso v Italy*.[65] The approach is consistent with the conclusions outlined above under which a viable fetus has the protection of a right to life but this does not prevent a woman refusing to provide the use of her body in order to ensure the continued preservation of that life. While states are typically given a wide discretion to resolve maternal–fetal conflicts in a manner appropriate to the state's social and religious preferences, no international body has upheld the right to life of a fetus, even a viable one, in circumstances where that would involve a restriction of the rights of the pregnant woman. There also appears to be a trend in international law towards increasing recognition of the rights of a pregnant woman in respect of abortion. While only one international treaty, the Protocol on the Rights of Women in Africa, expressly recognizes abortion as a human right in itself,[66] it has been argued that, in other treaties, 'a constellation of human rights, including the rights to privacy, liberty, physical integrity, non-discrimination and health, support the notion that abortion on request is a human right'.[67] Although this has not manifested itself in practice yet, cases such as *KL v Peru*[68] under the ICCPR and *Tysiac v Poland*[69] under the ECHR hint that, at least where the pregnant woman's right to health is at stake, access to abortion takes on the status of a human right. In *KL v Peru*, the HRC held Peru to be in violation of a number of Covenant Articles, including Article 7's prohibition of cruel, inhuman and degrading treatment, due to failure to permit a 17-year-old girl, pregnant with an anencephalic fetus, to obtain an abortion. She was forced to carry the fetus to full term and to watch it die four days after birth. Her severe depression substantiated a finding that the state's failure to permit her to terminate her pregnancy endangered her mental health. In *Tysiac v Poland*, the threat to the woman's health related to her eye condition. She was advised that pregnancy and delivery would threaten her eyesight but was denied access to a termination of pregnancy. The European Court of Human Rights did not find a substantive violation of the ECHR in respect of this denial, but did find a procedural violation of Article 8 due to the absence of any means of challenging the refusal of an abortion. This trend towards regarding abortion itself as an aspect of a pregnant woman's human rights, when coupled with a refusal to exclude the possibility of a fetal right to life, demands a nuanced approach to maternal–fetal conflicts. The ethical approach outlined above, under

---

[63] (1980) 3 E.H.R.R. 408.   [64] (1992) 73 DR 155.   [65] ECHR 2002—VII.

[66] Article 14.2(c): 'State Parties shall take all appropriate measures to . . . protect the reproductive rights of women by authorising medical abortion in cases of sexual assault, rape, incest, and where the continued pregnancy endangers the mental and physical health of the mother or the life of the mother or the foetus.' See C. Zampas & J.M. Gher, 'Abortion as a Human Right: International and Regional Standards' [2008] H.R.L.R. 249 for discussion.   [67] Zampas & Gher, ibid, p. 255.

[68] 1153/2003.   [69] (2007) 45 E.H.R.R. 42.

which the (viable) fetus' right to life does not include a power to compel its mother to provide continued use of her body, in violation of her own rights, is one possible solution.

Finally, the case of *Vo v France*[70] under the ECHR illustrated that a fetal right to life, even subject to the restriction outlined above, can still be a valuable and necessary protection. In *Vo*, the fetus was damaged by a doctor who, in a case of mistaken identity, attempted to remove a coil from a woman who was six months pregnant. A termination of pregnancy subsequently became necessary due to the damage suffered by the fetus. The mother lodged a criminal complaint alleging, inter alia, the unintentional homicide of her child but the French criminal courts held that a fetus could not be a victim of homicide. The European Court of Human Rights, while regrettably declining to decide whether a fetus has any protection under Article 2 ECHR, nevertheless found that if the fetus had a right to life it had not been violated in this case due to the availability of civil law remedies, such as negligence, against the doctor. The failure of the majority of the Court to decide the crucial issue in the case—does a fetus have a right to life—is a disappointing, if understandable, abdication of judicial responsibility. However, a number of lessons can be drawn from the *Vo* judgment. First, as the judges who gave individual opinions all agreed, discussing the procedural requirements of Article 2, as the majority judgment does, presupposes the applicability of that Article to the fetus. Second, the (implicit) recognition of the applicability of Article 2 is only the first step in resolving the conflict; the next step is to consider what exactly is required by the right to life. In *Vo*, a civil law remedy for the destruction of a life through negligence was regarded as sufficient protection by the state for the fetus' right to life. Similarly, it might be argued that a fetal right to life does not encompass an obligation on another person to undergo, against her wishes, a substantial invasion of her own rights. Thirdly, the facts of the *Vo* case remind us that the right to life of a fetus is not always in conflict with the rights of the mother. In this case, both fetus and mother were harmed by a third party. While a fetal right to life may not require that the fetus be carried to term in violation of its mother's rights, it will require that its life be protected from attack. A state that compelled a pregnant woman to undergo an abortion which killed the fetus would undoubtedly be violating the fetus' right to life (in addition to numerous rights of the mother), as would a state that failed to hold an individual accountable for killing a fetus, for example, by stabbing the mother or negligently performing a medical examination on the mother. The right to life for a viable fetus has many uses beyond compelling a violation of its mother's bodily integrity.

Typically, right to life provisions are ambiguously drafted and interpreted in respect of the right to life of a fetus. They leave considerable room for ethical debate. A number of points are clear, however: there is no explicit protection for

[70] (2005) 10 E.H.R.R. 12.

the fetus, although it may (and, it has been argued, after viability should) be accorded protection under the right; and there is no express procedure for reconciling a mother's right to life with the right to life of the fetus within her, in the rare cases in which they conflict. The right to life is limited in some contexts, as we are investigating throughout this book, but in the context of a fetal right to life, the necessary limitation should be seen as an element of the boundary of the right (namely that it does not compel other members of society to suffer violations of their own rights in order to ensure that your life is preserved), rather than as the consequence of a conflict of two rights.

D. Conclusion

This chapter has considered a number of specific situations in which a right to life may conflict with another person's rights, including the trolley problem, hijacked planes, conjoined twins and late pregnancy, and has sought to draw some general conclusions on when such conflicting rights may outweigh an individual's right to life. In line with previous chapters, it has been argued that the right to life can only be overridden as a last resort. While the previous chapter discussed situations where an individual has lost the protection of the right to life due to violating another's right, in this chapter there is no question of anyone losing the protection of the right to life. Instead, the focus has been on those rare situations in which tragic choices have to be made between lives, all of which benefit from the protection of the right to life. It has been argued that three strict conditions exist before an individual's right to life can be violated in order to save another individual's life: there must be a net gain in human life; and the intervening action diverts an existing threat to life, rather than creating a new one, and does not treat the person(s) killed as merely means to an end. Whether or not these conditions are satisfied may be difficult to determine, particularly if there remains some uncertainty about the factual situation, as will inevitably be the case in respect of a hijacked plane. These conditions only apply in circumstances where a proposed intervention, usually by the state, will kill at least one life in order to save more lives. Another important conclusion of this chapter, however, is that what may sometimes appear to be a conflict of rights may in reality be better defined as an issue about what is required by the right to life. We already know, and will investigate further in the following chapters, that the right to life extends beyond merely a negative right not to be killed and requires a state to take reasonable measures to preserve life. It cannot be assumed, however, that the right to life extends to the imposition of a legal obligation on other individuals to permit a violation of their rights, for example of bodily integrity, in order to help preserve that life. Termination of pregnancy (after viability) is not permissible on the grounds that a woman's rights to autonomy or bodily integrity or health outweigh a viable fetus' right to life, for they could not do so, but rather it is permissible because the fetus' right to life does not require that another individual suffer an infringement of bodily integrity. Similarly, an individual who will die without a kidney transplant does not suffer a violation of his right to life merely because the state does not compel another individual to suffer a violation of bodily integrity in order to provide a spare kidney. The right to life neither compels, nor permits, the state to require other members of society to suffer infringement of rights, or be used as means to an end, in order to ensure the preservation of an individual's life. And that general rule applies to the viable fetus, as much as to any other beneficiary of the right to life. This chapter has focused on situations where the right to life may come into conflict with the rights of others; the next chapter will turn attention to situations where an individual's right to life may conflict with the other rights of that individual, particularly the right of autonomy.

7

The Right to Life and Autonomy

In the previous two chapters, we have looked at potentially conflicting interests that might provide exceptions to the general negative obligation not to kill under the right to life. In this, and the following two, chapters, attention will turn to interests that may conflict with a state's positive obligations to preserve life under the right to life. This chapter focuses on the interest and right of autonomy which may conflict with the right to life in the context of suicide and other life-threatening autonomous actions. First we will briefly investigate the two concepts of the value of life and autonomy. Then the positive obligations imposed upon states under the right to life in this context will be identified, including the special duties imposed in relation to individuals under the control of the state, such as prisoners and mental patients. Finally, the issue of assisted suicide will be considered which will lead into the following chapter's discussion of the quality of life as another potentially conflicting interest to the preservation of life. It will be seen that the exceptions to the general obligation to take steps to preserve life are significantly broader than the very narrowly drawn exceptions to the duty not to kill which have previously been identified.

A. The value of life and autonomy

When considering the potentially conflicting interests of a right to life and autonomy, an important starting point is the issue of the value of life. In chapter 1, some consideration was given to why human life is valuable, and this is an issue to which attention will return in the next chapter. The focus here, however, is not so much on why life is valuable, but rather to whom is that life of value. If we accept that human life has some inherent value, is it solely to the individual who is enjoying that life or is there some broader state or societal benefit in that life? If life is of value only to the person living it, then this may elevate the importance of individual autonomy. It may even suggest that it is an individual's desire for respect for his or her own life that provides the inherent value in that life. On the other hand, it might be argued that the protection of human life is, at least partly, a matter of public interest. Whether it is to the state, or other members of society, or only an individual's own family and friends, there is an argument that a human life is a thing of value to others beyond the individual living that life. These two different views have particular significance to the issue of suicide because if life is legally and ethically protected in deference to the individual's wish for respect for that life, the protection would logically cease when an autonomous choice is made to bring the life to an end. If, however, the life is protected, at least partly, due to the legitimate interest in that life enjoyed by the state or other (perhaps select) members of society, then the individual's autonomous choice to end his or her life is not necessarily the decisive factor in determining whether legal and ethical protection for that life should continue.

Support for the proposition that an individual's life is of value to persons beyond that individual can be drawn from a variety of religious and philosophical thought. Perhaps most obviously, Christian thought, as discussed in chapter 1, regards human life as a gift from God and thus, as the giver of the gift, God retains an interest in how the gift is treated and ultimately disposed of. There is also an old belief that the state has a similar interest. In an old English case on suicide, the act of self-murder was described as 'an offence against nature, against God, and against the King. Against nature, because it is contrary to the rules of self-preservation... Against God, in that it is a breach of His commandment, thou shall not kill... Against the King in that hereby he has lost a subject...'[1] The introduction of the state, in the form of the King, as a body with a legitimate interest in the continuation of the lives of its citizens can also been seen in Blackstone's writings: 'the suicide is guilty of a double offence: one spiritual, in evading the prerogative of the Almighty, and rushing into his immediate presence uncalled for; the other temporal, against the king, who hath an interest in the preservation of all his subjects.'[2] This state interest has only strengthened since this time. In the intervening centuries, states around the world have criminalized suicide and spent public money on efforts to save lives, even when the individual concerned no longer valued his or her own life. They did so because they recognized the contribution to society that can be made by the lives of its members: economic contributions through paying taxes and adding to the gross domestic product; military contributions by serving in the armed forces, fighting and dying in the interests of defending, or expanding, their country; humanitarian contributions by caring for other members of society so that the state does not have to do so; educational contributions by furthering the sum of human knowledge in disparate fields, with tangible, often profitable, results for the state. A human life learns, builds, thinks, cares, shares, nurtures, buys, pays, and fights its way through the years. No one can realistically claim that the state, and its citizens, lack an interest in that life, for the state is built upon just such lives. And most lives will contribute more than they take. A life that ends prematurely is one less worker, one less shopper, one less carer, and, in times of emergency, one less

---

[1] *Hales v Petit* (1562) 1 Plowden 253, at 261; 75 Eng.Rep. 387, at 400.
[2] *Blackstone's Commentaries on the Laws of England*, Volume IV, p. 189.

soldier. It is not surprising that, as recently as the 1980s, a US court has explicitly recognized that the preservation of life 'has a high social value' and described suicide as a 'grave public wrong'.[3]

The argument that the state has a legitimate interest in the lives of its citizens, when coupled with legal protection offered to life by the right to life, suggests that a state has both a power and a duty to take steps to protect life. In previous chapters, discussion has focused on the state's legal duty not to kill except in very narrowly drawn exceptional circumstances. The state's duty to protect life goes beyond this, however, and extends to a positive obligation to take steps to preserve life. This legal obligation, outlined in chapter 3, requires a state to do all that is reasonably required in order to preserve life in circumstances where there is a real and immediate risk to life. In determining what is reasonable, a number of factors will come into play that may be regarded as limitations upon a general state duty to preserve life. One influential factor will be the allocation of finite resources. Because positive obligations to preserve life in general cost more than a negative duty not to kill, the allocation of public resources is often at the very core of decisions of what is reasonably expected of the state in its duty to preserve life. More police officers, shorter hospital waiting lists and better medical treatment may all save lives but they do so at a financial cost to society. Striking an appropriate balance is often difficult. We will investigate this potential economic limitation on the state's duty to preserve life in chapter 9. Another factor that may be relevant to this duty is quality of life. Should the state be obligated to take steps to preserve all human life even if the quality of an individual life is so poor that it no longer brings any benefit to the individual involved? Again this issue will require a delicate balancing of potentially conflicting considerations (which will be considered in chapter 8). The factor of concern to us in this chapter is individual autonomy. While there is some merit in the argument that the state has an interest in the lives of its citizens, we must not forget that the human life that contributes so much to society is also an individual whose autonomous choices are what create and sustain that life. The state's duty to preserve life cannot be enforced in total disregard of the relevance of the autonomous choices of the living entity.

B. Autonomous choices to die

The meaning and relevance of the principle of autonomy has been hotly debated over many years. The general idea that an individual should be free to make his or her own choices about how to live is an important foundational concept for the law of human rights, with only the principle of human dignity presenting a meaningful challenge to autonomy's reign. There is little agreement, however, on the exact definition and hence the boundaries of autonomous choice. The

---

[3] *Von Holden v Chapman* (1982) 87 A.D. 2d. 66, at 68; 450 N.Y.S.2d. 623, at 626.

Kantian conception of autonomy requires that a person be entirely lacking in personal interests before a truly autonomous choice can be made. This reflects a common difficulty encountered when dealing with autonomy: our choices are rarely independent of external influences, whether in the form of well-meaning advice from friends or family, societal expectations, religious faith, or a myriad of other hidden biases. To give an example, I am about to stop writing this chapter in order to drink a cup of coffee and that is a decision only partly of my own making: it is influenced by the societal convention of elevenses (it is currently 10.55am); by the easy availability of coffee in my house in the West Midlands (would I be stopping to drink coffee if I was in the Saharan desert or if I was living in a cardboard box on the street?); by a family tradition of mid-morning drinks; and, perhaps most pressing of all, because I am a creature of habit: I always drink a cup of coffee at 11.00am. So my choice to do so again today is not really a completely free choice, influenced as it is by so many factors, perhaps the least of which is that I am thirsty. If we perform a similar analytical exercise for our other daily choices, both the trivial (such as drinking coffee) and the major (such as moving to a new job), we can soon see that very few choices, if any, are devoid of external influences: we do not make choices, even trivial ones, on a whim, however much we may like to think that we do. In English medical law, a doctrine of undue influence ensures that a patient's consent or, more commonly, refusal of consent is not regarded as autonomous if the decision has been reached as a result of undue influence of another person, such as a relative.[4] Although recognizing that some apparently autonomous choices may be based upon an unacceptable degree of external persuasion, this doctrine of undue influence ignores the other influences likely to be affecting the very same patient, such as the influence of the doctors and nurses, or of religious doctrine. If autonomy were truly to mean a decision reached without any internal bias or external influence, it would be of little utility. It may be, however, that autonomy is of its greatest value in respecting the myriad of individual influences that operate upon a person and lead to a choice that may not be free but is uniquely our own, reflecting our society, religion, family and values.

A further difficulty with autonomy, however, is the question of rationality. Some commentators, such as Julian Savulescu, argue that our autonomous actions are only those which are based upon rational desires.[5] This is an approach that can most clearly be seen in the medico-legal context. When a patient refuses life-sustaining medical treatment, the decision will often be challenged on the basis that the patient lacks mental competence, not because of any independent evidence of mental illness, but because the decision to refuse treatment appears to be irrational and might be evidence in itself that the patient's capacity to make

---

[4] *Re T (adult: refusal of treatment)* [1992] 4 All ER 649.
[5] J. Savulescu, 'Rational Desires of the Limitation of Life-Sustaining Treatment' (1994) 8 Bioethics 191.

decisions is currently impaired. For example, there is a series of cases in which a pregnant woman has refused a Caesarean section delivery against the advice of the doctors. When the judge has been faced with an emergency application in which the medical evidence has been that both the woman and her unborn child will die without the operation, the judges have invariably allowed the operation to go ahead, usually on the basis that the woman is mentally incompetent to give or refuse consent, and thus should be treated in her best interests.[6] While it is true that the higher courts have criticized any first instance judge who overrules the refusal of consent without finding that the woman lacks competence,[7] it is hard to rule out the possibility that an irrational (and selfish) refusal of treatment is surreptitiously regarded as evidence of a lack of competence. This creates a danger that agreeing with the doctors proves that a patient is competent, while disagreeing, particularly without any objectively reasonable reason for doing so, suggests that a patient is incompetent. This is problematic because the choice of the patient is not being respected. If we have only the freedom to say yes, we do not have a freedom to choose, and that applies even, and most importantly, when yes is the objectively reasonable choice. Autonomy to agree with everyone else is of limited use; the times when we need to demand respect for autonomy are when we disagree with the majority opinion or with the reasonable conclusion. If evidence were needed that this is a real danger it can be found in the actions of the medical teams in the Caesarean section cases. In *Rochdale Healthcare NHS Trust v C*,[8] a pregnant woman declared that she would rather die than repeat her previous experience of a Caesarean section under epidural anaesthetic. C's obstetrician confirmed that her mental capacity was not in doubt and she was fully competent but Johnson J, during a two minute *ex parte* hearing, inexplicably took the opposite view and held C to be mentally incompetent. During the time of the hearing, however, the woman changed her mind and consented to the Caesarean section. Immediately, her competency, and right of autonomy, was restored. Once she had agreed to the operation her consent was considered to be a valid exercise of her autonomy and the doubts about her competency vanished. A similar development occurred in respect of the *St George's* case when, just before the operation was performed non-consensually under a court declaration, the patient was asked once more if she consented. If she was indeed incompetent, as the judge's issuing of the declaration suggested, it would be futile for medical staff to seek her consent to the procedure. The fact that they did so clearly re-iterates that these pregnant women were being found to be incapable of making a choice merely because of the choice which they had made.

It appears that anyone who regards death as an acceptable outcome compared to the available alternatives is vulnerable to an assumption that they are mentally impaired. Historically, this has meant that those who attempt suicide were frequently regarded as insane. Even more contemporary reasoning, under which it is more widely recognized that there may exist some good reasons for preferring death to the alternative, such as unbearable pain, continues to regard rationality as a key factor. For example, Battin recognizes a recent move 'from the recently predominant view that there is *no* good reason for suicide (and hence that all suicide is irrational or insane) to the view that there is after all one adequate reason for suicide: extreme and irremediable pain in terminal illness'.[9] This only raises the question, however, of why autonomous choice, in the context of choosing death, is repeatedly subjected to tests of rationality. It may indeed be true that there are some rational reasons for choosing to die—such as terminal illness—and also some irrational reasons—such as breaking up with a boyfriend—for making this choice. But should the rationality of a choice really affect the way in which we treat the autonomous choice, provided always that it is truly autonomous? There is plenty of evidence that the law, including, but not restricted to, human rights law, rejects a rationality restriction on autonomy. For example, in the English case of *Re T (adult: refusal of treatment)*, Lord Donaldson MR declared that a competent adult's right to choose medical treatment is 'not limited to decisions which others might regard as sensible. It exists notwithstanding that the reasons for making the choice are rational, irrational, unknown or even non-existent.'[10] If autonomy has value that value is to be found in the choices available to the individual, not in acting rationally. Many of our choices, both trivial and major, are irrational; they are no less worthy of respect for this.

Rather than rationality, perhaps we should be searching for intention when assessing whether a choice or action is autonomous. In recent years, conceptions of autonomy have taken on an individualistic nature whereby a person's desires or actions are regarded as autonomous to the extent that they originate in some way from his or her motivational set.[11] Gerald Dworkin's hierarchical approach to autonomy is one influential example of this. His explanation of autonomy is that of 'second order capacity of persons to reflect critically upon their first-order preferences, desires, wishes and so forth'.[12] For example, an individual may have not only a desire to smoke but also simultaneously a desire that he not have that desire. This capacity to reflect upon our instant desires distinguishes autonomy from mere voluntariness.[13] Dworkin's theory is based on self-reflection about our desires. It clearly has relevance to the question of suicide: is the choice to die the result of a second order reflective process, or merely a first order instinct? But how realistic is a requirement of self-reflection? Beauchamp queries whether

---

[9] M. Battin, *The Least Worst Death: Essays in Bioethics on the End of Life* (Oxford: Oxford University Press, 1994), pp. 198–9.   [10] [1992] 4 All ER 649, at pp. 652–3.
[11] J.S. Taylor (ed.), *Personal Autonomy: New essays on Personal Autonomy and Its Role in Contemporary Moral Philosophy* (Cambridge: Cambridge University Press, 2005), p. 1.
[12] G. Dworkin, *The Theory and Practice of Autonomy* (Cambridge: Cambridge University Press, 1988), p. 20.   [13] ibid, p. 15.

the non-repudiation of the values underlying a choice would be a more realistic alternative.[14] Certainly we make many choices without reflecting on them but there may be some merit in an approach that accords particular weight to those choices, decisions and actions that are the result of serious self-reflection. Under such an approach, a choice to die would attract greater protection under the label of autonomy if it is the outcome of self-reflection rather than an impetuous or unintended action. Indeed, using a similar approach to the topic, Kay Wheat has argued that many apparent suicide attempts are not necessarily true suicide cases because they lack considered and firm decisions to abandon life, whereas many cases of refusal of life-sustaining medical treatment would more appropriately be regarded as suicides (despite the law's reluctance to so regard them) because they are evidence of an unambiguous intention to die, usually following a lengthy period of self-reflection.[15]

It is interesting that, in general, refusals of medical treatment are not regarded as suicide attempts, even when the treatment is essential in order to preserve life. The same is generally true of refusals of food. They are treated as manifestations of autonomy that may or may not be respected by the law depending upon the individual's mental state. The apparently key issue of whether death is the intended result is often overlooked. In the English case of *Secretary of State for the Home Department v Robb*, for example, a prisoner on hunger strike was recognized as having a right of self-determination and there was held to be no countervailing state interest to balance against this because, while the state does have an interest in preventing suicide, it was held to be 'of no application in cases such as this where the refusal of nutrition and medical treatment in the exercise of the right of self-determination does not constitute an act of suicide'.[16] Why is this so? If judged on the basis of self-reflection and intention, there seems to be no reason to distinguish such a case from a person who takes an overdose of pills or jumps from a bridge. But the explanation is not hard to discern. If a patient who refuses life-sustaining medical treatment is attempting suicide, then a doctor who helps him or her will be assisting a suicide, which, as we shall see, remains a criminal offence in many countries (even those, such as the UK, which no longer criminalize suicide itself). Hence when Ms B was permitted, in line with well-established English medical law principles, to refuse consent to the continuation of artificial ventilation, it was categorically stated that she was not committing suicide, and the doctors who turned off the ventilator would not be guilty of a criminal offence.[17] Her case is thus distinguished from that of Dianne Pretty who was refused permission to commit suicide with the assistance of her husband.[18] The

[14] T.L. Beauchamp, 'Who Deserves Autonomy and Whose Autonomy Deserves Respect?' in Taylor, n. 11 above, pp. 320–1.

[15] K. Wheat, 'The Law's Treatment of the Suicidal' (2000) 8 Med.L.Rev. 182.

[16] *Secretary of State for the Home Department v Robb* [1995] 1 All ER 677.

[17] *Re B (adult: refusal of medical treatment)* [2002] 2 All ER 449.

[18] *R (on the application of Pretty) v Director of Public Prosecutions* [2002] 1 All ER 1 (HL); *Pretty v United Kingdom* (2002) 35 E.H.R.R. 1 (ECtHR).

intentions of both women are identical: to choose death as a preferable alternative to their current state of living. The cases should not be distinguished on that basis. (There is, however, a more convincing distinction that arguably justifies the different outcomes, namely that the doctors were committing a battery upon Ms B by subjecting her to artificial ventilation against her wishes. Such a blatant infringement of physical integrity must negate any general rules against actions that assist a person to commit suicide.)

If self-reflection culminating in a clear intention to die is the basis on which an act of suicide is judged to be autonomous and thus deserving of greater respect than mere instinctive actions, one might query whether sacrificial deaths are not of the same class. Battin queries why self-inflicted deaths intended to benefit others, such as Captain Oates walking into the Antarctic blizzard, are generally excluded from the category of suicides.[19] Why is this death seen as an heroic exercise of autonomy, while we are so readily inclined to regard most self-inflicted deaths as a symptom of mental illness and thus not autonomous at all? Williams argues that it is 'only the emotive effect of the word "suicide" that leads one to wish to withhold it from situations of this type'[20] but if the category of acts labelled suicides are to be treated differently from other self-inflicted deaths, a much clearer distinction between the two will be needed than can be discerned from Captain Oates' desire to help others. While this was undoubtedly honourable, so too may be other self-inflicted deaths, at least in the eyes of the person committing the act. An argument is being developed here that rationality, and related ideas such as reasonableness of objective and honourable choice, should be rejected when considering the issue of autonomous choices to die. Instead, we should focus only on intention: does this person really intend to die, and is this the result of at least a degree of reflection? While this will group honourable sacrifices of life together with selfish, irrational wishes to die, there is no acceptable justification for separating these two categories if both evidence an autonomous intention to die. On the other hand, the focus on intention allows us to distinguish another category of autonomous choices: those involved in undertaking risky behaviour.

To some extent, life itself is a risky business. We encounter potential threats to the continuation of our lives every day, such as crossing a street, eating fatty foods, or living in cities with high crime rates. However, some people voluntarily undertake greater than normal risks, such as smoking, participating in dangerous sports or driving recklessly. Assuming that this behaviour is undertaken on the basis of an autonomous choice, and assuming also that there is a demonstrable threat to life inherent in the behaviour, the question arises whether the state has an obligation, and/or a power, to take steps to prevent such behaviour. It seems to be well established that a state has both a power and a duty to intervene when one person's behaviour poses a threat to the life of another. This is inherent in the obligation under the right to life that homicide be criminalized, and

---

[19] Battin, n. 9 above, p. 188.
[20] G. Williams, *The Sanctity of Life and the Criminal Law* (London: Faber & Faber, 1958), p. 242.

it can also be seen through state interventions in our autonomous actions such as the imposition of speed limits on the roads. If I am legally required to drive at under 70mph on a motorway, it is primarily because of a belief that driving faster is more likely to cause accidents in which other people may die (or be seriously injured). My autonomy is restricted—perhaps if given the choice I would like to drive at 100mph—but it is a justifiable restriction in a society that values human life. There may also be other justifications for the restriction beyond protecting the lives of others. Road traffic accidents are expensive, both in terms of public costs for emergency services and medical treatment and also in terms of costs to business through delays and disruption. Furthermore, the restriction on my autonomy when driving also serves the purpose of protecting my own life. If my speed causes an accident, the life most likely to be endangered is my own. So in imposing speed limits, the state is not only protecting the lives of other members of society from my autonomous actions for it also has the effect of protecting my own life, which as was discussed above is something of value to society as a whole. A more ethically challenging situation arises if a state intervention cannot be, even partly, justified on the basis of saving the lives of others. In the driving context, a speed limit may save others, so too might a law requiring the use of seatbelts, but what about a law requiring that motorcyclists wear helmets? This will not save anyone's life other than that of the motorcyclist him/herself. Should the state restrict the motorcyclist's freedom to drive without a helmet? If so, does it logically follow that the state should also ban smoking even in private places, prohibit hang-gliding, and criminalize suicide? As Glover recognizes, 'We are used to paternalistic laws making motorcyclists wear crash helmets, but the idea of laws forbidding people to smoke cigarettes shocks us as an infringement of traditional liberties.'[21] The key, as Glover also recognizes, is to strike a balance between 'minimizing risks and minimizing the kinds of restrictions that frustrate people in things that really matter to them'.[22] While the state has an obligation to take steps to protect life, it is only required to take such steps as are reasonable and this means that it must weigh in the balance the infringement of personal autonomy that such intervention will cause. Wearing a helmet when driving a motorcycle is an infringement of autonomy but a relatively minor one in that a desire to drive without a helmet is unlikely to be a particularly strongly held principle and its denial will not impact on other aspects of the individual's life. A freedom to smoke may be rather more central to an individual's life and lifestyle, although here there will be a threat to the lives of others to be taken into account as well. Suicide is a different matter entirely. Here a decision to end one's life may (although will not always) be well considered and strongly held. A decision to kill oneself will rarely be taken lightly. A denial of autonomy in that context will impact in a major way on the entirety of the individual's life. Indeed, every day lived after a choice to commit suicide has been denied, will be an ongoing

---

[21] J. Glover, *Causing Death and Saving Lives* (London: Penguin, 1977), p. 180.   [22] ibid.

infringement of autonomy. A decision to kill oneself is more fundamental to a person than a decision not to wear a helmet and therefore being prevented by the state from making that decision would be a far greater interference with individual autonomy. Furthermore, because a decision to commit suicide is more fundamental to a person, a law prohibiting it is less likely to be effective, and, if not effective in preventing the suicide attempt, criminalization of the attempt will then impose an additional ordeal on those already suffering. Thus, a clear distinction can be drawn between state intervention to reduce the dangers both to others and to oneself from undertaking risky behaviour and state intervention to prevent suicide. In Glover's words, 'There is nothing to be said for a substantial erosion of autonomy that is also ineffective. There is a lot to be said for saving many people who want to live, but who, for trivial advantages, thoughtlessly gamble with their lives.'[23] This returns us to the idea of self-reflection and intention as the key to determining whether a restriction on autonomy in respect of a choice to die will be justified. The state has a positive obligation to take reasonable steps to preserve life and so should intervene when it is practicable to do so in order to seek to save the lives of those who thoughtlessly endanger it, but when an individual takes actions with a clear intention of ending his or her life, for whatever reason, an infringement of that person's autonomy is not justified even in order to save life, and would not be required even under the right to life. We will now look at the specific obligations that the right does impose in this context.

C. Positive obligations to prevent suicide

(1) Criminalization of suicide

Within Western countries,[24] there is a long, although not unchallenged, tradition of condemnation of suicide. While the Greek and Roman Stoics were sympathetic, even positive, about suicide,[25] the Christian Church from the time of Augustine has condemned it as a sin. Williams explains that the prohibition of

---

[23] ibid, p. 181.

[24] There are some examples of cultures that emphasized the honour aspect of ritual suicides such as in respect of the Japanese practice of suppuku (in which a samurai would kill himself by means of a sword to the abdomen) and the Hindu funeral practice of sati (in which a widow immolates herself on her husband's funeral pyre).

[25] Seneca, a Roman Stoic philosopher, regarded death as something we could, and should, control: 'Just as I choose a ship to sail in or a house to live in, so I choose a death for my passage from life. Moreover, whereas a prolonged life is not necessarily better, a prolonged death is necessarily worse…A man's life should satisfy other people as well, his death only himself, and whatever sort he likes is best' (Seneca, Letters to Lucilius, excerpt from Letter 70, in *The Stoic Philosophy of Seneca*, quoted in M.P. Battin, *Ending Life: Ethics and the Way We Die* (Oxford: Oxford University Press, 2005), p. 4). Battin explains Seneca's view that a self-embraced death is not a premature end to a complete life: 'It isn't like a journey cut short, which is so incomplete because you don't get there; rather, Seneca maintains, a life cut short can still be complete if it has been lived well—you do get there, so to speak; you've actually lived your whole life.' (Battin, p. 4.)

suicide was a 'necessary corollary of the church's other teaching, which would, without this corollary, have operated, and did in fact operate, as an incitement to suicide.'[26] In other words, for religious believers, suicide might appear to be a good option in order to avoid sin and ensure entry to heaven unless suicide is itself treated as a sin. So, while suicide was regarded as a sin, suffering, martyrdom and dying at God's will were to be rewarded. Perhaps as a legacy of this Christian condemnation, the punishments for suicide preceded the criminal prohibition of it.[27] Punishments for suicide took two forms: against the body and against property. The 15th Canon of the Council of Braga in 563 AD denied the usual funeral rites to suicides. Canon law was adopted into England in 673 AD and the denial of burial rites was expressly affirmed by canon of King Edgar in 967 AD. This was followed by secular laws enforcing the forfeiture of the property of suicides. Originally such forfeited property went to the suicide's immediate lord but this changed once suicide was held to be a felony so that it was the King that would benefit from the forfeiture.[28] However, the enforcement of these laws was problematic because coroner's juries were reluctant to impose a severe penalty upon the friends and family of the deceased. The best way to avoid this was for a finding of insanity to be brought. Hoffmann and Webb explain that: 'If the finding were that the deceased was "sane" at the time of the suicidal act, Christian burial could be denied and property could be confiscated. Conversely, a finding of insanity absolved the suicide of criminal responsibility, and thus allowed the family to evade the punitive consequences of their loved one's self-destruction.'[29] By the end of the eighteenth century, a suicide was rarely pronounced sane, and thus 'the public, acting through the coroner's jury, in effect obstructed the administration of the law'.[30] During the nineteenth century this led to a movement for legal reform, led by Sir Samuel Romilly, who 'contended that the extreme severity of the criminal code led to its nonenforcement'.[31] The reform movement succeeded and, through the Right to Burial Act 1823 and the Abolition of Forfeiture Act 1870, both burial and property penalties were removed. Suicide remained a felony, however. In other European countries, suicide was being legalized. France led the way in 1790, followed by many other countries, including Germany, Italy and Switzerland. But in England it remained a felony at common law for a sane person of the age of responsibility to kill himself, either intentionally or in the course of trying to kill another. Of greater practical significance, it was a misdemeanour to attempt to commit suicide. Even at the beginning of the twentieth century, imprisonment remained a common punishment for attempted suicide, and a second attempt might be punished by as long as six months in prison.[32] During the next few decades, however, prosecutions became rarer. In part this

---

[26] Williams, n. 20 above, p. 231.
[27] D.E. Hoffman & V.J. Webb, 'Suicide as Murder at Common Law' (1981) 19 Criminology 372, at p. 374.   [28] ibid, p. 376.
[29] ibid, p. 378.   [30] ibid, pp. 378–9.   [31] ibid, p. 379.
[32] Williams, n. 20 above, p. 249.

was due to a new police policy of prosecuting only where there was some definite circumstance calling for punishment, or where the order of the court constituted the only chance of refuge and asylum for one too weak to stand alone.[33] Later further procedural changes such as permitting the charge of attempted suicide to be tried summarily by magistrates and a sentence of absolute or conditional discharge, or probation with a condition of mental treatment, to be imposed after a finding of guilt all lessened the severity of the action taken against those who tried, but failed, to end their lives.

In 1961, legislation was finally introduced which, by implication, repealed the offence of attempted suicide, together with the explicit repeal of the felony of suicide. The Suicide Act 1961 states that 'The rule of law whereby it is a crime for a person to commit suicide is hereby abrogated.' There were a number of sound reasons for this legislative intervention. As David Ormerod explains: 'The felon was beyond the reach of punishment; the legal sanction was not an effective deterrent—there were some 5,000 suicides a year; and the effect was merely to add to the distress and pain of the bereaved relatives.'[34] Lord Bingham has also more recently identified the pressing reasons why an autonomous choice to kill oneself should no longer be subject to criminalization:

Suicide itself (and with it attempted suicide) was decriminalised because recognition of the common law offence was not thought to act as a deterrent, because it cast an unwarranted stigma on innocent members of the suicide's family and because it led to the distasteful result that patients recovering in hospital from a failed suicide attempt were prosecuted, in effect for their lack of success.[35]

It is interesting to note that respect for individual autonomy is nowhere to be found in these justifications. Suicide was decriminalized because criminalizing it was not an effective deterrent and punishing either directly someone who has failed in a suicide attempt or indirectly the family of one who has succeeded was seen to be distasteful and unnecessarily harsh. But there is another equally convincing reason for not criminalizing the act or attempt of suicide: it may (there will be exceptions) represent an intentional exercise of autonomous choice. This should be a good enough reason for the state not to intervene to save life, provided that no one else—who has not made the same autonomous choice—is harmed, and provided also that the choice is truly an autonomous one, which means not one reached on the basis of duress or mental illness. The absence of autonomy from the list of justifications for the legalization of suicide reflects the strongly held opinion that suicide remains something to be prevented and, perhaps, condemned, even if it no longer attracts legal culpability. Despite some academic attempts to recognize a 'right to suicide',[36] the courts remain adamant

[33] ibid.
[34] Smith & Hogan, *Criminal Law* (12th edn., ed. D. Ormerod) (Oxford: Oxford University Press, 2008), p. 554.   [35] *Pretty* (HL), n. 18 above, para. 35.
[36] See, for example, M.P. Battin, 'Suicide: A Fundamental Human Right?' in *The Least Worse Death*, n. 9 above.

that there is no such right. Lord Bingham explained in *Pretty* that 'while the 1961 Act abrogated the rule of law whereby it was a crime for a person to commit (or attempt to commit) suicide, it conferred no right on anyone to do so'.[37] This is undoubtedly a correct reading of the implications of the 1961 Act. Not every activity which is not a criminal offence can be regarded as a positive right. Furthermore, Lord Bingham justifies his conclusion by noting that the 1961 Act creates an offence of assisting suicide which demonstrates that the 'policy of the law remained firmly adverse to suicide'.[38] The fact that there is no specific right to commit suicide within English law is not the end of the issue, however, as there is a right to autonomy within English law, albeit one that is extremely limited. And committing suicide will in some circumstances be a manifestation of the right to autonomy.

Autonomy is protected in various ways in English law but of particular significance is Article 8's right to respect for private life, which embodies a general right to autonomy. It has been accepted, at both domestic and ECHR level, that this right of autonomy applies to choices as to how and when to die, as well as to choices of how to live. Lord Hope stated in respect of Dianne Pretty that 'The way she chooses to pass the closing moments of her life is part of the act of living, and she has a right to ask that this too must be respected.'[39] This statement was expressly approved by the European Court of Human Rights.[40] This Court has made clear that when the state intervenes in such a way as to prevent by law an individual 'exercising her choice to avoid what she considers will be an undignified and distressing end to her life', this may constitute an interference with Article 8.[41] In the case of *Pretty*, as will be discussed below, the choice to commit suicide required assistance from another and thus the Court was not prepared to find the UK's laws to be an infringement of Article 8. Nevertheless, a law that prohibited suicide itself would be much harder to justify under Article 8(2) as necessary in a democratic society. It would be a clear violation of the right to respect for private life and it is unlikely that any of the legitimate aims under Article 8(2) could be said to require a blanket prohibition. This conclusion is supported by the European Court's recognition that laws which prohibit dangerous activities are likely to violate the first paragraph of Article 8 and require justification in terms of the second paragraph: 'the ability to conduct one's life in a manner of one's own choosing may also include the opportunity to pursue activities perceived to be of a physically or morally harmful or dangerous nature for the individual concerned.'[42] The Court continued by expressly stating that 'even where the conduct poses a danger to health or, arguably, where it is of life-threatening nature, the case-law of the Convention institutions has regarded the state's imposition of compulsory or criminal measures as impinging on the private life of the applicant'.[43] While some such measures may be justified under

[37] *Pretty* (HL), n. 18 above, para. 35.   [38] ibid.   [39] ibid, para. 100.
[40] *Pretty* (ECtHR), n. 18 above, para. 64.   [41] ibid, para. 67.   [42] ibid, para. 62.
[43] ibid.

Article 8(2), for example by reference to the rights of others or the protection of health or morals, the fact that life-threatening behaviour which is not the result of an intention to die may be protected in this way, only strengthens the argument that suicide itself may be an exercise of autonomy worthy of protection as a limitation upon the state's obligation to protect life. In a conflict between a state's positive obligation to take reasonable steps to preserve life under the right to life and a state's negative duty not to infringe an individual's autonomy, a clear suicide attempt by a competent adult is so fundamental an exercise of autonomous choice, that it should require a state to refrain from criminalization of suicide. There will remain circumstances, however, in which the state's obligations under the right to life do require some intervention in order to seek to prevent a suicide.

(2) Obligations to prevent suicide in detention

While there is no general obligation under the right to life for suicide to be criminalized, a state will face specific obligations to take reasonable steps to prevent the suicide of a person over whom it is exercising control. The most obvious example of such a person is a prisoner. When dealing with a prisoner suicide the key questions will be whether the authorities knew (or should have known) that there was a real risk of suicide and, if so, whether they did all that could reasonably be expected of them in order to prevent that risk. These two questions stem from the general positive obligations inherent in the right to life discernible from cases such as *Osman v United Kingdom* under the ECHR. It will be recalled that in this case the European Court of Human Rights outlined the positive obligation upon a state party to the ECHR to preserve the lives of those in its jurisdiction. The Court established an important principle that state authorities must do all that could reasonably be expected of them to avoid a real and immediate risk to life of which they have or ought to have knowledge.[44] In cases specifically on the suicide of detained persons, the Court has applied this principle to impose a burden on state authorities to take reasonable steps to prevent the suicide of a known suicide risk. In the case of *Keenan v United Kingdom*,[45] a prisoner suffering from a mental illness which, the Court concluded, posed a potential risk of suicide was awarded an additional twenty-eight days in prison and seven days in segregation for a disciplinary offence. The prisoner hanged himself from the bars of his cell using a ligature made from a bed sheet. The Court found that the prison authorities knew of the potential risk to the life of this prisoner (by his own hand) although it was held that the risk to life varied and was not always an immediate risk. The Court said that 'It cannot be concluded that he was at immediate risk throughout the period of detention. However, the variations in his condition required that he be monitored carefully in case of sudden deterioration.'[46] The Court then moved

---

[44] (1998) 29 E.H.R.R. 245; Reps 1998-VIII, at para. 116.   [45] ECHR 2001-III.
[46] ibid, para. 96.

on to consider whether the authorities did all that could reasonably be expected of them to prevent the risk of suicide and concluded that they did respond in a reasonable way by placing him in hospital care and under suicide watch when he evinced suicidal tendencies.[47] There was therefore no violation of Article 2's protection for the right to life, although the Court did find a violation of Article 3 due to the lack of effective monitoring and psychiatric input, and the imposition of a disciplinary punishment, in relation to a mentally ill person known to be a suicide risk. While this indicates that greater steps should have been taken by the prison authorities in order to prevent this suicide, such steps were not required under the right to life. The key issue will be the reasonableness of the authorities' intervention. Some subsequent cases that have applied the approach developed in *Keenan* have resulted in a violation of Article 2. For example, *Renolde v France* also involved a suicide in prison of a prisoner with a known mental illness and who had previously attempted suicide.[48] The Court held that the prison authorities not only knew of the suicide risk, but also (unlike *Keenan*) failed to take reasonable steps to protect life. This failure was evidenced by the lack of discussion of admission to a psychiatric institution,[49] the lack of supervision of the medication prescribed,[50] and the severe disciplinary punishment imposed only three days after a suicide attempt which led to the prisoner being isolated and was thus likely to aggravate the existing risk of suicide.[51] (There was in addition a violation of Article 3 in this case as the imposition of the punishment fell short of the standards of treatment required under this Article.)

The duty on state authorities to do all that is reasonably expected of them in order to prevent a suicide in prison also applies in other contexts where an individual is under the control of the state. In *Abdullah Yilmaz v Turkey*, a young man committed suicide while performing his compulsory military service.[52] The suicide was provoked by a sergeant who verbally and physically abused the conscript at a time when his vulnerability was obvious. It was held by the European Court of Human Rights that the Turkish authorities had violated Article 2's right to life because the regulatory framework had proved deficient in protecting the conscript from such provocation. Turkey had not done all that could reasonably be expected of it in order to prevent the suicide of a known suicide risk within its military. The recent English case of *Savage v South Essex NHS Trust* extends the *Keenan* principles to a mentally ill patient detained under the mental health legislation.[53] It was made clear by the House of Lords in this case that such patients are in the same category as prisoners and conscripts in respect of the positive obligation owed by the state to take reasonable steps to prevent suicide when there is a known risk. The Lords in this case recognized two levels of suicide prevention. First, for all persons in these categories, there is a general obligation on the state

---

[47] ibid, para. 99.   [48] Application no. 5608/05 (Judgment of 16 October 2008).
[49] ibid, para. 97.   [50] ibid, para. 105.   [51] ibid, paras 106–7.
[52] Application no. 21899/02 (Judgment of 17 June 2008).   [53] [2009] 2 WLR 115.

authorities to prevent suicide. This is joined, however, by a second more onerous obligation where an individual presents a real and immediate risk of suicide. In this latter situation, there is what the House of Lords called an 'operational' obligation to do all that is reasonably expected of the authorities:

> This obligation is distinct from, and additional to, the authorities' more general obligations. The operational obligation arises only if members of staff know or ought to know that a particular patient presents a 'real and immediate' risk of suicide. In these circumstances Article 2 requires them to do all that can reasonably be expected to prevent the patient from committing suicide.[54]

The general obligation can be satisfied by the existence of proper systems and procedures but the operational obligation involves a specific duty to protect a particular individual from his or her own life.[55] Where, we might ask, does autonomy lie in respect of these obligations? Why are detained persons not accorded the same respect for an autonomous choice to die as are the rest of society?

In *Keenan*, the European Court of Human Rights recognized the need to balance the right to life with other Convention rights, including in this specific situation, the principle of autonomy, as protected under Articles 5 and 8. The Court stated that prison authorities must discharge their duties to protect life 'in a manner compatible with the rights and freedoms of the individual concerned. There are general measures and precautions which will be available to diminish the opportunities for self-harm, without infringing on personal autonomy. Whether any more stringent measures are necessary in respect of a prisoner and whether it is reasonable to apply them will depend on the circumstances of the case.'[56] This clearly suggests that there will sometimes be circumstances in which it will be both necessary and reasonable to infringe the personal autonomy of a prisoner in order to prevent him ending his own life. The reason why such a balance must be struck for classes of persons such as prisoners is well investigated in the *Savage* judgments. It is acknowledged in this case that in general adults, unlike children, do not need to be protected from themselves: 'Their personal autonomy is entitled to respect subject only to whatever proportionate limitations may be placed by the law on that autonomy in the public interest. The prevention of suicide, no longer a criminal act, is not among those limitations.'[57] Prisoners are in a distinct situation, however, for two related reasons. First, their personal autonomy has already been legitimately restricted by the state and, secondly, because of this restriction, prisoners are particularly vulnerable to depression and thoughts of suicide. Lord Rodger explains that it is these two factors that have led the European Court of Human Rights to interpret Article 2 as imposing an obligation on states to take reasonable steps to prevent those in detention from committing suicide. In his words, this is done 'because they are under the control of the

---

[54] ibid, para. 72, per Lord Rodger of Earlsferry.
[55] ibid, para. 97, per Baroness Hale of Richmond.   [56] *Keenan*, n. 45 above, para. 92.
[57] *Savage*, n. 53 above, para. 11, per Lord Scott of Foscote.

state and placed in situations where, as experience shows, there is a heightened risk of suicide'.[58] Thus, there is an emphasis on the vulnerability of prisoners and suicide prevention is regarded simply as one aspect of the broader obligation on state authorities to protect those within its detention. A person detained within a prison is likely to face a much greater risk to his life than those not detained both because of the threat posed by other prisoners and also by the impact of detention (and other factors such as remorse and loneliness) on the prisoner's own mental state. The person so detained should be protected, so far as it is reasonable to do so, by the state authorities from these threats. But while the prisoner's autonomy and liberty are inevitably restricted by detention, personal autonomy will not be completed destroyed. Lord Rodger confirmed that 'the need to respect the autonomy of prisoners remains'.[59] Therefore, the threat to life from the prisoner himself remains distinct in nature from the threat posed by other persons. There is no reason why the usual principles identified in the previous sections should not apply equally to prisoners. A suicide attempt that is intentional and based upon genuine self-reflection is not a threat to life that the authorities need to prevent under the right to life. The fact that it is disruptive to the prison or enables a prisoner to escape from his court-imposed punishment are not factors of relevance in this debate. It is unfortunate that the House of Lords in *Savage* favoured a more interventionist approach. Having confirmed that a prisoner's autonomy should be respected, Lord Rodger immediately proceeded to hold that, when a real and immediate risk of suicide has been identified, the protection of life must take precedence over other considerations such as autonomy: 'the immediacy of the danger to life means that, for the time being, there is, in practice, little room for considering other, more general, matters concerning his treatment. There will be time enough for them, if and when the danger to life has been overcome. In the meantime, the authorities' duty is to try to prevent the suicide.'[60] This is a very narrow view of the life versus autonomy debate. It suggests that an autonomous choice to die should always be set to one side in favour of saving the life involved, after which autonomy can be restored. While there is a sense in which this approach can be useful in determining that a suicide attempt is genuine and enabling an individual to have a second chance at life should he or she wish to take it, its use for subsequent attempts begins to look like a setting aside of autonomy in favour of the sanctity of life, merely because the individual concerned is being held in detention. This is regrettable.

There is one context, however, in which such an approach has considerably more merit, and it is the one that was actually the subject of the *Savage* case: the compulsory detention of a mentally ill person under the mental health legislation. On the one hand, the fact that a person is detained because of illness rather than criminality suggests that greater respect should be accorded to their autonomy. As Lord Scott said, the patient 'will be there for their protection,

---

[58] ibid, para. 39.   [59] ibid, para. 42.   [60] ibid.

not as a punishment' and thus the hospital authorities are 'entitled to place a value on her quality of life in the hospital and accord a degree of respect to her personal autonomy above that to which prisoners in custody could expect'.[61] On the other hand, but stemming from this very point, the patient is detained for their own protection and the risk of suicide is more likely to develop from the very mental illness that has justified detention. Only choices to die made by mentally competent individuals can present issues of autonomy; if a wish to die is a symptom of an illness, it is not an autonomous choice (and, applying the tests developed in this chapter, is not truly intended nor based on genuine self-reflection). Thus the positive obligation to protect life does not need to be balanced against the important principle of autonomy. The state authorities will still be judged on whether they have taken the steps that could reasonably be expected of them. The level of risk for any particular patient will fluctuate and in deciding what precautions are necessary the doctors must take into account 'both the potentially adverse effect of too much supervision on the patient's condition and the possible positive benefits to be expected from a more open environment'.[62] As was recognized in *Savage*, such decisions will involve clinical judgement. This balancing exercise is vital both to ensure that the state meets its positive obligations under the right to life to take reasonable steps to preserve life and also to ensure that a patient's autonomy is respected to the greatest degree possible given the limitations of autonomy imposed by the patient's mental illness. It is important to bear in mind, however, that other persons detained or under state control, such as prisoners or conscripts, may or may not be suffering from a mental illness and a choice to commit suicide will not always be a mere symptom of such an illness. The competence of the person involved must be a relevant factor. In *Reeves v Commissioner of Police of the Metropolis*,[63] however, the House of Lords held that competence was irrelevant in this context. The court accepted the authorities' admission of a duty of care to prevent the suicide of persons detained, regardless of their mental competence. While this will not be a relevant factor for most aspects of the authorities' duty of care towards the detainee, it should be very relevant indeed to the prevention of suicide. As Wheat argues, there is a distinction between 'a duty to take reasonable care to prevent external harm coming to a prisoner and a duty to prevent the prisoner from harming himself. In the case of the former, it must be right to assume that there is no conflict between this and a prisoner's competent and autonomous wishes; no such assumption can be made in respect of

---

[61] ibid, para. 13. Baroness Hale expands on this point, recognizing that respect for autonomy can be particularly valuable in a mental health hospital: 'Developing a patient's capacity to make sensible choices for herself, and providing her with as good a quality of life as possible, are important components in protecting her mental health. Keeping her absolutely safe from physical harm, by secluding or restraining her, or even by keeping her on a locked ward, may do more harm to her mental health' (ibid, para. 100). [62] ibid, para. 50.
[63] [2000] 1 A.C. 360.

the latter.'[64] An assumption that life should always be saved first and then considerations of autonomy can come back into play is both simplistic and objectionable. The underlying principle that should not be overlooked even within a detention context is that an autonomous choice to die is not always a matter in which the state should intervene even if it is able to do so. If the choice is reached with due consideration and respect for the gravity of the matter, while still a regrettable choice, it is not necessarily one for which the state should hold, or seek to hold, any responsibility.

D. Assisted suicide

So far in this chapter it has been proposed that an autonomous choice to commit suicide is a sufficiently weighty conflicting interest so that the state is not obliged under its positive right to life obligations to take steps to prevent such a suicide. The only proviso so far, and in practice it is a significant one, is that the choice to die will only be autonomous if it is competently made and therefore suicide as a symptom of a mental illness should be prevented by the state where it is reasonable to do so (and even here the reasonableness will take into account residual autonomy and physical liberty, as well as resources).[65] The question that arises now is whether this autonomy exception to the state's obligations to act to preserve life also imposes an obligation on the state to assist in giving effect to an autonomous choice to die. The English approach is strongly opposed to such assistance. The Suicide Act 1961, which abrogated the offence of suicide (and by implication attempted suicide), created a new statutory offence of assisted suicide. Section 2(1) states that 'A person who aids, abets, counsels or procures the suicide of another or an attempt by another to commit suicide, shall be liable on conviction on indictment to imprisonment for a term not exceeding 14 years.' This is a highly unusual offence because it imposes criminal liability for assisting an act that is not in itself unlawful. The justification for it stems from the law's strong rejection of any third party involvement in causing death. Indeed, there can at times be a fine line between murder and assisted suicide, such as when an overdose of pills are placed in the mouth of the person wishing to commit suicide: does the person who places them there face liability for assisted suicide or for murder? Furthermore, a charge of murder will be reduced to manslaughter if the person who killed another was acting in pursuance

---

[64] Wheat, n. 15 above, p. 188. It is interesting to note that the case of *Reeves* not only held that the police are under a duty to take reasonable measures to prevent the suicide of those in detention, regardless of their mental competence, and that a breach of that duty of care may be a cause of death despite the deliberate act of the prisoner, but also found that the prisoner's suicide attempt amounts to contributory negligence. The latter point relies upon a finding that suicide amounts to 'fault' under section 4 of the Law Reform (Contributory Negligence) Act 1945. It is not clear why an action that is entirely lawful should be regarded as fault.

[65] The latter point will be investigated in chapter 9.

of a suicide pact, defined as 'a common agreement between two or more persons having for its object the death of all of them'.[66] Again, the distinction between complicity in suicide and manslaughter is not always clear. The latter is a more serious crime but the defendant must intend to die as well, whereas a person who assists suicide may wish to live and profit from the deceased's death.[67] Ormerod gives an example of how fine the distinction can be between these two offences: 'if D and V agree to gas themselves and D alone survives, it appears that he will be liable under the Homicide Act if he turned on the tap, and under the Suicide Act if V did.'[68] What is clear is that the offence under the Suicide Act not only prohibits active involvement in the ending of life but also, most significantly, in persuading another person to end their life. It was made clear in *AG v Able* that even the distribution of a booklet advising on methods of committing suicide can amount to an offence under section 2(1) provided that the distributor intends the information to be used by someone contemplating suicide who would be, and was, assisted or encouraged by it.[69]

It is, however, the fear that vulnerable persons, especially the elderly or those suffering from a terminal illness, will be bullied into ending their lives that provides the strongest principled need for this offence. The state's obligations under the right to life are complicated in this context. On the one hand, an offence of assisted suicide can serve to protect the life of vulnerable persons in society; on the other hand, the offence may prevent the exercise of autonomy where a person wants to die but needs assistance to do so. If autonomy is a weightier interest than the preservation of life in this context, and it was argued above that, in respect of intentional suicide, it is, then it could be argued that the state owes a duty to facilitate, rather than hinder, the suicide. This was the argument put forward in the *Pretty* case. Dianne Pretty was suffering from motor neurone disease and, facing a lingering death, she wanted to commit suicide but was unable to do so unaided. Her husband was willing to assist her but they both sought a guarantee in advance that he would not be prosecuted for the offence of assisted suicide. The Director of Public Prosecutions refused to issue a guarantee that a prosecution would not be brought against Mr Pretty, arguing that there was no such power to grant immunities from prosecution in advance of the prohibited activities being initiated. Mrs Pretty sought to challenge the DPP's refusal as contrary to the Human Rights Act 1998, alongside a supplementary argument that the offence of assisted suicide found in section 2(1) was itself contrary to the HRA. Various Convention rights were relied on by Mrs Pretty's lawyers, including Articles 2, 3, 8 and 14. As mentioned above, the European Court of Human Rights concluded that the right to respect for private life protected under Article 8 was engaged by the prohibition of assisted suicide. In other words, the offence in section 2(1)

---

[66] Section 4(3) Homicide Act 1957.
[67] See discussion in Smith & Hogan, *Criminal Law*, n. 34 above, p. 558.   [68] ibid.
[69] [1984] QB 795; 1 All ER 277.

infringes the autonomy of persons who want to commit suicide but are unable to do so unaided. However, the Court held that this was a permissible interference with the right to respect for private life because, under Article 8(2), it was necessary in a democratic society in order to protect the rights of others. The Court was particularly concerned here about the rights of vulnerable members of society who might be pressured into ending their lives in the absence of an offence of assisted suicide. The Court recognized 'clear risks of abuse' in any relaxation of the prohibition on assisted suicide and concluded that it is a matter for each state to assess in its own way.[70] The UK's approach, although not regarded as essential under the Convention, was found to be consistent with it: 'It does not appear to be arbitrary to the Court for the law to reflect the importance of the right to life, by prohibiting assisted suicide while providing for a system of enforcement and adjudication which allows due regard to be given in each particular case to the public interest in bringing a prosecution, as well as to the fair and proper requirements of retribution and deterrence.'[71] It is clear from this that procedural safeguards are essential for any offence of assisted suicide; the need to consider the public interest in bringing a prosecution helps to ensure that the offence is enforced in a proportionate manner.

A more recent legal challenge has focused on this issue of prosecuting discretion. *R (on the application of Purdy) v Director of Public Prosecutions*[72] offered the opportunity for the courts to consider the legal position of persons who accompany and assist terminally ill relatives to travel abroad to countries, such as Switzerland, in which assisted suicide is lawful. While the House of Lords left open the question of whether section 2(1) applies to acts performed within the jurisdiction of the English criminal law regardless of where the final act of suicide is to be committed, it was prepared to depart from its previous decision in *Pretty* to the extent required by the Strasbourg Court in relation to Article 8(1). In *Purdy*, the Lords accepted that Article 8(1) confers a right to make autonomous choices about when and how to die. Instead of reopening the issue of whether a limitation on that right is necessary in a democratic society in order to protect the rights of others, the Lords proceeded to focus on the question of whether the limitation derived from section 2(1) was in accordance with the law (as required by Article 8(2)). This was an issue for the court because 115 cases of assisted journeys to undertake assisted suicide in countries where it is lawful had so far been identified and no prosecutions had followed. In most cases, the failure to prosecute was due to insufficient evidence but, in some cases, the DPP had declined to prosecute on the basis that a prosecution would not be in the public interest. On one occasion, when declining to prosecute on this ground, the DPP had admitted that the usual guidelines, contained in the Code for Crown Prosecutors, were unhelpful in the context of this offence.[73] This led the Lords to

---

[70] *Pretty* (ECtHR), n. 18 above, para. 74.   [71] ibid, para. 76.   [72] [2009] UKHL 45.
[73] ibid, para. 30.

conclude that the offence of assisted suicide failed the accessibility and foresee-ability tests inherent in Article 8(2)'s requirement that any limitation on the right to respect for private life be in accordance with the law. The DPP was required to set out an offence-specific policy identifying the facts and circumstances that he will take into account in deciding whether to consent to a prosecution under sec-tion 2(1) in cases such as *Purdy*.[74] Public consultation on this is now being under-taken. The House of Lords judgment in *Purdy* makes clear that flexibility coupled with consistency is essential in relation to the offence of assisted suicide. As the Strasbourg Court had recognized in *Pretty*, the offence itself can be justified but prosecutions under it must be individually justified in terms of the public interest because, unusually, the offence relates to assisting someone to do something to which there is a right under Article 8.

It is also worth noting that Pretty's argument that the right to life itself pro-tects autonomous choices as to how to die was categorically rejected by both the House of Lords and the European Court of Human Rights. The state is under no obligation, therefore, under either the right to life or autonomy-related rights, to provide or permit assistance in committing suicide, regardless of the wishes of the person wanting to die. It is important to protect vulnerable members of society from being pressured or persuaded into ending their lives before they truly wish to do so and, therefore, a general criminal prohibition on assisted suicide is a valu-able protection for the right to life. However, it is arguable that a limited excep-tion to this general prohibition could be justified to cover cases such as Dianne Pretty's in which her autonomy is so severely overridden by the existing law. To permit physician assisted suicide in tightly defined circumstances, including only where there is unbearable suffering and the patient is unable to take his or her own life unaided, would seem a sensible solution. And it is one that draws support not only from the principle of autonomy but also from quality of life consider-ations, both of which present weighty challenges to the preservation of life and when combined reveal a strong conflicting interest to the state's positive obliga-tions under the right to life. The issue of the quality of life, in contrast with the sanctity of life, will be considered in the following chapter.

E. Conclusion

The right to life's protection for human life extends far beyond a mere negative obligation upon the state not to kill. State authorities must also take reason-able steps to preserve life and this will include taking steps to prevent suicide by individuals who are not mentally competent to make autonomous decisions. However, when an autonomous choice to die is made by a mentally competent adult it acts as a very strong conflicting interest that will outweigh the state's

---

[74] ibid, para. 56.

duty, and power, to preserve life. This is true regardless of such considerations as the rationality, reasons or reasonableness of the choice. One factor that will be relevant when a balance is being sought between the preservation of life and the protection of autonomy, however, is whether the choice to die is really intended and the result of at least a degree of self-reflection. The state's duty to take reasonable steps to preserve life may encompass the need to protect individuals from their own recklessness or unthinking behaviour, but it should not empower the infringement of personal autonomy when a clear decision has been taken, by a mentally competent adult, to end his or her life. While it does appear that both English law and the ECHR draw a distinction between this general approach and the approach fitting for a person under the control of the state, such as a prisoner, it has been argued in this chapter that the fact of detention (or other control) does not justify the overriding of autonomy in respect of the ending of life, provided that the usual requirements of competence, intention and reflection are satisfied. In addition, while the state's duty to respect autonomy does not require the provision of assistance to commit suicide, even if necessary in order to give effect to an individual's autonomous choice to die, because of the need to ensure adequate protection for the preservation of the lives of the vulnerable, it has been argued here that a narrowly drawn exception to a general prohibition of assisted suicide may be justified. The balance between the need to respect autonomy and the need to take steps to preserve life, both legitimate and important obligations imposed upon the state, must also take into account considerations of the quality of life for, while this chapter has recognized that a human life is of value both to the state and to the person living that life, it is possible that a poor quality of life may negate the value in a life, leading to a further limitation upon the state's obligation to preserve life. It is to this issue that the next chapter will now turn.

8

The Right to Life and the Quality of Life

In the previous chapter it was argued that the state's duty to take reasonable steps to preserve life under the right to life does not permit the infringement of personal autonomy when a clear decision has been taken, by a mentally competent adult, to end his or her life. Decisions at the end of life can be more ethically problematic, however, when the individual is no longer mentally competent to make his or her own decisions. In this context, the state's duty to take reasonable steps to preserve life will not come into conflict with autonomy considerations (unless a decision was expressed by the individual prior to the loss of competence) but potentially conflicting considerations remain, including the human right to be free from degrading treatment. This chapter will first consider whether the right to life continues to offer protection for incompetent patients with negligible quality of life and will then proceed to consider the requirements of the right if its protection is applicable. This discussion should be read in light of the conclusions reached in the first chapter in which the value of human life was investigated.

A. Persons and humans: the application of the right to life

The core question to be addressed in this chapter is whether a very poor quality of life impacts upon the value of that life to such an extent that it reduces, or even extinguishes, the protection for that life offered by the right to life. We are thus concerned with why life is valued and whether the protection afforded by the right to life is contingent upon a certain quality (whether objective or subjective) of life. These are issues that have been raised less in the human rights arena than in the medical law and ethics arena, especially in relation to end of life decisions. The most famous case on this issue, *Airedale NHS Trust v Bland*,[1] provided an opportunity for members of the House of Lords to contemplate the meaning of life:

What is meant now by 'life' in the moral precept which requires respect for the sanctity of human life? If the quality of life of a person such as Anthony Bland is non-existent since he is unaware of anything that happens to him, has he a right to be sustained in

---

[1] [1993] 1 All ER 831.

that state of living death and are his family and medical attendants under a duty to maintain it?[2]

The judges in *Bland* had no difficulty in regarding Anthony Bland, a patient in persistent vegetative state (PVS) and thus with a negligible (if any) quality of life,[3] as still living,[4] but they implied that he may no longer have a 'life'. Lord Goff, for example, described Bland as alive but in a 'living death'[5] and Hoffmann LJ in the Court of Appeal stated that 'the very concept of having a life has no meaning in relation to Anthony Bland. He is alive but has no life at all.'[6] Similarly, the Irish Supreme Court in *Re a Ward of Court* described a patient in a condition falling just short of PVS as 'not living a life in any meaningful sense'.[7] O'Flaherty J said further that the patient 'may be alive but she has no life at all'.[8] This apparent ambiguity about when life, or at least the legal protection for life, ends is untenable. There is little of more import than the question of when human life should be protected by the state and when it may be left exposed. And yet legal declarations of the right to life are themselves vague on this issue. The Article 2 Handbook published by the Council of Europe recognizes that in the absence of a European or worldwide legal or scientific consensus, the Strasbourg institutions are 'unwilling to set precise standards in these regards'.[9] The ECHR does not clarify either what 'life' is nor when it, or the protection under Article 2, begins or ends.[10] No other international manifestation of the right to life provides any clearer guidance. The American Convention on Human Rights does expressly protect the right to life from 'the moment of conception' but the clarity provided by this is undermined by the proviso 'in general'.[11] What is clear, however, is that it is possible to distinguish two questions here: the question of when life ends, and the question of when the protection for life ceases. These dual questions reflect the increasingly influential ethical theory of personhood. Perhaps best explained by John Harris, a medical ethicist, the personhood theory begins with a recognition of the two relevant questions: 'what we need to know is not when

---

[2] ibid, p. 878.   [3] This issue will be discussed thoroughly below.
[4] Lord Browne-Wilkinson, for example, stated unambiguously that '[h]is brain stem is alive and so is he...' (*Bland*, n. 1 above, p. 878) and Lord Goff said 'I start with the simple fact that, in law, Anthony is still alive' (p. 865).   [5] ibid, p. 865.
[6] ibid, p. 853. At other points in his judgment, Hoffmann LJ repeated this theme: 'the stark reality is that Anthony Bland is not living a life at all' (p. 855); 'His body is alive but he has no life...' (p. 850).   [7] [1995] 2 ILRM 401, at para. 195 (per O'Flaherty J).
[8] ibid, para. 193.
[9] D. Korff, *The Right to Life: A Guide to Implementation of Article 2 of the European Convention on Human Rights* (Human Rights Handbook No. 8) (Strasbourg: Council of Europe, 2006).
[10] The Handbook proceeds to the reasonable conclusion that, on the question of the end of life, the European Court of Human Rights would adopt a similar approach to its approach to abortion, namely to leave the answer primarily to states to determine for themselves.
[11] See ACHR Article 4(1). In addition, the Cairo Declaration on Human Rights in Islam states that 'The preservation of human life throughout the term of time willed by God is a duty prescribed by Shari'ah.' (Article 2(c).) This might perhaps imply that excessive means of preserving life are not required under this manifestation of the right to life.

life begins, but rather when life begins to matter morally. And the correlated question is not "when does life end?" but rather "when does life cease to matter morally?"[12] For Harris the answer to when life ceases to matter morally is when the human being is no longer capable of valuing his or her own existence. This conclusion stems from Harris' view that the question of what makes life valuable is 'so difficult and so profound as to be almost absurd' because there are a myriad of different ways in which life can be valuable to the individual living it.[13] Instead of asking why this life is valuable, we should, in Harris' view, ask: is this individual capable of valuing life? If the answer is yes, then the individual is classed a 'person' and is entitled to legal and ethical protection for his or her life. If the answer is no, then despite being both a human being and alive, the individual is not a person and has no rights. The implications for the right to life from such a view are significant. As Harris explains, 'The wrongness of killing another person is, on this view, chiefly the wrongness of permanently depriving her of whatever it is that makes it possible for her to value her own life.'[14] A non-person, and this would include someone such as Anthony Bland who is no longer capable of valuing his existence due to a permanent loss of consciousness and capacity, 'cannot be wronged in this way because death does not deprive them of anything they can value'.[15] The personhood theory, as argued by Harris, therefore draws a stark distinction between the moral importance of the lives of persons and the lives of other human non-persons. For Harris, the key is not respect for human life, but respect for persons and the only value that life has is the value that we give to our lives.[16] It should be obvious that such an approach is not only ethically controversial but also legally problematic. At the crux of both objections is the argument that the personhood theory downplays the importance of human life, in and of itself. John Finnis, in response to Harris, argues that the personhood theory's attempt to distinguish human bodily life from person or selfhood leads to the identification of 'two things, one a nonbodily person and the other a nonpersonal body, neither of which I can recognise as myself'.[17] Human bodily life, in Finnis' view, has some intrinsic value and is not a mere instrument for the person. This view has some merit. A human being is comprised of the combination of a human person and a human body; it is vital for the law to provide protection not only for the person's wishes and choices (although these must be protected) but also for the human body which is just as important an aspect of the human being as the capacity to value. Finnis argues that 'In sustaining human bodily life, in however impaired a condition, one is sustaining the person whose life it is.'[18] If we could add the words 'one aspect of' to this quotation (i.e. 'one is sustaining one aspect of the person whose life it is') we can begin to see that a stark distinction between

---

[12] J. Harris, *The Value of Life: An Introduction to Medical Ethics* (London: Routledge, 1985), p. 8.
[13] ibid, p. 15.   [14] ibid, p. 17.
[15] This is Keown's interpretation of Harris's theory (J. Keown (ed.), *Euthanasia Examined: Ethical, Clinical and Legal Perspectives* (Cambridge: Cambridge University Press, 1997), p. 9).
[16] Harris, n. 12 above, p. 11.   [17] ibid, p. 32.   [18] ibid.

personhood and human life is flawed. When the human entity is viewed as a whole, we can identify a variety of valuable interests, including (and indeed perhaps most important) a capacity to value life, but also including bodily integrity, human dignity and the right to life. The human body is an inherent part of the person and its continued life should never be regarded as a matter of indifference to the entity that inhabits, or used to inhabit, it.

Thus, even when an individual's capacity to value his or her life has ceased, the individual may retain other interests because the capacity to value life is only one of the plethora of interests enjoyed by a human being. One important enduring interest will be autonomy based: the respect owed to the previously expressed wishes of the now permanently incapacitated individual. One possible view would be that this is the only enduring interest for such a patient. However, many of the other interests, and indeed rights, enjoyed by individuals are not logically restricted to competent, or conscious, individuals. Human dignity, for example, if inherent in humanity, would seem to endure beyond consciousness, as too would bodily integrity. An individual such as Anthony Bland, therefore, who no longer has any capacity to value his life, nevertheless has enduring interests in how his still living body is used. The use of his body in a humiliating or degrading manner is contrary to his interests, as too would be his treatment in a manner inconsistent with his previously expressed wishes. Any alternative view is founded upon a stark division between his personhood and enduring human bodily life and, as argued above, such an approach gives insufficient weight to the connection between the two, and to the diverse nature of the interests that human beings enjoy, extending beyond those that are inextricably tied to our mental capacity and/or awareness.

The ethical difficulties posed by the personhood theory, and specifically its denial of the moral worth of non-person humans, is supplemented by the difficulty in reconciling the theory with the concept of human rights and its implementation in international and national law. The principle of equality is at the heart of human rights law and the idea of excluding a category of human beings, for whatever reason, cannot be compatible with this body of law. All living human beings are entitled to the protection afforded by a right to life. It could be argued, however, that the personhood theory is less concerned with legal requirements to protect all human life and more concerned with the treatment of individual patients. A case such as that of *Bland* includes explicit reference to the right to life but also authorized the withdrawal of artificial hydration and nutrition from an irreversibly comatose patient. If, on paper, patients like Anthony Bland have a right to life, but in practice their lives can be ended in this way by the state, perhaps the personhood theory's view of Bland as a non-person human offers a possible explanation for this treatment. As David Price has argued, 'Although the law formally adopts a biological conception of persons, it might nevertheless be perceived that in juridical practice, patients without certain capacities are afforded a diminished right to life in so far as treatment may be more easily withdrawn from them resulting in death, and that legal and moral conceptions of personhood have been conflated.'[19] This can be seen in cases such as *Bland* where life-sustaining treatment is withdrawn from an irreversibly comatose patient, and also in cases involving severely disabled neonates where only basic nursing care is provided. There is little doubt that decisions about the appropriate medical treatment to be provided are taken not in isolation on the basis of some general concept of equal treatment for all but in conjunction with a detailed assessment of a patient's current condition. While it is the value of the treatment, and not the value of the patient's life, that should be assessed, as Price notes 'the condition of the patient, which would include underlying impairments and handicaps, is an essential pre-requisite of assessing the former'.[20] So it is the plethora of interests attaching to all living human beings, regardless of physical or mental condition, that is crucial in determinations of appropriate state intervention in terms of the provision of life-sustaining medical treatment. John Keown takes issue with this point, highlighting the potential danger of taking into account matters such as physical or mental disabilities when making decisions about continuation or withdrawal of life-sustaining treatment.[21] Keown is correct that such considerations should not affect the value of a patient's life, and they should certainly not exclude the patient from legal and ethical protection as the personhood theory suggests, but they may affect the extent and nature of the state intervention which will be appropriate in order to preserve life. The key here is not whether such patients are still afforded the protection of a right to life but rather what that protection entails. Does it require the state to take all possible measures to preserve life for as long as possible? The answer to this is almost always no. At the other end of the spectrum, however, it is only in extremely rare situations that an individual's right not to be killed by the state is not assured by the right to life (and we have identified those rare circumstances in earlier chapters). If someone had walked into Anthony Bland's hospital room and shot him at close range, there is little doubt that he would have committed murder and that a failure to impose appropriate sanctions would amount to a violation of Bland's right to life. This scenario alone should remind us that Bland retained a right to life. He had enduring interests in certain matters pertaining to his human body even though he was incapable of valuing his life at that stage. The question remains what steps will be reasonable for the state and its agents in order to preserve the life of such a patient?

[19] D. Price, 'What Shape to Euthanasia after Bland? Historical, Contemporary and Futuristic Paradigms' (2009) 125 L.Q.R. 142, at p. 169.

[20] D. Price, 'Fairly Bland: An Alternative View of a Supposed New "Death Ethic" and the BMA Guidance' (2001) 21 L.S. 618, at p. 643.

[21] J. Keown, 'Restoring the Sanctity of Life and Replacing the Caricature: A Reply to David Price' (2006) 26 L.S. 109, at p. 111.

B. The duty to take reasonable steps to preserve life

The act/omission distinction is notorious in relation to end of life decision making. English law embeds the distinction by permitting the refusal or withdrawal of life-sustaining treatment in cases such as *Bland*, but prohibiting any positive assistance to cause or assist death as in the *Pretty* case. The issue was highlighted by Lord Browne-Wilkinson in *Bland*:

> the conclusion I have reached will appear to some to be almost irrational. How can it be lawful to allow a patient to die slowly, though painlessly, over a period of weeks from lack of food but unlawful to produce his immediate death by a lethal injection, thereby saving his family from yet another ordeal to add to the tragedy that has already struck them? I find it difficult to find a moral answer to that question. But it is undoubtedly the law...[22]

Whatever the merits or demerits of an act/omission distinction in relation to legal liability in general, its application to situations such as healthcare where there is a duty of care in existence is problematic. As Finnis argues 'What is misshapen and indefensible is a law that treats as criminal a harmful "act" while treating as lawful (and indeed compulsory) an "omission" with the very same intent, by one who has a duty to care for the person injured.'[23] English law focuses on whether or not a duty to treat exists (which will be dependent on whether treatment is regarded as in the patient's best interests), but arguably a more pertinent duty is the duty of care that continues to exist regardless of the incompetent patient's best interests. In the case of Bland, whether or not continued treatment would be in his best interests, the doctors and hospital could be regarded as continuing to owe a duty of care to their patient which would prevent them, for example, from abandoning Anthony Bland on the pavement outside the hospital. A duty of care still existed even if the duty to treat had ceased, and thus a stark distinction between an act and an omission is hard to justify. As Price has argued, 'in view of the duty of healthcare professionals to aid patients and relieve suffering, the alleged primacy of the duty not to harm over the duty of beneficence is not only dubious, but these are arguably not discrete notions at all and exist along a spectrum. The boundary between them is fluid to accommodate changing perspectives as to where the extent of obligatory duty lies.'[24] Once we accept that there are continued obligations in the healthcare context, we can see that the act/omission distinction may at times be too rigid to reflect the variety of decisions about a patient's care. Harris is correct to recognize that the 'day-to-day care of most patients will involve innumerable decisions to do and not to do various things, and each will have its effect

---

[22] *Bland*, n. 1 above, p. 884.
[23] J. Finnis, 'Bland—Crossing the Rubicon?' (1993) 109 LQR 329, at p. 333.
[24] Price (2009), n. 19 above, p. 157.

on the course of the patient's illness and on his chances of recovery'.[25] He may go too far in dismissing the act/omission distinction in its entirety, for arguably there is a moral, and should be a legal, distinction between an act causing death and an omission causing death. Throwing a person in a river to drown may be regarded as morally worse than failing to jump in to save him, even if there is malicious intent in both cases.[26] The taking of a positive step to bring about a person's death entails not only a morally blameworthy thought, but also the initiation of a blameworthy action. A decision not to take action to save someone (even when reached with malicious intent) does not require the manifestation of that thought into action and it is that manifestation that provides a final opportunity to reconsider. Nevertheless, in the healthcare context (and others in which a duty of care continues to exist), the situation is different and the view of all actions and non-actions as manifestations of care decisions is to be preferred.

The dismissal of the relevance of an act/omission distinction in this context is complemented by the two types of obligations inherent in the right to life. The prohibition of intentional or arbitrary deprivation of life is, as we have seen, strictly enforced but the positive obligation to take steps to preserve life is of a more conditional nature. It has already been discussed in the previous chapter that a state's duty to preserve life is subjected to a reasonableness test. State authorities are obligated under the right to life to do all that could reasonably be expected of them in order to preserve human life, and both the public interest and the other rights of the individual whose life is at risk, will be relevant to the assessment of what is reasonable. The prohibition on the deprivation of life by the state is not concerned with issues of reasonableness, assuming instead that all such deprivations are unreasonable if they are intentional and arbitrary (and/or without a justification, such as the last resort to save the life of another innocent human being). The relatively extensive caselaw under the ECHR on the issue of positive obligations to preserve life has made clear that such obligations apply in the healthcare context. In the case of *Velikova v Bulgaria*[27] a failure to provide adequate medical treatment for a seriously injured detainee was regarded as a contributory factor for a finding of a violation of Article 2, while in *Anguelova v Bulgaria*,[28] such a failure was regarded as amounting to a separate breach of the right to life. In *Cyprus v Turkey*, a rare inter-state complaint, an argument was raised that the authorities in Northern Cyprus had failed to provide adequate medical services to Greek Cypriots and Maronites living there. The Court observed that 'an issue may arise under Article 2 of the Convention where it is shown that the authorities of a Contracting State put an individual's life at risk through the denial of health care

---

[25] Harris, n. 12 above, p. 32.
[26] The influential article by Rachels takes a different view: J. Rachels, 'Active and Passive Euthanasia' (1975) 292 New England Journal of Medicine 78.
[27] ECHR 2000-VI.
[28] ECHR 2002-IV.

which they have undertaken to make available to the population generally'.[29] The Court in this case was not prepared to examine the question of whether the right to life may impose an obligation on a state to make available a certain standard of healthcare, but this question was left open and remains undecided.[30] In his book on positive obligations under the ECHR, Alastair Mowbray has recognized that the positive obligation regarding the provision of medical care is at 'an early stage of development under Article 2'.[31] This is true, even though it is at a considerably more advanced stage than under any other international protection for the right to life. However, the cases so far have indicated that the positive obligation under Article 2 applies in the healthcare context[32] and, when coupled with the clear guidance in cases in other contexts that state authorities face specific obligations to take reasonable steps to ensure the preservation of particular lives (as we saw in the previous chapter in relation to prison suicides), it is not too great a leap of faith to assume that the right to life may be engaged by the withdrawal of life-sustaining treatment. The key will remain the question of the reasonableness of such a withdrawal. And this question remains relevant regardless of whether the withdrawal can itself be regarded as a deprivation of life (and that is a question which inevitably raises the act/omission distinction once more) or arbitrary. If we assume that such a withdrawal is either not a deprivation of life because it is an omission,[33] or is not an arbitrary deprivation,[34] it may still amount to a violation of the right to life if it signifies a failure on the part of the state to take steps (in this context, the provision of life-sustaining treatment) that are reasonable in the circumstances to preserve life.

When considering what is reasonable in the circumstances, both the public interest and the other rights of the patient must be taken into account. Jeremy McBride, although not writing in a specifically healthcare context, has identified a number of important considerations:

Awareness of a substantiated risk to life does not mean that it must be eliminated; there is at least implicit recognition that this might be impossible. Moreover even if some potential solutions are available, there may still be no obligation to pursue them all and there is certainly no duty to attempt those suggested by the potential victim...Although it is clear that there is a very substantial duty to protect life, it is also evident that this is not one that is to be fulfilled regardless of all other considerations.[35]

When applied to the healthcare context, this quotation reminds us first, that efforts to save life may be futile for the risk to life may not be eliminated by

---

[29] *Cyprus v Turkey* ECHR 2001-IV, para. 219.   [30] ibid.

[31] A.R. Mowbray, *The Development of Positive Obligations under the European Convention on Human Rights by the European Court of Human Rights* (Oxford: Hart Publishing, 2004), p. 26.

[32] This was explicitly confirmed in *Calvelli and Ciglio v Italy* (ECHR 2002-I).

[33] This was the view of Dame Butler-Sloss in *NHS Trust A v M; NHS Trust B v H* [2001] 2 WLR 942.

[34] This is the view of G. Zdenkowski, 'The International Covenant on Civil and Political Rights and Euthanasia' (2007) 20 U.N.S.W.L.J. 170.

[35] J. McBride, 'Protecting Life: A Positive Obligation to Help' (1999) 24 E.L.R. Supp. 42, at pp. 51–2.

any form of medical treatment; secondly, there is no right to demand specific treatment; and thirdly, 'other considerations' beyond the obligation to preserve life must be taken into account. These other considerations will include financial considerations because, within the public health sphere, limited resources are a constant restraint upon the state's duty to save lives,[36] but they may also include factors specific to the individual patient. McBride proceeds to recognize that the *Osman* case had established that other human rights, such as rights to liberty and privacy, cannot be flouted in order to investigate a perceived risk to life, and other rights 'could also be invoked as a constraint on affording protection once that risk has been established'.[37] In the policing context of *Osman*, a suspect's rights could not be infringed merely to investigate a possible risk to life of a potential victim, while in the healthcare context, it is the potential victim's own rights which should be taken into account before the state intervenes to seek to preserve life. For example, a patient will enjoy the benefits of the prohibition of degrading treatment and the right to respect for private life, as well as the right to life. And if life-sustaining treatment will potentially violate those other rights, then that will be a relevant factor in any determination of the reasonableness of its imposition by the state. Another way of looking at this issue might be in terms of proportionality. The state's treatment of those individuals unable to make decisions for themselves should be proportionate to the duty on the state to preserve life, which will involve a balancing exercise in respect of the entirety of that patient's human rights. This balancing exercise is unique to the positive obligations inherent in the right to life, because the negative obligation on the state not to kill will not present the same potential for conflict between different rights of the same individual (although it may, as we have seen in previous chapters, present a conflict between rights of different individuals). This balancing exercise is not entirely self-contained, however. Not only must it be placed alongside consideration of wider public interests (such as limited resources) but it may also be affected by the type of treatment necessary to preserve life. Specifically, it may be that the provision of basic care such as artificial nutrition and hydration (ANH) presents distinct issues from the provision of more extensive medical treatment. These issues will be considered in the following two sections.

C. What is reasonable to preserve life?

Keown's concept of the sanctity of life is described by him as the 'middle way' but this view depends upon the use of the strawman of the vitality principle[38] and it is more accurately regarded as a principle in favour of the preservation of

---

[36] This will be considered more fully in the next chapter.

[37] McBride, n. 35 above, pp. 52–3.

[38] Keown's vitality approach regards human life as an absolute moral value and considers it always to be wrong to either shorten life or fail to lengthen it, regardless of considerations of pain, suffering, or expense. This is such an extreme position that even Keown dismisses it summarily as

life in most circumstances, in contrast to the quality of life approach that he rejects. Even so, Keown's sanctity of life principle permits the withdrawal of life-sustaining medical treatment whenever that treatment is disproportionate. Keown defines this key term as follows: 'A treatment may be "disproportionate" either because it would be futile or excessively burdensome. A treatment is futile if it offers no reasonable hope of therapeutic benefit, and excessively burdensome if, for example, it would cause great pain.'[39] Whatever criticisms might be made of Keown's approach to end of life issues in general, and to the principle of sanctity of life in particular, this definition at least is a useful starting point for consideration of when life-sustaining treatment might legitimately be withdrawn. It has already been argued in the preceding section that the concept of proportionality will be fundamental to any such decision, and Keown's focus on whether continued treatment would be excessively burdensome to the patient is an indirect means of bringing other human rights considerations into the picture. Keown suggests that a burden imposed by treatment might be excessive in absolute terms—i.e. because it would impose unbearable pain—or in relative terms—i.e. because 'the pain imposed would be bearable but not worth enduring in view of the minimal improvement the treatment would purchase'.[40] Both of these approaches to the excessive burden concept seem appropriate. They imply that a balancing exercise is always appropriate in which the benefits to be gained from the treatment will be balanced against the pain and discomfort that will be caused by it. Sometimes the harm done to the patient in terms of the causation of pain will negate any benefit in terms of continued life, at other times the harm caused may be less but the benefit achieved minimal. In both situations the withdrawal of the treatment will be a proportionate response and would not cause the state to infringe its positive obligation under the right to life. The key factor is that the balancing exercise is in relation to the various rights of the patient to live, be free of pain and degradation, and to enjoy respect for bodily integrity. It is worth noting that awareness may strengthen both sides of the argument when assessing the burden from continued treatment. On the one hand, awareness will increase the value in life to the patient but, on the other hand, it also increases the significance of any pain or degradation flowing from the treatment. This was expressly recognized in the Irish case of *Re a Ward of Court*. The patient in this case was described as 'nearly, but not quite' in PVS.[41] Hamilton CJ argued that 'if such minimal cognition as she has includes an inkling of her catastrophic condition, then I am satisfied that that would be a terrible torment to her and her situation would be worse than if she were fully PVS'.[42] It should be noted, however, that some level of awareness will be

'ethically untenable' (J. Keown, 'Restoring Moral and Intellectual Shape to the Law after Bland' (1997) 113 LQR 481, at p. 482).

[39] J. Keown, 'Beyond Bland: A Critique of the BMA Guidance on Withholding and Withdrawing Medical Treatment' (2000) 20 L.S. 66, at p. 71.   [40] ibid.

[41] *Re a Ward of Court*, n. 7 above, para. 38.   [42] ibid, para. 41.

essential in order for a patient to gain additional benefit (beyond that of mere life) from the continuation of life. Thus, an irreversibly comatose patient is both less harmed and less benefited from continued treatment. A balance must be struck in both situations, and must focus upon the specific circumstances of the individual case.

Keown's approach to this issue thus far appears sound. However, shortly after outlining this approach, he sought to apply it to the controversial BMA guidance on withholding and withdrawing medical treatment.[43] He argues that the guidance condones the withdrawal of treatment on the grounds that the patient's life is no longer thought worthwhile. Keown is consistently critical of assumptions that a human life lacks worth and such an assumption would also cause significant problems under the right to life approach. However, there is doubtful evidence that the BMA guidance was adopting such an approach. While it refers to cases such as *Re J* in which the quality of life test seemed to refer as much to an assessment of the worth of the patient's life as to continued treatment, this may be regarded as an aspect of the assessment of the burden on the patient from the treatment, which is accepted as proper by Keown. The relevant question under English law will be whether the consequences of continued treatment, which will include the continuation of life in the patient's condition, is going to be proportionate. In other words, when assessing the burden of the treatment on the patient, as Keown argues is appropriate, it will be necessary to take into account the benefits that the preservation of life will entail. There will undoubtedly be some benefit, but if the only possible life available to the patient will be one full of pain and suffering, then that will be a factor to be weighed in the balance when determining the proportionality of continued treatment (and thus the state's right to life obligation). So it could be argued that, while Keown's basic argument on withdrawal of life-sustaining treatment is sound, his critique of the BMA guidance, and more generally his application of the principles, does not sufficiently apply the argument, settling instead for an instinctive revulsion at the idea of negating inherent value in human life.

The argument that there will always be some (minimal) benefit from the preservation of life is not without its detractors. The Irish Supreme Court's decision in *Re a Ward of Court* was based upon the controversial proposition that the right to life includes a right to die a natural death. While, as we discovered in the previous chapter, the right to respect for private life under the ECHR has been interpreted to include a right to make autonomous choices about the dying process,[44] the right to life is not generally regarded as incorporating a right to any particular form of death. Hamilton CJ explained the Irish Supreme Court's approach as follows:

As the process of dying is part, and an ultimate, inevitable consequence, of life, the right to life necessarily implies the right to have nature take its course and to die a natural death

---

[43] *Withholding and Withdrawing Life-Prolonging Medical Treatment: Guidance for Decision-Making* (London: BMJ Books, 1999).   [44] *Pretty v United Kingdom* (2002) 35 E.H.R.R. 1.

and, unless the individual concerned so wishes, not to have life artificially maintained by the provision of nourishment by abnormal artificial means, which have no curative effect and which is intended merely to prolong life.[45]

The result achieved by this approach, namely the withdrawal of life-sustaining treatment, could have been achieved by other reasoning. The right to life does not require all possible steps to preserve life and the patient in this case gained little benefit and suffered some burden from the treatment. The benefit/burden equation, and its focus on what is proportionate, is a preferable means of determining when life need no longer be preserved by artificial means than the inclusion of a right to die a natural death within the right to life. Not only does the natural death approach raise the query of when a death is 'natural', but it is also built upon an assumption that there is no inherent value in the preservation of human life. Hamilton CJ took the view that the patient's rights to privacy and dignity (which he rightly recognized as continuing despite her incapacity) faced no conflict in this case with the right to life, which here served only to produce a right to die a natural death and not to protect life.[46] Lord Clyde in the Scottish case of *Law Hospital NHS Trust v Lord Advocate* took a similar view when he stated that there would be no benefit at all in continuing life-sustaining treatment that served 'no purpose beyond the artificial prolongation of existence'.[47] This is overstating the point. The benefit to be obtained from the preservation of life for patients in PVS or a similar condition may be minimal but the preservation of human life is always in itself of some benefit, even though that may easily be outweighed by conflicting interests. A proportionality assessment is to be preferred.

It was mentioned above that Keown's definition of disproportionate treatment comprised not only the concept of excessively burdensome treatment but also treatment that is futile. It is this aspect of the definition that has been most heavily criticized due to its ambiguous nature and potential for misuse. Price has argued that 'futility is a nebulous concept applied too sweepingly and without sufficient care, including by the judiciary'.[48] In Price's view, futility should apply only to treatment that will not achieve its intended clinical effect. This is not the sense in which the term is often used, however. Price argues that even Keown misuses it, as for example when he claims that treatment such as antibiotics or ventilation are futile for patients in PVS when, in reality, they may achieve their intended clinical effect.[49] What Keown and others mean when they refer to futile treatment is rather that the treatment will not achieve the desired effect of returning the patient to full, or significantly restored, health.[50] As Price argues, 'the expression is often employed in circumstances where it is intended to imply that

---

[45] *Re a Ward of Court*, n. 7 above, para. 139.   [46] ibid, para. 165.   [47] 1996 SC 301.
[48] Price (01), n. 20 above, p. 626.   [49] ibid, pp. 626–7.
[50] Keown defends his view of futility against Price's criticism by seeking to redefine the meaning of the word. He says that, according to his sanctity of life principle, a treatment may be futile even if it can achieve its physiological effect (Keown (06), n. 21 above, p. 112). If a word has to be redefined in this way to serve its desired role, then perhaps a different word might be more appropriate.

relief will only prove temporary or where the patient's life will be enhanced to no, or only a very limited, degree by it'.[51] In other words, futility is often used to refer to the conclusion of a balancing exercise in which it has been determined that the treatment imposes an excessive burden on the patient for no significant benefit. In this way, the concept of futility adds nothing to the balancing exercise that has already been identified. If treatment is genuinely futile, i.e. will not achieve its intended clinical effect, then its continuation cannot be regarded as a proportionate requirement in order to preserve life because it is ineffective. If, however, the treatment is not in this sense futile but will provide no benefit or only a slight benefit which is outweighed by the burden imposed by it, then its continuation will also not be required under the proportionality test.

Price cautions that even the other string of Keown's definition of disproportionate treatment has no meaning in a vacuum.[52] Merely focusing on medical benefits and burdens imposed by the treatment itself does not present the full picture. He argues that the benefits and burdens inherent in continued existence in a particular condition must be taken into account also. This is an important gloss upon the balancing exercise outlined above, but it does tread a fine line. It is, as Price recognizes, important to take into account what the preservation of life will truly mean for the specific patient, and that will include both the specific benefits (for example, Is the patient conscious? Is the patient able to experience pleasure, or recognize loved ones?) and the burdens (for example, Will the patient experience pain or discomfort? Will the patient's body be subjected to degrading treatment?) But it is also important to avoid any implication of an individual's life being completely devoid of value or, worse yet, rights and interests. Price is right to point out that an excessive burden may result either from a treatment itself which generates intolerable pain, or by means of a treatment facilitating the continuation of a life full of pain and suffering.[53] Either burden can, and should, be taken into account when treatment decisions are made, but neither should be conclusive without recognition that the patient retains a right to life, as well as a right to be free from degrading treatment, and that even a life full of pain and suffering may have some value that will not easily be outweighed. Keown's distrust of an assessment of the worth of an individual patient, rather than of the value of continued treatment, has some justification, and provided that all of the relevant circumstances (including what life will entail for the individual should it endure) form part of the balancing exercise, then it provides a useful restraint upon the withdrawal of life-sustaining treatment.

A distinction between ordinary/extraordinary treatment may be too stark but life-sustaining treatment should always be subjected to a test of proportionality and it may be harder for more excessive measures to be justified if the benefit/burden balance reveals that continued life will be bought at too high a cost in terms

[51] Price (01), n. 20 above, p. 626. [52] ibid, p. 629.
[53] Price (09), n. 19 above, p. 152.

of pain and suffering. This approach reflects the human rights approach in which rights often require offsetting with other potentially conflicting rights. The right to life imposes, as we have seen, an obligation upon states to take whatever steps are reasonable in order to preserve life. That reasonableness will be determined by the balancing exercise envisaged here. The question that must now be addressed is whether the same approach applies to all forms of medical care, or whether the provision of artificial nutrition and hydration (ANH), which is the subject of many judicial cases, requires a different approach, in which its withdrawal is harder to justify.

D. The provision of food and water: always reasonable?

Patients in PVS often require little intervention in order to remain alive. For example, often they will be able to breathe without assistance. However, they will all require the provision of ANH. Therefore in cases such as *Bland* when issues of withdrawal of treatment are considered, it is not the switching off of a life support machine, but rather the withdrawal of food and water that is being proposed. Does this raise any specific concerns? It might appear that in terms of the right to life, it does. No human being is more vulnerable than those in PVS, or otherwise permanently unconscious, and it might be argued that the provision of food and water to such a vulnerable individual is the least that the state should be obligated to do in order to preserve life. While many aspects of the positive obligations on states under the right to life can impose onerous requirements, ensuring nutrition and hydration for those unable to do so for themselves seems to be a minor imposition on a state that values human life. The fundamental issue here is whether ANH is merely a form of medical treatment like any other, and should thus be subject to the benefit/burden balancing exercise outlined above, or whether it is better described as a form of basic care, to which different rules might apply.

Various commentators have argued that ANH is a form of basic care. John Finnis, for example, argues that food, water and cleaning that one can provide at home (as distinct from more technical medical care received in hospital) should be provided to everyone for whom one has responsibility. As the state will ultimately bear responsibility for an incompetent patient in hospital, this suggests that the withdrawal of ANH by the state cannot be justified. Finnis bases this argument upon his view that a failure to provide such basic care amounts to a decision that the patient would be better off dead and such a decision would violate the intrinsic good of human life and violate the right to life.[54] Keown also regards feeding by a nasogastric tube as basic care rather than medical treatment. The conclusion is supported by the BMA's definition of basic care as 'those

---

[54] J. Finnis, 'A Philosophical Case Against Euthanasia' in Keown (97), n. 15 above, p. 33.

procedures essential to keep an individual comfortable' which is said to include 'warmth, shelter, pain relief, management of distressing symptoms...hygiene measures (such as the management of incontinence) and the offer of nutrition and hydration'.[55] It should be noted, however, that all of the judges in the *Bland* case regarded ANH as a form of medical treatment, and this precedent has been followed in subsequent caselaw. In the judges' view, artificial feeding by means of a tube could be distinguished from other means of providing nutrition. Sir Thomas Bingham MR attempted to explain this distinction by claiming that the insertion of the tube requires skill and knowledge, that the tube is invasive, and that the mechanical pumping of food through the tube is an unnatural process.[56] There was considerable support for this view from the medical experts in the case. However, the provision of food and water, through whatever means, is distinct in pertinent ways from the provision of other forms of medical treatment. It does not 'treat' any underlying medical condition, it is essential for all human life, and in no other context is it regarded as in any way a medical need. While the artificial provision of nutrition and hydration by means of a tube is more clinical in nature, this should arguably not be permitted to transform the nature of the care being provided.

The significance of the debate about whether ANH is basic care or medical treatment relates to whether it should be judged on the same basis as other forms of life-sustaining medical treatment, and thus subject to the need to balance with other potentially conflicting interests, or whether the provision of food for an incompetent patient is such a basic expectation within an affluent society that it should not be compared with the more extraordinary means of artificially preserving life. Certainly the denial of basic care such as food and water from a patient who otherwise requires no medical intervention to support life can be regarded as a distinctly different issue to a decision that medical treatment is no longer in a patient's best interests. Likewise in right to life terms there is a convincing argument that such basic care should be assumed always to be a reasonable step in order to preserve life. Largely this conclusion stems from the fact that competing public interests are likely to be less pressing, but is also influenced by the consideration that this minimal level of state support for the preservation of life may be easier to justify in terms of the rights and interests of the patient. This point is perhaps overlooked by Price who argues that the contention that ANH should only be withheld when it is futile (which he takes to mean that the patient can no longer metabolize) or where it is unduly burdensome is too restrictive. He emphasizes that for a patient who is permanently unconscious, the withholding of nutrition and hydration will not produce any discomfort and therefore Price

[55] BMA guidance, para. 3.3. Keown expressly compares a feeding tube with a catheter: 'the former allows liquid to pass into the stomach, the latter allows it to pass out of the bladder. And catheters (especially those already in place) are surely basic care rather than medical treatment' (Keown (2000), n. 39 above, p. 70).   [56] *Bland*, n. 1 above, p. 836.

argues that the continuation of ANH can only be justified 'on the basis of its symbolic significance for society in general or on the basis of potential distress to carers or relatives/friends . . . not for the benefit of the patient'.[57] This view is problematic from a right to life perspective. While Price is correct to draw attention to the impact upon others in society, including most importantly the patient's loved ones, from any decision to withdraw or continue ANH, the interests of the patient should not be negated, despite the lack of competence and consciousness. Even if there is no tangible benefit, in terms of relief of suffering, from ANH, there is usually the benefit of the preservation of life.[58] While it has been recognized that that benefit may be outweighed in some situations, it is still a factor to be placed in the balance as long as the patient retains rights and interests. And as long as the patient remains alive, then such rights and interests endure. The Court of Appeal's approach in the *Burke* case illustrates a very different starting point from Price's view that continuation of ANH produces no benefit for the patient.[59] The Court in this case was particularly concerned with the withdrawal of ANH from a competent patient who wished to remain alive but it took the view that, as long as ANH is prolonging the life of the patient, then there is a continuing duty to provide it, stemming not from the demands of the competent patient but from the law's presumption in favour of the preservation of life. This presumption will obviously be strengthened by a patient's expressed desire to continue to live in the condition in which he now finds himself. But the presumption is an important starting point, regardless of the patient's wishes. If there is an expressed desire not to continue life in a PVS or comatose state, then that will outweigh the basic presumption; if there is no evidence of the patient's wishes, then the presumption in favour of the preservation of life by ANH is a useful starting point which can then be challenged by other potentially conflicting factors, such as the right to be free from degrading treatment and the presumption in favour of bodily integrity. It is the starting point, then, that distinguishes ANH from other forms of life-sustaining treatment. The balancing scales start equally balanced for other forms of treatment, but for ANH (and other forms of basic care, such as the provision of warmth and shelter) the scales begin weighted in favour of life.

E. The balancing exercise

Regardless of the starting point, it has been concluded that a balancing exercise is vital when determining whether the withdrawal of life-sustaining treatment will amount to a violation of the right to life. On the one side of the balance is the

[57] Price (01), n. 20 above, p. 632.

[58] In very rare cases, it is possible for the provision of ANH to hasten death. See the Court of Appeal's judgment in *R (Burke) v The General Medical Council* [2005] 3 WLR 1132, para. 54.

[59] *Burke,* ibid. See C. McIvor, 'The Positive Medical Duty to Provide Life-Prolonging Treatment' (2006) P.N. 59 for discussion.

enduring value in the preservation of life. This is an issue that has been considered in various places in this book. It encompasses both the inherent value of any human life and the instrumental value of life to the individual concerned and to his or her loved ones. On the other side of the balance are considerations such as dignity of the human person, protection of bodily integrity and respect for privacy. Of particular significance in this regard will be the international prohibition of inhuman or degrading treatment. This protection is to be found in Article 3 ECHR, Article 7 ICCPR, Article 5 ACHR and Article 5 AfCh. Typically, it is an absolute prohibition, which is non-derogable even in times of war or public emergency. As such it can be contrasted with the more flexible protection of the right to life which, as we have seen, envisages many potential limitations upon the right. It is of particular relevance in this context that, in the case of *D v United Kingdom*,[60] the European Court of Human Rights made clear that Article 3 not only prohibits inhuman and degrading treatment from being imposed by the state, but also applies to situations where the suffering from a natural illness is exacerbated by the treatment of an individual by national authorities. In this case, the applicant was dying of AIDS and his complaint related to the British authorities' attempts to deport him to the island of St Kitts where he would be denied the medical care and attention he was able to enjoy in the UK. In the Court's view such a deportation would expose the applicant to 'a real risk of dying under most distressing circumstances' and this would amount to inhuman treatment, contrary to Article 3.[61] While the Court has been reluctant in later cases, such as *Pretty v United Kingdom*, to recognize a right to die under Article 3, the earlier case of *D v United Kingdom* can be distinguished from the *Pretty* assisted-suicide situation. In the former case, the UK sought to take a positive step to intervene in the applicant's life (deportation) and that step, it was concluded, would cause suffering to the applicant during his dying process. In *Pretty*, however, the state's only action was to prohibit assisted suicide so, while D's human dignity could be assured by the state refraining from deporting him, Pretty's dignity, she argued, could only be assured by her death. Whatever the merits or demerits (considered to some extent in the previous chapter) of an argument that international human rights law should protect Pretty's desire to obtain dignity *by* dying, there is a much stronger argument that D's desire to obtain dignity *in* dying is already protected under human rights law. This distinction is crucial for the issue of withdrawal of life-sustaining treatment. Even without legal recognition of a right to die, existing human rights norms protect human dignity at all stages of life, including during the final dying stage. The state's actions in the *D* case of seeking to deport a dying man with the foreseeable outcome that the suffering imposed by his disease would be increased, could arguably be compared to a decision to continue the provision of degrading treatment in a way that, while preserving life, would cause the dying process to lack basic dignity. While this only provides one side of

---

[60] [1997] 24 EHRR 423.   [61] ibid, para. 53.

the balancing scales (the other being the enduring value in human life), it illustrates the conflicting interest that may outweigh the right to life in this context.

F. Conclusion

To some extent, the conclusions reached in this chapter may appear non-specific. The key consideration is the reasonableness of the continuation of life-sustaining care or treatment and this can only be determined on a case by case basis. Not only will the burdens imposed by specific treatment vary according to the nature of the treatment and the condition of the patient, but also the benefits to be obtained by continuing the life-sustaining treatment will depend upon the type of life that can be preserved. While all human life has an inherent value, one that endures no matter how poor the quality of a particular life, it will not always be proportionate or reasonable to expect the state to provide the treatment necessary for its continuation. The inherent value in the preservation of life will serve, not as a conclusion, but as either a factor to be placed on one side of the balancing scales (in respect of the continuation of life-sustaining medical treatment) or as a prima facie assumption that basic care (such as ANH) should be provided by the state. There will be a number of potentially conflicting factors that will strengthen the argument for withdrawal and the most significant of these will be the public interest in the allocation of limited resources and the private right to be free from degrading treatment. (The relevance of the latter has been considered here and the next chapter will turn to the issue of public resources.) Once more, however, the reasonableness of withdrawal must be decided on a case by case basis, a task which is made both easier and more important by the recognition that any living human being retains both a right to life and other human rights. Because all human life has value, all living human beings, even those in PVS or an irreversible coma, retain interests in what is done to their bodies, as well as in whether previously expressed wishes are respected. It is worth bearing in mind that ironically it is in part because such interests endure that life continues to have value.

9

Protecting the Right to Life with Limited Public Resources

The previous two chapters have focused upon positive obligations under the right to life and the way in which the conflicting interests of autonomy and quality of life may limit the type and extent of life-saving interventions by the state. Finally in this chapter we will consider a very real practical restraint upon the duty to take positive steps to preserve life: that of limited public resources. It is a fact of life that acting to save lives often costs money. Whether it is the provision of food, shelter, healthcare or police protection, when the state is under a duty to take a positive step to save life, it must draw upon public resources in order to do so. And public resources are, and will always be, finite. While there is scope to argue that a greater proportion of a national budget should go towards the fundamental public duty to preserve human life, the amount of money available will always be limited. What we must consider in this chapter is whether the fact that resources are limited provides an excuse for a failure on the part of the state to intervene to save life. We are concerned here with a collision between human rights theory and the practical limits of real life.

A. Positive obligations and their cost

There is no doubt that the positive obligations imposed under the right to life can extend to actions necessitating extensive public funding. This was made clear by the HRC in its General Comment on Article 6 ICCPR in which it criticized narrow interpretations of the obligations imposed by the right to life and stated that 'it would be desirable for States parties to take all possible measures to reduce infant mortality and to increase life expectancy, especially in adopting measures to eliminate malnutrition and epidemics'.[1] While this might, perhaps, be viewed as a desirable aim rather than a legally enforced (or enforceable) obligation, the treaty bodies under a wide range of human rights treaties, as well as some domestic courts, have been willing to recognize some quite extensive obligations upon

---

[1] General Comment No 6: The Right to Life (1982), para. 5.

states. For example, in the case of *Villagran Morales v Guatemala*, the Inter-American Court of Human Rights opined that 'Owing to the fundamental nature of the right to life, restrictive approaches to it are inadmissible.'[2] It proceeded to recognize that the right includes 'not only the right of every human being not to be deprived of his life arbitrarily, but also the right that he will not be prevented from having access to the conditions that guarantee a dignified existence'.[3] The Court also recognized that the state has an 'obligation to guarantee the creation of the conditions required in order that violations of this basic right do not occur'.[4] This judgment makes clear, therefore, that an obligation inherent within the right to life (at least under the ACHR) is that states commit to creating the conditions that guarantee an individual a dignified existence. This must, at its minimum, incorporate a basic standard of living including access to essential food, shelter and medical care, and arguably could cover far more. In the case in which the Inter-American Court made these statements, it was the abduction, torture and killing of a number of street children in Guatemala City that led to findings of widespread violations. The wide reach of the right to life's positive aspect, as recognized by the Court, however, implies that the everyday lives of such street children may in itself raise arguable issues under the right to life even in the absence of the persecution and mistreatment of the children by agents of the state revealed in this case.

The African Commission on Human and Peoples' Rights has also adopted an expansive view of the right to life. In the case of *Social and Economic Rights Action Center v Nigeria*, the Commission recognized the existence of different levels of duties for states that undertake to adhere to a rights regime, including not only a duty to refrain from interfering but also a positive expectation to move state machinery towards the actual realization of rights, which may include the direct provision of basic needs such as food.[5] The Commission's finding of a right to life violation in this case was coupled with the implication that pollution and environmental degradation may contribute, or even amount, to a violation.[6] It should be noted that the Commission is interpreting a right to life located within a Charter containing other rights such as a right to enjoy the best attainable state of physical and mental health and a right of all peoples to freely dispose of their wealth and natural resources. Within this context, and with the socio-economic history and culture of the states committed to the Charter, the recognition of extensive and meaningful positive duties upon states is not surprising, and, of course, their judicial recognition is a long way from practical impact. Even the European Convention on Human Rights, however, which in general is more focused upon civil and political rights and the negative obligations found at the core of such rights, has been interpreted by the European Court of Human Rights as imposing extensive positive obligations upon states. While the case of *Osman v United*

[2] Series C, No. 77 (1999), para. 144.   [3] ibid.   [4] ibid.
[5] No. 155/1996, paras 44–47.   [6] ibid, para. 67.

Kingdom[7] initially demonstrated the extent of the positive duty under the right to life in the policing context, later cases such as *Öneryildiz v Turkey*[8] recognized its application in the context of the destitute who face special dangers due to their inadequate living conditions. The case concerned individuals who were residing in slums near a household-refuse tip. The tip was destroyed, along with much of the slum housing, in a methane explosion and the Court interpreted the right to life as imposing a duty on the state to safeguard the public from the possibility of such a lethal explosion, both by means of providing appropriate legal regulation of such hazardous waste sites, and also by ensuring the observance of these regulations and informing the public about risks. While this case falls short of imposing a general obligation on state parties to the ECHR to protect or guarantee the lives of the poor, it does imply that a specific responsibility may emerge in particular circumstances to protect the destitute from perceptible threats to their lives.[9]

Whether the European Court would be prepared to include the threat of starvation in that approach remains uncertain but some domestic courts have adopted this approach. The best example of this, and of the potentially extensive and expensive positive obligations implied by the right to life, is a series of cases in India in which the Supreme Court of India has interpreted the right to life to encompass a more general right to livelihood. Both a right to healthcare and a right to food have also been recognized by the Indian courts. Article 21 of the Indian Constitution states that 'No person shall be deprived of his life and personal liberty except according to procedure established by law.' In *Maneka Gandhi v Union of India*[10] the Supreme Court introduced the idea of substantive due process and asserted that the right to life includes the right to a life with human dignity. In *Francis Coralie Mullin v The Administrator, Union Territory of Delhi*[11] the Supreme Court expanded on this idea: 'The right to life includes the right to live with human dignity and all that goes with it, namely, the bare necessaries of life such as adequate nutrition, clothing and shelter and facilities for reading, writing and expressing oneself in diverse forms, freely moving about and mixing and comingling with fellow human beings.'[12] In this manner, the Court was able to introduce subsidiary economic and social rights into the ambit of the right to life. As developed in subsequent caselaw, these have included a right to shelter, a right to healthcare, a right to education, a right to food and a right to a clean and healthy environment.

The potential reach of the right to life in guaranteeing a minimum standard of living in order to ensure adequate protection for human life is well demonstrated by the cases considered so far. Whether expressed in terms of a right to livelihood, a right to food, protection from specific threats to life or the guarantee of

---

[7] (1998) 29 E.H.R.R. 245; Reps 1998-VIII.

[8] [2004] ECHR 657; (2005) 41 E.H.R.R. 20.

[9] See C. O'Cinneide, 'A Modest Proposal: Destitution, State Responsibility and the European Convention on Human Rights' [2008] E.H.R.L.R. 583, at p. 590.   [10] (1978) 1 SCC 248.

[11] (1981) 2 SCR 516.   [12] ibid, p. 529.

a dignified existence, the right to life has been described as a potentially useful mechanism for improving, and thus going some way towards protecting, the lives of individuals. Such obligations do not come cheap, however, and a variety of courts have also accepted that limitations upon the reach of the right to life's positive obligations may stem from the reality of finite public resources.

In *Osman*, the European Court of Human Rights made clear that the positive obligation that it had just identified as inherent within the right to life 'must be interpreted in a way which does not impose an impossible or disproportionate burden on the authorities'.[13] It recognized that, in the context of policing, there are a number of factors to be taken into account by the authorities, including the 'difficulties involved in policing modern societies, the unpredictability of human conduct and the operational choices which must be made in terms of priorities and resources'.[14] The latter factor is one of huge significance not only, or even especially, in the context of policing but more broadly whenever a positive obligation arises. For example, the provision of healthcare is a significant component of the protection of human life but will inevitably involve choices about the allocation of resources. In *Pentiacova v Moldova*,[15] the European Court heard a complaint about insufficient public funding of a specific treatment (haemo-dialysis for chronic renal failure). The Court regarded the applicant's claim as a call to public funds which, in light of the scarcity of public resources, would require the diversion of funds from other worthy needs. It considered the main issues under Article 8 (on its own initiative) and concluded that 'In view of their familiarity with the demands made on the health care system as well as with the funds available to meet those demands, the national authorities are in a better position to carry out this assessment than an international court.' In other words, the Court regarded a wide margin of appreciation as key to its findings on the positive obligations imposed on the state in this context under Article 8. The granting of a broad discretion to state authorities to determine the appropriate division of very limited public funds is an easily justifiable approach. However, having concluded that it 'cannot be said that the respondent State failed to strike a fair balance between the competing interests of the applicants and the community as a whole', the Court felt able to dismiss the application as inadmissible on the basis that it was manifestly ill-founded. This is much harder to justify as there are clearly arguable issues involved here that might be said to deserve a hearing on merits. Furthermore, the dismissal of the application under Article 8 was followed by a summary dismissal of Article 2 on the basis that issues related to positive obligations had already been examined under Article 8 and the Court saw no need to reach a different conclusion under Article 2. The Court's conclusions under Article 8, however, were based solely upon the application of a very

---

[13] *Osman*, n. 7 above, para. 116.
[14] ibid.
[15] (2005) 40 E.H.R.R. SE23.

wide margin of appreciation which is commonly found to attach to consideration of what is necessary in the particular democratic society of the respondent state. Under the right to life, the need for a margin is less clear. It should be remembered, however, that any positive obligation to preserve life under Article 2 is restricted to what is reasonable and it may be that the view of what is reasonable is an issue that an international court wishes to leave to national authorities. It will be vital, however, that the discretion given to states on this issue is not absolute. What is reasonable should be determined on an objective basis, albeit taking into account the specific situation pertaining in the respondent state (for example, a scarcity of public resources). Arguably the European Court did not adequately perform this crucial oversight role in this case.

The case of *Öneryildiz*, also before the European Court of Human Rights, indicated that the Court will sometimes perform such a role. The respondent state reminded the Court in this case that an impossible or disproportionate burden should not be imposed upon the authorities without consideration being given to the operational choices that they must make in terms of priorities and resources. The Court eagerly accepted this point and indeed emphasized that it is not its task to substitute its own views of the policy related questions for the views of the national authorities. However, the preventive measures that could have been taken to counter the risk to life evident on the facts of this case were, in the view of the Court, reasonably regarded as suitable means of averting risk and, crucially, 'would not have diverted resources to an excessive degree or give rise to policy problems'.[16] Therefore, despite the wide margin of appreciation that the Court again in this case regarded as appropriate in relation to positive obligations under the right to life, there are clearly defined limits to that discretion if the diversion of resources is not excessive and if no policy problems are created by such diversion. This is a constructive approach that will be considered further below.

The Human Rights Committee has taken a potentially even more interventionist approach by explicitly denying that limited resources serve as a reason for failing to meet positive obligations under the right to life. In *Lantsova v Russian Federation*[17] the HRC recognized the duty on states to protect the lives of its detainees. The case concerned a man held in pre-trial detention who was healthy upon admission but became ill, received no medical attention, and died, while being detained in a seriously overcrowded and under-resourced detention centre. The HRC concluded that, by detaining individuals, the state takes on the responsibility of caring for their lives and that the national authorities must therefore organize detention facilities in a manner that enables it to know about the state of health of its detainees so far as may be reasonably expected. In relation to this, the Court firmly held that 'lack of financial means cannot reduce this responsibility'.[18] This is in stark contrast to the approach of the European Court

---

[16] *Öneryildiz*, n. 8 above, para. 107.   [17] Communication 763/1997.
[18] ibid, para. 9–2.

of Human Rights that expressly recognizes the need to grant a degree of discretion to the states to determine how best to allocate finite resources. It may be that the situation in *Lantsova* was closer to that in *Öneryildiz* than *Pentiacova* due to the possibility that relatively inexpensive measures could have been taken to avert the risk to life without significant inroads into the state's general allocation of public resources and thus without creating difficult policy issues that are best determined by national authorities. It may also be that steps to protect the lives of detainees will always be more rigorously enforced due to the state's assumption of responsibility for the life of that individual. In general it seems clear that the issue of allocating public resources to avert risks to life is a factor that will be taken into account by courts enforcing the right to life, even if in some limited circumstances the court feels justified in discounting the difficulties raised by this factor.

One reason for judicial reluctance to intervene when the state relies upon limited resources as a reason for failing to take steps to avert a risk to life is that the judiciary may regard itself as not best placed to make decisions about allocating resources. As Fredman explains, 'Positive duties are often thought to be better suited to the political than the judicial arena, because decision-makers are accountable to the electorate for their decisions as to how to balance competing claims on resources.'[19] This may be described as a separation of powers perspective. The judiciary is well suited to determining issues of legal rights and duties where its independence and impartiality are an asset, but in relation to issues of economic and social policy a body that is elected by, and accountable to, the public is better suited to making decisions. This view has been repeatedly outlined by Lord Hoffman in domestic caselaw[20] but is no less (and may be more) relevant to the international arena, where a margin of appreciation given to national authorities will only enhance the restraint imposed upon international courts by separation of powers considerations. The obvious difficulty with this approach is distinguishing between issues of rights and issues of policy, a task that is particularly problematic in the context of positive obligations to preserve life. As O'Cinneide remarks, 'Judges often fear that applying human rights law to plug gaps in complex systems of executive-bureaucratic welfare provision will resemble setting a bull loose in a delicate china shop.'[21] It need not be this way, however. As suggested above, in relation to the *Öneryildiz* case, it is possible for a court to enforce a positive obligation without intervening significantly in decisions about allocation of resources. This is also demonstrated by the Indian cases, which, despite recognizing the broadest of all obligations under the right to life, rarely impose significant resource burdens upon the Indian authorities. As Fredman

---

[19] S. Fredman, 'Human Rights Transformed: Positive Duties and Positive Rights' [2006] P.L. 498, at p. 512.

[20] See Lord Hoffmann's judgments in *R (Alconbury Developments) v Secretary of State for the Environment* [2001] 2 All ER 929 and *R (ProLife Alliance) v British Broadcasting Corporation* [2003] 2 All ER 977.   [21] O'Cinneide, n. 9 above, p. 601.

recognizes the 'affirmation of wide duties is often used to counter maladministration rather than to initiate new projects'.[22] Even in relation to the recognition of a right to food under the right to life, this occurred in the context of a finding by the Indian court that half of a food subsidy was being spent on holding excess stocks and so reducing that stockpile would free up resources to provide food to those who needed it.[23] It is, therefore, possible for courts to enforce positive obligations to take reasonable steps to preserve life, even when they appear to involve some expenditure, without overstepping their bounds of responsibility and expertise, either by pointing to pre-existing maladministration or by leaving the specifics of expenditure to national authorities but enforcing the need for some consideration to be given to the provision of public funds to avert specific risks to life. While there is sound justification for judicial reluctance to second guess decisions about the allocation of limited public resources, therefore, this should not preclude the recognition and enforcement of positive duties to take steps to avert risks to life merely because some cost may be involved. As was originally stated in *Osman*, an impossible or disproportionate burden should not be placed on authorities, but this does not amount to a blanket exception to duties under the right to life whenever the issue of funding is raised.

B. Allocating resources to save lives

The understandable reluctance of a court (particularly an international court) to second guess decisions about the allocation of resources must be balanced against the need to enforce, in a meaningful way, the state's positive obligations under the right to life. The key to striking this balance, in this context as in others, will be reasonableness. The right to life typically requires that a state take reasonable steps to preserve the lives of individuals within its jurisdiction. The allocation of public resources within a state will impact upon its ability to meet this obligation and a failure to allocate resources in a reasonable manner might amount to a failure to take reasonable steps to preserve life. We will investigate, in turn, two contexts in which resource issues may hamper efforts to preserve life: policing and healthcare.

(1) The application of the *Osman* test to policing in England and Wales

The *Osman* case before the European Court of Human Rights set out the authoritative test for determining whether a state has fulfilled its positive obligations under the right to life. In a number of domestic cases, however, it had been

---

[22] Fredman, n. 19 above, p. 514.   [23] See Fredman, ibid, for discussion of this.

suggested that the test was variable and that the threshold of what is reasonable can be lowered where it is the conduct of state authorities that has exposed the individual to the risk to his life.

R (on application of A) v Lord Saville of Newdigate,[24] involved a challenge by a British soldier against a decision of the Bloody Sunday Inquiry compelling him to give evidence in Londonderry, while both *R (on application of DF) v Chief Constable of Norfolk Police*[25] and *R (on application of Bloggs 61) v Secretary of State for the Home Department*[26] concerned applications by prisoners challenging decisions about placements in protected witness units. In all these cases, the courts departed from the *Osman* test when considering the extent of the positive obligation under Article 2 ECHR under the Human Rights Act 1998 and applied instead a lower threshold, opening the door to greater expenditure. The courts held that a common-sense approach was needed in determining whether a risk to life existed; if the authorities were responsible for the creation of the risk, then a lower threshold than outlined in *Osman* is appropriate. There are a number of potentially relevant issues raised by this approach. First, there is the possibility that a special relationship exists between the state (and its agents) and the person in danger in these cases, whether a prisoner or soldier (or, as in *Van Colle*, discussed below, a prosecution witness). If such a special relationship exists, then a risk to life may be more readily identified and the expectation of preventative action, whatever the resource implications, may be heightened. Alternatively, it may be that the distinguishing factor of these cases is the potential vulnerability of the individual. It was discussed in a previous chapter that prisoners, in particular, are in a peculiarly vulnerable position in respect of the right to life and that the state's positive obligations to take reasonable steps to preserve life may be more stringent in this context. Finally, these cases raise the possibility that a state has greater obligations to act to preserve life if it has been a contributory factor in creating the risk to life. This is certainly true of prisoners who are detained by the state in a dangerous and potentially life-threatening environment, but may also be true of witnesses being compelled to testify for the prosecution or soldiers being compelled to give testimony in a hostile environment. All of these factors, either together or alone, may contribute to an argument that the seemingly high threshold imposed by *Osman*, under which there must be a real and immediate risk to life that the state must know or should have known before any legal expectation of a preventative duty will arise, may be lowered depending on the facts of the case.

The case of *Van Colle v Chief Constable of Hertfordshire* presented another opportunity for consideration of this issue. The case involved a man due to appear as a prosecution witness in a theft trial who was shot and killed by the accused two days before the trial. The Police Complaints Authority upheld a complaint about the police officer in charge who had failed to identify the risk to life or to protect the witness, and a case was brought under the Human Rights Act claiming a

---

[24] [2002] 1 WLR 1249.   [25] [2002] EWHC 1738.   [26] [2003] 1 WLR 2724.

violation of the right to life of the witness. The claimants sought to distinguish the *Osman* requirement of a real and immediate risk to life on the basis that the state contributed to the risk to life by requiring the man to act as a witness. The Court of Appeal accepted this argument but the House of Lords overturned this judgment and explicitly rejected the idea that the *Osman* test is variable in any way. Lord Hope of Craighead explained that 'The way the test was expressed in *Osman* offers no encouragement to the idea that where the positive obligation is invoked the standard to be applied may vary from case to case.'[27] The Lords rejected any notion that the threshold could be lowered where the conduct of state authorities has exposed the individual to a risk to his or her life. This may seem a harsh approach. It fails to take into account any degree of responsibility on the part of the state to avoid placing individuals at risk. However, Lord Brown of Eaton suggested that it is hardly surprising that the *Osman* test is so stringent because there are potential resource, and other policy, issues involved in meeting positive obligations.[28] Lord Hope also commented on the explicit reservation expressed in the *Osman* case that any positive obligation under the right to life must be interpreted in a way which does not impose an impossible or disproportionate burden on the authorities. He noted that the European Court of Human Rights could have said that the question of whether the imposition of a positive obligation would be an impossible or disproportionate burden was a matter to be decided on the facts of each case, but instead the Court defined the limits of the positive obligations imposed under the right to life and required that those limits be observed in every case.[29] In other words, the test of whether a positive obligation exists or not is not variable on a case by case basis. While this may make it more difficult for an individual to succeed in establishing the existence of a positive obligation in cases where the state may be regarded as having contributed to the circumstances that created a threat to life, it may also mean that there is less discretion on issues such as limited resources. In cases where a real and immediate risk to life is shown to have existed, it is not for the individual court hearing the case to assess whether the recognition of a positive obligation would impose an impossible burden on the state, but rather the court should enforce that obligation to do all that is reasonable in the circumstances. It is only in relation to the assessment of reasonableness that the question of impossible burdens, including financial burdens, on the state arises, and not on the earlier question of whether a positive obligation exists in the circumstances or not.

(2) The allocation of resources in healthcare: NICE and QALY

One particularly interesting example of the challenges posed by the allocation of finite public resources, and its implications for the preservation of life, is the funding of healthcare. This presents challenges to all governments, although the

[27] [2002] 1 WLR 1249, para. 70.   [28] ibid, para. 115.   [29] ibid, para. 70.

nature of the challenge varies considerably depending upon the socio-economic conditions of the state, and other factors such as its political tradition and population size. So, for example, in many third world countries, the challenge is to provide a basic level of healthcare to a large, and predominantly poor, population; in many European countries, the challenge is to provide a high standard, and equitable, public health service; while in the United States, the challenge is to ensure adequate healthcare for all within a system developed upon a private insurance scheme. The US is alone amongst advanced industrialized countries in not having universal coverage, with an estimated 45 million Americans left without health insurance.[30] The US is also distinct in that limited resources are not seen as the crucial, or even a relevant, issue there.[31] Nonetheless, decisions about allocating resources to healthcare take place at many different levels of priority setting. They begin at a macro level of decisions about what share of national resources should be allocated to health, which is ultimately a political decision. They then proceed to incorporate decisions about the distribution of that finite budget between different geographical areas and health services; about the allocation of resources to particular forms of treatment; choices of which patients should receive treatment; and decisions on how much to spend on individual patients.[32] Such decisions have always had to be made but in recent years the light of publicity has illuminated their nature. In more prosperous states, this has occurred in large part due to a more explicit recognition of the restraints imposed by limited resources.[33] As Coulter and Ham have argued 'Implicit decision making has come under pressure in the face of resource constraints and rising patient expectations. This has led politicians in a number of countries to address the challenge of rationing more explicitly by setting up committees and expert groups.'[34] One good example of this is the National Institute for Health and Clinical Excellence (NICE) in the UK and a closer investigation of its role and its implications for the preservation of life will present a useful case study of

---

[30] See N. Daniels & J. Sabin, *Setting Limits Fairly* (Oxford: Oxford University Press, 2002), p. 150, for discussion. The immense difficulties in reforming the US system have become increasingly apparent in recent months.

[31] ibid. Daniels and Sabin explain that 'To Americans, the message that costs are rising too rapidly does not translate in the public mind into the understanding that resources are limited...Instead, it translates into other messages: employers do not want to pay enough; taxes are too high; or companies are seeking to raise profits' (p. 151).

[32] These five levels of priority setting are identified by R. Klein, 'Dimensions of Rationing: Who Should Do What?' (1993) BMJ 307, at pp. 309–11.

[33] Daniels and Sabin argue that until the 1990s, the rationing process in the UK 'was almost entirely implicit, carried out by physicians through the potentially beneficial treatments they did not offer and the referrals they chose not to make, and by capacity limits and waiting lists' (n. 30 above, p. 178). Then the NHS changes made by Prime Minister Thatcher, including the purchaser–provider split and the creation of general practitioner fundholders, introduced market values into the NHS and led to a more public debate about the allocation of funds and rationing.

[34] A. Coulter & C. Ham, 'International Experience of Rationing (Or Priority Setting)' in Coulter & Ham (eds), *The Global Challenge of Health Care Rationing* (Oxford: Open University Press, 2000), at p. 1.

how resource allocation impacts upon a state's ability to meet its positive obligations under the right to life.

NICE is a body created by delegated legislation under the NHS Act 1977.[35] It began work in April 1999. Described by Mason and Laurie as 'something of a brave attempt to rationalise, and nationalise, our health care',[36] it was created with two main purposes in mind: to address the problem of a postcode lottery (a term meaning that certain treatments were available on the NHS in some areas but not in others) and to make hard choices on questions of the allocation of resources. It was charged with providing the NHS with guidance on best practice in three areas: clinical guidelines on management of specific conditions; recommendations on audit methods which enable monitoring of clinical performance; and appraisals of clinical and cost-effectiveness of health technologies. It is the latter aspect of NICE's work that has proved most controversial. Initially, the guidelines issued by NICE in all aspects of its work provided mere guidance and were not binding upon the NHS. However, since 2002 Health Authorities and Trusts have been required to make funds available to ensure that technologies approved by NICE can be provided where recommended by clinicians. This has meant that the third aspect of NICE's work—the appraisal of new technologies—has become all the more important. And a crucial aspect of this task is a decision about cost-effectiveness of treatments. NICE has explicitly recognized that this involves 'balancing the needs and wishes of individuals and the groups representing them against those of the wider population. This sometimes means treatments are not recommended because they do not provide sufficient benefit to justify their cost.'[37] It is clear that in this respect NICE plays a crucial role in determining the positive steps taken by the state (in this context, the NHS) to save lives. If a potentially life-saving treatment is not cost-effective, it will not be recommended for use. Deciding on the cost-effectiveness of treatment requires, as NICE acknowledges, a balancing of the rights of individuals whose lives may be saved or prolonged by the treatment with the rights of other individuals whose lives can only be saved or prolonged, or improved, by the provision of other treatments. If the overall healthcare budget is finite, such choices have to be made. The existence of NICE enables both politicians and healthcare managers to avoid making the choices themselves. But how does a body like NICE make such difficult choices?

NICE has adopted the QALY approach to rationing decisions. It describes this as a 'common currency' that allows comparisons to be made across different conditions.[38] The QALY, or Quality Adjusted Life Year, is based on the principle that

[35] National Institute for Clinical Excellence (Establishment and Constitution) Order (SI 1999 No. 220).

[36] J.K. Mason, A. McCall Smith & G. Laurie, *Law and Medical Ethics* (Oxford: Oxford University Press, 2006, 7th edn.), p. 423.

[37] NICE, 'Social Value Judgements: Principles for the Development of NICE Guidance' (NICE 2005), para. 4.2.   [38] ibid.

it is not just the saving of lives that matters, but rather the saving of life years, the value of which is adjusted to take into account the quality of those years. (A numerical value is placed on the quality of an individual's life so that a year of full health is valued as 1; death is valued at 0, and a year of reduced health will be valued at somewhere between 0 and 1.) For a state that is usually suspicious of quality of life considerations, the UK has eagerly endorsed their use in the context of allocating resources to healthcare. In the words of the Chairman of NICE, Sir Michael Rawlins, the QALY 'embodies the important social value judgment that to count only gains in life expectancy, without considering the quality of the additional life years, omits important dimensions of human welfare.'[39] The official NICE document on Social Value Judgements re-iterates this point: 'In addition to recognising that much of healthcare is concerned with improving people's quality of life, it also reflects the value judgement that mere survival is an insufficient measure of benefit.'[40] There is an opposing viewpoint, however, that reminds us that 'mere survival' is about saving lives and that this should indeed be prioritized over other health gains. Intuitively we may feel that the right to life would favour this view. Syrett has queried whether the NICE approach is consonant with societal values on how scarce resources should be distributed within the healthcare context, suggesting that NICE's utilitarian assumption may not be 'unequivocally shared by the British population, which regards equity considerations as of considerable significance and which accords particularly high priority to life-saving interventions'.[41] Some valuable research into this question has been undertaken by Cookson and Dolan who first identified five main classes of rationing principles in the relevant literature and then asked focus groups to make choices on the allocation of limited resources based on specific (hypothetical) case studies.[42] The five rationing principles identified were: (1) lottery principles or the 'not playing God' approach; (2) distribution according to immediate need or the 'rule of rescue'; (3) health maximization across the community; (4) equalizing lifetime health or the 'fair innings' approach; (5) equalizing opportunity for health or 'choicism' (i.e. giving priority to those whose ill health is caused through no fault of their own). During Cookson and Dolan's research, they discovered that the focus groups favoured principles one and five less than the others. So, there was no widespread support for applying lottery principles to resource allocation or for discriminating against those whose actions bear some responsibility for their ill health.[43] The other three rationing principles received relatively equal support, however, suggesting the favouring of an essentially pluralistic approach encompassing a broad rule of rescue (to cover not just threats

---

[39] M.D. Rawlins & A.J. Culyer, 'NICE and its Value Judgements' (2004) 329 BMJ 224, at p. 226.   [40] NICE, n. 37 above, para. 4.2.
[41] K. Syrett, 'NICE and Judicial Review: Enforcing "Accountability for Reasonableness" through the Courts?' (2008) 16 Med.L.R. 127, at p. 138.
[42] R. Cookson & P. Dolan, 'Public Views on Health Care Rationing: A Group Discussion Study' (1999) 49 Health Policy 63.   [43] ibid, p. 69.

to life but also those in immediate pain and suffering); health maximization, including concerns to make savings for the NHS in the long run (for example, reducing long-term nursing costs by providing a hip replacement); and reducing inequalities in people's lifetime experience of health by prioritizing younger patients, especially children.[44] Each element of this pluralistic approach requires some further consideration.

As mentioned above, the so-called rule of rescue serves as an opposing viewpoint to the common currency of the QALY. It seeks to prioritize saving lives that are under threat rather than giving equal weight to all quality-adjusted life years and, as such, is a more comfortable fit with the right to life and its positive obligations to preserve life. In the mid-1990s, the Swedish Parliamentary Priorities Commission asserted that a first principle of distribution of healthcare should be to help the most vulnerable and seriously ill regardless of issues of cost or even benefit.[45] However, in the UK, NICE is adamant that it does not recognize any such rule of rescue. Its rejection is based upon the argument that limited resources mean that prioritizing one patient whose life is in threat inevitably means that other anonymous present and future patients will be denied the treatment they need.[46] This argument, however, represents a more general rejection of the adoption of any priorities other than cost-effectiveness as determined by QALY. What would be more helpful is an unpicking of what exactly a rule of rescue would entail and how it could be implemented. First, it should be noted that the rejection of a rule of rescue is just as much a prioritization as the adoption of such a rule. As Coulter and Ham have recognized, 'the relative priority attached to different types of treatments or services (for example, to palliative care for the terminally ill as opposed to intensive care for those with life-threatening conditions) depends in part on the value attached to different outcomes (such as improving the quality of life as opposed to increasing the length of life)'.[47] The QALY approach prioritizes both quality and length of life, while the rule of rescue prioritizes the saving of as many lives as possible. While the right to life is not immune from quality of life considerations (as seen for example in the context of justifying the withdrawal of life-sustaining treatment), at its core is the protection of each human life in equal terms. The positive obligations imposed upon state governments by the right to life could be regarded as the right's very own rules of rescue: the state must do all that could reasonably be expected of it in order to preserve the lives of those within its jurisdiction. While what is reasonable is, as we have seen, open to some interpretation, taking steps to save lives that can be saved by prioritizing life-saving treatment when allocating limited public resources seems a logical expectation. The difficulty might be in determining what exactly is meant by saving life. It could be argued that many forms of medical treatment serve to save life by improving health and thus prolonging life. There is an important distinction,

---

[44] ibid, p. 71.   [45] See Daniels & Sabin, n. 30 above, p. 3 for discussion.
[46] NICE, n. 37 above, para. 4.5.   [47] Coulter & Ham, n. 34 above, p. 10.

however, between treatment that immediately saves life and treatment that may have a beneficial effect upon the preservation of life at some future indeterminate stage. The distinction is not unique to this context. In more general terms, the positive obligations to preserve life imposed under the right to life are restricted to actions with an imminent and tangible impact on human life. For example, a healthy diet would have a beneficial effect upon life expectancy but, at most, the right to life would seek to impose a right to a basic food ration. The reasonableness requirement is used in these wider contexts to limit the ambit of the right to life's positive obligations. In addition, it should be noted that the rule of rescue will be at its most significant if confined to life saving rather than life prolonging interventions. Its use as a prioritizing principle depends upon it giving priority to the saving of one life over the improvement (and implicit prolongation) of another life. If interpreted too broadly, it loses any value that it may have as a prioritizing principle. A rule of rescue as a prioritizing principle enables considerations of life expectancy, quality of life, and competing calls on resources to come into play. Its role as a prioritizing principle is much more justifiable, however, than a rule of rescue acting as an absolute restraint upon the allocation of resources. What is reasonable to prolong a life by a matter of hours may not be the same as what is reasonable to prolong it by twenty years; similarly the preservation of a life full of pain and suffering may not require the same positive intervention by the state as the saving of a potentially healthy life if such intervention inevitably prevents similar interventions to save, or improve the health, of other patients. It will not always be reasonable to take whatever steps are possible in order to rescue an individual patient from death because such choices are not, and cannot, be made in isolation, but rather as one thread of a complex tapestry of public funding. Nevertheless, a rule of rescue has something to offer as a reminder that the state should, if it reasonably can, intervene to save lives.

The other two aspects of the pluralistic approach to resource allocation mentioned above also deserve some consideration. First, the so-called fair innings principle suggests that priority should be given to younger patients, especially children. This accords with intuitive reaction and, indeed, research by Lewis and Charney has confirmed that when asked to choose between two patients with identical clinical needs, a significant majority of the public will choose the younger patient for treatment (except, interestingly, if the choice is between a two-year-old and an eight-year-old when the majority chose the older child for treatment).[48] It is not entirely clear, however, whether giving priority to a younger patient results from an implicit acceptance of the fair innings argument or is instead derived from a QALY-like approach in which the potential benefits of treatment are compared.[49] An older patient is likely to gain fewer

---

[48] P. Lewis & M. Charney, 'Which of Two Individuals Do You Treat When Only their Ages are Different and You Can't Treat them Both?' (1989) 15 J Med Eth 28.

[49] P. Dolan et al, 'QALY Maximisation and People's Preferences: A Methodological View of the Literature' (2005) 14 Health Economics 197, at p. 205, make this point.

life years from the provision of treatment than a younger patient and thus the QALY approach itself prioritizes the younger (as well as healthier) patient. Nevertheless, NICE explicitly rejects the notion that an NHS patient would be denied treatment due to their age, although it does accept that age may be a relevant factor in their treatment appraisals in a number of ways. For example, age may sometimes be a good indicator of health status or of the likelihood of adverse effects of specific treatment or there may be good grounds for believing that patients will respond differently to treatment due to their age.[50] More crucially, however, age inevitably impacts upon the QALYs saved by any particular treatment and so a treatment aimed at the elderly will have a starting point of a lower QALY compared to treatments aimed at younger patients and indeed this is one of main, and most convincing, arguments against the use of a QALY approach.

The final aspect of the pluralistic position evident from Cookson and Dolan's research, discussed above, is the principle of health maximization. While their research study emphasized the benefits of allocating funds now to fix an ongoing problem that will otherwise require continuous funding for nursing care, the health maximization approach also applies across society so that the benefits of treating one patient can be offset against the benefits of treating a different patient. This is a vital, if dangerous, principle. As argued above, choices about what treatments are to be funded cannot be taken in isolation from the implications for other treatments from such choices. When NICE recommends one treatment (and encourages the state to act to preserve the lives of the patients who can be saved from that treatment), it is also inevitably failing to recommend a different treatment (and thus providing the state with an excuse not to fund intervention that may save the lives of other hypothetical patients). There will be no solution to the allocation of finite public resources to healthcare that does not involve, either explicitly or implicitly, the balancing of benefits from one treatment to one set of patients with the benefits from another treatment to a different set of patients. As stated above, the advantage of the QALY approach is that it enables such a balancing exercise to be performed, although it may be criticized for defining the terms of the balance as an equal playing field when in fact some priorities could, and should, be written into the terms. While we might all agree that limited resources should be used in a way that best maximizes healthcare across society, and even accept that this will sometimes mean that treatment we or our loved ones need is not funded, we may not all agree that each QALY is equal; we may want to use those limited resources in a way that saves as many lives as possible; to prioritize those most in need of live-saving intervention. All potential patients are equal but are all life years (or days) really equal or should some count for more than others, such as the extra year of life given to a cancer sufferer by a radical new treatment? That extra year might be one filled with some

---

[50] NICE, n. 37 above, para. 6.3.

suffering but it might also be the most valuable year of that patient's life both for the patient and for his or her family.

The approach of NICE has traditionally avoided such considerations, instead using an incremental cost-effectiveness ratio (ICER). The ICER is the ratio of (a) to (b), where (a) is the difference in the mean costs of a proposed intervention compared with the next best alternative and (b) is the difference in the mean health outcomes. NICE has traditionally rejected any absolute threshold but acknowledged that 'As the incremental cost effectiveness ratio increases, the likelihood of rejection on grounds of cost ineffectiveness rises.'[51] Furthermore, some guideline ranges have been provided by NICE, thus an ICER of less than £20,000 per QALY gained is generally considered to be cost-effective, while an ICER of above £30,000 per QALY gained will require an increasingly stronger case for supporting the intervention as an effective use of limited NHS resources.[52] In recent years there has been some disquiet about such an approach, including from government ministers.

In conclusion, it is clear that NICE serves an important role in providing guidance about new and existing medical technologies. Comparisons between the costs and benefits of one treatment compared to another are inevitable and should not be avoided because, while limited resources exist, the state must take great care to ensure that it funds the treatments that will bring the most benefits to its citizens. The positive obligations under the right to life do support, however, a greater priority than currently seems to exist for treatments that are capable of saving lives. The rule of rescue, as a prioritization principle and not an absolute rule, has something valuable to offer to the balancing exercise that NICE undertakes at the government's behest. Perhaps the greatest achievement of NICE, however, is in enabling funding decisions to be taken in a transparent and procedurally fair manner. As we will now see, it may be that this in itself contributes to the state's satisfying its obligations to do all that is reasonable to preserve life.

C. Procedure matters: accountability for reasonableness

There is no doubt that seeking substantive solutions to questions of allocation of resources is a difficult challenge. The courts, in the UK and elsewhere, are reluctant to become involved and the framework used by bodies such as NICE is, as we have seen, subject to some criticism. Recognition of the difficulty of finding agreed substantive solutions has led to an increased focus on the question of procedural fairness. While the courts are reluctant to second guess substantive decisions, they are much more familiar with assessing questions of procedure, and thus within English law we see an increasing emphasis on requiring funding

---

[51] Rawlins & Culyer, n. 39 above, p. 224.   [52] NICE, n. 37 above, para. 4.2.

bodies to provide an explanation of their reasoning.[53] This may be regarded as a legacy of the increased importance of proportionality within English law due to the Human Rights Act, although it is an approach with a much longer history. Laws J's judgment in *R v Cambridge District Health Authority ex parte B*, for example, was immediately overturned by the Court of Appeal and subjected to extensive criticism but his demand for an explanation from the health authority as to the conflicting priorities which had led it to refuse potentially life-saving treatment for a ten-year-old leukaemia patient is nothing more than an early attempt to enforce proportional decision making: 'Where the question is whether the life of a 10 year-old child might be saved, by however slim a chance, the responsible Authority must . . . do more than toll the bell of tight resources. They must explain the priorities that have led them to decline to fund the treatment.'[54] The proportionality test, which is such a fundamental part of the protection of all human rights, always requires explicit reasoning and its relevance to the question of what positive steps are reasonably required under the right to life should not be underestimated. Dembour, writing more generally on human rights, recognizes the difficulty courts (specifically the European Court of Human Rights) often face in applying the proportionality test. She argues that while they talk of weighing different interests in the balance, instead they implicitly classify them as either important or not important.[55] The solution, for Dembour, is 'striving to achieve more transparency in the operation of a utilitarian calculus'.[56] This search for transparency is vital in the context of allocating resources to enable public bodies to act to save lives.

Transparency is one aspect of a broader approach developed by Daniels and Sabin in the context of funding for healthcare which has become extremely influential in recent years. Their approach, called 'accountability for reasonableness', is based upon an understanding that a lack of consensus on substantive solutions requires increased focus on procedural fairness. Daniels and Sabin put this argument as follows: 'When we lack consensus on principles that tell us what is fair, or even when we have general principles but are burdened by reasonable disagreements about how they apply, we may nevertheless find a process or procedure that most can accept as fair to those who are affected by such decisions. That fair process then determines for us what counts as a fair outcome.'[57] The

---

[53] A similar approach can be discerned in Israel. Recent research by Gilbar and Bar-Mor has revealed that in Israel the courts tend to reject patient complaints about lack of access to healthcare because (1) the courts must take into account limited resources; (2) the decision-making process has been adequate; and (3) the decision was reasonable and professional. Complaints are only upheld if the decision-making process has been inadequate or, in contrast to the approach in England, where the treatment is the only way of saving a patient's life (in which case the principle of the sanctity of life is relied upon). See R. Gilbar & H. Bar-Mor, 'Justice, Equality and Solidarity: The Limits of the Right to Health Care in Israel' (2008) 16 Med.L.R. 225, at pp. 245–50.

[54] [1995] 25 BMLR 5, pp. 16–17 of judgment.

[55] M-B. Dembour, *Who Believes in Human Rights? Reflections on the European Convention* (Cambridge: Cambridge University Press, 2006), p. 89.   [56] ibid, p. 91.

[57] Daniels & Sabin, n. 30 above, p. 4.

approach developed by Daniels and Sabin recognizes four conditions which must be met if a decision-making process about healthcare limits is to be legitimate (and these conditions could equally apply to similar allocation of limited resource decisions in other contexts). The first condition is called the publicity condition and requires that both the decisions and the grounds for making them must be accessible to the public. This ensures the transparency which was identified above as an important aspect of proportionate decision making. The second condition is the relevancy condition. This is potentially the most significant condition and requires that the grounds for the decision must be ones that fair-minded people can agree are relevant to meeting healthcare needs under reasonable resource constraints. This means that the rationale for a decision about healthcare limits must be reasonable, a requirement that Daniels and Sabin further explain in the following terms: 'a rationale will be reasonable if it appeals to evidence, reasons, and principles that are accepted as relevant by fair-minded people who are disposed to finding mutually justifiable terms of cooperation'.[58] While the inclusion of terms such as 'fair-minded people' is always problematic, this requirement helpfully focuses not on the final decision made but on the reasons on which the decision is based, and requires that they, if not the conclusion, are ones on which there is a general consensus. So, for example, a refusal to fund treatment because the patient is of a particular race would clearly fall at the relevancy hurdle, while a refusal to fund because the treatment will provide little or no clinical benefit would clear this hurdle. The successful implementation of this condition requires the publicity condition also to be met so that the rationale for the decision is in the public domain and can thus be assessed for its reasonableness. What is crucial is that it is not the final decision that must be reasonable but rather the grounds on which it was made. The focus is on the decision-making process and not its substance. Nevertheless, there is an assumption underlying this approach that regards a fair process as a guarantee of a reasonable, but not necessarily consensual, outcome. It is for this reason that it holds such potential for assessing positive obligations under the right to life. The final two conditions seek to ensure a framework is in place to review the process. The third condition requires that decisions be subject to revision and appeal, while the fourth condition requires that some form of regulation exists to ensure that the other conditions are met.[59] In combination the four conditions comprise the accountability for reasonableness theory which Daniels and Sabin admit may seem esoteric but argue is all the more vital in countries where public resources are very scarce.[60] It is intended to offer justification for rationing decisions and is thus most important in states, and contexts, in which limited resources impact most detrimentally upon the lives of individuals.

[58] ibid, p. 45.
[59] The four conditions are outlined at pp. 11–12 in Daniels and Sabin, ibid.
[60] ibid, p. 164.

Within the UK, the accountability for reasonableness approach has gathered much support. It is in line with the courts' approach to allocation of resource challenges. As Syrett explains, 'the courts have shown a preparedness to oversee the process by which limit-setting decisions are reached in a manner which broadly corresponds with enforcement of compliance with the requirements of "accountability for reasonableness"'.[61] For example, in 2007 the first judicial review of NICE occurred in *Eisai Ltd v NICE*.[62] The case involved a challenge to NICE's decision not to recommend a new Alzheimer's drug to be available under the NHS for newly diagnosed patients. At first instance, the grounds for review ranged from procedural impropriety (due to the supply of a read only version of the economic model used by NICE rather than a fully executable version that would have allowed alternative assumptions to have been re-run), to rationality-based challenges (such as an argument that excluding patients with mild dementia failed to reflect the cumulative benefits from the treatment) to breach of statutory duties to promote equal opportunities and eliminate discrimination (due to the failure to address with sufficient clarity the special position of patients with learning difficulties or for whom English is not a first language). At first instance this final ground succeeded and NICE was required to amend its guidance to ensure compliance with its statutory duties. An appeal on the narrow first ground was rejected. It will immediately be obvious that this case was fought on a procedural battleground. There was no discussion of whether NICE's use of a cost-effectiveness analysis or QALYs was appropriate, no doubt because the claimants knew that the courts would refuse to be drawn into such issues. The only reasonable chance of bringing a successful challenge against NICE guidance is to challenge it under one of the accountability for reasonableness conditions. The relevance of these conditions may be implicit in the English courts' approach to such cases, but significantly it is also explicitly recognized by NICE.

NICE has explicitly adopted a procedural justice approach that focuses on ensuring that the processes by which healthcare decisions are reached are transparent and the reasons explicit.[63] The document 'Social Value Judgements' refers to the accountability for reasonableness approach explicitly and in some detail.[64] It seems clear that the four conditions set out above are the standard by which NICE accepts that it will be judged. This raises the question of whether the approach to funding decisions adopted by NICE is capable of meeting these conditions. In general, its approach ensures procedural fairness: decisions are undoubtedly reached in a transparent manner with a regulatory framework in place and the possibility of judicial review ever present. However, there remains a question of whether the cost-effectiveness requirement meets the relevancy

---

[61] K. Syrett, 'Nice Work? Rationing, Review and the "Legitimacy Problem" in the New NHS' (2002) 10 Med.L.R. 1, at p. 24.   [62] [2007] EWHC 1941. See Syrett (2008), n. 41 above.
[63] NICE, n. 37 above, para. 2.2.   [64] ibid, para. 2.3.

condition of accountability for reasonableness.[65] On the surface, the need to ensure that limited public resources are allocated in a manner that seeks to ensure the greatest benefit to all seems to meet the reasonableness test. Most fair-minded people in Daniels' and Sabin's test are likely to accept the relevance of the need to select for public funding those treatments that offer the best ratio of expense to health benefit. However, it was argued above that the use of the QALY as the sole determinant of this issue is flawed. NICE could still perform its role of approving some (but not all) treatments for funding if a series of prioritizations were adopted as guidance. The rule of rescue, under which extra weight is given to a potentially life-saving treatment, is a principle that seems to have widespread public support and the (no doubt politically motivated) support of the government but is excluded by the application of a strict QALY approach. Within the context of the positive obligation to take reasonable steps to preserve life under the right to life, the rule of rescue as a prioritizing principle will help to ensure compliance. This must be backed up by emphasis on a fair decision-making process. But one element of the accountability for reasonableness approach which seeks to ensure a fair process is that the grounds upon which a decision about funding is reached must be regarded by fair-minded persons as relevant. The need to allocate limited resources as fairly as possible is one such relevant issue, but so too is the need for the state to do all that can reasonably be expected of it to save the lives of those facing an avoidable death. In a world of finite resources, the latter issue may sometimes mean that a little less money can be allocated to other health needs but, as regrettable as that is, it does not justify the omission of the special need to save lives from the decision-making process. If it does, and NICE's approach will sometimes have been guilty of that, the decision-making process arguably fails the accountability for reasonableness test despite its many procedurally fair aspects.

Daniels and Sabin have acknowledged the 'excellent fit' between their accountability for reasonableness theory and the human rights approach. The similarities include that both have transparency and public accountability as a hallmark; both involve relevant stakeholders in vetting reasons underlying rationales for choices; and both rest on evidence-based approaches. What accountability for reasonableness adds in addition to these shared elements is 'a coherent rationale for combining them into a fair process, given the moral disagreement about rights claims that infects the priority-setting process'.[66] The impossibility of obtaining a consensus either on how to allocate public resources, or when finite resources prevent the need for the state to take positive steps to preserve life, has been acknowledged above. The right to life is, as always, an important starting point when decisions about allocating resources are likely to cost lives but the requirement that a state act reasonably in taking positive action can be given more tangible meaning by

---

[65] Daniels himself thinks that it does (N. Daniels, 'Justice, Health and Healthcare' (2001) 1 Am. J. of Bioethics 2, at p. 12).   [66] Daniels & Sabin, n. 30 above, p. 227.

the application of the accountability for reasonableness requirements including, of particular significance, the requirement that the grounds for funding decisions are relevant. If nothing more, it is a way of keeping governments honest.

D. Conclusion

The last few chapters have investigated the potential restraints upon a state's positive obligations to take reasonable steps to preserve the life of those within its jurisdiction. No restraint is more significant than the practical restraint imposed by the need to allocate limited resources. However well meaning a state, difficult questions of rationing services, including healthcare, policing and social services, will inevitably arise and will impact upon the state's ability to act to preserve life. While the negative obligation not to kill can be enforced in an absolute manner in most circumstances (with only a few very narrowly drawn exceptions permissible), positive obligations are far more conditional with their boundaries ill-defined. Dembour has accurately described positive obligations as appearing 'in shades of grey rather than in black and white' and for this reason proportionality tests become essential.[67] Dembour further explains that positive obligations 'derive from a consequentalist philosophy which does not hold that an action is good or bad in itself but which assesses the moral status of an action by reference to the circumstances prevailing at the time'.[68] This can be seen clearly in respect of protection of the right to life by means of limited resources. What can reasonably be expected of a state will depend entirely upon the prevailing circumstances. When resources are limited, any expenditure to save life in one context will represent a choice not to save life in another context. Which life should be saved and how will depend upon considerations such as life expectancy, potential quality of life, and maximum benefit. National authorities, especially transparent bodies such as NICE, are best placed to make detailed allocation of resource choices but this does not mean that international (or national) bodies enforcing a right to life should abdicate all responsibility for such issues. Limited resources is not a blanket excuse for the state failing to intervene to save a life and the courts should investigate the specific circumstances prevailing in each case. When doing so, it will be helpful for the court to consider the accountability for reasonableness conditions, such as transparency of the decision-making process and the relevancy of the grounds for the decision. Failings on these issues can lead to a conclusion that the national body has not done all that could reasonably be expected of it under the right to life. In addition to these important procedural considerations, it has been argued in this chapter that the rule of rescue should be used as a prioritization principle. This means that when allocating limited resources in contexts such as healthcare, funding bodies should ensure that life-saving measures are given

<hr/>

[67] Dembour, n. 55 above, p. 83.   [68] ibid, p. 87.

a priority. This does not require that every possible step that might prolong an individual life must be provided by the state, but merely that the funding body starts from an assumption that spending money to save a life is of greater importance than spending money to improve a life. That assumption can be rebutted, for example, if many lives could be improved significantly for the cost of an extra day of suffering for a terminally ill patient. But it is an assumption that is arguably vital under the right to life because a failure to accord any special recognition to life-saving measures does not satisfy the reasonableness requirement imposed upon state actions by the positive limb of the right to life.

10

Conclusion: The Right to Life and Conflicting Interests

This book has sought to investigate the right to life in the context of the other interests that may conflict with the right. Taking into account the scientific, religious and philosophical origins of the concept of the value of human life, it has sought to identify the nature and ethos of the legal protection for human life and the circumstances in which such protection may legitimately be restricted.

The first section of this book focused upon outlining the concept of a right to life. It was first argued that the key factor in the special legal and ethical protection accorded to human life is the high level of consciousness the species enjoys compared to most other species. This high level of consciousness was said to justify greater protection being given to human beings than to most other species. However, it was also argued that, once it is accepted that human life in general deserves such protection, it should also be accepted that each and every human life deserves it, regardless of whether an individual enjoys full, limited, or no consciousness. Instead of consciousness, the key requirement for an individual to qualify for the special legal and ethical protection given to human life was said to be integrative function of a human organism. Such integrative function will be governed by the brain and will require sufficiently developed lungs to supply oxygen to the major bodily organs. Based on this argument, it was concluded that a human organism has the potential to function in an integrative manner from viability to brain death and thus should enjoy the special protection accorded to the human species during that period, regardless of considerations of birth or consciousness.

The history of this special protection accorded to human life was then investigated and it was discovered that a concept of the sanctity of human life is not specific to any single human culture. All major religious traditions, as well as primitive societies without formal religions, can be seen to place a high value on human life. (It was noted, even at this stage, however, that such high value is never regarded as absolute.) For a period in ancient times, death was often viewed as a welcome refuge from life but a wide range of influential thinkers since that time (including Kant, Locke and Dworkin) have recognized a special value inherent in human life; a value that mirrors but is distinct from religious belief. This universally recognized value in human life, when combined with a natural law philosophy and widespread moral revulsion at the disregard for human life during the Holocaust, cemented itself into a legally recognized international human right to life in the mid twentieth century. The rhetoric of the value in human life was then joined by practical enforcement, albeit one that is severely hampered by financial and political restraints. It was recognized in chapter 3 that the most effective means of protecting the right to life will be by means of domestic law, including by means of the core requirement of a criminal prohibition of killing. However, it is at a domestic level in which the threat to human life usually arises and so international oversight is essential. The various means of implementation of the right at international law, including reports and complaints, are also joined by non-legal mechanisms especially in relation to armed conflicts. At times, it is political negotiation rather than international law that serves as the most pressing defender of the right to life, although the tragic history of conflicts and genocides reveals that the international community has a long way to go before its protection for human life is adequate.

Chapter 3 on the practical enforcement of the right to life also provided the opportunity to investigate the scope of the international right. Three core obligations imposed upon states under the right were identified: not to arbitrarily/intentionally kill individuals; to set up effective investigations into deaths and disappearances; and to take all reasonable measures to prevent a real and immediate risk to life. In addition, it was determined that the right to life has potential application to the use of non-lethal force but does not extend to a right to die. Furthermore, it is clear that the right's application pre-birth remains uncertain in international law, while its reconciliation with the death penalty remains controversial. The enforcement of the right to life is problematic not only because the bodies enforcing the right often lack the financial means and/or political will to enforce it, but also because the nature of the right to life means that other interests not infrequently conflict with it. From the very beginnings of a religious belief in the sanctity of life, through the rhetoric of philosophers and lawmakers, to the pronouncement of international judges, it is clear that legal protection for human life cannot, and should not, be absolute. Throughout the remaining chapters of this book, a diverse range of conflicting interests were seen to outweigh the right to life in certain narrowly defined circumstances.

The first situation identified as involving a conflict with the right to life was wartime or other armed conflicts. The issue of whether human rights law continues to apply in its usual form during times of conflict is an increasingly controversial one, but it was argued in chapter 4 that this branch of law should still have application. However, it was recognized that in practice the issue of jurisdiction causes considerable difficulties in applying human rights law during wartime. While extra-territorial jurisdiction does exist if effective control is being exercised by one state in the territory of another, this limited exception must be rigorously enforced. Any suggestion of a special European territory category was strongly rejected. Whatever the difficulties in establishing extra-territorial jurisdiction when a state kills individuals in another state's territory, it was argued that, at the very least, a state's own soldiers should be regarded as within the state's jurisdiction. Assuming that jurisdictional issues can be overcome, a death in wartime will not violate the right to life if it is in accordance with the rules of international humanitarian law. This branch of law requires a deviation from the general equality which underlies the right to life. Individuals are accorded varying levels of legal protection for their lives depending upon their classification (for example, as lawful combatants, unlawful combatants, prisoners of war or civilians). While the lives of lawful combatants may be regarded as legitimate military targets, civilians are generally protected from deliberate attack, although their lives may become 'collateral damage' if a proportionality test is satisfied. Proportionality, and military necessity, are the key restraining factors upon legitimized state killing during wartime, and these considerations fit well with the prohibition of arbitrary deaths under human rights law. It was recognized in chapter 4 that, despite the argument that human rights law still applies during times of war and armed conflict, more effective protection for the right to life may be provided by means of international humanitarian law and/or international criminal law at this time. Under all three branches of international law, the loss of human life must be regarded as necessary and proportionate in order to be lawful. In the unusual circumstances of armed conflict, however, those tests are far more easily satisfied than in peacetime because concepts such as collective self-defence and acting in the national interest come into play as interests which conflict with the right to life. When the state itself is under threat, the right to life, while still important, becomes in practice much harder to enforce.

Returning to the relatively more straightforward circumstances of peacetime, chapter 5 considered the challenges to the right to life in the context of the prevention of crime. First, looking at the death penalty, it was recognized that international law is moving towards abolition of this penalty but that this movement is independent of the right to life which, for historical reasons, seeks to reconcile the protection of human life with judicial killing. However, the death penalty is not just about death: collateral human rights abuses inevitably accompany the penalty (such as degrading punishment prior to or during the execution; due process failures; and arbitrariness or discrimination in the discretionary imposition of the penalty) while an additional punishment beyond mere death is also inherent within the penalty. Both retributive and deterrence arguments in favour of the death penalty were rejected in chapter 5. In terms of retribution, even if death is deserved, respect for human life cautions against its imposition by the state, and the idea of forfeiting the right to life by past actions should be categorically rejected. The right is not subject to acceptable behaviour. That would be an extremely dangerous road on which to proceed. The evidence of deterrent effect remains ambiguous and controversial but, even if deterrent effect can be established, the death penalty remains an unjust punishment and one that is easily distinguishable from the use of lethal force to prevent crime. The distinguishing factor is that the imposition of death as a punishment can never be regarded as a last resort, and yet the only circumstances in which state agents (or others) can legitimately use lethal force against an unjust aggressor is when that is the only means of saving innocent life. The use of lethal force in the context of prevention of crime must be confined to circumstances where there is a perceived threat to life. In this situation, the unjust aggressor may lose the protection of the right to life if death is the only reasonable means of saving the potential victim's life. Even in this situation, however, the aggressor does not forfeit his or her right to life, nor is death imposed as a punishment. In practice, perceptions of threats to life can sometimes be mistaken. Contrary to the current approach in English law, a mistake as to the perception of a threat to life must be based on good reason if it is to excuse the use of lethal force. In addition, a mistake about the degree of force that is necessary must also be reasonable. And these requirements must be most stringently enforced against agents of the state. Where the lethal force is imposed by a state agent, not only must there be a strict requirement of necessity, but also the armed operation as a whole must be planned, controlled and conducted in a manner that reduces the risk to life, so far as possible, to both the suspect and the public. This requirement recognizes that the state is responsible not just for its agent's last-minute decision to kill or not to kill, but also for a series of previous decisions that have contributed to the need for such a life or death choice. While death can never be necessary as a punishment, it may sometimes be necessary as a means of saving another innocent life but only in very tightly defined circumstances.

These narrowly defined circumstances do not permit the taking of one life merely because it is necessary in order to save another life. In chapter 5 the additional factor of an unjust aggressor who can only be prevented from taking an innocent life by the use of lethal force justified taking one life to save another. In chapter 6 a further additional reason was identified. It was argued that one life may be taken to save another if there will be a net gain in human life, provided that two conditions are met. First, the intervening action must only divert an existing threat, not introduce a new threat to an individual's life. Secondly, the intervening action must not entail an infringement of an individual's rights and thus treat him or her as a means to an end. If these conditions are met, then a utilitarian action to ensure a net gain in human life will be justified but, just as the forfeiture argument was rejected in the previous chapter, here the designated for death argument was rejected. We are all designated for death and a short life expectancy will not, by itself, lessen the legal and ethical protection afforded to an individual's life. Chapter 6 also considered the potential conflict of interests between a viable fetus and its mother. In line with the earlier conclusions, it was acknowledged that a viable fetus enjoys the protection of a right to life but it was argued that this does not obligate the fetus' mother to permit it to continue to use her body in order to preserve its life. A viable fetus should not be killed, and doing so potentially violates its right to life, but it is no more entitled to compel others in society to suffer infringements of their rights or be used as means to an end in order to preserve its life than any other beneficiary of the right to life. The permissibility of terminations of pregnancy is, therefore, better determined as an issue of the appropriate boundary of a right to life rather than as a conflict of the right to life with other rights.

In chapter 7, the focus turned to conflicts between the right to life and other rights of the individual, specifically the right to autonomy. Rationality was regarded as irrelevant to the appropriate state response to an autonomous choice to die. The key instead was recognized to be intention. If an autonomous choice to die is intended and the result of a degree of self-reflection, then any state intervention is not justified under the right to life. In respect of a clear suicide attempt by a mentally competent adult, the state's negative duty not to infringe an individual's autonomy will outweigh its positive obligation to take reasonable steps to preserve life under the right to life. Suicide should not, therefore, be criminalized. If, on the other hand, the individual is not capable of exercising autonomy due to mental incapacity, or if an individual thoughtlessly endangers his or her life, then the state should intervene to offer protection. Some interpretations of the right to life (such as under the ECHR) suggest that the state is obligated to take reasonable steps to prevent the suicide of those under its control (such as prisoners), but it was argued in chapter 7 that the requirements of intention/self-reflection should still apply and that the state should only have a duty to intervene where a suicide is a symptom of mental illness. Even in that situation, the state will be confined to act in a reasonable manner and must take into account the residual autonomy of the individual. Finally it was recognized in this chapter that the state's duty to respect individual autonomy, which outweighs its positive obligations under the right to life in this context, does not require the provision of assistance in committing suicide. The need to ensure adequate protection for the preservation of the lives of the vulnerable in society justifies the criminalization of assisted suicide, although arguably a narrowly drawn exception to it would be justified in circumstances where an individual is enduring unbearable suffering and is unable to take his or her own life unaided.

Chapter 7 identified autonomy as the first of three interests that potentially conflict with the state's positive obligations to preserve human life. In chapter 8, the potentially conflicting interest of quality of life was investigated. The person/human distinction was rejected in the context of human rights law, although it may have some relevance in helping to explain the treatment of individual patients; for example it might be relevant to explaining why Anthony Bland had a right to life and yet was allowed to die. The key issue in withdrawal of life-sustaining treatment is not whether the right to life is applicable (for, in respect of a not yet brain dead human being, it will always be applicable) but rather what steps will be reasonable for the state to take in order to preserve the individual's life. While there is some value in the act/omission distinction generally, it is not helpful in the healthcare context where all actions and non-actions are manifestations of care decisions made under a duty of care. In determining what steps are reasonable in the circumstances in order to preserve life, the other rights of the patient must be taken into account, including of particular relevance the right to be free from degrading treatment and the right to privacy and autonomy. Proportionality will be the appropriate test in this context and an important factor to be taken into account here will be whether life-sustaining treatment will be excessively burdensome for the patient. Both the benefits and the burdens of the proposed treatment must be weighed in the balance, and the focus must always be on the specific patient involved, but it should also be borne in mind that life itself has some value regardless of factors such as consciousness and suffering. While that inherent value may be outweighed by other considerations, such as the burden that will be caused by life-sustaining treatment, the relevance of the right to life should never be overlooked. In respect of ANH and other forms of basic care, the right to life will play an even more crucial role by ensuring that, rather than the scales being equal, they begin weighted in favour of the preservation of life.

A final factor of relevance in the healthcare context and elsewhere is the existence of limited public resources. By its nature, the right to life involves potential public expenditure. While the courts (both international and domestic) are reluctant to overstep their judicial boundaries by second guessing allocation of resource issues, it is possible for the positive obligations inherent in the right to life to be enforced by the courts even when they involve expenditure. The courts may identify pre-existing maladministration or they may leave the specifics of expenditure to the national authorities while requiring that some consideration be given to the provision of public funds to avert a specific threat to life, and neither of these approaches will require the courts to overstep their boundaries of responsibility or expertise. It is vital that there is not perceived to be a blanket exception to the duty to take reasonable steps to preserve life whenever the issue of limited funds is raised. The positive obligation upon the state exists regardless of the financial, or other, burdens caused by it, but such burdens will be highly relevant to a determination of what can reasonably be expected of a state. Chapter 9 proposed that the rule of rescue should be a prioritizing principle within the balancing exercise which should be performed when allocating public funds. It should not serve as an absolute rule because in this context, as in others, the duty to act to preserve life may be outweighed by other considerations, including the rights of others to life and health, but some weight must be given to the importance of allocating finite funds in a way that saves lives. Given the difficulties in obtaining a consensus on how exactly finite funding should be allocated, there is a need for focus on issues of procedural fairness in the allocation. The application of the 'accountability for reasonableness' theory will provide a useful check in this context. Of particular significance will be the application of a relevance condition that ensures that the rationale for decisions about allocating public funds is reasonable. It was argued in chapter 9 that the omission of any emphasis on a rule of rescue from allocation decisions may not be regarded as reasonable. There are interests more important than the preservation of life in certain circumstances but due weight should be given to the right to life whenever it is in issue. The need to preserve life should always be the starting point and weighty reasons will be required to overturn this basic right.

One underlying theme of this book is that the legal protection for human life cannot be, and should not be, absolute. There are some conflicting interests that should, albeit in tightly defined circumstances, outweigh the value in human life. A closer look at these interests reveals, however, that they do not include some of the more commonly identified conflicting principles. The right to life is not, for example, subject to acceptable behaviour. The right cannot be forfeited by an individual whatever onerous crimes he or she commits. It applies to everyone and thus protects even those lives that bring little of value to society. Similarly, the right to life cannot be removed as a punishment for past crimes, nor to deter future crimes by other individuals. In addition, a short life expectancy in no way reduces the protection provided by the right to life. Any concept of some individuals being designated for death, and thus not needing their life protected, must be unambiguously rejected. As the right to life is a fundamental human right it should also not be subject to any personhood requirement. Even human beings lacking consciousness, mental capacity and/or self-awareness are beneficiaries of this right. The rejection of these various arguments reveals both that life should not be used as a reward for good behaviour, and that the right to it should not be a reward for a certain level of capacity. The right to life is not, in any sense, something to which we must aspire to qualify. Once a viable human being, we can be assured of the right until our brain dies.

Despite the rejection of the arguments in the previous paragraph, it must be re-iterated that the right to life is not absolute. Therefore, despite all human beings enjoying its protection, sometimes the state will be justified in either killing or letting die. For this to happen, however, a specific conflicting interest must be identified and sufficient interests are rare. In terms of the negative obligation on the state not to deprive an individual of his or her life, only three exceptions exist, and the broadest of these is restricted to times of international armed conflict where despite the best efforts of international law, life is inevitably treated cheaply. The wartime exception covers deaths that are necessary and proportionate in the national interest and/or for collective self-defence. In times of peace, the only circumstances in which the state may legitimately kill are (a) where it kills an unjust aggressor who is threatening an innocent life or lives, and the killing is both necessary and the last resort in order to avert the threat, and (b) where there will be a net gain in human life from the killing and the killing takes the form of diverting an existing threat to life and does not use any individual as a means to an end. Any other state killing should not be regarded as legitimate under the right to life. In terms of the positive obligation on the state to take reasonable steps to preserve life, the inclusion of the reasonableness requirement immediately ensures that the obligation is less onerous and represents a realistic obligation on state authorities.

Again, however, the circumstances in which the state may decline to take available intervening action in order to save a life are limited. The three circumstances are as follows: (a) where there has been an autonomous choice to die; (b) where the intervening action would not be proportionate because it would amount to an excessive burden on the individual and one that outweighs the benefit to be gained; and (c) where the financial cost to society would not be a reasonable use of limited public funds. These three circumstances all encompass a great deal of room for interpretation but this is not necessarily undesirable. All require the state authorities, and any body reviewing the actions of the state, to assess the reasonableness of any positive steps to save life. The right to life, and its development, reminds us that there is an inherent value in all human life and so there will always be a benefit in any steps that will preserve life. But we must accept also that there may be some harm done by life-sustaining actions, either to the individual whose life is preserved (perhaps by restricting his or her autonomy, or by being subjected to degrading treatment or pain and suffering) or to wider society if the intervening action will inevitably reduce the protection available for other lives. These various conflicting interests have a common theme. They emphasize the need to balance one right to life with the lives and rights of others, as well as the other rights of the individual concerned. However, the fundamental distinction between negative and positive obligations within the right to life should not be underestimated. The exceptions to the negative obligation are all in one sense about saving other lives, while the positive obligation exceptions introduce other rights both of the individual and others in society. There is little doubt, therefore, that the most important interest that may conflict with a right to life is the rights to life of others. Other rights beyond the right to life will only come into play when the threat to the right to life comes from a failure on the part of the state to intervene, not when the threat is from the use of lethal force by an agent of the state. Only human life itself can outweigh the state's duty not to kill the individuals in its jurisdiction.

Bibliography

An-Na'Im, A.A. & Deng, F.M., (eds), *Human Rights in Africa: Cross-Cultural Perspectives* (Washington DC: Brookings Institution, 1990)

Baderin, M.A., *International Human Rights and Islamic Law* (Oxford: Oxford University Press, 2003)

Battin, M.P., *The Least Worst Death: Essays in Bioethics on the End of Life* (Oxford: Oxford University Press, 1994)

—— *Ending Life: Ethics and the Way We Die* (Oxford, Oxford University Press, 2005)

Becker, C., *The Declaration of Independence: A Study in the History of Political Ideas* (New York: Peter Smith, 1933)

Bedau, H.A., 'An Abolitionist's Survey of the Death Penalty in America Today' in H.A. Bedau (ed.), *Debating the Death Penalty: Should America have Capital Punishment? The Experts on Both Sides make their Best Case* (Oxford: Oxford University Press, 2004)

Bernat, J.L., 'Refinements in the Definition and Criterion of Death' in S.J. Younger, R.M. Arnold & R. Schapiro (eds), *The Definition of Death: Contemporary Controversies* (Baltimore: Johns Hopkins University Press, 1999)

Beauchamp, T.L., 'Who Deserves Autonomy and Whose Autonomy Deserves Respect?' in J.S. Taylor (ed.), *Personal Autonomy: New essays on Personal Autonomy and Its Role in Contemporary Moral Philosophy* (Cambridge: Cambridge University Press, 2005)

Blackstone's Commentaries on the Laws of England, Volume IV (edited by W. Morrison, London: Cavendish Publishing, 2001)

Bohlander, M., 'In Extremis: Hijacked Airplanes, "Collateral Damage" and the Limits of the Criminal Law' [2006] Crim.L.R. 579

—— 'Of Shipwrecked Sailors, Unborn Children, Conjoined Twins and Hijacked Airplanes: Taking Human Life and the Defence of Necessity' (2006) 70 J Crim. L. 147

Bossuyt, M.J., *Guide to the 'Travaux Preparatoires' of the International Covenant on Civil and Political Rights* (Dordrecht: Martinus Nijhoff, 1987)

Bostock, D., *Plato's Phaedo* (Oxford: Clarendon Press, 1986)

Brody, B.A., 'How much of the Brain must be Dead?' in S.J. Younger, R.M. Arnold & R. Schapiro (eds), *The Definition of Death: Contemporary Controversies* (Baltimore: Johns Hopkins University Press, 1999)

Capron, A.M., 'The Bifurcated Legal Standard for Determining Death: Does it Work?' in S.J. Younger, R.M. Arnold & R. Schapiro (eds), *The Definition of Death: Contemporary Controversies* (Baltimore: Johns Hopkins University Press, 1999)

Case, P., 'Police Liability for Failing to Prevent Criminal Assaults' [2008] Professional Negligence 242

Cerone, J., 'Jurisdiction and Power: The Intersection of Human Rights Law and the Law of Non-International Armed Conflict in an Extraterritorial Context' (2007) 40 Isr.L.Rev. 396

Coates, A.J., *The Ethics of War* (Manchester: Manchester University Press, 1997)

Collier, C. & Collier, J.L., *Decision in Philadelphia: The Constitutional Convention of 1787* (New York: Ballantine Books, 1986)

Cookson, R. & Dolan, P., 'Public Views on Health Care Rationing: A Group Discussion Study' (1999) 49 Health Policy 63

Coulter, A. & Ham, C., (eds), *The Global Challenge of Health Care Rationing* (Oxford: Open University Press, 2000)

Daniels, N., 'Justice, Health and Healthcare' (2001) 1 Am. J. of Bioethics 2

Daniels, N. & Sabin, J., *Setting Limits Fairly* (Oxford: Oxford University Press, 2002)

Davis, N., 'Abortion and Self-Defense' (1984) 13 Philosophy and Public Affairs 175

Dembour, M-B., *Who Believes in Human Rights? Reflections on the European Convention* (Cambridge: Cambridge University Press, 2006)

Deng, F.M., 'A Cultural Approach to Human Rights among the Dinka' in A.A. An-Na'Im & F.M. Deng (eds), *Human Rights in Africa: Cross-Cultural Perspectives* (Washington DC: Brookings Institution, 1990)

Dennett, D.C., *Consciousness Explained* (London: Penguin, 1991)

Dennis, M.J., 'Non-Application of Civil and Political Rights Treaties Extraterritorially during Times of International Armed Conflict' (2007) 40 Isr.L.Rev. 453

Diamond, J., *The Third Chimpanzee: The Evolution and Future of the Human Animal* (New York: HarperCollins, 1992)

Dinstein, Y., *The Conduct of Hostilities under the Law of International Armed Conflict* (Cambridge: Cambridge University Press, 2004)

Dolan, P. et al, 'QALY Maximisation and People's Preferences: A Methodological View of the Literature' (2005) 14 Health Economics 197

Donald, M., *A Mind So Rare: The Evolution of Human Consciousness* (New York: W.W. Norton & Co, 2001)

Droege, C., 'The Interplay between International Humanitarian Law and International Human Rights Law in Situations of Armed Conflict' (2007) 40 Isr.L.Rev. 310

Dworkin, G., *The Theory and Practice of Autonomy* (Cambridge: Cambridge University Press, 1988)

Dworkin, R., *Taking Rights Seriously* (London: Duckworth, 1977)

—— *Life's Dominion: An Argument about Abortion and Euthanasia* (London: HarperCollins, 1993)

Evans, M., 'Against the Definition of Brain Stem Death' in R. Lee & D. Morgan (eds), *Death Rites: Law and Ethics at the End of Life* (London: Routledge, 1994)

Evans, M.D. & Murray, R., (eds), *The African Charter on Human and Peoples' Rights: The System in Practice 1986–2000* (Cambridge: Cambridge University Press, 2002)

Feldman, D.J., *Civil Liberties and Human Rights in England and Wales* (Oxford: Oxford University Press, 2002, 2nd edn.)

Finkelstein, C., 'Two Models of Murder: Patterns of Criminalisation in the United States' in J. Horder (ed.), *Homicide Law in Comparative Perspective* (Oxford: Hart Publishing, 2007)

Finnis, J., 'Bland—Crossing the Rubicon?' (1993) 109 LQR 329

—— 'A Philosophical Case Against Euthanasia' in J. Keown (ed.), *Euthanasia Examined: Ethical, Clinical and Legal Perspectives* (Cambridge: Cambridge University Press, 1997)

Fredman, S., 'Human Rights Transformed: Positive Duties and Positive Rights' [2006] P.L. 498

Fuller, L.L., 'The Case of the Speluncean Explorers' (1949) 62 Harv.L.R. 616

Gardner, J. & Shute, S., 'The Wrongness of Rape' in J. Horder (ed.), *Oxford Essays in Jurisprudence, 4th Series* (Oxford: Oxford University Press, 2000)

Gardner, S., 'Necessity's Newest Inventions' (1991) 11 O.J.L.S. 125

Gilbar, R. & Bar-Mor, H., 'Justice, Equality and Solidarity: The Limits of the Right to Health Care in Israel' (2008) 16 Med.L.Rev. 225

Glover, J., *Causing Death and Saving Lives* (London: Penguin, 1977)

Greer, S., *The European Convention on Human Rights: Achievements, Problems and Prospects* (Cambridge: Cambridge University Press, 2006)

Gurnham, D., 'Kantian Principle and the Right to Life in Legal Judgement: The Case of the Conjoined Twins' (2003) 14 Kings College Law Journal 21

Hannikainen, L., *Peremptory Norms (Jus Cogens) in International Law: Historical Development, Criteria, Present Status* (Helsinki: Finnish Lawyers' Publishing Company, 1988)

Happold, M., '*Bankovic v Belgium* and the Territorial Scope of the European Convention on Human Rights' (2003) 3 H.R.L.R. 77

Harris, J., *The Value of Life: An Introduction to Medical Ethics* (London: Routledge, 1985)

Harris, D., 'The ICCPR and the UK: An Introduction' in D. Harris & S. Joseph (eds), *The International Covenant on Civil and Political Rights and United Kingdom Law* (Oxford: Clarendon Press, 1995)

Heffernan, L., 'A Comparative View of Individual Petition Procedures under the European Convention on Human Rights and the International Covenant on Civil and Political Rights' (1997) 19 H.R.Q. 78

Hodgkinson, P. & Schabas, W.A., (eds), *Capital Punishment: Strategies for Abolition* (Cambridge: Cambridge University Press, 2004)

Hoffman, D.E. & Webb, V.J., 'Suicide as Murder at Common Law' (1981) 19 Criminology 372

Hood, R. & Hoyle, C., *The Death Penalty: A Worldwide Perspective* (Oxford: Oxford University Press, 2008, 4th edn.)

Horder, J. & Hughes, D., 'Comparative Issues in the Law of Homicide' in J. Horder (ed.), *Homicide Law in Comparative Perspective* (Oxford: Hart Publishing, 2007)

Howard, R.E., 'Group versus Individual Identity in the African Debate on Human Rights' in A.A. An-Na'Im & F.M. Deng (eds), *Human Rights in Africa: Cross-Cultural Perspectives* (Washington DC: Brookings Institution, 1990)

Johnson, S., *Mind Wide Open: Why You Are What You Think* (London: Penguin, 2004)

Joseph, S., 'The Right to Life' in D. Harris & S. Joseph (eds), *The International Covenant on Civil and Political Rights and United Kingdom Law* (Oxford: Clarendon Press, 1995)

Joseph, S., Schultz, J. & Castan, M., *The International Covenant on Civil and Political Rights: Cases, Materials and Commentary* (Oxford: Oxford University Press, 2004, 2nd edn.)

Kant, I., *Groundwork of the Metaphysics of Morals* (edited by L. Pasternack, London: Routledge, 2002)

Keown, J., (ed.), *Euthanasia Examined: Ethical, Clinical and Legal Perspectives* (Cambridge: Cambridge University Press, 1997)

—— 'Restoring Moral and Intellectual Shape to the Law after *Bland*' (1997) 113 LQR 481

—— 'Beyond *Bland*: A Critique of the BMA Guidance on Withholding and Withdrawing Medical Treatment' (2000) 20 Legal Studies 66

—— 'Restoring the Sanctity of Life and Replacing the Caricature: A Reply to David Price' (2006) 26 Legal Studies 109

Klein, R., 'Dimensions of Rationing: Who Should Do What?' (1993) BMJ 307

Korff, D., *The Right to Life: A Guide to Implementation of Article 2 of the European Convention on Human Rights* (Human Rights Handbook No. 8) (Strasbourg: Council of Europe, 2006)

Lackey, D.P., *The Ethics of War and Peace* (New Jersey: Prentice-Hall, 1989)

Lamb, D., *Death, Brain Death and Ethics* (London: Croom Helm, 1985)

Lauren, P.G., *The Evolution of International Human Rights: Visions Seen* (Philadelphia: University of Pennsylvannia Press, 2003, 2nd edn.)

Leckie, S., 'The Inter-State Complaint Procedure in International Human Rights Law: Hopeful Prospects or Wishful Thinking?' (1988) 10 H.R.Q. 249

Lee, R. & Morgan, D., (eds), *Death Rites: Law and Ethics at the End of Life* (London: Routledge, 1994)

Lepsius, O., 'Human Dignity and the Downing of Aircraft: The German Federal Constitutional Court Strikes Down a Prominent Anti-terrorism Provision in the New Air-transport Security Act' (2006) 7 German Law Journal 761

Leverick, F., *Killing in Self-defence* (Oxford: Oxford University Press, 2006)

Levy, L.W., *Origins of the Fifth Amendment: The Right Against Self-incrimination* (New York: Macmillan, 1986)

Lewis, P. & Charney, M., 'Which of Two Individuals Do You Treat When Only their Ages are Different and You Can't Treat them Both?' (1989) 15 J Med Eth 28

Lizza, J.P., *Persons, Humanity and the Definition of Death* (Baltimore: Johns Hopkins University Press, 2006)

Locke's *Two Treatises of Government* (ed. P. Laslett) (Cambridge: Cambridge University Press, 1988)

Mason, J.K., *Medico-Legal Aspects of Reproduction and Parenthood* (Aldershot: Dartmouth Publishing, 1998, 2nd edn.)

May, L., *War Crimes and Just War* (Cambridge: Cambridge University Press, 2007)

Mayer, D.N., *The Constitutional Thought of Thomas Jefferson* (Charlottesville: University Press of Virginia, 1994)

McBride, J., 'Protecting Life: A Positive Obligation to Help' (1999) 24 E.L.R. Supp. 42

McGoldrick, D., *The Human Rights Committee: Its Role in the Development of the International Covenant on Civil and Political Rights* (Oxford: Clarendon Press, 1994)

McIvor, C., 'The Positive Medical Duty to Provide Life-Prolonging Treatment' [2006] Professional Negligence 59

—— 'The Positive Duty of the Police to Protect Life' [2008] Professional Negligence 27

McMahan, J., 'Brain Death, Cortical Death and Persistent Vegetative State' in H. Kuhse & P. Singer, *Companion to Bioethics* (Oxford: Blackwell, 1998)

—— *The Ethics of Killing: Problems at the Margins of Life* (Oxford: Oxford University Press, 2002)

—— 'The Ethics of Killing in War' (2004) 114 Ethics 693

Michalowski, S., 'Sanctity of Life: Are Some Lives More Sacred than Others?' (2002) 22 Legal Studies 377

Morgan, P. & Lawton, C., (eds), *Ethical Issues in Six Religious Traditions* (Edinburgh: Edinburgh University Press, 2007, 2nd edn.)

Morsink, J., *The Universal Declaration of Human Rights: Origins, Drafting, and Intent* (Philadelphia: University of Pennsylvania Press, 2000)

Mowbray, A.R., *The Development of Positive Obligations under the European Convention on Human Rights by the European Court of Human Rights* (Oxford: Hart Publishing, 2004)

Ni Aolain, F., 'Truth Telling, Accountability and the Right to Life in Northern Ireland' (2002) 5 E.H.R.L.R. 572

Novak, D., *The Sanctity of Human Life* (Washington DC: Georgetown University Press, 2007)

O'Cinneide, C., 'A Modest Proposal: Destitution, State Responsibility and the European Convention on Human Rights' [2008] E.H.R.L.R. 583

Otsuka, M., 'Killing the Innocent in Self-Defense' (1994) 23 Philosophy and Public Affairs 74

Paust, J.J., 'The Right to Life in Human Rights Law and the Laws of War' (2002) 65 Saskatchewan Law Review 411

Pernick, M.S., 'Brain Death in a Cultural Context: The Reconstruction of Death 1967–1981' in S.J. Younger, R.M. Arnold & R. Schapiro (eds), *The Definition of Death: Contemporary Controversies* (Baltimore: Johns Hopkins University Press, 1999)

Plato, *Five Dialogues: Euthyphro, Apology, Crito, Meno Phaedo* (translated by G.M.A. Grube) (Indianapolis: Hackett Publishing, 2002)

Plomer, A., 'A Foetal Right to Life? The Case of *Vo v France*' [2005] H.R.L.R. 311

Pojman, L.P., 'Why the Death Penalty is Morally Permissible' in H.A. Bedau (ed.), *Debating the Death Penalty: Should America have Capital Punishment? The Experts on Both Sides make their Best Case* (Oxford: Oxford University Press, 2004)

Pojman, L.P. & Reiman, J., *The Death Penalty: For and Against* (Lanham: Rowman & Littlefield Publishers, 1998)

Price, D., 'Fairly *Bland*: An Alternative View of a Supposed New "Death Ethic" and the BMA Guidance' (2001) 21 Legal Studies 618

—— 'What Shape to Euthanasia after *Bland*? Historical, Contemporary and Futuristic Paradigms' (2009) 125 L.Q.R. 142

Rachels, J., 'Active and Passive Euthanasia' (1975) 292 New England Journal of Medicine 78

Ramcharan, B.G., (ed.) *The Right to Life in International Law* (Dordrecht: Martinus Nijhoff, 1985)

Rawlins, M.D. & Culyer, A.J., 'NICE and its Value Judgements' (2004) 329 BMJ 224

Robertson, G., *Collected Edition of the Travaux Préparatoires* (The Hague: Martinus Nijhoff, 1977), Vol. 2

Rodley, N.S., 'Rights and Responses to Terrorism in Northern Ireland' in D. Harris & S. Joseph (eds), *The International Covenant on Civil and Political Rights and United Kingdom Law* (Oxford: Clarendon Press, 1995)

Rogers, J., 'Necessity, Private Defence and the Killing of Mary' [2001] Crim.L.R. 515

Savulescu, J., 'Rational Desires of the Limitation of Life-Sustaining Treatment' (1994) 8 Bioethics 191

Schabas, W.A., '*Soering's* Legacy: The Human Rights Committee and the Judicial Committee of the Privy Council Take a Walk Down Death Row' (1994) 43 I.C.L.Q. 913

—— *The Abolition of the Death Penalty in International Law* (Cambridge: Cambridge University Press, 2002, 3rd edn.)

Searle, J.R., *The Mystery of Consciousness* (London: Granta Books, 1997)

Silverstein, H.S., 'On a Woman's "Responsibility" for the Fetus' (1987) 13 Social Theory and Practice 103

Simpson, A.W.B., *Human Rights and the End of Empire: Britain and the Genesis of the European Convention* (Oxford: Oxford University Press, 2001)

Singer, P., *Rethinking Life and Death: The Collapse of Our Traditional Ethics* (Oxford: Oxford University Press, 1995)

Skinner, S., 'Citizens in Uniform: Public Defence, Reasonableness and Human Rights' [2000] P.L. 266

Smith, S.W., 'How We Value Life: George Bailey and the Life not Worthy of being Lived' in J. Yorke (ed.), *Orientations of the Right and Value of Life* (Farnham: Ashgate, 2009, forthcoming)

Smith & Hogan, *Criminal Law* (ed. D. Ormerod) (Oxford: Oxford University Press, 2008, 12th edn.)

Sorell, T., *Moral Theory and Capital Punishment* (Oxford: Basil Blackwell, 1987)

Spencer, J.R., 'Intentional Killings in French Law' in J. Horder (ed.), *Homicide Law in Comparative Perspective* (Oxford: Hart Publishing, 2007)

Steiker, C.S. & Steiker, J.M., 'The Seduction of Innocence: The Attraction and Limitations of the Focus on Innocence in Capital Punishment Law and Advocacy' (2005) 95 Journal of Criminal Law and Criminology 587

Steiker, C.S., 'No, Capital Punishment is Not Morally Required: Deterrence, Deontology, and the Death Penalty' (2006) 58 Stan.L.Rev. 751

Steinbock, B., *Life Before Birth: The Moral and Legal Status of Embryos and Fetuses* (Oxford: Oxford University Press, 1992)

Steiner, H.J., Alston, P. & Goodman, R., *International Human Rights Law in Context: Law, Politics, Morals* (Oxford: Oxford University Press, 2008, 3rd edn.)

Sunstein, C.R. & Vermeule, A., 'Is Capital Punishment Morally Required? Acts, Omissions, and Life-Life Tradeoffs' (2005–06) 58 Stan.L.Rev. 703

—— 'Deterring Murder: A Reply' (2006) 58 Stan.L.Rev. 847

Syrett, K., 'Nice Work? Rationing, Review and the "Legitimacy Problem" in the New NHS' (2002) 10 Med.L.Rev. 1

—— 'NICE and Judicial Review: Enforcing "Accountability for Reasonableness" through the Courts?' (2008) 16 Med.L.R. 127

Tadros, V., 'The Scots Law of Murder' in J. Horder (ed.), *Homicide Law in Comparative Perspective* (Oxford: Hart Publishing, 2007)

Taylor, J.S., (ed.), *Personal Autonomy: New essays on Personal Autonomy and Its Role in Contemporary Moral Philosophy* (Cambridge: Cambridge University Press, 2005)

Thomson, J.J., 'A Defence of Abortion' (1971) 1 Philosophy and Public Affairs 47

—— *Rights, Restitution and Risk: Essays in Moral Theory* (ed. W. Parent) (Cambridge: Harvard University Press, 1986)

—— 'Self-Defense' (1991) Philosophy and Public Affairs 283

Tooley, M., 'Abortion and Infanticide' (1972) Philosophy and Public Affairs 37

Uniacke, S., *Permissible Killing: The Self-defence Justification of Homicide* (Cambridge: Cambridge University Press, 1996)

—— 'Was Mary's Death Murder?' (2001) 9 Med.L.Rev. 208

Veatch, R.M., 'The Conscience Clause: How much Individual Choice in Defining Death can our Society Tolerate?' in S.J. Younger, R.M. Arnold & R. Schapiro (eds), *The Definition of Death: Contemporary Controversies* (Baltimore: Johns Hopkins University Press, 1999)

Waddington, P.A.J., 'Overkill or Minimum Force?' [1990] Crim.L.R. 695

Walzer, M., *Just and Unjust Wars: A Moral Argument with Historical Illustrations* (New York: Basic Books, 2006, 4th edn.)

Warren, M.A., *Moral Status: Obligations to Persons and Other Living Things* (Oxford: Clarendon Press, 1997)

Wasserman, D., 'Justifying Self-Defence' (1987) 16 Philosophy and Public Affairs 356

Watkin, K., 'Controlling the Use of Force: A Role for Human Rights Norms in Contemporary Armed Conflict' (2004) 98 Am.J.Int.L. 1

Wheat, K., 'The Law's Treatment of the Suicidal' (2000) 8 Med.L.Rev. 182

Wicks, E., 'The Greater Good? Issues of Proportionality and Democracy in the Doctrine of Necessity as Applied in *Re A*' (2003) 32 Common Law World Review 15

—— 'Terminating Life and Human Rights: The Foetus and the Neonate' in C.A. Erin & S. Ost, *The Criminal Justice System and Healthcare* (Oxford: Oxford University Press, 2007)

—— *Human Rights and Healthcare* (Oxford: Hart Publishing, 2007)

Williams, G., *The Sanctity of Life and the Criminal Law* (London: Faber & Faber, 1958)

Williams, N., *The Right to Life in Japan* (London: Routledge, 1997)

Wiredu, K., 'An Akan Perspective on Human Rights' in A.A. An-Na'Im & F.M. Deng (eds), *Human Rights in Africa: Cross-Cultural Perspectives* (Washington DC: Brookings Institution, 1990)

Yeo, S., 'Fault for Homicide in Singapore' in J. Horder (ed.), *Homicide Law in Comparative Perspective* (Oxford: Hart Publishing, 2007)

Younger, S.J., Arnold, R.M. & Schapiro, R., (eds), *The Definition of Death: Contemporary Controversies* (Baltimore: Johns Hopkins University Press, 1999)

Zampas, C. & Gher, J.M., 'Abortion as a Human Right: International and Regional Standards' [2008] H.R.L.R. 249

Zdenkowski, G., 'The International Covenant on Civil and Political Rights and Euthanasia' (2007) 20 U.N.S.W.L.J. 170

Zinn, H., *A People's History of the United States: 1492-Present* (New York: HarperPerennial, 1999)

Zohar, N.J., 'Collective War and Individualistic Ethics: Against the Conscription of "Self-Defense"' (1993) 21 Political Theory 606

Index

Printed and bound by CPI Group (UK) Ltd, Croydon, CR0 4YY